THE UNIVERSITY OF
WINCHESTER

Music Wars
1937-1945
First published 2012 by
EAST & WEST PUBLISHING LIMITED
London
ISBN 978 1 907318 07 8

www.eastandwestpublishing.com

Produced by Melisende UK Limited
Printed and bound in Malta at the Gutenberg Press
Cover design and layout by stuartpolsondesign.com

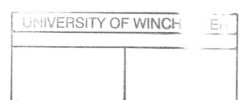

Contents

PHOTO CREDITS

Anthony Wong Photography: p. 400 centre.

© BFI, p. 336 all.

Cine Mondial: p. 305.

© English Heritage: p. 250.

Foto Quick: p. 325.

Harcourt: p. 252, 332.

Illustrated London News: p. 385.

Illustrated London News/Mary Evans Picture Library: p. 249.

Match: p. 62 top and below, 154, 269.

Parade: p. 207 top, 226, 353, 400 below.

© RMN/Dist. RMN © Studio Harcourt/Paris, Médiathèque de l'Architecture et du Patrimoine: p. 252.

Scherl/Süddeutsche Zeitung Photo: p. 109.

Signal: p. 297, 368 below.

Traumerei: p. 24.

UFA: p. 304 top left.

FOREWORD

The idea for this book arose from a chance conversation with my publisher Sahar Huneidi. I had recently translated two booklets that accompanied an issue of four CDs of live recordings of concerts given in Paris in 1944 by the great Dutch conductor Willem Mengelberg. I had been struck by the palpable shared emotion of performers and listeners at these concerts and pondered the heightened response to music in times of war. Sahar encouraged me to explore this idea further and commissioned this book.

The first thing to say about it is that it differs from most other books about the history of music and indeed about the Second World War, in that the primary source material is recorded sound. It is a sign of the astonishing times in which we live that I was able to listen to almost every one of the thousands of recordings cited in this book without leaving my own home. My own collecting activities stretch back over more than half a century to the time when my grandparents passed on their collection of 78 rpm records to me when they replaced them with LPs. A number of records mentioned, including Joan Hammond's 'O my beloved father' and many popular songs, were already in this collection. Over the years I acquired tens of thousands of records on shellac, vinyl and CD, always tending to focus on the period of recording covered by this book.

The Second World War was truly a war of the airwaves. Vast quantities of wartime broadcast material have now been issued on LP or CD, often illegally or semi-legally by small private companies. What I did not already possess, I was able to track down quite easily over the internet. Similarly, I did not need to make great use of libraries for the written source material. Once again I was able to rely on a fairly comprehensive collection of biographies and autobiographies that I had built up over many years. I made one trip to Colindale in search of British newspaper articles and my local library located Tully Potter's monumental two-volume biography of Adolf Busch for me. Otherwise, flea markets across Europe proved a valuable source of printed material, as did the remarkable Parisian shop La Galcante, where it would seem that almost every newspaper and periodical published in France in the past two centuries can be found in a warren of ancient cellars and tunnels under the Rue de l'Arbre Sec.

With the exception of a handful of reference books and biographies in Italian, all the published material I used for this book was in English, French or German (I made my own translations where necessary). This inevitably limited the scope of the book. I decided to concentrate on France, Britain and the German Reich and occupied territories. The United States and the Soviet Union are largely viewed from a Western and Central European perspective. I was particularly intrigued by the clash of musical cultures in North Africa and the Middle East. This is something I hope to be able to explore in greater depth in the future. There is undoubtedly an interesting book to be written about the role of music in the Pacific and Far Eastern theatres of war, but not by me.

For the illustrated material, I once again relied heavily on my own collections.

I have used a smattering of personal testimony throughout the book. I was able to draw upon recalled conversations with Arletty, Erna Berger, Hilde Zadek, Renée Doria, Kyra Vayne, Spoli Mills (daughter of Mischa Spoliansky), Ernst Gombrich, Friedlinde Wagner, and above all, of course, with my own parents. Both served in the British armed forces and indeed one could say that Hitler brought them together. They met in Palestine in 1944. The Second World War was a very frequent topic of conversation during my childhood. For my father it was undoubtedly the most vividly experienced period of his life. Sadly he died before I began work on this book, but my mother, who is working on her own memoirs of the war, provided me with a great deal of material. Two greatly loved friends assisted me with insights from very different points of view. One of these, Trude Levi, a woman of inspiring courage and resilience, is a survivor of Auschwitz-Birkenau. The other, Balbina, Gräfin Otting, who with characteristic fearlessness took great risks to help persecuted Jews in wartime Paris, had served in the German Wehrmacht.

First and foremost, I would like to thank Sahar Huneidi. Sahar is a woman of shining intellectual integrity and generosity who gave me complete freedom to write as I wished even when we did not see eye to eye on certain points. My editor Louise Stein not only greatly improved my written English but went well beyond the role of editor by providing me with many valuable gobbets of information. Two German friends, Renate Rauch and Dr Thomas Roeske, acted as unofficial editors in the early stages of the book, correcting not only my factual information but even my written English! Among the many friends who helped with this book, I would like to single out my fellow collectors Dr. Richard Copeman and Professor Stanley Henig, both of whom shared their collections and their knowledge with me.

An important element that has fed into this book is the experience of 15 years teaching (or should I say learning) at the London Jewish Cultural Centre. Many of the lectures I have given at the LJCC relate to the subject matter of this book. I would like to acknowledge the contribution of the challenging and stimulating audiences I have encountered there.

My last thank you goes to the great Italian soprano Magda Olivero, who more than anyone else has helped me to understand the power of music to move and uplift.

Patrick Bade
February 2012

Chapter 1
MUSIC:
THE MIRACLE WEAPON

In 2009, two recorded broadcasts of wartime concerts, long believed to have been destroyed with the entire archives of the notorious German controlled Radio Paris, mysteriously reappeared. They were discovered by chance in an antique shop at Lyons with no indication of how they got there or how they escaped the conflagration that destroyed the premises of Radio Paris during the Liberation of Paris.

From 1940 to 1944 Radio Paris had engaged in a duel over the airwaves with the Free French broadcasting from the BBC in London. The French comedian Pierre Dac invented a jingle to be sung to the tune of 'La Cucaracha' that ran 'Radio Paris ment, Radio Paris ment, Radio Paris est Allemand' ('Radio Paris lies, Radio Paris lies, Radio Paris is German').

Radio Paris sweetened the poisonous pill of Nazi propaganda with a cultural programme of extraordinary richness and diversity intended to ensure the loyalty of French listeners. The musical programmes included popular dance bands, stars of Variétés (the French equivalent of Music Hall) and classical concerts of the highest quality. Poaching the finest instrumentalists from the other Parisian orchestras, Radio Paris created its own first-rate orchestra. The classical concerts were broadcast live from the elegant Théâtre des Champs-Elysées. The concerts were free and members of the Parisian public could mingle with the German military in their grey-green uniforms.

The two surviving concerts date from 16 and 20 January 1944, during the fourth and final winter of the German Occupation. It was a particularly harsh winter, with food, fuel and clothing all in short supply. The poor health of the audience is evident in the amount of coughing in the background of the recording. The choice of programmes is hardly what we would expect for concerts given under

Photos Boerthelé Radio-Paris

Ci-dessus, le grand orchestre de Radio-Paris. Au pupitre, le maî-
tre W. Mengelberg. Devant le micro, Mona Laurena.
Ci-contre, José Beckmans étudiant une partition à l'occasion
du cycle Beethoven. auquel il a pris une part brillante.

Photo Harcourt.

The Beethoven Cycle at Radio Paris. Willem Mengelberg rehearsing at the Théâtre
*des Champs Elysées. (*Vedette*)*

the aegis of the Nazis. None of the music presented was from the
Austro-German tradition. The four main works were Franco-Belgian
(César Franck, Symphony in D Minor) Czech (Dvořák Cello Concerto)
Polish (Chopin Piano Concerto in F minor) and, most surprising of
all, given that the Red Army was pushing back the German front line
relentlessly in the east, Russian (Tchaikovsky 'Pathétique' Symphony).
By a peculiarly fateful coincidence Leningrad had been liberated on 19
January, the day before the Tchaikovsky symphony was performed.
The two soloists in the concertos were the veteran pianist Alfred Cortot
and the youthful and as yet little known cellist Paul Tortelier.

But the main interest of these concerts lies in the participation of
the great Dutch conductor Willem Mengelberg, who had been chief
conductor of the Amsterdam Concertgebouw for nearly half a century.
Mengelberg was a revered figure on a level with Toscanini and
Furtwängler. Even in a period in which a conductor's megalomania was
freely indulged, Mengelberg was feared by his players and regarded as
a martinet. Furtwängler's assistant Bertha Geissmar commented that
Mengelberg's 'rehearsal manners are notorious, and his interminable
lectures are torture to orchestral musicians.'[1] The peremptory tapping

of the conductor's desk, familiar to New York audiences from Mengelberg's tenure of the New York Philharmonic Orchestra and hilariously spoofed by the Marx Brothers in *A Night at the Opera*, is clearly audible at the start of each movement. It was perhaps only through such rigid and dictatorial methods in lengthy and gruelling rehearsals that Mengelberg was able to hold his musicians together in performances of quite extraordinary wilfulness and freedom. Every phrase sounds as though newly invented or improvised. When in 1938 he conducted Wagner's 'Vorspiel und Liebestod' from *Tristan und Isolde*

Willem Mengelberg. Cover of Les Ondes, *13 December 1942.*

with the London Philharmonic Orchestra, Bertha Geissmar tells us that he 'treated the orchestra as if they had never heard or played this music before.'[2] Irritating though this undoubtedly was to the musicians, it was integral to his approach to music making and perhaps the secret of his magic as a conductor. What these broadcasts convey in sound of exceptional vividness for the period is the breathless involvement of musicians and audiences in his performances.

It would have been apparent to everyone sitting in the Théâtre des Champs-Elysées in January 1944, whether German or French, that the war was about to enter its final phase and that all their lives and the fate of the city of Paris itself hung by a thread. Under these circumstances the baleful utterances of Tchaikovsky's symphony must have taken on a very intense and personal meaning for everyone present. After the fireworks of the third movement, there is a little burst of applause that is quickly brought to order by the tapping of Mengelberg, but at the end of the final movement there is a moment of awed silence before a prolonged frenzy of clapping and cheering—Parisians and their German oppressors united in common emotion.

Mengelberg's performance of the César Franck symphony is perhaps even more remarkable. Headlong and tumultuous, this performance is quite different from the fine but far more measured performance that Mengelberg had given of this symphony in a recording studio with the Concertgebouw Orchestra in 1940. The great surprise comes when the timings of the two performances are compared. The live performance in Paris feels very much faster but is in fact slower by more than two minutes than the studio recording.

Furtwängler conducting. (Signal)

It has often been remarked of Wilhelm Furtwängler that his wartime broadcasts of live performances were charged with greater emotion and excitement than earlier or later recorded performances in times of peace. An outstanding example is a recently published recording of Furtwängler conducting Beethoven's Ninth Symphony on 19 April 1942. Through a mixture of naivety and vanity, Furtwängler had allowed himself to be trapped into serving a regime that he knew to be evil, although this was the only occasion when he failed to evade conducting a concert to celebrate the Führer's birthday. His conflicting emotions come through in the frenetic quality of the performance. In the words of the critic Michael Tanner, the final bars of the choral movement are a 'nightmare of nihilism, a stampede towards the abyss'.[3]

If the horrors of war blunt human feelings, what Noel Coward described in a wartime diary as 'the enforced contact with the sterner realities of life and death'[4] can also sharpen musical sensibilities. Numerous memoirs and reminiscences from the Second World War bear witness to the fact that people experienced music more intensely in war than they did at other times in their lives. In her autobiography Joyce Grenfell spoke of being 'nourished' by the famous wartime concerts organised by the pianist Myra Hess:

> Music was particularly important in the terrible (beautiful) Spring of 1940—continuing days of cloudless blue skies and more and more tragic news … On the day that Holland fell I heard Mozart's clarinet quintet (K.5810). I was behind the platform curtain with my shoes off and my feet up on a chair. As I listened I had an intuitive feeling of hearing beyond the

music to some sense of infinity. It was 'evidence of things not seen'—or heard. I cannot put it more plainly but I believe anyone who has had this experience will know what I mean. It was first a recognition and then an acknowledgement. There was no picture in my mind, nor were there any words; but I had a glimpse of unchanging limitless life, of spiritual being that no war or misery of uncertainty and fear could ever touch.[5]

A similar experience is described in a memoir by the cellist Anita Lasker-Wallfisch, who played in the women's orchestra at Auschwitz. It is all the more telling because the tone of the book is one of blunt factuality and truthfulness and she was clearly not a woman given either to flights of fancy or gushing emotion. She recalled taking part in a quartet arrangement of Beethoven's 'Pathétique' sonata. 'It may not sound very extraordinary; it was just a chamber music evening. But it was one with a difference. We were able to raise ourselves high above the inferno of Auschwitz into spheres where we could not be touched by the degradation of concentration camp existence.'[6]

Janina Bauman experienced her first symphonic concert in the Femina cinema on Leszno Street in the Warsaw Ghetto in the winter of 1941-42. It was a revelation to her. 'There were enough prominent musicians who happened to be Jews to set up a first-rate symphony orchestra in the ghetto; it was conducted by Szymon Pulman. I knew nothing about classical music. I had never in my life been to a concert before. The orchestra played Tchaikovsky's "Pathétique" Symphony. Everyone sat still in the dark, profoundly moved. Then an eighteen-year-old girl sang "Ave Maria" by Schubert. She had a strong clear voice that seemed to hurl through the wall of the hall and rise high above our world with all its daily troubles. The audience cried and I cried myself.'[7]

From this moment Janina Bauman craved the spiritual nourishment of great music as much as she did the physical nourishment of food. She managed to get hold of a portable gramophone and took it to friends who still possessed a few records:

> Some other young people were already waiting for us and we all went to a strange place next door; it was an empty room half demolished by fire and terribly cold. We sat down on the floor and our host brought out two records—

the only two he had not yet sold. One was Beethoven's Fifth Symphony first and second movements; the other Beethoven's Fifth Symphony third and fourth movements. [This was presumably an abridged version as most complete versions on 78 rpm records required 8 sides, or in the case of Furtwängler, nine.] Freezing in our coats and gloves, we spent all evening listening to these two records. When the fourth movement was over we started with the first again, until it was nearly curfew time. After that we met at the same place again and listened to the same records once a week until the end of the winter. We had no other records of classical music. We had just the Fifth Symphony.[8]

In Hans Fallada's powerful quasi-documentary novel of German resistance *Alone in Berlin* published in 1947, the working class hero Otto Quangel discovers the solace of classical music while sharing a cell on death row with the former orchestral conductor Dr Reichhardt, who hums as he paces up and down the cell.

In the course of his morning walk, which lasted from ten to eleven, Dr Reichhardt would sing to himself. Generally he confined himself to humming softly, because a lot of warders wouldn't allow it, and Quangel got used to listening to this humming. Whatever his poor opinion of music, he did notice its effect on him. Sometimes it made him feel strong and brave enough to endure any fate, and then Reichhardt would say, 'Beethoven'. Sometimes it made him bafflingly lighthearted and cheerful, which he had never been in his life, and then Reichhardt would say, 'Mozart', and Quangel would forget all about his worries. And sometimes the sounds emanating from the doctor were dark and heavy, and Quangel would feel pain in his chest, and it would be as though he was a little boy again sitting in church with his mother, with something grand—the whole of his life—ahead of him, and then Reichhardt would say 'Johann Sebastian Bach'.[9]

It was not only the great masterpieces of the classical tradition that evoked such heightened emotion in wartime. Almost anyone who lived through those years will have powerful musical memories and these are often associated with popular songs or dance music. To the day he died, my own father recalled the emotion he felt when he unexpectedly heard the voice of Vera Lynn on a gramophone record

6

emanating from an invisible foxhole in the wilderness of Persia.

When asked for her musical memories of the war, Anne Cookson gave an account that could speak for a generation of British women:

Anne Cookson and a fire warden.
Private photo.

> I was still at school when the Second World War started and not terribly interested in the 'pop' music of the day. I was concentrating—or trying to—on learning boring piano pieces because my mother wanted me to learn. I didn't until I found that if I signed up for music lessons at school I would miss religious instruction … Through my brother who was two years older, I gradually started listening to the popular dance music because all the time he was at home, the radio was on. The favourites were Geraldo, Henry Hall (who started the programme saying 'THIS IS Henry Hall speaking'), Harry Roy, Ambrose, Joe Loss. When America entered the war my greatest favourite of all was Glenn Miller and his Orchestra.
>
> I was in hospital in, I think, 1941, with diphtheria and I was terribly homesick and allowed no visitors. There was at that time a young American singer and her record of 'Harbour Lights' was played a lot on the radio and I was nearly convinced it had been written just for me! It went 'I can see the harbour lights of home, shining brightly o'er the foam' etc. Tears ran freely every time I heard it. Her name was Deanna Durbin.[10]

To judge from the number of picture postcards of Deanna Durbin to be found in German flea markets, there must have been a great many young German girls who felt the same way about Deanna Durbin.

Deanna Durbin.
A German postcard.

Dodgie Shaffer, a beautiful girl in Alabama who enjoyed herself despite the 'late unpleasantness' of the Second World War.

For Dodgie Shaffer, a lady from Montgomery, Alabama, of undiminished charm and joie-de-vivre, the dance music of the Second World War evokes the headiest moments of her life. After listening to a CD of hits of 1945 she wrote: 'I have been transported back to Lake Rhea (in actuality an oversized pot hole with a high diving board and bare lights strung about. To me at that time the most romantic place on earth). The jukebox in the dancing pavilion was a roiling band of lights and for "3 for a quarter" you selected your tickets to heaven! A beautiful long line of teenaged boys snaked about the dance floor and competition was fierce to attract them to

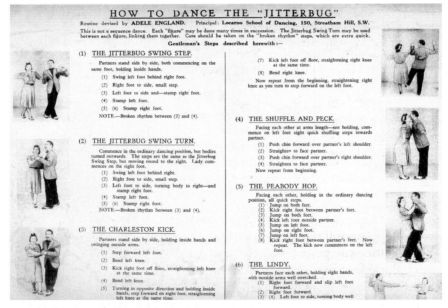

How to dance the 'Jitterbug' from a 1940s dance manual.

"break" on you and, pray God, only dance a few steps before somebody else came along. I have thought that, having lived through that terror, nothing later should have been daunting! But the terror was laced with the smell of gardenias blossoming all around, the athletic workout of the "jitterbug" where one was thrown over shoulders and the hope for grace in the "slow dances". My mother would say when I got home hot and tired, "Young lady, if I made you work that hard, you would sue me under the child labour laws."'[11]

For Dodgie, the war she refers to as 'that late unpleasantness' was also 'the last of the romantic wars!' evoked most potently by the song 'Don't Sit Under the Apple Tree, with anyone else but me'. It is hardly surprising that Dodgie Shaffer, who was a lovely young girl living far from any war zone, should feel that way, but a great many people who experienced the horror and tragedy of war more directly also grow misty-eyed and nostalgic when they hear the songs of the period.

When asked which song had meant most to her during the Second World War, Balbina, Gräfin Otting, born in Augsburg in 1918, immediately cited Schubert's 'An die Musik' and especially the text of its first verse:

> Du holde Kunst, in wieviel grauen Stunden
> Wo mich des Lebens wilder Kreis umstrickt,
> Hast du mein Herz zu warmer Lieb' entzunden,
> Hast mich in eine bessre Welt entrückt!

> (Oh lovely Art, in how many grey hours,
> When life's fierce orbit ensnared me,
> Have you kindled my heart to warm love,
> Carried me away into a better world!)

Gräfin Otting loved the voice of the Swedish film star Zarah Leander and sings along happily with all the *Schläger* (hits) of the war period but it is not so much these that recall the experiences of the war years to her as the folk songs with titles such as 'Der Jäger in den grünen Wald' (The Huntsman in the Green Forest) that were sung communally. Over 60 years later at the age of 92, she could still sing them off the top of her

Balbina, Gräfin Otting, who loved to sing Schubert and traditional folk songs during the war.

head over the telephone.

During the war, simple and banal songs were often invested with an intensity of emotion quite beyond their intrinsic merit. The intensity of feeling provoked by these songs did not have to be positive. Janina Bauman developed a deep loathing for the song 'Bel Ami', popularised throughout occupied Europe in the early stages of the war by the German movie of the same name. Bauman wrote:

> Regina, the girl who worked with me in the field, was singing all the time we were weeding. She has a nice voice and knows many of the pre-war hits. I was really quite enjoying it until she started on 'Bel Ami'. Suddenly I became hysterical and yelled at her to shut up. The reason is that I've been forced to listen to this stupid song day in day out in the early evenings. A beggar woman sings it endlessly down the street, just under my open window where I sit, trying in vain to concentrate on my reading. And how she sings it, my goodness. With a harsh, broken voice, Polish, Yiddish, French words all mixed up together. Her face is swollen so I can't tell her age. She has two children with her, one in her arms, the other clinging to her filthy clothes. Their feet are bare. When I drop down a coin or a bit of bread for them, or if someone else does, she stops for a second, then carries on with her 'Bel Ami' even louder and harsher. I really hate her, I hate all of them.[12]

There are many stories of music inspiring noble deeds during the war and the period leading up to it. Perhaps the most famous is that of the German officer who saved the life of the Polish pianist Wladyslaw Szpilman after hearing him play the Chopin C sharp minor Nocturne in the ruins of Warsaw.[13] There is also the story of two unobtrusive English spinsters, Ida and Louise Cook, who constantly travelled to Germany in the years leading up to the war to hear opera performances given by the conductor Clemens Krauss and the soprano Viorica Ursuleac, and at the same time organised escape routes for German Jews. Ida Cook wrote: 'I very much doubt if we should have been able to force ourselves to go on with this harrowing and arduous task if the whole experience had not been irradiated for us by Krauss and Ursuleac's superb operatic performances. Just as the pursuit of opera had originally brought us to the refugee work, so the pursuit of the refugee work was made possible only by the support (or if you like, the bribe) of great operatic performances which brought us back again and again.'[14]

Music did not always serve a 'nourishing', comforting or uplifting purpose. Like religion, music can be harnessed to any cause, good or bad. In an article entitled 'The Mission of Music' published in the *New York Times Magazine* in March 1944 in tribute to the conductor Bruno Walter, Thomas Mann commented on the dual nature of the impact of music: '… it is both moral code and seduction, sobriety and drunkenness, a summons to the highest alertness and a lure to the sweetest sleep of enchantment, reason and anti-reason'.[15] Fascism was primarily interested in exploiting music's power of seduction and its ability to overcome reason when not using it for utilitarian purposes. According to Anita Lasker-Wallfisch, the main function of the Auschwitz orchestra was to 'go to the Main Gate every morning and every evening and play marches for the thousands of prisoners who worked outside the camp, at places like I G Farben *inter alia*. It was imperative that these columns of prisoners should march neatly and in step, and we provided the music to achieve this.'[16] A particularly pointed use of music as a weapon of deception and propaganda was Goebbels's faked broadcast of soldiers in besieged Stalingrad singing Christmas carols in the winter of 1942.[17]

The endless stream of military marches broadcast from German radio stations was intended to induce a state of mindless obedience and aggression in the German military and civil population, particularly towards the end of the war when authorities feared a breakdown of resolution and discipline. Though more benign, the 'Music While You Work' programmes broadcast by the BBC fulfilled a similar purpose of encouraging concentration and productivity in factory workers.

There is a chilling and disturbing photograph taken in May 1942 of Reinhard Tristan Heydrich, 'protector' of Bohemia and Moravia and one of the principal authors of the 'final solution' against the Jews, on the eve of the attack by partisans that eventually resulted in his death. In full uniform and accompanied by his plump blond wife trotting docilely behind him, Heydrich is striding out of a concert hall in Prague where he had been listening to a concert of chamber music by his father. Heydrich's father, Richard Bruno Heydrich, was a minor German composer working in a post-Wagnerian idiom (hence his son's middle name). Heydrich senior wrote an opera with the curiously prophetic name of *Reinholds Verbrechen* ('The Crimes of Reinhold').

The works of Heydrich père are unlikely to see the light of day again. This will probably be no great loss to the world of music. Heydrich's music made little headway even under the propitious circumstances of the Third Reich. Nevertheless morbid curiosity, if nothing else, might encourage a music lover to wonder what a string quartet by the father of one of history's greatest criminals could possibly sound like.

We are presented here with a conundrum—the juxtaposition of art and crime. The classical musical tradition was arguably the greatest achievement of Western culture. The great French soprano Germaine Lubin asserted '… it is inconceivable that Schumann, Brahms, Wagner or Strauss had any connection with the horrors perpetrated by the Nazis.'[18] The Nazis themselves saw it differently and attempted to appropriate the work of these composers and bring it into alignment with their ideology of nationalism, hatred and aggression.

The women's orchestra of Auschwitz is perhaps the most notorious example of music being performed in circumstances of great horror, but there were many other juxtapositions equally bizarre and incomprehensible. In May 1943 a company from the Czech town of Ostrava (Mährisch-Ostrau) arrived at Auschwitz in order to entertain Waffen-SS in the camp with a performance of the operetta *Bezauberndes Fräulein* ('Enchanting Lady') by Ralph Benatzky, best known for his pre-war hit *White Horse Inn*, and then a refugee with his Jewish wife in America.[19] Hans Frank, the governor general of occupied Poland and ultimately responsible for the Polish death camps, was a passionate lover of music (and according to rumour of a much respected German soprano of the post-war period). Frank was the dedicatee of works by the two leading, living German composers, Pfitzner and Strauss, and continued to sponsor musical events in Crakow till close to the end of the war, including what must have been an exceptionally fine performance of Strauss's *Ariadne auf Naxos* on 24 June 1944, with Julius Patzak and Viorica Ursuleac.[20]

It was in the nineteenth century that music was first widely used to enhance a sense of national identity and to quicken patriotic fervour. The inflammatory power of opera was demonstrated in a spectacular way on 25 August 1830 by a performance of Auber's *La muette de Portici* at the Théâtre de la Monnaie in Brussels. The patriotic duet 'Amour sacré de la patrie' sparked uproar in the audience, and in turn led to riots in the streets and the eventual creation of an independent Belgium. After this incident, repressive and authoritarian regimes all over

Europe became anxious about the potential of opera to fuel populist and nationalist sentiment. For over twenty years Verdi battled with authorities in various parts of Italy who attempted to censor the plots of his operas. Often their efforts were in vain. Longing for the freedom and unity of their country, Italians identified with the oppressed Jews in Verdi's *Nabucco,* premiered in 1842, and 'Va pensiero', 'The Chorus of the Hebrew Slaves', became the anthem of the Risorgimento and an unofficial Italian national anthem.

In Poland in 1865, the Russian authorities suppressed Stanislaw Moniuszko's opera *The Haunted Manor* because of its nationalist sentiment. But in neighbouring Bohemia, the authorities of the Habsburg Empire seem to have regarded Smetana's great epic operas *Dalibor* (premiere 1868) and *Libuše* (premiere 1881) as safety valves for the expression of Czech nationalism and made no attempt to prevent performances.

It was in the nineteenth century, too, that the singing of national anthems became common practice. A handful of nations adopted their anthems even earlier. The Dutch 'Het Wilhelmus', dating back to the sixteenth-century Dutch Revolt, is regarded as the earliest, though not officially adopted till 1932. The British used 'God Save the King' from 1745. The 'Marseillaise' was written in 1792, briefly adopted as a national anthem in 1795 and in 1830, and finally and permanently from 1879. Haydn's graceful melody used by the Austrians until 1918, was taken over by the Germans in 1922 for 'Deutschland über alles'. The Russians used the 'Internationale' from 1917 to 1944 when a competition was held to replace it. America's 'Star-Spangled Banner' underwent some strange vicissitudes during the war. Toscanini re-arranged it for inclusion in Verdi's 'Hymn to the Nations'. Stravinsky was less successful when he attempted to re-arrange it to express his gratitude at becoming an American citizen in 1943 and, as he put it, to do his 'bit in these grievous times toward fostering and preserving the spirit of patriotism'. Objections were raised to his dissonant harmonies and a police raid prevented a public performance in Boston on 15 January 1944.[21] There must have been even more dissonant harmonies when André Kostelanetz conducted it on a Far Eastern tour in February 1945 and the Chinese insisted on playing their own anthem simultaneously in order to avoid questions of precedence.[22]

Needless to say, all these anthems were widely used during the Second World War, but in this war of anthems the French had an undoubted advantage. The inflammatory 'Marseillaise' with its

In the war of national anthems, the French had the advantage.

exciting upward leaping melody proved a highly effective weapon for the Free French and a thorn in the flesh for the authorities in both Vichy and Occupied France. The communal singing of the 'Marseillaise' was always a potential flashpoint between German occupiers and the French population. The famous scene in the movie *Casablanca* when the customers of Rick's bar join together in an emotional rendering of the anthem must have been repeated countless times in reality. The Vichy regime attempted to promote 'Maréchal nous voilà' as an alternative to their official anthem, as did the Italians with the Fascist hymn 'Giovinezza', and the Germans with the 'Horst Wessel Lied'. The English and the Americans also had their popular and unofficial anthems in 'There'll always be an England' and 'God Bless America' though there were no government attempts to sponsor either.

The emotive power of national anthems was demonstrated in April 1945 in a broadcast around the world of the moment that the French pianist and singer Fania Fénelon was rescued at the Bergen-Belsen concentration camp. Fénelon was close to death from the effects of typhus and starvation. She wrote:

> Someone handed me a microphone.
> It was strange. The process of breathing exhausted me, my heart was positively economising its beats, life had become a remote possibility, yet I straightened up, galvanised by joy, and I sang the 'Marseillaise' again. This time it emerged with a violence and a strength that I had never had before which I shall probably never have again …
> The microphone holder insisted: 'Please, miss, it's for the BBC.'

I sang 'God Save the King' and tears filled the soldier's eyes.
I sang the 'Internationale' and the Russian deportees joined in.[23]

All countries involved in the Second World War attempted to harness the power of music and to use it to reinforce a sense of identity. But music was not always so easily channelled or controlled. It could cross borders and serve the interest of either or both sides. In popular music the most remarkable example of this was the song 'Lili Marleen'. In classical music the most telling example was the opening motto theme of Beethoven's Fifth Symphony—three short notes followed by a longer one that conveniently also formed the letter 'V' in Morse Code. Though written by a German, this music became a potent symbol of faith in the ultimate victory of the Allies over the Axis powers. Played on a kettledrum and repeated with pregnant pauses, Beethoven's theme was used to introduce the legendary BBC broadcasts to the French Resistance. During the 1941 campaign, run from the BBC in London, to incite French civilians to inscribe defiant 'V' signs in public places, the French makers of the radio programme 'Les Français parlent aux Français' ('Frenchmen speak to the French') devised a cheeky text to be sung to the opening melody of the Fifth Symphony that must have struck many Germans as a blasphemy.

Il ne faut pas désespérer
On les aura
Il ne faut nous arrêter de resister
Et n'oublie pas la lettre 'V'.[24]

After the opening drum signals, the programmes of the London-based Free French continued with the announcement 'Ici Londres' ('This is London') followed by a snatch of the 'Water Music' by another German composer, Georg Friedrich Händel (known in England as George Frideric Handel). It does not seem to have struck anyone as odd that this 'English' music was by a native of the German city of Halle, which would resist Allied conquest with house-to-house fighting in the very last days of the war. The composer Ralph Vaughan Williams wrote to the BBC objecting to the use of the Bach chorale 'Ein feste Burg', virtually a German national anthem—at least in the Protestant north, in a service broadcast from St Paul's Cathedral on D-Day, but no one else seems to have noticed the incongruity.

Nazi attempts to re-appropriate Beethoven's Fifth Symphony

for the German cause and harness it to their own war effort were ineffective and the music remained stubbornly associated with the Allies. The nearest equivalent on the German side was the use of the fanfares from the tone poem 'Les Préludes' by the Hungarian composer Franz Liszt. In continental Europe at least, this music became indelibly associated with radio announcements of Nazi victories in the early stages of the war. However, this did not prevent 'Les Préludes' from being programmed three times during the war at Prom concerts in London where audiences would have been more likely to associate the music with the wobbly take-off of Buster Crabbe's space ship in the pre-war science fiction *Flash Gordon* movies than with Nazi news bulletins.[25]

The wartime prestige of classical music is demonstrated by a mini-war of commemorative postage stamps. In 1941 and 1942 the French issued stamps honouring Debussy and Chabrier, two composers who were believed to represent Gallic rather than Teutonic musical virtues. In November 1942 the German government of Poland issued a commemorative stamp of the obscure ethnic German composer Josef Elsner, who had been Chopin's teacher, in an attempt to claim Poland's great national genius for themselves. In 1941 the German authorities in Bohemia issued a set of stamps dedicated to Mozart in commemoration of the 150th anniversary of his death, but also as part of their programme to germanize Czech culture. Two years later in 1943 the Czechs were forced to endure a stamp celebrating Wagner. The Quisling government of Norway, and the Soviets, got in on the game with commemorative stamps of Grieg and Rimsky-Korsakov respectively.[26]

Throughout the war in every Western country, Austro-German classical music remained as dominant in the concert hall as American-style popular music was in the dance hall. In the Prom concerts that continued in London every summer from 1940 to 1944, and which themselves became an important symbol of British defiance of the Nazi bombing of London, works by Austrian and German composers outnumbered those by British and Commonwealth composers by a factor of three to one (595 to 191). The most frequently performed composers were Beethoven (128 works) and Wagner (111 works); their nearest British competitor was Elgar with a mere 33 works performed. Amongst the composers still living at the end of the war, the most frequently performed (with 15 works) was another German, Richard Strauss.[27] In Paris, Arthur Honegger was a lone and brave voice protesting in an article of September 1941 in the journal *Comoedia* that there was too much German classical music being foisted on the French public by the Paris orchestras: 'More than ever in the winter of 1940-41 the festival of Beethoven followed the festival of Wagner which preceded the festival of Wagner-Beethoven.' Honegger's point was that this showed laziness on the part of concert programmers but there was also perhaps an implication of excessive deference towards the German occupiers.

Beethoven Cycle. Paris 1943. (Les Ondes)

From the very first, the Nazi regime relentlessly exploited the richness of the Austro-German musical tradition to promote the idea of German cultural superiority. For the operetta composer Robert Stolz, speaking over the radio to his Austrian compatriots from New York in 1942, it was as if the Nazis had 'planted a steel helmet on the head of Mozart, had strapped a sabre to Schubert's side and wound barbed wire round the throat of Johann Strauss.'[28] In a speech broadcast on 8 November 1939, Hitler mocked English cultural inadequacy and proclaimed: 'Ein einziger Deutscher, sagen wir Beethoven, hat mehr geleistet als alle Engländer zusammen' ('One single German, shall we say Beethoven, achieved more than all the English put together'). Musicology in Germany was subverted to create a version of musical history that accorded with Nazi ideology. Inconvenient details, such as Johann Strauss's Jewish ancestry, were airbrushed from sight.[29] On a more populist level, the lives of composers such as Mozart, Beethoven and Schumann were celebrated in movies that presented them as heroes of German culture.

In fact, the lives and works of nearly all the great German and Austrian composers, from Handel and Bach to Schumann and Brahms and even Wagner, were problematic to Nazi ideologues in various ways. In the case of Handel and Bach it was largely their engagement with Biblical texts from both Old and New Testaments. With Handel there was also the uncomfortable fact that he deserted his native

Wounded German soldiers at a performance of Mozart's Die Zauberflöte. *(Signal, 1943)*

Germany for England, the country that remained, throughout the early part of the war at least, the most stubborn and implacable of Germany's enemies. The debate about the 'Aryanisation' of the texts of Handel's oratorios, in which Rosenberg and Goebbels took opposite sides, is discussed authoritatively in Erik Levi's book *Music in the Third Reich*. The popular oratorio *Judas Maccabeus* in particular received several Nazi makeovers. With Bach it was the Jewish references in the Cantatas and Passions that caused problems for the Nazis. Two recordings of the *St Matthew Passion* were made in Germany during the Second World War—a near complete version under Bruno Kittel in August 1942 and a more heavily cut version under Günther Ramin in 1941. The cuts in the Ramin version, which comprises thirty-one 78 rpm sides, are largely down to the exigencies of space. But cuts of certain phrases in some of the recitatives that are common to both, such as 'von den Kindern Israel' ('from the children of Israel') and

'Dies ist Jesus, der Judenkönig' ('This is Jesus, King of the Jews') show that even minor references to the Jews were unacceptable to the Nazis.[30] Similar minor changes were made even to the Latin text of Bruno Kittel's wartime recording of the Mozart *Requiem* in order to avoid the words 'Sion' and 'Jerusalem'.

Despite the famous *Requiem*, Mozart was never primarily a religious composer and the problems he presented to the Nazis were of quite a different order. Firstly, there was his very active involvement in Freemasonry—Freemasons being only a little lower down the Nazi hate list than Jews. Connected with Mozart's interest in Freemasonry was his espousal of 'enlightened' ideals of brotherly love, tolerance and pacifism that sat ill with Nazi ideology. These ideas were expressed not only in the numerous works that Mozart wrote for the Freemasons but also in two of his greatest operas, *Die Entführung aus dem Serail* (composed 1781-82, some time before Mozart became a Freemason) and above all *Die Zauberflöte*. (Ironically, because of the casual and clumsy racism of Emanuel Schikaneder's text, *Die Zauberflöte* is the only work in the standard operatic repertoire that is routinely censored in modern performance.)

The knottiest problem for the Nazis concerning Mozart was what to do about the three masterpieces that he wrote to texts of Lorenzo da Ponte—*Le Nozze di Figaro*, *Don Giovanni* and *Così fan tutte*. That Da Ponte was a renegade Catholic priest did not excuse him from also being a renegade Jew. The Nazis in any case favoured the performance of Mozart's Italian operas in German translation, but this did not help, as the standard translations in use since the late nineteenth century were by another Jew, Hermann Levi. Alternative 'Aryanised' translations were produced though it is not clear how much German audiences noticed.[31]

The 150th anniversary of Mozart's death fell in 1941. The Nazis attempted to capitalise on this event to the maximum, staging commemorative concerts around the Reich, climaxing in a 'Mozart Week' in Vienna at the beginning of December to which musicians and composers from all over the Nazi empire were summoned. Commemorative performances of the *Requiem* took place around the globe on both sides in the conflict, with Furtwängler leading the performances in Vienna and Berlin, Bruno Walter in New York and Victor de Sabata in Rome. In an exciting dramatic performance, remote from anything considered Mozartian today, De Sabata conducted the gargantuan forces of the combined orchestras and choirs of Turin and Rome radio in the echoing spaces of the Basilica di Santa Maria degli Angeli, with Beniamino Gigli, Maria Caniglia, Ebe Stignani and Tancredi Pasero as soloists. Excerpts of the prestigious concert are preserved in contemporary newsreel footage. The following day De Sabata made a commercial recording of the work for the Italian state firm of CETRA. Somewhat oddly, considering that Italy and Britain were now at war, the exclusive contracts of Gigli, Caniglia and Pasero with the British firm of HMV were honoured and they were replaced on the CETRA recording by Ferruccio Tagliavini, Pia Tassinari and Italo Tajo.

It was above all Beethoven who was presented by the Nazis as the supreme expression of 'Aryan' genius. This version of Beethoven accorded well with the frowning 'superman' to be found in countless plaster busts sitting on pianos in middle class households and on popular picture postcards of Beethoven dating back to the end of the nineteenth century. The more bombastic elements in the music of *Fidelio* and the Ninth Symphony enabled the Nazis to overlook the liberal and humanistic sentiments expressed in these works and to adopt them as talismanic works of the regime. *Fidelio* was chosen to reopen almost every major German opera house after the war and according to Germaine Lubin, who sang the role of Leonora in occupied Paris, its message of freedom was not lost on wartime audiences either. 'When

Cover of Les Ondes *16 May 1943.*

Fidelio was revived, there was an interminable ovation after the "Abscheulicher", whose text is a hymn of defiance towards injustice. With so many Germans in the audience, I did not want to create an incident and refused to take my usual solo bow.'[32] In an article published in a German language magazine in New York in September 1945, Thomas Mann famously asked how it was possible that *Fidelio* could be performed under the Third Reich. 'It was a scandal that it was not forbidden, that highly refined performances were given, that there were singers

20

prepared to sing it, musicians prepared to play it and a public prepared to listen.'[33]

The appeal of Beethoven during the Second World War was universal. He was the most frequently performed classical composer in every country. Above all, the Ninth Symphony seemed to offer a universal message of hope. Many fine live recordings of this symphony survive from the war years, including several by Furtwängler, Toscanini and Mengelberg. Janine Micheau, who sang the soprano part in the final public performance given by Mengelberg at the Théâtre des Champs-Elysées on 18 June 1944, not long after sang in one of the first performances to be given in liberated Paris under Serge Koussevitzky.

Beethoven is the composer most frequently and movingly referred to in the diary of the young French Jewish violinist, Hélène Berr, as she gradually came to the realisation that her death at the hands of the Nazis was inevitable. On 26 November 1943 she wrote: 'I must have a fever. I felt odd all day. All the same I went to see Nadine. The Adagio from Beethoven's Trio No. 5. What beauty!'[34] But Beethoven's music could increase the pain as well as providing solace. In February 1944 shortly before her arrest and deportation, it prompted a heartfelt outburst in her diary.

> I had been at Nadine's. Lessons have been suspended yet again. The pianist who played with us was arrested on Monday evening with his sister and has surely been deported. Denounced. Mme Jourdan and Nadine played a Beethoven sonata. Suddenly during the Adagio, the cruelty and lunatic injustice of this new arrest—after a thousand others—seared my heart. A boy of such talent, a boy able to offer the world such pure joy through an art oblivious to human malice—up against brutality, matter devoid of spirit. How many souls of infinite worth, repositories of gifts others should have treated with humility and respect, have been similarly crushed and broken by Germanic brutality? Just as a precious violin, full of dormant capacities to awaken the deepest and purist emotions, may be broken by brutal, sacrilegious force.[35]

It was ironic that it was precisely the beauty of this most German music that should elicit her denunciation of German brutality.

Both Schumann and Brahms were potentially tainted for the Nazis by their Jewish connections. Schumann wrote some of his greatest songs to texts of Heine (as had Schubert towards the end of his short life) and Brahms had formed a lifelong friendship and musical partnership with the violinist Joseph Joachim. There was even the dreadful prospect that Wagner might turn out to have been half Jewish. Wagner's mother's lover, Ludwig Geyer, may or may not have been the composer's true father and may or may not have been a Jew. All this was anxiously investigated under the Nazi regime.

Richard Wagner is the classical composer most closely associated in popular imagination with Hitler and the Nazi war effort. Hitler is often quoted as having said 'Whoever wants to understand National Socialist Germany must first know Wagner.' Woody Allen quipped: 'Every time I hear Wagner I feel like invading Poland.' This might seem like a rather glib equation of Wagner's music and Nazism, but does in fact identify perhaps the most salient characteristic of Wagner's music, the ability to stir emotion and arouse passion in a visceral and quite unthinking way, something that was ruthlessly exploited by the Nazis, and not only by them as we see from the frequency of Wagner's name in wartime Prom programmes in London. The virulence of Wagner's anti-Semitism is evident in both his published writings and his private correspondence. A direct line can be drawn from Wagner to Hitler through the racist theorizing of the composer's son-in-law Houston Stewart Chamberlain.

To what extent Wagner's stage works are infected by his racism and anticipate or conform to Nazi ideology is currently a matter of intense debate. Wagner's granddaughter Friedlinde, the 'black sheep' of the Wagner clan who bravely rejected her family's association with Hitler and emigrated to America, was adamant that Wagner's operas had nothing to do with Nazism. Interviewed on 14 February 1943 during a broadcast of *Tannhauser* from the Metropolitan in New York (commemorating the 59th anniversary of the composer's death), Friedlinde Wagner indignantly refuted any link between Wagner and Nazi ideology.

> My grandfather is dead and cannot defend himself against the abuse. But I, his granddaughter, speak in his spirit and with his convictions when I tell you that 'Senta's pure love', as well as *Lohengrin* and *Parsifal* arise from a landscape where no Nazi jackboot ever trod.[36]

While Hitler and Nazi ideologues paraded their love of Wagner it is not clear how much they understood or even liked his operas. It is perhaps significant that the operas of Verdi were more frequently performed in Nazi Germany than those of Wagner. If the nobility of Verdi's idealism is not in doubt, the black and white certitudes of his operas may have been easier for Fascists to comprehend than the moral complexities and contradictions of Wagner's.

Benno von Arent's design for the final scene of Die Meistersinger *made it look like a Nuremberg rally.*

Die Meistersinger von Nürnberg became quite literally the party piece of the Nazi regime, wheeled out for party rallies and festivities. Benno von Arent's design for the final scene of *Die Meistersinger* (which was illustrated in a wartime Bayreuth programme), looks remarkably like Albert Speer's design for the Zeppelinfeld I Nuremberg, where the party rallies were actually held, and makes the connection obvious. Hans Sachs's peroration in this last scene leaves an unpleasant taste, but is essentially an expression of nineteenth-century nationalism rather than twentieth-century racism and not necessarily more sinister than a xenophobic speech at a Tory party conference. Otherwise, *Die Meistersinger*'s insistence on freedom of expression and artistic innovation was more in tune with the ethos of Weimar Germany than Nazi Germany.

In the *Ring* cycle, the depiction of the Nibelungen may well have anti-Semitic undertones but the themes of the corrupting influence of power and the redemptive power of love are hardly in accordance with Nazi ideology. If the *Ring* is indeed a blueprint for the Nazi regime as some believe, then it was all too accurate in its prediction of how it would end. For wartime listeners in democratic countries, even the most thunderously monumental sections of the *Ring* did not necessarily bring associations of Nazism to mind. When the émigré conductor Bruno Walter included 'Siegfried's Funeral March' in a concert given in Los Angeles in July 1939, a local critic wrote that the 'emotions this performance aroused brought tears' as the 'fate of the country where this music was created came to mind and the orchestra reflected the life tragedy that is in our hearts and minds at this moment.'[37]

The fact that *Parsifal* was more or less dropped from the repertory throughout the German Reich during the war years (although recorded fragments exist of what was evidently a fine performance, conducted by Knappertsbusch in Vienna on 10 November 1942) is indicative of the problems that the Nazis had with their favourite composer. With its quasi-religious celebration of purity of blood, *Parsifal* has been identified by Robert Gutman and several more recent commentators as the most proto-Nazi of all Wagner's operas.[38] It would seem that the Nazis mistook *Parsifal*'s veneer of Christian piety for the real thing and failed to understand the opera's underlying meaning.

Though wounded soldiers from the Eastern Front were forced to endure performances of *Die Meistersinger* and *Götterdämmerung* at Bayreuth, it is likely that many of the Nazi top brass (including perhaps Goebbels and Hitler) secretly preferred *The Merry Widow*. Albert Speer recalled that during the gala performance of *Die Meistersinger* that opened the 1933 Nuremburg Rally, patrols had to be sent out to the beer halls and cafes to press-gang Nazi officials into turning up at the opera, and the following year Hitler had to issue orders for party chiefs to attend. 'They showed their boredom; many were visibly overpowered by sleep. Moreover, to Hitler's mind the sparse applause did not do justice to the brilliance of the performance.'[39] With the impending disaster of Stalingrad in the back of everyone's minds, the gala performance of *Die Meistersinger* staged at Goering's behest

on 12 December 1942 in order to celebrate the restoration and re-opening of the Berlin State Opera House after its first destruction by British bombers was a particularly glum and hollow occasion. Albert Speer wrote in his autobiography: 'In gala uniforms or full dress we took our seats in the Führer's big box. The jovial plot of the opera painfully contrasted with the events at the front so that I kept chiding myself for having accepted the invitation.'[40]

Wagner continued to figure prominently in the programmes of the Prom concerts in London and

A wartime Wagner Festival at Bayreuth.
(Signal)

the Metropolitan Opera in New York (not to mention the concert halls and opera houses of occupied France). It was only in France during the *drôle de guerre* that there was a debate as to whether the playing of Wagner's music was appropriate in wartime or not. The Parisian daily newspaper *Le Jour* thought not: 'Wagner's art is a mirror of the brutal and rapacious German soul. Now that the front line, where our sons may be fighting tomorrow, bears the name of Siegfried, it seems hardly fitting for us to participate in Wagner's glorification.' Even here though, the debate went Wagner's way, and on 10 March 1940 Paul Paray conducted a concert with the combined members of the Colonne and Lamoureux orchestras who had not been conscripted, in which they played the Overture to Wagner's *Tannhäuser* alongside French works.

It is a measure of the importance given to music in wartime Germany that musical performances continued until the very last days of the war. In 1944 the French edition of the Nazi propaganda magazine *Signal* boasted of seven premieres given in Germany in one week and illustrated a performance of Mozart's *Die Zauberflöte* that took place in Hamburg on 16 May 1944, nearly a year after the destruction of its opera house and most of the city by firestorms caused by a series of bombing raids in the week of 25 July to 2 August 1943.

Die Zauberflöte *performed in the ruined city of Hamburg in 1944 after the destruction of the opera house.* (Der Adler)

Erna Berger as Gilda in Verdi's Rigoletto.

Even after theatres were closed down in August 1944, German radio stations continued to record and broadcast concerts and complete operas with Germany's top artists. Two surviving opera broadcasts from the final months of the war stand out— *Tosca* with Hildegarde Ranczak, Helge Rosvaenge and Georg Hann conducted by Leopold Ludwig in October 1944, and *Rigoletto* with Heinrich Schlusnus, Erna Berger and Helge Rosvaenge, conducted by Robert Heger, in November. By coincidence, in both recordings small roles are sung by Margery Booth, an English singer who was later revealed to have been a spy working for the British throughout the war.

In *Tosca*, the Act II scenes between Tosca and the evil police chief Scarpia are played with a brutal realism unequalled in any other recording, suggesting that the lurid melodrama of Puccini's 'shabby little shocker' had become the reality of daily life for many in the German Reich by this time. It was a thought that certainly occurred to the baritone Tito Gobbi when he performed the role of Scarpia in a performance of *Tosca* presented to the German Wehrmacht in Rome in May 1944. 'Many times during those months of the Occupation it seemed that nothing which we acted out on the operatic stage could surpass the drama in our everyday lives ... The performance was a great success in spite of the nervous tensions among the cast and the inevitable reflections among us that Scarpia had become a disagreeably topical figure.'[41]

It seems remarkable that by late November 1944 a functioning studio with a roof on it could have been found in Berlin for the making of what turned out to be one of the finest of all recorded performances of *Rigoletto*. The deeply felt and smoothly sung Rigoletto of Heinrich Schlusnus and the touchingly girlish Gilda of Erna Berger remain exemplary.

It is even more bizarre that in January 1945, German sound engineers were still experimenting with improved recording techniques. On 23 January 1945, four days before the liberation of Auschwitz and the revelation of the ultimate horror of the Nazi regime, a stereo recording was made in Berlin of Beethoven's 'Emperor' Concerto with Walter Gieseking as soloist. By this time the Nazis' last vain hope of avoiding defeat lay in the prowess of German engineers, and Hitler's final secret weapon—the V2 rocket—was about to be unleashed on London. The sound quality of this Beethoven is astonishing. In a quiet passage of the first movement cadenza the sound of distant anti-aircraft fire is captured with perfect clarity.

As the Soviet troops closed in on Vienna in March 1945 the Gauleiter of the city, Baldur von Schirach, made a speech in which he claimed: 'This war has a profoundly mysterious and strange meaning in that … it is also being fought for art against a nation that has no feeling for the arts' ('gegen eine amusische Nation geführt wird'). In a last flamboyant gesture he commissioned a gala performance of *Götterdämmerung* that was to be recorded and filmed for posterity. His son Richard von Schirach has written a detailed and vivid description of the increasingly desperate attempts to complete this quixotic project in a city stricken by bombing raids and on the point of surrender.[42]

Appropriately enough it was the Berlin Philharmonic Orchestra, the flagship of Nazi musical life, that gave the last concerts of the regime, continuing into the second half of April 1945. The very last, which included Strauss's tone poem *Tod und Verklärung* ('Death and Transfiguration'), was given on 20 April 1945, ten days before Hitler's suicide and eighteen days before the final surrender.[43]

The First World War had cost the lives of three fine composers. The Catalan Enrique Granados, a citizen of neutral Spain, was drowned when the passenger ship on which he was travelling was torpedoed by a German submarine. The 31-year-old English composer George Butterworth was killed on the Western Front in 1916, having produced a handful of hauntingly sad works that with hindsight seem to have anticipated his own death. The French composer Albéric Magnard staged his own immolation and the destruction of the manuscript of his unperformed operatic masterpiece *Guercoeur* by firing on the German troops who surrounded his house in 1914. The Austrian pianist Paul Wittgenstein compensated for the tragic loss of his right arm by commissioning a series of left-hand piano works from leading composers.

The annual lists of prizewinners at the Paris Conservatoire published in the magazine *Le Théâtre* in the years immediately preceding the First World War reveal a characteristic pattern. Most of the female singers went on to have significant careers at one or other of the two main Paris opera houses but almost none of the men. The presumption must be that the young male singers were killed or had their careers blighted by four years on the Western Front. In the First World War it was overwhelmingly young men of military age who died. In the Second, with both sides waging a ruthless and indiscriminate war against civilian populations, the toll of musicians and the consequent loss to music was much higher.

The most significant factor in the death toll of musicians was undoubtedly the Nazi Holocaust. Czechoslovakia, the first country to be occupied by the Nazis, lost more of its musical talent than any other. In 1942 Erwin Schulhoff, who had been a leading figure of the inter-war avant-garde, died in the Wülzburg concentration camp. The three days of 16 to 18 October 1944, during which the Czech Jewish composers Hans Krasa, Viktor Ullmann and Pavel Haas were transported along with many other musicians from Theresienstadt to Auschwitz and gassed, may be deemed the most tragic in the history of music. In occupied Croatia, the partisan composer Vojislav Vuckovic was shot dead by Nazi police on 25 December 1942. Two noted German musicologists were executed for their opposition to the Nazi regime, Kurt Huber on 13 July 1943 and P Kilian Kirchhoff on 24 April 1944.

In addition to these composers who had already had the opportunity to demonstrate if not to fully develop their talents, there must have been thousands about whose potential one can only speculate. In an interview given in 2009, the eminent Dutch conductor Bernard Haitink, who was brought up in Nazi-occupied Holland, said modestly: 'These are very dangerous and unpleasant thoughts— but I would never have been a conductor if all these catastrophes had not happened. There would have been more talented conductors than me.'[44]

Two factors worked in favour of musicians. All sides in the war regarded musical talent as an asset to be exploited for political ends and tended to protect their more gifted composers and musicians. Though Shostakovich was photographed in a fire helmet doing fire service on the roof of the Leningrad Conservatoire, he was in fact carefully looked after by the Soviet regime that recognised his propaganda value. In the German Reich, members of the Berlin Philharmonic led something like a charmed existence until the very end of the war. In his book *The Reich's Orchestra*, Mischa Aster calculates that six members of the orchestra died in its final chaotic days.

Secondly, musical talent was the best of all passports and certainly enabled many musicians to escape Nazi persecution. The composer Mischa Spoliansky always referred to his 1932 international hit song 'Tell me tonight' as his 'passport'.[45] Others discovered that their 'musical passport' had run out. The great Wagnerian mezzo Ottilie Metzger, the dramatic soprano Henriette Gottlieb, the coloratura soprano Grete Forst and the dapper baritone Louis Treumann (the original Danilo in *The Merry Widow*) all died because they were too old to continue their careers somewhere safer. Gershon Sirota, known as the 'Jewish Caruso' and perhaps the greatest cantor to have made records, could easily have found refuge in America but was caught in Warsaw when he returned to be with his sick wife and died with the rest of his family in the Warsaw Ghetto.

The fine dramatic soprano Henriette Gottlieb who died in a concentration camp in 1943.

A number of Jewish musicians who fell into Nazi hands, such as the cellist Anita Lasker-Wallfisch, and the pianists Fania Fénelon and Alice Herz-Sommer, survived thanks to their musical talents. The most famous case of a life saved by music is that of the Polish composer and pianist Wladyslaw Szpilman, whose memoir *Death of the City* provided the basis for the film *The Pianist*.

Considering the devastation meted out to so many European cities, the number of musicians who were casualties of bombing raids was relatively small. The privileged status of the Berlin Philharmonic was not enough to protect all its members from Allied bombs. The violinist Alois Ederer and the timpanist Kurt Ulrich were both killed in Allied bombing raids as were two noted Italian singers—the famously beautiful Lina Cavalieri and the fiery mezzo Irene Minghini-Cattaneo, and the French composer Raoul Laparra.

In London the popular crooner Al Bowlly was killed on 17 April 1941 by a landmine that fell close to his flat. In one of the worst incidents of the Blitz, the Café de Paris received direct hits from bombs that killed the bandleader Ken 'Snakehips' Johnson and many of his musicians.

We cannot know how many young servicemen killed in the war might have gone on to have significant musical careers. Relatively few who had already established themselves took part in the war as combatants. The German baritone Karl Hammes, who had been a noted Don Giovanni in the 1930s, volunteered as a pilot at the start of the war and was killed during the initial invasion of Poland. The British composer Walter Leigh died at the age of 37 while fighting in North Africa in 1942 just as his music was beginning to take on a more personal voice. The gifted composer of film music Maurice Jaubert died of wounds on 19 June 1940. The death of the 29-year-old French composer Jehan Alain, killed on 20 June 1940 while acting as a despatch rider when France was already defeated, was a grievous and senseless loss. The promising Schoenberg pupil Peter Schacht died in the closing months of the war, in the service of the Nazi regime that had banned his music and that of his teacher.

At the end of the war there were a number of musicians on the Axis side, including three members of the Berlin Philharmonic and the conductor Oswald Kabasta, who committed suicide. Perhaps the best known musician to die in uniform was Major Glenn Miller, whose big band provided the soundtrack of the war for so many and whose disappearance over the English Channel in December 1944 has provoked wild and unlikely theories. Though a commissioned officer, Glenn Miller's value to the war effort was as an entertainer and morale booster.

Hundreds of other musicians and entertainers from the greatest to the most amateur put their lives in danger by travelling to war zones to entertain troops. The memoirs of these entertainers are full of anecdotes of hair-raising adventures and narrow escapes. Basil Dean recalled the dangers endured by ENSA (Entertainment National Service Association) stars in North Africa, when artistic temperament and military discipline did not always sit comfortably together:

> The rough flights over the desert tried the nerves of some of the party … En route for Tripoli, the port engine of the Dakota began to splutter and finally gave out altogether. One of the girls became hysterical:
> 'This is frightful. What will happen if we crash?' she cried.
> 'Two minutes' silence in the Ivy, dear,' remarked Bea [Beatrice Lillie] with admirable calm.[46]

One popular performer on the Axis side did indeed forfeit her life—the Austrian-born film star La Jana (real name Henny Hiebel), best known for her scantily-clad exotic dancing. She caught cold while entertaining the Wehrmacht on the Eastern Front in the winter of 1940 and died of double pneumonia.

For the history of twentieth-century music, the most serious loss of the Second World War was the death in September 1945 of the composer Anton Webern, shot as he stepped out into his son-in-law's garden after curfew to smoke a cigar, by a nervous and trigger-happy American soldier. The conductor Leo Borchard, who had survived Nazi persecution and taken

Viennese exotic dancer La Jana who died of pneumonia after catching cold on the Eastern Front.

an active role in German resistance, suffered a similar fate, shot dead by an American sentry on 23 August 1945.

An opera score I acquired a few years ago tells a heartening story of endurance and survival from the Second World War. It is an object that touches on and embodies many of the complexities and contradictions of twentieth-century musical history. The score in question is of the opera *Tiefland* by the Glasgow-born composer Eugen d'Albert, who had controversially repudiated his Scottish background to adopt Germany as his cultural and musical homeland. *Tiefland*, his greatest success, was premiered in the German Opera House in Prague in 1907.

Despite its Jewish librettist Rudolph Lothar (Rudolph Spitzer), *Tiefland* was apparently a favourite opera of Hitler and much performed during the Nazi period. During the war it travelled in the baggage of the German army. In the spring of 1944 it was performed in occupied Athens with the 20-year-old Maria Callas in the role of Marta. The theme of the purity of the mountains pitted against the corruption of the lowlands (Tiefland) fitted in comfortably with Nazi ideology. Though *Tiefland* continued to be performed in provincial German theatres after the war, it has never completely recovered from its associations with the Nazi period and has rarely been performed outside of Germany.

This particular score belonged to one Esther George Blum who lived in Budapest and who proudly inscribed her name twice on the score. She noted the names of the cast of a performance broadcast on Radio Budapest in 1932, including the fine Wagnerian bass-baritone Hans Hermann Nissen in the role of Don Sebastiano. The most telling feature of this score is the translation of parts of the German text that Esther Blum made into Swedish. These pencilled inscriptions suggest that Esther Blum may have been one of those Hungarian Jews issued with protective passports by the diplomat Raoul Wallenberg in 1944. How this much-travelled score arrived in London and what became of Esther Blum, remain a mystery. The score was offered to me by the dealer Eva Hornstein, a colourful and much loved personality on London's musical scene who supplies singers and musicians with rare scores. Eva's 'biological father', as she likes to call him, was himself a composer and a refugee from Nazi Germany.

In January 1941 the Austrian conductor Bruno Walter contributed an article to the journal *Decision* entitled 'About war and music' in which he expounded on the importance of music in wartime. 'I wanted to make up my mind whether now, when the battle of humanity is being fought, music should be allowed to retain the same importance as before. I began to see that music does not mean escape from world affairs; it can, in fact, play an active role in them ... To cultivate those things which have given meaning to our lives, and will redeem our future after the war, is the highest service to the good cause ... the voice of music brings in those who can hear it a message of hope. It is the high duty of the musician today unflatteringly to spread its gospel of promise to all mankind.'[47]

1   Bertha Geissmar, *The baton and the jackboot*, 1988, p. 321.
2   Ibid., p. 321.
3   CD, ARPCD 0270. Sleeve notes.
4   Noel Coward, *Middle East Diary*, 1944, p. 64.
5   Joyce Grenfell, *Joyce Grenfell Requests the Pleasure*, 1976, p. 149.
6   Anita Lasker-Wallfisch, *Inherit the Truth*, 2000, p. 84.
7   Janina Bauman, *Winter in the Morning*, 1986, p. 53.
8   Ibid.
9   Hans Fallada, *Alone in Berlin*, 2009, p. 473.

10 Letter to the author, 10 February 2010.
11 Letter to the author, 3 March 2010.
12 Bauman, p. 51.
13 Wladyslaw Szpilman, *Le Pianiste*, 1998.
14 Ida Cook, *We Followed Our Stars*, p. 190.
15 *New York Times Magazine*, 19 March 1944, p. 14.
16 Lasker-Wallfisch, p. 76.
17 Antony Beevor, *Stalingrad*, 1988.
18 Lanfranco Rasponi, *The Last Prima Donnas*, 1994, p. 93.
19 Ernst Klee, *Kulturlexikon zum Dritten Reich*, 2009, p. 38.
20 Ibid., p. 407.
21 Nicolas Slonimsky, *Music since 1900*, 1972, p. 779.
22 James A Drake and Kristin Beall Ludecke, *Lily Pons*, 1999, p. 149.
23 Fania Fénelon, *The Musicians of Auschwitz*, 1977, p. 18.
24 Aurélie Luneau, *Radio Londres, 1940-44*, 2005, p. 101.
25 BBC Proms Archive.
26 Slonimsky, p. 721 ff.
27 BBC Proms Archive.
28 Robert and Einzi Stolz, *Servus Du*, 1980, p. 377.
29 Erik Levi, *Music in the Third Reich*, 1994, p. 67.
30 I would like to thank Timothy McFarland for alerting me to the nature of the cuts in the Ramin recording of the *St Matthew Passion*.
31 Levi, p. 75-77.
32 Rasponi, p. 91.
33 Thomas Mann, *Essays. Volume 6. 1945-1955*, 'Warum ich nicht nach Deutschland zürück gehe', pp. 33-42. Originally published in *Aufbau*, 28 September 1945.
34 Hélène Berr, *Journal*, 2008, p. 219.
35 Ibid., p. 253.
36 Brigitte Hamann, *Winifred Wagner, a life at the heart of Hitler's Bayreuth*, 2005, p. 346.
37 *Los Angeles Times*, July 27, 1940, Section II, p. 7.
38 Robert W Gutman, *Richard Wagner*, 1968, pp. 589-616.
39 Albert Speer, *Inside the Third Reich*, 1970, p. 103.
40 Ibid., p. 346.
41 Tito Gobbi, *My Life*, 1979, p. 58.
42 Richard von Schirach, *Der Schatten meines Vaters*, 2005.
43 Mischa Aster, *The Reich's Orchestra*, 2010, p. 219.
44 *The Guardian*, 23 September 2009, Arts section, p. 20.
45 Conversation between the author and the composer's daughter Spoli Mills, 18 September 2003.
46 Basil Dean, *The Theatre at War*, 1956, p. 362.
47 Erik Ryding and Rebecca Pechefsky, *Bruno Walter, a world elsewhere*, 2001, p. 272.

Chapter 2
PRELUDE TO WAR 1937-40

The Second World War began formally on 3 September 1939. Informally, it could be said to have started as early as 1936 (or earlier still in the Far East) with Mussolini's invasion of Abyssinia, and with Hitler and Stalin fighting one another by proxy in Spain. Musically speaking, manoeuvres began in earnest in 1937. The Italian invasion of Abyssinia had immediate diplomatic and musical consequences which, though trivial seeming at the time, should have been a warning that in an age of totalitarian regimes, the fiction that art and politics can be kept separate from one another could no longer be maintained.

In reaction to French and British sanctions against Italy, the leading Italian tenor Beniamino Gigli indignantly declined to sing in Britain, and the French opera *Mignon* was precipitously dropped from the schedule at La Scala, to be replaced by Cilea's *L'Arlesiana*. Though dating back to 1897, *L'Arlesiana* had failed to catch on and had never been performed at Italy's premiere opera house. It was chosen quite simply because it had suitable roles for the two principal singers already booked for *Mignon*, Tito Schipa and Gianna Pederzini. The extraordinary success of these performances, fuelled in part by patriotic fervour, established *L'Arlesiana* as a firm favourite with Italian audiences for the rest of the Fascist period and some years beyond, and the lovely tenor aria known as the 'Lamento di Federigo' is a standard of the lyric tenor repertoire to this day.

More significantly, Anglo-French moves against Italy pushed Mussolini into the arms of Hitler, bringing about a political alignment between the two nations with the most important operatic traditions. Mussolini sealed the Axis by sending the company of La Scala to Munich and Berlin in June 1937 on a cultural goodwill mission. La

35

Tito Schipa as Federigo in Cilea's L'Arlesiana *at La Scala in 1936.*

The conductor Victor de Sabata who led the official visit of La Scala to Germany in 1937.

Scala fielded the best casts at its disposal—Beniamino Gigli, Gina Cigna, Ebe Stignani and Tancredo Pasero in the Verdi *Requiem*, Mafalda Favero and Giuseppe Lugo in *La Bohème*, and Gigli, Cigna, Stignani and Pasero again in *Aida*—all conducted by Toscanini's successor, the demonically brilliant Victor de Sabata.

The trip was celebrated with a lavishly produced official souvenir book. The cover is decorated with a border of fasces, theatrical masks, the swastika and the Italian national flag, and a photograph of Hitler and Goebbels applauding enthusiastically. Starting with the departure from Milan Central Station at 8.50 on 13 June 1937 of two trains loaded with scenery and equipment and almost 700 personnel (soloists, chorus, orchestra, dancers and technicians), we are taken through the 12-day tour day by day. Great pride is shown in the efficiency of the organisation, which we are told was admired even by the Germans.

In Munich where the company was quartered at the luxurious Vierjahreszeiten Hotel, the mayor gave a speech of welcome in which he lauded Munich ('capitale del movimento') and Milan as cultural capitals that had played a key role in the 'regeneration' of their respective nations.

The book is punctuated with images of smiling faces and right arms raised in the 'German greeting'. But the trip was not without some strange contradictions. Though Maestro de Sabata was brought up as a Catholic, his mother was Jewish, enough under the Nuremburg laws to ban him from cultural activities and later could have earned him a place in the gas chambers. In view of his close relationship with Mussolini and above all his value as a counterweight to the virulently anti-Nazi Toscanini, the Nazis

Cover of the souvenir booklet of the Scala visit to Germany in 1937.

were evidently happy to overlook De Sabata's Jewish ancestry and two years later would accord him the extraordinary honour of an invitation to conduct *Tristan* at Bayreuth. The celebrated chorus master Vittore Veneziani, who is repeatedly praised in the book for his contribution to the Verdi *Requiem*, was also Jewish but would lose his job the following year as a result of the racial laws introduced by Mussolini in imitation of Hitler. In a ceremony broadcast over the radio, intended as a homage to German culture and the new German Reich, the entire Scala company gathered round the monument to Richard Wagner for the laying of a wreath. In a moment of sublime and unconscious irony, the company burst into a rendition of 'Va, pensiero!' ('The Chorus of the Hebrew Slaves') from Verdi's *Nabucco*.

Reviews from German newspapers extensively quoted in the souvenir book are uniformly positive. It could hardly have been otherwise at this point with the German press so firmly under the control of Goebbels. Nuances of opinion can only be deduced from what is not said rather than from what is said.

The train carrying the Scala company leaves Milan railway station.

The company of La Scala pays homage to Wagner with a rendition of the Chorus of the Hebrew Slaves from Verdi's Nabucco.

The cast of La Bohème *takes a bow.*

It is noticeable for example that Mafalda Favero's Mimi elicits a great deal less comment than the Rodolfo of Giuseppe Lugo. The neutral comment from one German critic that her voice was 'typically' Italian may offer a clue. Her pointed, slightly acidulous tone and her lively and passionate manner would have differed greatly from the creamy timbre, and the droopy and pallid femininity, of the typical German lyric soprano of the period, reflecting the Nazi ideal of womanhood.

The final performance, of *Aida*, took place in Berlin on 22 June 1937 in the presence of Hitler and Goebbels. As we hear from extended surviving fragments of a radio broadcast, it was a passionately driven performance with all the performers responding to the excitement of the occasion. The audience, too, displays a frenzied enthusiasm more in keeping with a football match or a political rally than an opera performance. The Nile Scene is interrupted in mid-flow by wild applause in what would have been judged a major lapse of taste by serious Wagnerians. Gigli, at the end of a long career packed with triumphs, still remembered the applause on that night in Berlin: 'I had seen plenty of enthusiastic German audiences before, but never quite such frantic delirium. At the end of each act the entire audience was on its feet, shouting and waving handkerchiefs. Hitler applauded tirelessly, and at the final curtain he sent enormous bouquets tied with the national colours of Germany and Italy to all the principal artists. This provoked the audience to new outbursts of applause.'[1]

Berlin 22 June 1937. The singing of the German and Italian national anthems before the performance of Aida.

Even Goebbels was impressed by the occasion. He noted laconically in his diary: 'In the evening German Opera House, La Scala guest performance. The Führer there too. Splendid audience ... Gigli, Cigna. Quite magnificent.'[2]

On the homeward journey, as the two trains entered the Brenner Pass, the company broke into a spontaneous rendering of the Fascist hymn 'Giovinezza'. Using a metaphor that once again strikes us as incongruous, the book's author compares the return of La Scala to Milan to the arrival of Crusaders in Jerusalem.

Verdi's tub-thumping *Aida* and the French-born soprano Gina Cigna both did good service for Italy in 1937. In February Cigna sang Aida in New

Hitler and Goebbels at the performance of Aida.

Gina Cigna and Beniamino Gigli in the Triumph Scene from Aida.

Hitler congratulates De Sabata after the performance of Aida.

York alongside her compatriots Giovanni Martinelli, Bruna Castagna and Ezio Pinza to the ecstatic applause of New York's Italian community as we hear from a recording of a broadcast performance. With war approaching, Mussolini realised that vocal talent was a valuable national asset not to be squandered, and restricted the travel of top singers such as Mafalda Favero, Maria Caniglia, Ebe Stignani and Galliano Masini.

Hitler was less successful in attempting to ingratiate himself with London audiences by offering to send the much admired new Bayreuth production of *Lohengrin*, starring Franz Völker and Maria Müller under the baton of Furtwängler, with handsome designs by Emil Praetorius in a style that could be termed Fascist Deco, for the Coronation Season at the Royal Opera House. Hitler's offer was politely declined. According to Sir Thomas Beecham's biographer John Lucas, the reasons for the rejection were as much practical as political. Designed for the larger stage of Bayreuth, the *Lohengrin* production was simply too big for Covent Garden. The new king, Edward VIII, suspected by many of pro-Nazi sympathies, had no objection to accepting the Bayreuth *Lohengrin* as long as he did not have to go to 'the damned opera' himself.[3]

We know something of what London audiences missed from a surviving radio broadcast of extracts from Act III of one of the 1936

40

Bayreuth performances. The contrast between the peremptory barking of the German announcer and the patronisingly languid style of BBC announcers of the same period already underlines the growing gulf between the two nations (the splendidly effete BBC commentator on the opening ceremony of the 1936 Berlin Olympics could have been enough to convince the Nazi hierarchy that the British empire was ripe for the taking). But Furtwängler's dazzling account of the Act III prelude and the superb singing of Völker and Müller, both of whom muster sufficient breath to cope with Furtwängler's languorous tempi in the Bridal Chamber duet, might have won a measure of sympathy for the German regime among London's opera lovers.

Mounting suspicion of Nazi Germany and new diplomatic alignments were reflected in the programming and casting of the Coronation Season. Since international opera had resumed in 1924 for the first time after World War I, the Covent Garden seasons had been dominated by German repertoire and German performers. When Hitler took power in 1933, the management of Covent Garden cravenly dropped the distinguished Hungarian bass baritone Friedrich Schorr, who had been acclaimed since 1926 as Wotan and Hans Sachs, for fear of offending Hitler, who had been outraged to find the Jewish Schorr singing Wotan at the Bayreuth Festival in 1925. At the same time Covent Garden was happy to pick up some of the other many fine singers forced to flee from Nazi Germany and to buy at bargain price a production of the opera *Schwanda* by the Jewish composer Jaromir Weinberger that was no long wanted by the Berlin State Opera.[4]

By 1936 worries about Nazi Germany had reached the point when a conscious decision was taken to make the following season less dependent on German repertoire and artists. Productions of Dukas's *Ariane et*

Programme for the Coronation Season at the Royal Opera House, Covent Garden in 1937.

Souvenir programme for the Coronation Season in 1937

OTHER CONDUCTORS
for the Coronation Season

Conductors in the Coronation Season.

Barbe-Bleue and Gluck's *Alceste*, both starring the noble-voiced French dramatic soprano Germaine Lubin, were imported from the Paris Opéra, and the French repertoire was boosted with performances of *Pelléas et Mélisande* and *Carmen*.

A fascinating memorandum written on 9 December 1936 by the director of the Royal Opera House, Sir Thomas Beecham, for the attention of the director of the Paris Opéra, Jacques Rouché, makes it clear that personal and sexual as well as international politics played a role in the negotiations between the London and Paris opera houses. Beecham's memorandum is also a perfect model of the kind of arrogant and clumsy diplomacy with which the British have so often offended continental Europeans. Beecham begins by commenting on the failure of French singers to find favour with London audiences in recent years and speculates about the lack of current French vocal talent in terms that Rouché can only have found gratuitously insulting. While it is true that French singers did not figure largely on the roster of Covent Garden or in other non-French opera houses in the 1930s, the period that heard the likes of Ninon Vallin, Germaine Lubin, Georges Thill and Vanni-Marcoux was, if not a golden age of French singing, then an afterglow of one. Certainly Britain had nothing like a similar array of vocal talent to offer.

If Rouché shared the traditional French opinion of English deviousness and sexual hypocrisy, he will have been highly amused if unsurprised by Beecham's shameless pitch to have his mistress Dora Labbette (aka Lisa Perli) cast in the role of Mélisande at the Paris Opéra.

Dora Labbette was a fine singer trained in the English concert and oratorio tradition. Her renditions on records of songs by Delius, accompanied by Beecham, are exquisite. Her contribution to Beecham's 1927 recording of Handel's *Messiah* (itself a monument to a now extinct performing style) is very lovely too. In 1935 Beecham decided to re-launch Labbette's career on the operatic stage, under the name of Lisa Perli (apparently inspired by the outer London suburb of Purley where she was born). In a recording of Act IV of Puccini's *La Bohème* made at the time under Beecham, Labbette makes a touching if unidiomatic

Mimi. She would have sounded strangely anaemic in Puccini to an Italian audience, and probably equally unsatisfactory to a French audience as Mélisande. However, this did not deter Sir Thomas, and the larger part of his memorandum to Rouché was devoted to promoting her:

Soprano Dora Labbette was a pawn in the musical diplomacy of the late 1930s.

> Together with all those who are acquainted with the work of this artist, for a long time I have held the view that Miss Perli is capable of being the Mélisande of our time. Having this conviction, I have engaged her definitely for Covent Garden next Summer (the Coronation Season) … I understand that there is some slight possibility of Mr Rouché considering this lady for his own production of *Pelléas et Mélisande* at the Opéra Comique … And, in connection with this, I should not like Mr Rouché for one moment to think that, because Miss Perli is singing Mélisande at Covent Garden in a French Season which would be largely his affair, that I am in any way hinting or designing that she take part in Mr Rouché's very own representation at the Opéra Comique. At the same time, so far as Miss Perli is concerned, it would undoubtedly be a high compliment to her and to what can be generally called English singing, if she were for some time to sing this role at a French theatre.[5]

Unsurprising, in view of the insults Beecham had heaped on French singing earlier in the memorandum, Rouché was unwilling to pay this compliment to English singing and Dora Labbette did not sing Mélisande in Paris.

As artistic and managing director of the Royal Opera in London, Sir Thomas Beecham played a pivotal role in the pre-war flurries of operatic diplomacy. Undeterred by the rejection of *Lohengrin*, the Nazi authorities continued to woo Sir Thomas by every means at their disposal. In 1937 Dora Labbette was offered major roles in all three of Germany's most prestigious opera houses, in Berlin, Dresden and Munich.

Beecham himself was invited to conduct performances of Gluck's *Orfeo* and Mozart's *Die Entführung aus dem Serail* at the Berlin State Opera towards the end of the same year. They also offered to make available to him the Berlin Philharmonic and the forces of the Berlin State Opera for a complete recording of Mozart's *Die Zauberflöte* to be made by HMV; the Nazis apparently believed that Beecham, through his other long-term mistress, Lady Cunard, had influence in the higher echelons of British society and might be of use in furthering their interests. Beecham liked to play the political innocent and assumed a mask of clownish insouciance in all things political (Toscanini nicknamed him 'Pagliaccio'). In fact he was a smart political operator and every bit as amoral and ruthlessly self-interested as Herbert von Karajan or Karl Böhm, currently establishing their careers in Nazi Germany. Taking heed of the damage that Richard Strauss did to his international reputation in 1933 by taking over from the exiled Bruno Walter, Beecham declined to accept the invitation to take over from Furtwängler when the Nazis forced his withdrawal from a planned Berlin Philharmonic visit to Britain in 1935.

In 1936, Beecham led the London Philharmonic Orchestra, including a number of Jewish players who must have felt deeply uncomfortable, on a triumphant concert tour of Germany. Shamefully, Beecham agreed to drop Mendelssohn's Scottish Symphony from the programme in order to avoid offending the Nazi hierarchy. Goebbels was unimpressed by the British orchestra and its conductor: 'It was painful, as we had to clap out of politeness. Also the Führer was very discontented. How high Germany's musical culture stands in contrast, what with the Berlin Philharmonic and Furtwängler! I'm working on the press—No tearing to shreds!'[6] The Nazi propaganda machine exploited Beecham's tour to the maximum, going so far as to publish a fake photograph of Beecham beside Hitler in his box. Even Beecham seems eventually to have become disgusted with the relentless politicising of the tour. Nevertheless, in 1937 the unprecedented honour for a British conductor to be invited to the Berlin State Opera was too great a temptation for Beecham to pass up, as was the opportunity to use the Berlin Philharmonic for his *Zauberflöte* recording even if it meant abandoning the great Jewish singers Richard Tauber and Alexander Kipnis and the political refugee Herbert Janssen, originally envisaged for the roles of Tamino, Sarastro and the Speaker.

A sign of the continuing value placed upon Beecham in Germany in the late 1930s is his inclusion as the only representative of 'Das

Land ohne Musik' in the prestigious 1938 volume *Künstler plaudern*, otherwise almost entirely devoted to musical personalities from the Axis powers of Germany and Italy. Given in that jocular tone that enabled him to skate unscathed through the political controversies of the period, Sir Thomas's interview is harmless enough and entirely apolitical in so far as giving an interview to a German publication in 1938 can be regarded as apolitical.[7]

The most important international cultural event of 1937 was the Paris World Exhibition. It was the final one of a series that dated back to 1855. That there have been no further Paris World Exhibitions is probably down to the fact that the 1937 one was perceived to have ended in ignominy and to have been a kind of fiddling before Europe burned in the Second World War. The most memorable image of the 1937 exhibition is of the Nazi German and the Soviet Russian pavilions, both in the classical monumental or 'totalitarian megalithic' style favoured by interwar dictators, facing up to one another like a pair of pugilists flexing their muscles. Other pavilions of ominous portent included that of the Spanish Republic, which showcased Picasso's *Guernica*, and the pavilion of a nascent Jewish state, bearing the inscription 'Israel en Palestine'.

The architectural duel between Germany and Russia was paralleled by a musical duel between Germany and the beleaguered Austrian Republic that took place in the elegant Théâtre des Champs-Elysées, earlier the scene of one of the most celebrated musical battles of the twentieth century when Stravinsky's *Sacre du printemps* was premiered there in 1913. (Fifty years later the composer Henri Dutilleux remembered his excitement as a young student at the Paris Conservatoire at being able to hear the two great conductors Bruno Walter and Wilhelm Furtwängler in quick succession.[8])

The conductor Bruno Walter brought the Vienna Philharmonic to Paris in 1937.

Austria went first in late June with performances of Bruckner's *Te Deum* and Mozart's *Requiem* given by the Vienna Philharmonic and chorus and soloists of the Vienna State Opera under

45

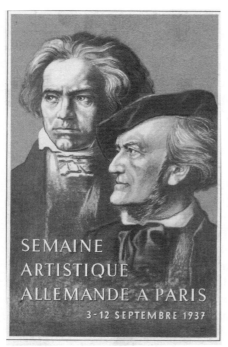

Cover of the souvenir booklet for the
Week of German Art in Paris in 1937.

Bruno Walter. The choice of the Berlin-born, Jewish Bruno Walter, recently exiled from Germany, would have been perceived as a provocation by the Nazis. The performance of the Mozart *Requiem* on 29 June was recorded by HMV with the intention of issuing it as the first-ever complete one. Walter vetoed publication because of technical and orchestral imperfections but we must be grateful that it was preserved and eventually issued, if only for the heavenly singing of the soprano Elisabeth Schumann, whose silvery voice rides easily and joyously over the orchestra and her larger-voiced colleagues. This fine performance by Viennese or Vienna-based artists gains added poignancy from the knowledge that the *Anschluss* was only months away and that three of the four soloists (Elisabeth Schumann, Alexander Kipnis and Kirstin Thorborg) as well as the conductor and a significant proportion of orchestra and chorus would be forced to flee.

In early September the Berlin State Opera took over the Théâtre des Champs-Elysées in the course of what was billed as a 'Week of German Art'. Hitler and Goebbels were well aware that music was Germany's most valuable cultural export. Bach, Mozart and Beethoven could reach a far wider international audience than Goethe, Schiller or Thomas Mann. Posters were printed with the image of a German eagle and stylised organ pipes, and with the English words 'Germany land of music'—an unkind reference perhaps to the common belief in Germany that England was 'das Land ohne Musik'.

Though somewhat depleted by Nazi racial policies, the Berlin State Opera was still commonly regarded as the finest operatic ensemble in the world. Amongst the artists who appeared at the Théâtre des Champs-Elysées were the conductors Wilhelm Furtwängler,

Karl Elmendorf and Heinz Tietjen, and the singers Frida Leider, Maria Müller, Viorica Ursuleac, Erna Berger, Margarete Klose, Franz Völker, Helge Rosvaenge (billed as Roswaenge during the Nazi period) and Rudolf Bockelmann. The repertoire consisted of two Wagner works: *Tristan und Isolde* and *Die Walküre*, two Strauss works: *Der Rosenkavalier* and *Ariadne auf Naxos* (still a novelty in France at the time) and Beethoven's Ninth Symphony.

The programme of the performance of Beethoven's Ninth Symphony given in the Salle Pleyel at 9 pm on Tuesday 7 September 1937 contains a rather woolly statement from Walther Funk, vice-president of the Reichskulturkammer, that nevertheless makes brutally clear the subservient role the artist was expected to play in the new Germany:

Photograph of Wilhelm Furtwängler in the souvenir booklet of the Week of German Art.

Ticket for the performance of Beethoven's Ninth Symphony conducted by Furtwängler at the Salle Pleyel on 7 September 1937.

> The International Exhibition of 1937 provides National Socialist Germany with the opportunity to present to the world a picture of its achievements, which should give a faithful idea of cultural and social life and activity in the Reich of Adolf Hitler. The new Germany appears in the 'German Pavilion' where she is represented by different examples of her artistic, technical and social progress. The 'Week of German Art' should give the world an impression of the current state of opera, song, dance and film in the new Germany from an artistic point of view.
>
> The national socialist state has invited artists to new and great tasks. These aim not only to respond to current needs

but also to re-awaken the great creative forces of the past, so that the young generation can measure its works against the eternal values of German culture. Art only becomes culture when it is the sublime expression of a people strong enough to impress on its period its own image. A truly great epoch assigns to Art and to artists tasks of proportionate greatness. The prodigious political and spiritual turnaround that national socialism has provoked in Germany has opened, equally in Art a new phase of development and assigned to the artist the duty to recast the new epoch in giving a nobility of form that will survive it!

The artist derives his artistic mission from the direction given by the state. He has a responsibility of a political order, by reason of the fact that the ensemble of spirit is based in the direction of the state; a profound and unanimous expression of the popular soul. *Thus the artist renders service to the nation.*

He brings Art to the people and the people to Art. It is in this cultural conception that the new creative activity of German art takes its point of departure and finds its achievement.

Goebbels's intention was to showcase Germany's two greatest living musicians, the composer Richard Strauss and the conductor Wilhelm Furtwängler. Both had recently been in disgrace with the Nazi

Frida Leider as Isolde.

authorities and it was an opportunity for both to prove their worth to the new regime and rehabilitate themselves. In the event, neither quite did so as hoped by Goebbels. Furtwängler very publicly failed to give the Nazi salute at a ceremony honouring the unknown soldier, and Strauss—who fell ill—failed to turn up at all. Goebbels noted in his diary on 27 August 1937: 'Richard Strauss is ill. Unfortunately he cannot conduct in Paris. A great loss for us.'

According to the critic of *Le Figaro*, the outstanding event of the week was the performance of *Die Walküre*, conducted by Furtwängler with the dream cast of Frida Leider as Brünnhilde, Maria Müller as Sieglinde, Margarete Klose as Fricka, Franz Völker as Siegmund and Rudolf Bockelmann as Wotan. Despite the praise heaped upon her, Frida Leider, who was married to the Jewish violinist Rudolf Deman and felt increasingly under threat, remembered the Week of German Art as an unhappy experience. 'Until 1933 I had sung, a free artist at the Paris Opéra where I was received by the French public with the greatest enthusiasm. This time we were appearing at the Théâtre des Champs-Elysées, a smaller theatre hardly suitable for Wagner. A few old Parisian friends came to greet me during the intervals, but others whom I had known so well were no longer to be seen. The discord between my work and my private life was becoming increasingly obvious. I avoided all official receptions and meetings.'[9]

For Leider, as for her French rival Germaine Lubin, performing the supremely testing role of Isolde brought its rewards. Soon after her Paris triumph Leider performed the role again in Berlin in a new production, again with Furtwängler. 'I was artistically at the finest point of my career, and my one thought was to make this Isolde, both musically and dramatically, come from the deepest springs of my being. It is difficult to explain how I managed to do this, but I succeeded in performing this miracle. Perhaps it was the purgatory of my life at this time, or perhaps the inexhaustible talent which nature had granted me. On that unforgettable evening, I felt that I had reached the pinnacle of my career.'[10]

It was not only around Frida Leider that the storm clouds were gathering, but around France itself. The French newspapers in September 1937 were full of troubling reports from every quarter of the globe and in particular from around France's borders—the deteriorating situation of the Spanish Republic, the refusal of Italy and Germany to abide by international agreements on non-intervention in the Spanish Civil War, mounting diplomatic tensions in the Mediterranean, atrocities in the Sino-Japanese war, alarming accounts of resurgent German militarism at the concurrent Nuremberg rally, and perhaps most worrying of all, a report on the front page of *Le Figaro* on 5 September of an open letter from Adolf Hitler to the British people, published in *The Daily Mail*, inviting alliance between the British and the Germans.

The popular song that in retrospect came to encapsulate this threatening moment in French history was Paul Misraki's 'Tout va très bien, Madame la Marquise'. In this song the increasingly distraught Marquise telephones each of her servants in turn, who assure her blithely 'Tout va très bien, Madame la Marquise' as they catalogue the disasters that have befallen her. In fact that song was written as early as 1935 and as far as it had any political sub-text referred to the impact of the Great Depression that hit France with belated force in the first half of the 1930s. In 1937, perhaps inspired by the Paris World Exhibition, the Ray Ventura band recorded a new version of the song, 'La marquise voyage', in which the Marquise travels the world still trailing bad news and disasters. Also in 1937 the popularity of the song inspired a movie of the same title, with the great character actress Marguerite Moreno as the embattled Marquise. Like many songs in this period, 'Tout va très bien, Madame la Marquise' picked up new layers of meaning in the light of later events and was exploited by both sides during the war with new propaganda texts.

Among the more successful popular vocal groups of the interwar period were the Berlin-based Comedian Harmonists. Between 1928 and 1933 the sound of this male sextet with its sophisticated combination of American, classical and folk elements, and its playful and witty hedonism, came to represent all that was most attractive about the culture of Weimar Germany. According to their own accounts, the close harmony of their voices was reflected in an easy working relationship between members of the group. The advent of the Nazi regime brought tensions, recriminations, betrayals and eventually litigation between the three 'Aryans' Robert Biberti, Erwin Bootz and Ari Leschnikoff, and the three Jews, Erich Collin, Roman Cycowski and Harry Frommermann.

Marguerite Moreno in the 1937 film Tout va très bien Madame la Marquise.

In 1934, while on their final tour of Germany, the Comedian Harmonists arrived in Munich to find that their sold-out concert had been banned. After representation to the Nazi authorities the concert was allowed to proceed but not before a uniformed official had gone on stage to say: 'This group of the Comedian Harmonists appears today in Munich for the last time. This is by special permission of the Gauleiter, even though this music no longer fits in with what is acceptable to National Socialism. Those of you who do not wish to sit through this degenerate "artistic entertainment" may reclaim the price of their tickets at the box office and leave quietly now.'[11] A few members of the audience did indeed get up and leave, but the majority remained and gave the performers a resounding ovation. There was deep emotion when the Comedian Harmonists sang Spoliansky's touching song 'Auf wiedersehen' as a final encore.

Similar scenes were re-enacted in other German cities as the tour limped to a close, but by 1935 it was clear that a rupture between the 'Aryan' and the Jewish members of the group was inevitable. Biberti, Bootz and Leschnikoff remained in Germany and re-formed the group with three new members, under the name of Das Meistersextett. Collin, Frommermann and Cycowski toured the world with three new members, under their old name of Comedian Harmonists (later Comedy Harmonists). Neither group was able to recapture their former success. The German-based group suffered from the change of name forced upon them by Nazi officials and also the political restriction of their repertoire, robbing it of its variety and charm. Both groups continued with diminishing conviction until 1941. The cosy humour of both was increasingly out of tune with a world hurtling inexorably towards war. In Germany in particular, the polished elegance of the Meistersextett came to be regarded as 'unmanly'.

In the 1970s, a series of penetrating interviews by the author Eberhard Fechner with the surviving members of the original group laid bare the mutual resentments that had simmered for forty years. Perhaps no story illustrates so poignantly the insidious impact of Nazism on the lives of ordinary musicians.

In the years immediately preceding and following the Spanish Civil War, the casting of artists (singers and conductors) at Spain's premier opera house, the Liceu in Barcelona, reflected the changing political developments elsewhere in Europe. In January 1936, months before the outbreak of the Civil War, the Liceu presented a festival of the operas of Mozart, Wagner, Smetana and Dvořák. In the Mozart operas the Jewish Lotte Schoene, who had been a great favourite in Berlin before her forced departure in 1933, found herself re-united with many of her former Berlin colleagues. The Czech operas were conducted by another refugee from Nazi Germany, Alexander von Zemlinsky. Five years later, with the Spanish Civil War now over and the European war raging, the Liceu was able to present an exceptionally brilliant programme over the winter season of 1941-2. Apart from the local stars Mercedes Capsir and Pablo Civil, the artists were drawn almost exclusively from the Axis nations of Germany and Italy. Refugees and artists from Allied or neutral nations were no longer in evidence.

From the beginning of 1938 until the eventual outbreak of war in 1939, politics intruded ever more insistently into the rarefied world of opera. At its most benign this was simply a matter of casting directors taking advantage of the flood of refugee talent. The two houses that benefited most from this were Glyndebourne and the Colon in Buenos Aires—the two great refugee conductors Erich Kleiber and Fritz Busch (neither Jewish but both outspoken critics of the Nazi regime) ensured that the German opera performances were of a particularly high standard, ending the earlier dominance at the Colon of Italian and French repertoire. As at Covent Garden, in these years Jewish artists found themselves thrown together with ardent Nazis.

Adolf Hitler had played a decisive role in the establishment of Glyndebourne as a serious and lasting cultural institution. Originally conceived by the wealthy country-house owner John Christie as a vehicle for the modest vocal talents of his soprano wife Audrey Mildmay, the Glyndebourne Festival would never have got off the ground without the sudden and cheap availability of first-class talent from Germany, including the conductor Fritz Busch (former chief conductor of the Dresden Opera), the producer Carl Ebert, and the ruthlessly efficient manager and administrator Rudolf Bing. The timing of the first festival could not have been more perfect. The special magic of Glyndebourne felt by all from the first resulted from the peculiar combination of Middle European professionalism and English amateurism. Rudolf Bing's memoirs contain many amusing anecdotes of the mutual lack of comprehension between the Europeans and their English hosts and employers. With remarkable modesty and generosity John Christie took a back seat and allowed Busch and Ebert near total artistic freedom, though on one occasion Ebert was forced to threaten suicide to prevent the re-engagement of an English singer of whom he did not approve. Bing recalled the embarrassment caused by his attempt to explain the indelicacies of the plot of Act I of *Der Rosenkavalier* to a group of English nurses who were listening to the famous 1933 abridged recording on 78 rpm records, when Glyndebourne was being used to shelter evacuee children during the war.[12]

From the first, the refugee artists had to deal with Nazi party members such as Willi Domgraf-Fassbaender, who sang Figaro in the opening performances of Mozart's *Le Nozze di Figaro*, or with artists from Fascist Italy such as Mariano Stabile who took over the same role. The intensely germanophile John Christie, who signposted the Glyndebourne toilets as 'Damen' and 'Herren' and strode over the Sussex Downs in lederhosen, remained sublimely oblivious to the darkening political situation. The great test came when the Nazis, continuing their operatic charm offensive against Britain, invited Audrey Mildmay to take part in the 1939 Salzburg Festival. Responding to the appalled reaction of her German Jewish colleagues and to advice from the Foreign Office, Mildmay reluctantly renounced what would undoubtedly have been the crowning glory of her career.

Towards the end of the final pre-war season in July 1939, Prime Minister Neville Chamberlain, attending a performance of the much-praised production of Verdi's *Macbeth*, was spontaneously applauded by the conservative Glyndebourne audience who presumably still supported his policy of appeasement. On 15 July 1939, the very last night of the season and with war only a few weeks away, Christie alarmed the jittery audience with the announcement that he had serious news for them. They were relieved to discover that the serious news was that Eton had beaten Harrow in their annual cricket match.[13]

At Covent Garden too, in the final pre-war seasons of 1938 and 1939 politics loomed ever larger. Again the casting of German operas threw together some unfortunate combinations of artists. After Beecham's brief flirtation with the French in 1937, German repertoire was once again in the ascendant, though according to Harold Rosenthal, the chronicler of Covent Garden, attendance figures for German operas were affected by mounting anti-German feeling.

The political situation also affected the programming in 1938 when Beecham was forced to drop his intention of giving the British premiere of Strauss's opera *Die Schweigsame Frau*. The opera had been banned in Germany owing to Strauss's refusal to suppress the name of his Jewish librettist Stefan Zweig, and Beecham found it impossible to find German artists who would have been willing or able to sing the opera.[14]

Programme for a performance of Die Zauberflöte *that united the refugee Richard Tauber with members of the Berlin State Opera.*

Programme for the performance of Der Rosenkavalier *during which Lotte Lehmann collapsed.*

The half-Jewish Richard Tauber, who had been dropped from Beecham's recording of *Die Zauberflöte* in order to appease the Nazis and who was currently being pilloried by them in the travelling exhibition of 'Entartete Musik', now found himself singing the role of Tamino in a production borrowed from Berlin and surrounded by some of the most esteemed artists of the Nazi regime, including Tiana Lemnitz, Erna Berger, Gerhard Hüsch and Wilhelm Strienz. One can only speculate on what backstage conversation must have been like, though Tauber no doubt brought his usual charm and aplomb to the situation.

Lotte Lehmann's very public collapse midway through Act I of a broadcast performance of *Der Rosenkavalier* in May 1938, murmuring audibly 'I can't go on … Finish', was widely attributed to bullying from Nazi members of the cast. Lehmann, as the Marschallin, had quite literally found herself in bed with Nazi party member Tiana Lemnitz singing the role of Octavian. Lehmann would later deny that this was the cause of her collapse, which seems to have resulted from a combination of travel fatigue and anxiety about the political situation in Austria.

Another notable performance in the 1938 season that brought refugees and citizens of the Reich to London was Strauss's *Elektra* with Rose Pauly in the title role and Hilde Konetzni as Chrysothemis. 'A cast and performance so superb come our way very few times in the course of a life-time', according to London's senior critic Ernest Newman.[15]

The 1939 season opened on 1 May with a German language performance of the Czech masterpiece *The Bartered Bride*, a matter of weeks after the Nazi invasion of the rump of Czechoslovakia that had remained after the Munich agreement. In the words of Harold Rosenthal: 'The opening opera was hardly a happy choice in view of the European situation; Smetana's *The Bartered Bride* sung in German as *Die verkaufte Braut* conducted by Beecham and a company of singers that included Nazi and Jew, Teuton, Briton and Slav.'[16] According to the baritone Marko Rothmüller, rehearsals were indeed very tense but the battle lines were drawn up not between Nazi and Jew but between Beecham and his European singers, all of whom were much more familiar with the score than was Beecham himself. Tauber gallantly came to the rescue of his colleague Hilde Konetzni when she was reduced to tears by the bullying of the irascible conductor. With exaggerated politeness Tauber leaned over the orchestra pit and said 'Please, Sir Thomas, you must be more patient with us. Having sung this opera incorrectly for the past twenty-five years you cannot expect us to adapt to the correct way immediately.' It was one of the few occasions when a singer got the better of Sir Thomas.[17]

Just over a year earlier in March 1938, as Hitler had made his triumphal entry into Vienna, by another macabre coincidence of programming the Vienna State Opera was due to perform another great Czech national opera, Smetana's rousingly patriotic *Dalibor*. At the last minute *Dalibor* was replaced by Beethoven's *Fidelio*. With its passionate denunciation of tyranny, *Fidelio* might be thought to have been even less suitable to celebrate the *Anschluss* but it was at least a German opera.

Of all the political events that led up to the Second World War, the *Anschluss* had the most immediate and dramatic effect from a musical point of view. There was a rapid and thorough culling of Jewish personnel from the Vienna Philharmonic and the Vienna State Opera. Overnight the latter lost not only its musical director Bruno Walter, but also many of the singers who had been most idolized by the Viennese public since the First World War, including Lotte Lehmann, Elisabeth Schumann, Alfred Piccaver, Richard Tauber, Alexander Kipnis and Emmanuel List. Tauber and Piccaver continued their careers in Britain. The other four crossed the Atlantic, with Lehmann, Kipnis and List devoting the final years of their distinguished operatic careers to the Metropolitan in New York and adding greatly to the glory of Wagner performances in that house.

Like the Colon and Covent Garden, the Met gained from the influx of refugees including, from 1938, the Czech soprano Jarmila Novotná and the German baritone Herbert Janssen.

Overall, the balance between imported and American singers tipped decisively in favour of the Americans in the late 1930s through a combination of different factors. The desire to give American-born singers a larger share of the cake at the Met reflected the mood of isolationism but was also a matter of economic necessity: a pre-requisite for the financial support from the Juilliard Foundation that had got the Met through the Depression and its aftermath was the increasing use of American artists.

The outbreak of war in Europe cut off the supply of Italian singers. Gigli, Cigna, Caniglia and Favero, who had all been cheered by Met audiences, failed to return to New York. The much anticipated debuts of Tiana Lemnitz and Germaine Lubin also failed to happen and two of the Met's biggest draws, the Norwegian Kirsten Flagstad and the Swede Jussi Björling, returned to their homelands. All of these absences provided an unprecedented opportunity for American singers who came to dominate the Met roster.

In London, owing to anxieties about the deteriorating political situation, it was far from certain that an opera season in 1939 would take place at all at Covent Garden. In January 1939 Sir Thomas Beecham (who when war eventually did break out would be one of the first to jump ship and go to America) berated the British public for its pusillanimity in an article published in *The Daily Telegraph*:

> It is seriously proposed that because we are suffering from a temporary access [*sic*] of jitters and jumps that would bring discredit upon a community of elderly nuns we should discontinue an event that is a regular a feature of our yearly calendar as the Royal Academy, the Military Tattoo, or the Eton and Harrow cricket match ... Let us on our part show that in matters of art and culture, and especially in music, which is the common property of the entire world, we can rise above the ephemeral conditions of purely political discord, and maintain our old reputation for national sanity and understanding. There must, and shall be, a season at Covent Garden; and I shall be surprised if it does not begin as usual on May 1 next, conducted on lines similar to those familiar to the world during the past two centuries.[18]

As predicted, the season did indeed take place, ending on 1 June with a performance of *Tristan und Isolde* conducted by Beecham with Germaine Lubin as Isolde. At the end of the evening Beecham told his final pre-war opera audience: 'I will do what I can to give the public an opera season [in 1940], although frankly, I do not think it deserves one.'[19] That 1940 season would have consisted of more of the same, though with a few novelties such as Puccini's *La Fanciulla del West*, with casts blending refugees with artists from the Axis countries—but it was not to be.[20]

At Bayreuth a few weeks later, the season also ended with *Tristan und Isolde* and once again starring Germaine Lubin. When she had first taken the role at Bayreuth in 1938, she was the first French artist to have sung a major role there and the event received a great deal of press coverage. The highly subsidized Bayreuth Festival had become one of the showpieces of the Nazi regime, and whatever her vocal and histrionic merits in the role the choice of a French singer was a political decision calculated to curry favour with certain elements in France. Widely publicized photographs of an admiring Hitler seated beside Lubin were a source of French national pride at the time, but later did immense harm to the singer's reputation and career.

The magnificent performances of *Tristan and Isolde* at Bayreuth in August 1939, with Lubin under the inspired direction of Victor de Sabata, supplied an appropriate musical background to a drama of mutual adultery being played out between Goebbels and his wife Magda. On the orders of Hitler, Goebbels had broken off his affair with the beautiful Czech film star Lida Baarova. Now, in order to facilitate a reconciliation with her erring husband, Magda Goebbels was forced to give up her own lover, a Nazi official called Karl Hanke. Wagner's highly charged music proved too much for her. Seated behind Hitler and her husband in the central box, Magda Goebbels cried openly throughout the performance. During the interval, according to Albert Speer, 'she sat racked with incessant sobs in the corner of one of the drawing rooms, while Hitler and Goebbels showed themselves to the audience through the window, and attempted to ignore the embarrassing display.'[21]

In parallel with all these international, operatic-political manoeuvres taking place in the late 1930s and into the early stages of the Second World War, opera and concert performances continued in Germany under the aegis of the Kulturbund der deutschen Juden ('Cultural Association of German Jewry'). This organisation was one of the more bizarre and perverse manifestations of Nazi racial policies. Jews were entirely excluded from the cultural life of Germany, but as a sop to world opinion, they were encouraged to organise and conduct their own performances with exclusively Jewish performers and audiences. The Berliner Theater in the Charlottenstrasse in Berlin was designated as a venue for these performances. An ambitious programme of opera and concerts continued until 1941 against a background of ever-diminishing resources that became a macabre game of musical chairs, as one by one the more gifted and better-connected performers managed to escape. These included the brilliant coloratura soprano Fritzi Jokl, the baritone Gerhard Pechner, who went on to a lengthy career as a *comprimario* in New York, and the conductors Joseph Rosenstock and Wilhelm (later William) Steinberg, who helped to found the Palestine orchestra. These performances were briefly interrupted by the increased repression of Jews following the violence of *Kristallnacht* in 1938, but they soon resumed under pressure from the Nazi regime in an attempt to deflect international criticism of their racist policies. The last opera to be fully staged was Verdi's *La Traviata* in March 1939. This was followed by numerous performances of Kálmán's operetta *Gräfin Mariza* and concert performances of *Cavalleria Rusticana* and *I Pagliacci* late in 1940. The final performance was a Verdi evening given on 12 June 1941. By this time France was conquered and Russia was about to be attacked, and there was little need to keep up pretences as far as the Jews were concerned. The remaining performers and audiences were soon liquidated.

When war was declared in Britain on 3 September 1939, the music stopped for a brief moment—or so it seemed to the popular English singer Vera Lynn. 'When it started, there was a general dither and *everything*, except radio, shut down completely. I think we must have been conditioned by German propaganda and the newsreels of the fighting in Spain to assume that the outbreak of war would be followed immediately by the destruction of most of our cities.'[22]

The highly successful 1936 science fiction movie *Things to Come*, based on a novel by H G Wells that predicted that a world war would start in 1940 with a bombing raid on London, had helped to persuade many people that London would be reduced to rubble within hours of the start of the next war. The entertainer Douglas Byng recalled: 'The night war was declared I was playing in non-stop revue at the Prince of Wales theatre. We closed the show at eight o'clock when orders came through that all lights were to be extinguished as an air raid on London was likely to happen. I immediately phoned my sister Amy and told her she had better come with me to my cottage in Surrey. She had nursed abroad all through the First World War and although her flat was on the seventh floor she seemed to be in no hurry to leave, insisting that she must first cover up everything with dust sheets. She kept us waiting until midnight before we could start. All the way in the car she was lamenting that she had forgotten her Alophen, her favourite laxative. I had become a little bored with this and after the fourth reminder I said, "Listen dear, if a bomb drops anywhere near us you won't need Alophen."'[23]

Sir Kenneth Clark, the director of the National Gallery recalled: 'Soon after the war was declared the air-raid sirens sounded and we all took our gas masks and went to our shelters. We were slightly nervous, but cheerful and excited like nuns in a new convent … Partly from prudence, partly from a feeling that something must be done to show that we were taking the war seriously, and partly in a spirit of contrition, the Home Office had decided to close down anything that could cheer and console us … For the first two or three nights the black-out was beautiful and poetic. Thereafter it combined with a lack of entertainment to make people irritable.'[24]

According to Vera Lynn, it was believed that 'any activity that gathered large crowds of people in one place was automatically doomed.' But, she continued, 'When it was realized that it wasn't going to be like that, and that ordinary people were going to need entertainment more than they'd ever done in their lives, the industry pulled itself together, the theatres gradually re-opened, the hotels re-started their dances, and there was a boom in the whole cheer-up business.'[25]

While ENSA and CEMA (The Council for the Encouragement of Music and the Arts) were still quite literally getting their acts together, John Christie of Glyndebourne did his bit to fill the cultural gap by hiring John Gielgud to create a touring production of John Gay's *The Beggar's Opera*. It was an inspired choice for that moment. It required modest resources and played well to national sentiment. *The Beggar's Opera* had been launched in 1728 as a self-consciously British form of musical entertainment in reaction to the Italian operas of the German composer Handel that had held the British aristocracy in thrall for the previous two decades. Though the melodies were arranged by yet another German composer (Johann Christoph Pepusch), they were borrowed from popular and traditional songs that would have been familiar to British audiences of the 1720s and indeed many would still have been familiar to British audiences in 1940. The version used by the Glyndebourne company had been created in 1920 by Frederic Austin and now sounds very much of that era. The recordings made of the Glyndebourne cast in 1940 have also become period pieces. The vocally untrained actor Michael Redgrave was cast as Macheath. His singing, in a voice described by Audrey Mildmay as 'rather Harris-tweed', is one of the chief attractions of the set. Mildmay herself, as Polly Peachum, offers a charming performance of considerable vocal accomplishment including some nicely turned trills. Starting out in Brighton in January 1940, the production travelled to Cardiff, Liverpool, Manchester and Edinburgh before playing in London from 5 March to 25 May 1940.[26]

Across the channel in France, most people felt reasonably safe behind the supposed impregnability of the Maginot Line. Two French composers of different generations, the veteran Reynaldo Hahn, and Francis Poulenc who was still of military age, both took a more pessimistic view. Hahn wondered only half-humorously what would happen if the German army turned out to be as excellent as German orchestras. He wrote to the conductor Désiré-Emile Inghelbrecht on 21 October 1939: 'And then, one suspects that the German army is perhaps just as perfect as the German orchestras, the German conductors and the German singers. Oh, the horrible Bruno Walter! And Monsieur Furtwängler?'[27] Hahn was out of date as far as Bruno Walter was concerned as he was no longer a 'German' conductor and was safely on the other side of the Atlantic, but within six months his suspicion that German Panzer divisions were as well-trained as Furtwängler's Berlin Philharmonic proved to be correct. As Poulenc anxiously awaited his call-up papers, he worried about his musical legacy and concentrated on polishing the orchestration of his ballet masterpiece *Les Biches* rather than embarking on new compositions.

In France too, popular entertainment continued on its cheery way with barely a nod towards the war. An anthology published in 1993 on CD of excerpts from surviving broadcasts from the commercial radio stations Radio-Cité and Le Poste Parisien offers a fascinating cross-section of popular entertainment over the airwaves at this time.

Record request programmes were staple fare and up to 70 percent of broadcast music was from commercial records. But each radio station had a roster of stars who could be heard live or in specially-made studio recordings. Radio-Cité offered Charles Trenet, Rina Ketty, Léo Marjane, André Claveau, Edith Piaf, Georgius, and the dance bands of Ray Ventura and Jacques Helian. Le Post Parisien offered Jean Sablon, Mistinguett, Marie Dubas, Damia, Georges Milton, Pils et Tabet and Lucienne Boyer. From 2 March 1940, courtesy of Radio-Cité, we can hear Fernandel entertaining troops at the Maginot Line and reducing his audience (amongst whom are a number of women) to helpless laughter with a rendition of the song 'Ne me dis plus tu' from his 1938 movie *Barnabé*. With his brilliant comic timing he manages to squeeze a laugh from the very first note.

The most popular programme on Radio-Cité was a brutally cruel talent show, based on the American 'Major Bowes Amateur Hour', the main purpose of which seems to be to inflict humiliation on the contestants. In a broadcast of 1940 we hear a matronly middle-aged housewife (she is 42, dressed in blue and does not wear lipstick) attempting to sing the sentimental song 'Tristesse'. She gets no further than the first couple of bars before being interrupted by the gong and breezily dismissed with the words 'Heureusement la tristresse n'a pas duré longtemps'.

Many of the songs of the Phoney War, or the *drôle de guerre*, are relentlessly cheerful and optimistic. 'The Lambeth Walk', which dated back to 1937, was especially popular on both sides of the Channel in the period leading up to and just after the outbreak of war. It was recorded in French by Ray Ventura et ses Collégians and broadcast live on the Post Parisien by the Pierre Zeppilli orchestra. Its brief pre-war popularity in Berlin provoked a Nazi official to denounce it as 'Jewish mischief and animalistic hopping'. Its most memorable wartime use was in a still funny 1942 propaganda short produced by the British Ministry of Information, in which doctored footage from Leni Riefenstahl's *Triumph of the Will* is used to make Nazi troops dance 'The Lambeth Walk'.

In the early months of the war the great Paris music halls continued to provide their traditional entertainments. Mistinguett, the undisputed queen of the music halls, appeared in a revue at the Étoile-Palace supported by the sultry, American style crooner Léo Marjane. A new star on the horizon was celebrated in an illustrated article in the April 1940 edition of *Match*, which hailed Edith Piaf as 'maintenant une grande vedette de la chanson française' ('now a great star of French song'). The Casino de Paris mounted a revue entitled *Paris-London* that promoted the soon-to-be ill-fated Franco-British alliance. It starred two

Maurice Chevalier performs in the revue
Paris-London *in December 1939.*

*Maurice Chevalier presents Gracie Fields to
the French public at the Paris Opéra during
the Phoney War.*

other great luminaries of the Paris music halls—Maurice Chevalier and Josephine Baker. Backstage rivalries between the two would turn to bitter enmity after the fall of France when Baker chose the path of resistance and Chevalier of collaboration. For the moment, though, they buried their differences sufficiently to travel together to the Maginot Line to entertain troops, recorded in contemporary newsreels. Anglo-French solidarity was cemented in a gala at the Opéra at which Gracie Fields sang for the President of France. Josephine's great hit in *Paris-London* was the wistful 'Mon Coeur est un oiseau des îles' during which she appeared for the last time on the Paris stage in a state of semi-nudity.

Classical music also continued more or less unabated in Paris during the *drôle de guerre*. Whereas the Royal Opera in London closed—for opera at least—for the duration of the war, the Paris Opéra re-opened on 16 November after a gap of two and half months. Classical recordings continued to be made as usual until the very eve of the French collapse and two in particular deserve special mention.

In January 1940 the great Polish Jewish harpsichordist Wanda Landowska continued with her pioneering series of recordings of Scarlatti sonatas. In her recording of the D Major sonata (Kk 490) she does not miss a beat, quite literally, and continues to play 'cantabile' as requested in the score as the boom of anti-aircraft fire is heard in the background. Four months later Landowska would be forced to flee, leaving behind her priceless collection of scores and keyboard instruments to be pillaged by the Germans.[28]

On 10 May 1940 as the German hordes poured into Belgium and the Netherlands on their way round the Maginot Line, Marguerite Long, doyenne of French pianists, respected colleague of Fauré, Debussy and Ravel and chosen performer of their music, entered a recording studio with the Pasquier Trio in order to record the first quartet of that most refined and Gallic of composers, Gabriel Fauré. It may not be too fanciful to imagine that under the grim circumstances this wonderful music may have meant even more to them than it normally would and that this shows itself in the unusually passionate quality of their performance.

Outside of France another especially poignant classical record was made in the closing days of the Phoney War. In Copenhagen on 26 March 1940, less than two weeks before the German invasion of Denmark, the great Danish tenor Aksel Schiøtz recorded the solo 'Comfort ye, my people' from Handel's *Messiah*. Whether or not the Danes had an inkling of what lay ahead, the choice of this title and the decision to record it in the original English cannot have been entirely divorced from political circumstance in the early months of the war. Nor is it merely hindsight that makes this version of the aria so moving. Schiøtz warms the opening declamatory recitative with the judicious use of gently drooping downward portamenti that enhance the effect of the repeated words 'Comfort ye'.

At La Scala in Milan, an exceptionally brilliant opera season was announced for the spring of 1940. Gigli was engaged to display the full range of his vocal talents from the lyrical to the heroic in *La Forza del Destino*, *Il Trovatore*, *Zaza*, *Manon* and *Maristella*. Other great Italian singers announced for the season included Gina Cigna, Maria Caniglia, Mafalda Favero, Iris Adami-Corradetti, Lina Bruna Rasa, Ebe Stignani, Carlo Galeffi and Tancredi Pasero. Events of particular interest were the heralded return of the veteran American-based tenor Giovanni Martinelli as Parsifal, and the debut of the young Jussi Björling opposite the exquisite Lina Pagliughi in *Rigoletto*. The season went ahead despite the outbreak of war but neither of the two latter tenors turned up.

Interventions by members of the audience in two musical performances in neutral countries in the early stages of the war that survive in recorded broadcasts provide interesting insights into the attitudes of the time. The first is a performance of Mahler's *Das Lied von der Erde* given at the Concertgebouw in Amsterdam on 5 October 1939, just over a month into the war. Owing to the indisposition of Willem Mengelberg, the orchestra was conducted by the German conductor Carl Schuricht. In a quiet passage of the final movement a woman heckler, apparently protesting against the willingness of a German to conduct the work of the Jewish composer, shouts out 'Deutschland über alles, Herr Schuricht!' to the very audible disapproval of the Dutch audience.

Months later in December 1940, after the fall of Holland and France but a year ahead of the entry into the war of the United States, Donizetti's *La fille du régiment* was programmed at the Met in New York. The choice of this patriotic French opera (albeit by an Italian composer) that had not been heard at the Met since the end of the First World War, was in itself an indication that American isolationism was not carved in stone. The popular soprano Lily Pons is greeted with prolonged and enthusiastic applause when she sings the 'Salut à la France' and in the final scene, when Pons waves the tricolour flag as the chorus launch into the 'Marseillaise', a spontaneous burst of applause in mid-scene demonstrates very clearly where the sympathies of the New York audience lay.

1   Beniamino Gigli, *The Memoir of Beniamino Gigli*, 1957, p. 195.

2   Ernst Klee, *Kulturlexikon zum Dritten Reich*, 2009, p. 166.

3   John Lucas, *Thomas Beecham*, 2008, p. 231.

4   Harold Rosenthal, *Two Centuries of Opera at Covent Garden*, 1958, p. 534.

5   Lewis Foreman, *From Parry to Britten*, 1987, p. 200.

6   Lucas, p. 232.

7   H E Weinschenk, *Künstler plaudern*, 1938.

8   Henri Dutilleux, *Mystère et mémoire des sons*, 1993, p. 34.

9   Frida Leider, *Playing my Part*, 1966, p. 170.

10 Ibid., 1966.

11 Eberhard Fechner, *Die Comedian Harmonists*, 1988, p. 225.

12 Sir Rudolf Bing, *5000 Nights at the Opera*, 1972, p. 98.

13 John Joliffe, *Glyndebourne: an Operatic Miracle*, 1999.

14 Rosenthal, p. 532.

15 Ibid., p. 535.

16 Ibid., p. 545.

17 Lucas, p. 238.

18 *The Daily Telegraph*, January 28, 1939, p. 19.

19 Rosenthal, p. 550.

20 Ibid., p. 549.

21 Anja Klabunde, *Magda Goebbels*, 2001, p. 281.

22 Vera Lynn, *Vocal Refrain*, 1975, p. 85.

23 Douglas Byng, *As You Were*, 1970, p. 148.

24 Sir Kenneth Clark, 'Music in Place of Pictures', in *Myra Hess by her friends*, ed. Denise Lassimore and Howard Ferguson, 1966, p. 56.

25 Lynn, p. 85.

26 Alan Strachan, *Secret Dreams: the biography of Michael Redgrave*, 2004, pp. 212-14.

27 Jacques Depaulis, *Reynaldo Hahn*, 2007, p. 129.

28 Willem de Vries, *Sonderstab Musik*, 1996, p. 217.

Chapter 3
DEFEATED FRANCE

On 16 January 1944, after three and half years of gruelling and increasingly rapacious German occupation of their city, the hungry and depressed Parisians could have cheered themselves with an extraordinary feast of music. At the Théâtre des Champs-Elysées there was a free concert conducted by Willem Mengelberg that included the Overture to *Anacreon* by Cherubini, the Dvořák Cello Concerto with Paul Tortelier as soloist, and the César Franck Symphony in D Minor. On the same day there were two performances at the Opéra Comique, a ballet at the Opéra, two concerts at the Salle Pleyel, and concerts at the Salle Gaveau, the Salle Debussy, the Salle du Conservatoire, the Théâtre du Chatêlet and the Palais du Chaillot. There was nothing exceptional about this. Mengelberg gave a total of twenty-eight free concerts at the Thêâtre des Champs-Elysées between 1942 and 1944; the weekly concert programmes published in Parisian newspapers through the grimmest years of the Occupation show the continuing richness of Parisian musical life. All this was in line with the policies of the German occupiers who wished to maintain Paris as a cultural beacon of the new European order and for the recreation of the German armed forces.

Despite their proclaimed belief in the superiority of German culture, the Nazis were not a little awed by Paris and its reputation as a cultural capital. On his one fleeting visit to the conquered city in the early hours of 23 June 1940, Hitler made straight for the Paris Opéra in the company of the architect Albert Speer and the sculptor Arno Breker. According to Speer, Hitler knew the building inside and out, from having studied plans of it. Shortly after, Goebbels made a more prolonged visit to the building during which he discussed with the dancer and ballet master Serge Lifar his plans for the cultural life of Paris.

Paris between the wars.

The centre of Paris was spared the destruction that rained down on London and other cities but performances could still be interrupted by air raid warnings, and performers and audiences could still be confronted with death and destruction on their way to and from cultural events. The composer Marcel Delannoy wrote: 'How to forget a certain Sunday when we passed in front of a building which seemed to have been scarcely touched and where several workers were busy clearing out the cellars. "Look at what they have found in there!" said one of them showing us through the cellar window a woman's hair, a poor scalp covered in dust! My two children—thank God—did not seem to understand. Some minutes later, in the company of Honegger, we were listening to a concert of "Ars Rediva" devoted to the music of Bach and Telemann and on the evening of the same day, the orchestra of Maurice Hewitt.'[1]

The cultural thirst of Parisian audiences combined with the sudden cessation of the import of American movies at the end of 1941 produced an unexpected golden age for French theatre and cinema. Writers and audiences found themselves in daily situations of profound moral and political choice. Because of Nazi censorship these dilemmas could only be dealt with in oblique and abstract terms. Out of this came a series of theatrical masterpieces such as Paul Claudel's *Le soulier de satin*, Jean Giraudoux's *Sodome et Gomorrhe*, Henri de Montherlant's *La reine morte*, Jean Anouilh's *Antigone* and Jean Paul Sartre's *Les mouches* and *Huis clos*, and films such as Clouzot's *Le corbeau* and Carné's *Les visiteurs du soir* and *Les enfants du paradis*.

The Nazi authorities were determined to keep the cultural life of Paris going as normally as possible until the very last gasp. Sartre's *Huis clos*, which can hardly have pleased the Nazi censors if they understood it at all, received its premiere on 10 June 1944, four days after the Normandy landings. Mengelberg's final Beethoven cycle continued until 18 June 1944, ending with a performance of the Ninth Symphony in the Théâtre des Champs-Elysées. The Paris Opéra only closed its doors on 22 July 1944 when supplies of electricity ran out and it could no longer utilize the elaborate and sophisticated stage lighting that had impressed even the Germans. Even then the Opéra managed to put on a performance of Gluck's *Alceste* at the Sorbonne on 13 August, just over a week before the liberation of the city.

After the great exodus from Paris in June 1940, a number of the musicians who had played a key role in the musical life of the city failed to return. The conductor Albert Wolff spent the war in Argentina. The composer Darius Milhaud, the influential teacher Nadia Boulanger, the cellist Gregor Piatigorski, the pianist Artur Rubinstein and the harpsichordist Wanda Landowska all fled to America. Paris lost two of its greatest patrons of modern music in Ida Rubinstein and the Princesse de Polignac, both of whom found refuge in London.

Many Jewish musicians who failed to escape were forced to disappear from view in a kind of 'inner immigration'. The Austrian soprano Lotte Schoene, who as a refugee from Berlin since 1933 had been an ornament of the Parisian musical scene, hid in the mountains of Savoie, singing Schubert *Lieder* to herself to maintain her spirits. Even a composer and conductor as well established as Maurice Rosenthal led an extremely precarious existence and only narrowly escaped deportation and death. His aged mother, who as a young woman had walked to France from Russia to escape persecution, died alone and abandoned during the panic-stricken flight from Paris in June 1940, like a character from Irène Nemirovsky's great novel *Suite française*. Some Jewish composers who remained, such as Joseph Kosma, were able to continue working for the film industry under pseudonyms and with the help of brave colleagues. On 1 June 1943 the organisers of a concert at the École Normale de Musique got away with programming the two-piano piece 'Scaramouche' by Milhaud, with the ingenious anagram of 'Mous-Arechac' by Hamid-al-Usurid.

In his book *Sonderstab Musik*, Willem de Vries has chronicled how the Germans pillaged the libraries of Milhaud and Landowska as well as Landowska's unique collection of historic keyboard instruments, and important musical manuscripts, trainloads of musical instruments and even gramophone records from all over France. In a display of dark humour not always attributed to the Germans, a score of Wagner's *Parsifal* was left on the mantelpiece of Milhaud's emptied apartment.[2]

Happily, Milhaud's friends and colleagues had been able to retrieve manuscripts and precious objects from the composer's apartment before the arrival of the Germans. Some of these were deposited for safekeeping in the apartment of Arthur Honegger, which happened to be on the same street. In a gesture of generous friendship that was also a demonstration of faith in the ultimate victory of France, the conductor Roger Désormière paid the rent on Milhaud's apartment over the four years of the Occupation.

Désormière was also central to a group of musicians who organised themselves into a cell of the 'Front national', a Resistance organisation that included the composers Henry Barraud, Georges Auric, Claude Delvincourt and Elsa Barraine, and the singer Irène Joachim.

The loss of the great musicians who fled across the Atlantic was to some extent mitigated by an influx of musicians from the German Reich and occupied countries, and by a number of gifted young French musicians such as the violinist Ginette Neveu and the cellist Paul Tortelier, who postponed their international careers and confined their activities to France. The great French soprano Germaine Lubin was forced to break her contract with the Metropolitan in New York and remain in Paris.

Apart from Mengelberg, musicians who arrived in France under the protection of the Germans included the conductors Herbert von Karajan, Hans Knappertsbusch, Clemens Krauss, Eugen Jochum, Hermann Abendroth, Hans Rosbaud, Fritz Lehmann and Carl Schuricht, and the pianists Wilhelm Kempff, Elly Ney and Walter Gieseking. The Berlin Philharmonic visited France in every year of the Occupation. Karajan, replacing Furtwängler who had moral scruples about conducting in occupied countries, took the first steps in what was to become one of the most important international musical careers of the twentieth century when he visited Paris in 1941.

The most prestigious German musical offering to France during the war years was a visit in May 1941 of the Berlin State Opera for performances of Mozart's *Die Entführung aus dem Serail* and Wagner's *Tristan und Isolde* at the Paris Opéra. The company comprising 250 personnel arrived at the Gare du Nord to be met by massed journalists and enthusiastic crowds of opera fans. The soprano Erna Berger, who sang Konstanze in *Entführung*, later denied any wrongdoing in taking part in these performances: 'That the Staatsoper with the entire ensemble went to occupied Paris in order to perform Mozart's *Entführung* and Wagner's *Tristan und Isolde* gave me nothing but pleasure. We could sing in the Grand Opera—otherwise reserved for French singers—which was a joy for every singer because of its unique acoustic. That this was at the same time a hostile demonstration of power towards a defeated enemy was not apparent to me. They had applauded me before the war in Paris as an artist and not as a German and why should it be different now?'[3]

On 22 May, Wagner's birthday, a performance of *Tristan und Isolde* was given in the presence of the composer's daughter-in-law Winifred Wagner, with Max Lorenz as Tristan and the French Lubin singing Isolde as a guest with the Berlin company. In an interview she gave towards the end of her life, Lubin claimed: 'I had no choice but to appear as Isolde' but also quoted her teacher Felia Litvinne saying: 'To sing Isolde is worth all the sorrow of living.' These particular Isoldes would certainly cost Lubin a great deal of sorrow at the end of the war. At the time though, the reaction was much as it had been when she sang the role at Bayreuth in 1938 and 1939, one of pride that a French woman could hold her own in the company of the finest German singers. The daily newspaper *La France au Travail* headlined 'Triomphe de Tristan et Isolde' on its front page and enthused:

The Parisian public are familiar with this magisterial work, so often performed on our stages. Nevertheless the crowds fell upon the humblest and the most expensive seats.

The interest of this occasion lay in the presence of Monsieur Herbert von Karajan at the conductor's desk. This conductor is

Winifred Wagner arrives in Paris to attend a performance of Tristan und Isolde *at the Opéra. May 1941.*

not yet 35 years old but had already conquered Paris last November with his interpretation of the Bach B Minor Mass at the Palais de Chaillot. One hardly knows how to describe the magic of such a performance because it is very clear that the elite troupe we have just received belongs amongst the very best current interpreters of Wagner. For this reason French artists were proud that the Staatsoper chose Mme Germaine Lubin, who generously accepted to sing the role of Isolde, that she had already interpreted on the stage of Bayreuth.

Even at this stage though, when Hitler had not yet attacked Russia and when resistance in France against the Germans was minimal, there were a few dissenting voices. Lubin was outraged to receive the following anonymous letter:

> Madame Germaine Lubin of the German company at the Opera. Madame, a German journal in the French language gives us today the two news items added here [the two cuttings have not survived]. Is it necessary to tell you that contrary to these people in the pay of our eternal enemy, French sympathies will not go to an adored actress who has sold herself but to these courageous men deemed traitors by these journalists without a country.[4]

A concert given on Saturday 24 May at the Palais de Chaillot by the Berlin Staatskapelle under Karajan, that included a Mozart symphony, the Strauss tone poem *Tod und Verklärung* and Beethoven's Seventh Symphony, elicited another ecstatic response from the critic of *La France au travail*: 'I had already expressed my inability to praise him [Karajan] as he deserves, in the feeble language of every day. I can only repeat that Monsieur Karajan exhausts all comparisons. He conducted the three works in the programme and the two demanded by the audience, arousing a delirious enthusiasm that can have been experienced by few conductors.'

The visit of the Berlin Staatsoper had been preceded in March by one from the Mannheim company that brought Wagner's *Die Walküre* under the conductor Karl Elmendorff, and was followed on 17 August by the Berlin Deutsche Oper with a performance of *Die Fledermaus* in which the young Elisabeth Schwarzkopf took part. As the latter was reserved for German military and civil personnel based in Paris, Parisians would have had to content themselves with fragments of the performance in a newsreel film. In 1942 the Cologne opera brought *Der fliegende Holländer* to the Paris Opera and in 1943 artists from Cologne and Vienna (including the radiant Hilde Konetzni as Sieglinde) presented *Die Walküre* once again. There were also a number of performances in the Palais Garnier by concert artists from the Reich: on the 31 March 1942, the Vienna Boys Choir, on 13 April 1943 the pianist Walter Gieseking, and on 14 September 1943 the Berlin Philharmonic under Hans Knappertsbusch.

Under pressure from the German authorities, the Palais Garnier hosted not only 'goodwill' visits from German opera companies and musicians but also presented a number of German works that in times of peace would not have seen the light of day in Paris. The most high profile of these productions was the French premiere of Hans Pfitzner's opera *Palestrina* on 30 March 1942. This opera had received its world premiere in Munich during the First World War, conducted by the now exiled Bruno Walter. In more conservative German cultural circles it gained cult status as a work of peculiarly German seriousness and profundity. It was never able to establish itself outside of German-speaking countries and the 13 performances at the Paris Opéra in 1942 were the first and last that have taken place in that city. It was performed in a French translation with a cast entirely drawn from the company of the Paris Opéra. It says much for the vocal resources of the Opéra at the time that this was possible, as it requires an enormous cast of male singers. Amongst the artists who took part were José de Trevi as Palestrina, José Beckmans as Cardinal Borromeo and Charles Cambon, Henri Medus, Jean Claverie, Henry Etcheverry, Georges Nore and Pierre Froumenty in smaller roles. The amount of attention that the *Palestrina* premiere received in German and collaborationist journals makes it clear that it was something like the musical equivalent of the exhibition of sculpture by Arno Breker at the Orangerie that opened a month or so later and which is generally regarded as the most important cultural event organised by the Nazis in Paris.

Under the circumstances it would have been impossible for any French critic to give *Palestrina* a bad review. In a review published in the arts journal *Comoedia* on 4 April 1942, Arthur Honegger chose his words gingerly and hedged his bets. Acknowledging that Pfitzner had an important reputation in Germany while being as yet virtually unknown and unperformed in France, he felt that many Frenchmen

The exhibition of sculpture by Arno Breker at the Orangerie in 1942 was the most prestigious cultural event in occupied Paris.

The premiere of Pfitzner's Palestrina *at the Opéra in 1942 received widespread publicity.*

would be likely to say 'Pfitzner is so specifically German as a musician that he will never be understood by the French any more than Fauré will ever be to the taste of the Germans.' With somewhat lukewarm praise he continued: 'Musically the work is written with an authority that commands respect. The orchestra, often massive, with dense polyphony that is sometimes laborious, does not however drown the voices.' He found the second act boring and far too long, while conceding that the German sense of scale is different from that of French musicians. He reserved his highest praise for the scene in the final act in which the divinely inspired Palestrina composes his famous papal mass. Honegger concludes: 'And now I would be very curious to know what sort of impression a work like Fauré's *Pénélope* would make in Berlin.' There was small chance of any French opera other than *Carmen* receiving a performance in Berlin during the war. Perhaps as a riposte to *Palestrina* the Paris Opéra itself staged *Pénélope* for the first time the following year with Germaine Lubin and Georges Jouatte.

There was also a great deal of coverage in the Nazi-controlled and collaborationist press of the presentation of two works at the Opéra by the German composer Werner Egk—the opera *Peer Gynt* which had been premiered in Berlin in 1938, and the ballet *Joan de Zarissa* which was presented with choreography by Serge Lifar on 10 July 1942, both under the baton of the composer. *Peer Gynt*, like Pfitzner's *Palestrina*, required an enormous cast and involved many of the best singers in the Paris company, including Jeanne Segala, Suzanne Lefort, Suzanne Juyol, José Beckmans, Edmond Rambaud and Etcheverry. It was given for a total of twelve performances between 4

October 1943 and 11 March 1944. A concert performance was broadcast from the Théâtre des Champs-Elysées on 10 October 1943.

During the war Egk was in the happy position of representing the acceptable face of modernism to the Nazis and the acceptable face of German musical culture to the French. An interview with Egk in the radio magazine *Les Ondes* on the day that *Peer Gynt* was broadcast is headed 'Werner

An article on the German composer Werner Egk in the radio magazine Les Ondes.

Egk. Compositeur moderne' and stresses his credentials as a modern composer. Though he was careful not to praise any composers who might have been objectionable to the Nazi authorities, Egk put the case for musical modernity with surprising forcefulness and gave the impression of being critical of German conservatism. During his visits to Paris, Egk was lionised by the political and cultural elite, including Serge Lifar and Jean Cocteau. In the pages of *Comoedia* Arthur Honegger received both of Egk's works with a great deal more enthusiasm than he had Pfitzner's *Palestrina*. On 2 May 1943, he wrote: 'M W Egk searches above all for a living, direct art, far from all formulae, whether romantic or neo-classical. He desires an art that is virile and healthy, hostile to all preciousness but constantly determined by a lucid intelligence at the service of a very decided will.' The German authorities could hardly have put it better to their own satisfaction. Egk repaid the compliment by writing a laudatory review of Honegger's opera *Antigone* for *Comoedia* in February 1943. This public display of mutual admiration between the German and the Swiss composers would bring Honegger into disrepute at the end of the war.

The Opéra Comique at the Salle Favart, despite being from 1941 under the direction of the composer Max d'Ollone who was an enthusiastic supporter of musical collaboration with the Germans—he published an article entitled 'Le role de la musique dans le nouvel ordre européen' in the journal *Collaboration* May-June 1943—was far more successful in maintaining its integrity as a French cultural institution. A somewhat exceptional placatory gesture towards the Germans was the first production in the house of Richard Strauss's opera *Ariadne auf Naxos*—or *Ariane à Naxos* in its French translation. On paper it would seem to have been a splendid performance with Germaine Lubin as Ariadne, Georges Jouatte as Bacchus, Janine Micheau as Zerbinetta, and Marisa Ferrer as the Composer, conducted by Roger Désormière. The only souvenir we have of this impressive cast is a recording of Zerbinetta's aria by Micheau, who negotiates the perilous altitudes of the aria with breathtaking ease and luminosity of tone but, as Honegger noted in his otherwise laudatory review in *Comoedia*, lacks the 'vivacity and malice' for the role. According to Germaine Lubin, Micheau earned a year-long performance ban at the end of the war for singing the role in a performance broadcast by Radio Paris.[5]

After the debacle of June 1940 and the desertion of Paris by a large part of its population, cultural life resumed a semblance of normality with remarkable speed. The much respected veteran administrator Jacques Rouché returned to his job as director of the Opéra despite his misgivings, believing that it would be better than allowing the Germans to take direct control of the institution. Rouché was allowed a measure of creative freedom but like every other administrator in Paris he was forced to conform to Nazi racial directives and dismiss approximately 30 members of the Opéra personnel.

The Opéra reopened its doors on 24 August 1940 after a gap of just over two months, with a performance of Berlioz's *La damnation de Faust*. This was evidently carefully considered. Not only was *La damnation de Faust* one of the few French works that could compete in scale and profundity with the greatest German musical masterpieces, it was also a setting of the most famous and admired work of German literature. As such, this choice could have been interpreted as a gesture of support for German domination of the 'new European order' about which so much was being spoken and in which France desired to play a leading role.

Berlioz was the one French composer during the war years to be accorded the heroic 'biopic' treatment (like Mozart, Beethoven and Schumann around the same time in Germany) with the film *La symphonie fantastique*, released in April 1942, which starred Jean-Louis Barrault as the composer. In an article in *Comoedia* on 1 August 1942 entitled 'Hector Berlioz—Romantic Hero', Adolphe Boschet praised the film. 'Certainly the cleverly chosen scenes, filmed in a picturesque way, the beauty of the extracts of music by a symphonist of genius exercise a powerful attraction. But Berlioz's life itself, the dramatic episodes of a

The Paris Opéra under new masters; A gala opening in December 1940.

The Paris Opéra in 1940.

passionate existence, the evocation of an epoch rich in contrasts and unexpected excess, also seduced the audience.' Answering those who found the film exaggerated, he wrote: 'If it seems like something out of fiction it is because Berlioz was so himself. And it is necessary that a portrait resembles its model.'

La damnation de Faust received no less than twenty performances during the German Occupation. In an undertaking that can only be described as heroic under wartime circumstances, the first complete recording of the piece was made between 15 and 20 September 1942 under the baton of Jean Fournet with the augmented orchestra of Radio Paris consisting of 95 players, the 80 singers of the Chorale Émile Passani, and the soloists Mona Laurena, Georges Jouatte and Paul Cabanel. It might seem surprising that neither Ninon Vallin nor Germaine Lubin, who were the two most admired exponents of the role of Marguerite and still at the height of their powers, was chosen for the recording. Mona Laurena sang at neither the Opéra nor the Opéra Comique and seems not to have had a significant pre-war or post-war career. She apparently owed her brief wartime prominence as a recording and broadcasting artist to her relationship with the German artistic director of Radio Paris, Otto Sonnen. However, her vocal talents are far from negligible and she does not let the side down.

Mona Laurena

The French soprano Mona Laurena came to prominence during the Occupation thanks to the patronage of the German director of Radio Paris.

Two months later on 17 November 1942, Fournet, a rigid musical disciplinarian according to the soprano Renée Doria, conducted *La damnation de Faust* at the Palais de Chaillot with even larger forces, combining three of Paris's five major orchestras—Lamoureux, Pasdeloup and Pierné (the former Orchestre Colonne, temporarily renamed because of Colonne's Jewish origins).

Berlioz's monumental *Requiem* also became a talismanic work under the Occupation. On 26 November 1943 a performance was presented at the Opéra with Charles Munch conducting 613

78

musicians and singers. Once again the seemingly inevitable soloist was Georges Jouatte who was received, we are told by the critic of *L'Illustration*, with 'frenetic ovations'. The performance was intended as a political demonstration. It was given in aid of the French Red Cross at a time when increasing numbers of French civilians were being killed or wounded in Allied bombing raids on French industry and strategic targets. Once again a pioneering recording was made, between September 1943 and May 1944, conducted by Fournet with Jouatte as soloist—

A wartime performance of Berlioz's Requiem *with over 600 performers.*

this time with a mere 290 soloists and singers involved. Just how remarkable these massive wartime Berlioz recordings were is shown by the fact that there was no complete recording of *La damnation de Faust* attempted for another twelve years and none of the *Requiem* for another 14 years.

It was the Opéra Comique rather than the Grand Opéra that had premiered the most characteristic works in the French operatic repertoire, including Bizet's *Carmen* in 1876, Offenbach's *Les contes d'Hoffmann* in 1881, Massenet's *Manon* in 1884 and Debussy's *Pelléas et Mélisande* in 1902.

Les contes d'Hoffmann by the Jewish Offenbach could not be performed under the German Occupation, nor works by composers such as Darius Milhaud, Reynaldo Hahn and Paul Dukas. But it is very clear that the repertoire was carefully chosen to reassert French cultural values.

The greatest wartime achievement of the Opéra Comique was the superb production of that most French of French operas *Pelléas et Mélisande* by that most French of French composers Claude Debussy, frequently referred to in many wartime articles as 'Claude de France'. It is no coincidence that in November 1940 the French post office issued two stamps commemorating Debussy.

The conductor Roger Désormière.

The first performance of this revival took place on 12 September 1940. Like many wartime performances it began early, at 5.45 pm. It was a sign of the times that the programme carried a résumé of the plot in German, rather than in English, as had been the custom before the war. The performance brought together two artists who were to be key elements in what came to be seen as a classic cast—the conductor Roger Désormière and the 27-year-old soprano Irène Joachim as Mélisande. Joachim later recalled of that night:

The curtain rose, the auditorium was absolutely packed. I immediately spotted a group in which I recognized faces, people of the theatre, actors and musicians, all friends of Déso [Désormière], Jouvet, etc. Everything was good. It made us feel good. But immediately I noticed to my horror, that the theatre was three-quarters full of German officers and soldiers. It was appalling! We had to prove, through Debussy's music that we were there, still capable of living for the greatest of music, to be the best for the sake of Debussy. But when Mélisande is beaten and thrown to the ground by Golaud who drags her by the hair 'Forwards and backwards' and Arkel says at last; 'If I were God I would take pity on the hearts of men,' I can say that the emotion was such that all the friends in the auditorium, the musicians in the orchestra and we singers on stage, we were all crying.[6]

The composer Henri Dutilleux who was in the audience remembered the occasion in very similar terms:

On this evening a public flocked in that was hardly ordinary. In the orchestra seats there was everyone in Paris who mattered in the world of theatre, literature and music—and then there were the others ... the uniformed officers that chance that evening had thrown together with the likes of Jouvet, Jean-Louis Barrault, Aragon and those who would soon re-group in the 'Front national', like Désormière himself at the conductor's stand.

The theatre was vibrant with emotion that grew unceasingly, from the interpreters to the public, throughout the work, whose spirit and mystery had never, it seemed, been more faithfully expressed. The orchestra interludes, impelled by Désormière, took on a passionate accent, but without exaggeration, that has only been achieved by him. And then in Act IV, after the long progression of the central scene in which Golaud's rage reaches its climax, Arkel implores 'If I were God, I would take pity on the hearts of men', the frisson that everyone always feels at this moment has never been as intense as it was on that September evening in 1940 in occupied Paris.[7]

Pelléas would be given 44 times at the Opéra Comique between 12 September 1940 and 1 January 1946 as well as being given in several other French cities with the same or similar casts. But Irène Joachim's Mélisande did not meet her ideal Pelléas till some months after the 12 September performance. This was in a matinee performance on 20 April 1941, which marked the debut at the Salle Favart of the young baritone Jacques Jansen. It was a rare concurrence of two singers who were perfect for their roles in voice, temperament and physical appearance. Both saw their casting in their respective roles in terms of destiny. In essays written for a CD reissue of the set, Jansen wrote: 'It was all a matter of chance. Everything was inextricably linked, as if one were putting together the crucial pieces of a puzzle.' And Joachim wrote: 'It must have been pre-destination—the force of destiny.'

On 18 December 1941, a few days after he had noted a sinister round up of Parisian Jews, the composer Georges Van Parys heard the new cast of *Pelléas* at the Opéra Comique and wrote in his diary: 'The Opéra Comique has revived *Pelléas* with a cast that is perfect in every way. Jacques Jansen is an admirable Pelléas, Irène Joachim and Etcheverry at his side are a Mélisande and a Golaud which you could not dream of bettering. Roger Désormière at the conductor's desk. I cannot believe

Baritone Jacques Jansen sang Pelléas in the legendary wartime performances of Debussy's opera.

81

Article in Comoedia *about the recording of* Pelléas et Mélisande.

that we shall see a performance as perfect as this for a long time.'[8]

Happily, the firm of Pathé-Marconi made the bold decision to record the whole opera in 1941 with the cast of the Opéra Comique. There had been two previous recordings of extracts of *Pelléas* but this was the first commercial attempt to record it complete. As such it was a considerable act of faith. On twenty, thick, double-sided 78 rpm shellac discs that weighed in at over twelve kilos, there was no foreseeable prospect of recouping costs with wartime restrictions on materials.

The recording was made over a period of just over a month, between 24 April and 26 May 1941. For a work whose salient characteristic is the continuous flow of its music, dividing it into approximately four-minute sections for the purpose of recording on 78 rpm discs was itself problematic. This task was entrusted to the composer Louis Beydts. Jansen recalled: 'Wax was so scarce—it was during the Occupation—there was no question of doing some bit over ten times.' Irène Joachim too asserted: 'The near absence of wax permitted very few retakes' and she attributed the spontaneity and naturalness of the performance to this fact. Interestingly, a review of the recording in *Comoedia* at the time stresses the exact opposite. 'How many waxes were wasted before the recording was definitive! Certain sides were remade up to six times before every scruple was satisfied.'

In addition to Joachim and Jansen in the title roles, every other role in the opera was definitively cast—Etcheverry as a powerful and tormented Golaud, Paul Cabanel as the noblest and most moving of Arkels, Germaine Cernay with her smooth legato and immaculate diction as Geneviève and the charming Leila Ben Sedira as Yniold.

On its appearance in January 1942, the Désormière *Pelléas et Mélisande* was recognised as a cultural landmark and a remarkable technical achievement, but it clearly meant different things to different commentators according to their differing political persuasions. For some it was a defiant assertion of French as opposed to German cultural values. Arthur Hoerée began his review of 24 January 1942 in *Comoedia*: 'After *Tristan* Wagner took opera under his yoke while taking it to sublime heights. Debussy delivered French opera from under this yoke in leaving us his imperishable masterpiece *Pelléas*. One feels the magnificent gift, the importance of fixing it complete in wax, the quiet audacity of M. Jean Bérard, the director of Pathé-Marconi, in undertaking and succeeding in such an enterprise under current circumstances.'

When it was first issued in January 1942 the set was accompanied by what was by the standards of the time a very lavish, illustrated booklet with an introduction by the Vichy minister of education, Abel Bonnard. 'At this moment when the Frenchman risks being entirely reduced to the concerns of his physical existence by privation, just as he was yesterday by an excess of pleasures, we must seize the opportunity imperiously to re-awaken that other hunger and compensate with ineffable feasts for the poor meals of which the body complains.' A further essay by the distinguished composer and musicologist Gustave Samazeuilh suggests a conservative and anti-modernist agenda in tune with the cultural policies of Vichy and even of the Germans. 'May the name and the work of Claude Debussy, who renewed our art, remain honoured in this country. May their example of taste, tact and sobriety never cease to be appreciated. They are amongst those things that affirm the immortal genius of our race and oppose the lifeless conventions of a tradition of pure form, of a second-hand aesthetic and of the already obsolete rigors of a certain superficial, surgical dynamic with a harmonious poetry, the evocative virtue and penetrating expression of genuine French music.' The targets here, though not named, are clearly Stravinsky and Schoenberg and the cosmopolitan avant-garde so abhorred by the Nazis.

The rabidly germanophile critic Lucien Rebatet, writing in the collaborationist journal *Je suis partout* on 24 January 1942, praised the technical quality of the recording but boasted that he preferred *Meistersinger* and *Tristan*. At the other end of the political scale, the Surrealist poet and Resistance martyr Robert Desnos wrote on the same day in *Aujourd'hui*: 'The choice of *Pelléas*, an internationally recognised French work, is not just a happy one but an inspiring one.'

Another composer who seemed to represent typically Gallic virtues of wit and insouciance as opposed to Teutonic heaviness was Emmanuel Chabrier. Like Debussy, he was honoured by the Vichy government with a pair of commemorative postage stamps. Chabrier came under the influence of Wagner, like many French composers at the end of the nineteenth century, but remained sufficiently detached to make irreverent use of themes from *Tristan* in a jaunty piece for two pianos entitled 'Souvenir de Munich'. Wagner's widow, Cosima, was appalled by what she regarded as the vulgarity and triviality of Chabrier's *Le roi malgré lui* when she heard it in Dresden in 1890 and would have been even more appalled if she had ever got to hear 'Souvenir de Munich'. The centenary of Chabrier's birth in 1941 offered an opportunity to mount a production of his neglected operetta *L'étoile* and also to record extensive excerpts. This delightful work, showcasing the lively talents of the popular mezzo Fanély Revoil, was given thirty times between 1941 and 1946 and must have lightened the hearts of many during the dark days of the Occupation.

Throughout the Occupation the Opéra Comique continued to present new works on a regular basis, much as it had done since the nineteenth century. In all there were seven premieres—André Lavagne's *Comme ils s'aiment* on 27 May 1941, Antoine Mariotte's *Nele Dooryn*, Francis Bousquet's *Mon oncle Benjamin* on 10 March 1942, Paul le Flem's *Le rossignol de St Malo* on 5 May 1942, Marcel Delannoy's *Ginevra* on 25 July 1942, Marcel Bertrand's *Amphytrion 38* on 25 January 1944 and Henri Sauguet's *La gageure imprévue* (delayed from the previous season) on the 4 July 1944, nearly a month after the Normandy landings.[9] While it is true that very few of the enormous quantity of operas premiered at the Opéra Comique in the first half of the twentieth century have established themselves in the international repertoire, it is striking that not one of these operas managed to outlive the war, though several were well received at the time. Amongst the composers only Henri Sauguet is likely to be familiar to even the best-informed music lover today.

The most successful of these forgotten operas was *Ginevra* by Marcel Delannoy, a composer second only to Arthur Honegger in prominence on the wartime Parisian musical scene. Delannoy was a former protégé of Honegger and would write the first biography of his mentor after the war. Based on a tale of Boccaccio, *Ginevra* has a most attractive musical score, as we can tell from recorded extracts with the excellent original cast—Irène Joachim, Etcheverry, Marthe Angelici and Camille Mauranne under the baton of Désormière.

In a lengthy review of *Ginevra* in *Comoedia* dated 1 August 1942, Arthur Honegger notes with a hint of irritation that all Paris has been talking about the opera for months in advance of the premiere. He places the work in a current tendency, both anti-Debussy and anti-Wagner, to write works of 'demi-caractère', i.e. of a light and populist nature. The last act contains a delightful 'rhumba' that according to Honegger greatly pleased the audience. (Rumbas were clearly

Marcel Delannoy's Ginevra *was one of the most successful wartime premieres at the* Opéra Comique.

in the air in 1942 on both sides of the Atlantic and the war. Arthur Benjamin's 'Jamaican Rhumba' was premiered in New York on 21 January under the baton of Alfred Wallenstein, and later in the same year Leopold Stokowski premiered Paul Lavalle's 'Symphonic Rhumba' in NBC's Studio 8H to the audible pleasure of the audience.)

Honegger criticised *Ginevra* and works of a similar tendency for being archaic and escapist in their subject matter and failing to engage with the reality of life in 1940, though how that could have been done under the German Occupation he does not elaborate. Nevertheless, Honegger praises the score as being 'rich in true and charming music'.

Despite these fine qualities *Ginevra* was doomed not only by the composer's high profile during the Occupation and the fact that he had contributed reviews to the ultra-Fascist journal *Je suis partout*, but still more by its librettist Julien Luchaire, father of the collaborationist journalist

The sculptor Arno Breker discusses a point with Jean Cocteau at the opening of his exhibition in 1942.

Jean Luchaire and grandfather of the film star Corinne Luchaire. The name of Luchaire on the score would have been advantageous in 1942 but fatal to post-war chances of revival after the execution of Jean Luchaire on charges of treason in 1946. Ironically, Julien Luchaire was involved in the Resistance and his notorious son gave employment and protection to the young Simone Signoret, knowing that she was half Jewish and that her father was working for the Free

Le programme de la saison

A L'OPERA

Reprises :

Joan de Zarissa, de M. Werner Egk ;
Palestrina, de M. Hans Pfitzner ;
Les animaux modèles, de M. Francis Poulenc ;
Marouf, de M. Henri Rabaud ;
Salammbo, de Reyer ;
La légende de saint Christophe, de Vincent d'Indy ;
Lohengrin, de Wagner ;
Othello, de Verdi ;
Freischütz, de Weber.
SUITE DU CENTENAIRE DE MASSENET : Thaïs.

Œuvres mises au répertoire :

Pénélope, de Gabriel Fauré ;
Antigone, de M. A. Honegger ;
L'oiseau de feu, de Stravinsky ;
Ballet de la Sylphide ;
Graziella, de M. Mazellier ;
L'amour sorcier, de M. Manuel de Falla.

Œuvres inédites :

Lucifer, livret de M. Dumesnil, musique de M. C. Delvincourt ;
Ballet Cercle enchante, de M. A. Jolivet ;
Ballet basque, de M. Ermend Bonnal ;
Ballet Le jour, de Jaubert.

A L'OPERA-COMIQUE

Reprises :

Ginevra, livret de M. Julien Luchaire, musique de M. Marcel Delannoy ;
Mon oncle Benjamin, livret de M. Ricou, musique de M. Franc's Bousquet ;
La lépreuse, de M. Sylvio Lazzari ;
Habanera, de M. Raoul Laparra ;
Lakmé, de Léo Delibes.
SUITE DU CENTENAIRE DE MASSENET : Grisélidis, Manon.

Œuvres remises au répertoire :

Ariane, de M. Richard Strauss.
Fragonard, livret de M A. Rivoire, musique de G. Pierné.

Œuvres inédites :

Amphitryon, d'après M. Giraudoux ; mus'que de M. Marcel Bertrand ;
Kermesse, ballet de M. Lavagne ;
Fantaisie nocturne, ballet de M. Bachelet ;
La gageure imprévue, livret de M. Bertin, musique de M. H' Sauguet.

Réouverture du Cours d'Art dramatique de MM. RAYMOND-GIRARD, CHAMARAT et Lucien PASCAL
du Théâtre National de l'Odéon
Studio : 18, r. de Condé, 6°, Jeud, Dim., 10 h. à midi. Rens. 'et Inscrip.: 26, r. Vavin.
(DAN. 48-16)

Le COURS PAUPELIX a lieu le dimanche et le jeudi matin de 10 heures à midi au Théâtre Monceau.

The programme announced for the 1942-43 season at the Opéra.

French in London, once again demonstrating the bewildering complexities of life under the Occupation.

Even outside the two national opera houses there was much opera of a high standard to be enjoyed in Paris under the Occupation. Two veteran sopranos familiar to record collectors, Ninon Vallin and Germaine Féraldy, appeared at the Gaîté-Lyrique. Féraldy signed for 30 performances of *La Traviata*, *Le barbier de Séville* and *Si j'étais roi* though illness prevented her from singing them all.[10] In September 1942, after a long absence from Paris, Ninon Vallin appeared at the Gaîté-Lyrique as the Countess in *Les noces de Figaro*. The critic of *Comoedia* enthused: 'In the secondary role of the Countess, she was able to give the full measure of her mastery of her rounded, easy and flexible voice that was nuanced with the most delicate inflections and used with consummate skill.' That the 56-year-old Vallin was still in ravishing voice can be heard in a transcript of a Swiss radio performance of *L'Étoile* dating from the same year.

When the repertoire of the Opéra and the Opéra Comique was announced for the season of 1942-43, *Comoedia* carried a front page article in which Jacques Rouché, 'administrateur général des théâtres lyriques subventionnés'—to give his full title, expounded at length on the difficulties of choosing a repertoire without touching on what must in fact have been one of his greatest difficulties—dealing with the German authorities and indeed with the Vichy authorities, who did not always want the same things. In 1942 Rouché had been forced to mount a production of the opera *Le drac* by the obscure Hillemacher brothers because the wife of the Vichy education minister Jérôme Carpino was related to them. What is most striking about the list of works announced for the 1942-43 season is how few of them would be familiar to the public today. There is also an interesting distinction between those composers who are given the title of *Monsieur* and a first name or initial and those who are clearly accepted as great masters who need neither. To the latter group belong Reyer, Wagner, Verdi, Weber, Massenet, and most surprisingly Stravinsky, who was not only the only one of these great masters still alive, but a Russian-born resident of the United States.

Surviving radio performances dating from the last weeks of the Occupation, of Sylvio Lazzari's *La tour de feu* and Boieldieu's *La dame blanche*, provide evidence of the high vocal standards of the time as well as offering fascinating glimpses of this now unfamiliar French repertoire. The broadcast of Lazzari's *La Tour de Feu* on 25 June 1944 was intended to commemorate the death of the composer two weeks earlier on 10 June. Sylvio Lazzari was born in Bolzano of Austro-Italian parentage, but was French educated and nationalized, and a prominent and respected composer in France in the first half of the twentieth century. His opera *La lépreuse* had been performed 70 times at the Opéra Comique. The revival in April 1943 was received with the greatest enthusiasm and was reviewed with a surprising degree of empathy and respect by the much younger composer Arthur Honegger, who represented a very different musical aesthetic.

The broadcast of *La tour de feu* reveals an exciting score in a post-Wagnerian vein that might be better described as French *verismo* with its melodic and high-pitched emotionalism. The recording also allows us to hear two very fine and unjustly forgotten singers at the height of their powers. The powerful dramatic soprano Marisa Ferrer was one of the leading singers at the Opéra for a quarter of a century from 1924 but strangely made only one commercial record. The Belgian baritone José Beckmans had the misfortune that his career peaked during the Occupation. He was one of the singers most in view in wartime Paris taking part in such high profile productions as Pfitzner's *Palestrina* and Werner Egk's *Peer Gynt*, and his post-war reputation suffered as a consequence.

La dame blanche was broadcast on 25 July 1944. The pointed and accomplished coloratura of Odette Turba-Rabier and the perfumed elegance of the tenor Louis Arnoult show the old Opéra Comique tradition at its very best. One cannot help wondering whether the broadcast of this opera with its Scottish subject at a time when Allied troops were well on their way to Paris was an oblique political gesture. Exactly one month later when Allied troops entered Paris, the bed-ridden author Colette told her husband Maurice Goudeket she would not believe it unless he could go out into the streets and fetch a soldier in a kilt.

Although new operas were premiered at the Palais Garnier, it was ballet rather than opera that went through a particularly creative phase at the Grand Opéra. This was largely due to the talents of the Ukrainian Serge Lifar as a dancer, choreographer and ballet master. In the 1920s Lifar was the successor to Nijinsky as star dancer of Diaghilev's Ballets Russes and as the great impresario's lover. In the 1930s he was engaged as ballet master at the Paris Opéra. The war years were his most creative period. According to the German composer Werner Egk, Lifar was accorded the status of 'demi-god' in wartime Paris. Among the ballets he choreographed were *Le chevalier et la demoiselle* in 1941 to a score by Philippe Gaubert, the musical director of the Opéra, Werner Egk's *Joan de Zarissa*, Poulenc's *Les animaux modèles*, Maurice Jaubert's *Le jour* and André Jolivet's *Guignol et Pandore*. The last only reached dress rehearsal before the Opéra was shut late in July 1944.

After the Liberation, because of his close collaboration with the Nazi authorities, Lifar was dismissed from his post and banned for life from employment at the Opéra and all other state theatres. The ban was soon reduced to a year and Lifar was back in his old job at the Opéra by 1947. In his autobiography *Ma vie* Lifar wrote pretentiously of 'my mission' as though he were personally responsible for saving French culture

The Russian dancer Serge Lifar was accorded the status of a 'demi-god' in occupied Paris.

from Nazi barbarism. The book reveals a man of such shallow narcissism and naïve boastfulness that one might be tempted to excuse his collaboration on grounds of diminished responsibility. Fascism and the conquering Wehrmacht held an allure for him that was aesthetic or even erotic. He was entranced by 'the young heroes who had conquered the world with a smile.' He designed and had made a fantasy Fascist uniform in which he proudly had himself photographed in 1939 and did not hesitate to include the photograph in his 1965 autobiography. He relates a comical incident when he was asked by a young German officer to provide proof of his Aryan origins. 'In my disarray I attempted to bring him physical proof of an integrity that Nazi racism would appreciate.' By which he presumably meant that he dropped his trousers. The outraged Nazi, misinterpreting or perhaps correctly interpreting Lifar's gesture, shouted: 'You are insulting the German army!'[11] Poulenc's charitable verdict on Lifar was that he had been 'childishly imprudent out of his fondness for publicity.'[12]

A typical week of concerts in Paris in 1942.

The repertoire in the concert hall was much more thoroughly germanised than that of the two Paris opera houses during the Occupation. The week of 6 to 13 April 1941 was fairly typical of the earlier part of the war when Germany and Russia were still nominally allies and Russian music could also figure prominently in concert programmes. On Sunday 6 April, four major symphonic concerts of what seem to modern eyes of inordinate length took place at the early evening time required for all public events. At 6 pm Charles Munch conducted the Conservatoire Orchestra at the Palais de Chaillot in a concert consisting of Weber's Overture to *Oberon*, Weber's Piano Concerto and Beethoven's Ninth Symphony. At the same time François Ruhlmann conducted the renamed orchestra of Gabriel Pierné (formerly Colonne) at the Théâtre du Châtelet in Beethoven's Eighth Symphony, Schubert's 'Der Erlkönig' ('Le roi des aulnes'), Canteloube's 'Poème' for violin and orchestra, Stravinsky's *Firebird*, and a selection of shorter Russian pieces. At the Salle Pleyel at 5.45 pm the Concerts Lamoureux under Eugène Bigot played an all-César Franck and Wagner concert, and at 5.30 pm at the Salle Gaveau the Concerts

Pasdeloup played Bach's Easter Cantata and short pieces by Wagner. On Friday 11 April the Concerts Gabriel Pierné gave an all-Beethoven concert at the Théâtre du Châtelet consisting of the Third, Sixth and Fifth Symphonies, and the Concerts du Conservatoire under Charles Munch performed Bach's *St John Passion* in the church of St Eustache; finally, on Easter Sunday the Concerts Lamoureux gave an all-Russian concert at the Salle Pleyel conducted by Eugène Bigot and consisting of music by Borodin, Rimsky-Korsakov, Moussorgsky and Stravinsky.

Following a policy launched under the Third Republic, the Vichy regime continued to commission new works from French composers but with a more overt and determined political agenda. Altogether fifty-seven composers received commissions. A number were openly propagandist, such as André Gailhard's 'Ode à la France blessée'. Preference was given to composers who had served in the armed forces and been repatriated from German prisoner of war camps, and also to composers who were Catholic, especially those who held posts as organists in the great metropolitan churches. Significantly, Olivier Messiaen, who qualified on all counts as he had been organist of the great Second Empire church of La Trinité since 1931, did not receive an official commission since his music did not conform to the conservative tendencies favoured by the regime.[13]

By no means all the composers favoured with Vichy commissions were servile hacks or hopelessly reactionary. Among the more distinguished beneficiaries of commissions were Marcel Delannoy and Paul Le Flem, as well as younger composers who would have successful post-war careers, such as Henri Dutilleux, André Jolivet and Henri Sauguet.

Of the more than fifty works sponsored by Vichy only one succeeded in establishing itself in the concert repertoire. This was Maurice Duruflé's *Requiem*. It was perhaps fortunate for Duruflé that he was a slow worker. The work was not ready for performance until 1947, which enabled it to escape, to some extent at least, the taint of association with Vichy. The austere melodic lines borrowed from Gregorian chants, clothed in the sensuous harmonies and instrumentation of Fauré, combining medievalism and restrained modernism and the mood of nostalgic Catholicism, made the Duruflé *Requiem* the perfect musical expression of the Vichy mentality, rather as the crude populism of Orff's *Carmina Burana* expresses certain aspects of the Nazi mentality.

French music like French theatre was profoundly affected by the moral dilemmas and ambiguities of the Occupation. Among the composers whose music reflected in more or less oblique ways the political situation of France were Arthur Honegger, Francis Poulenc, André Jolivet and Henri Dutilleux. Under such pervasively evil regimes as the German Occupation and Vichy it was impossible to survive without some form of compromise even if it was just the trivial compromises of daily life. With all of these composers, as with the French population at large, there were infinite shades of complicity and resistance, with the two not being mutually exclusive.

The most visible, performed and discussed composer in occupied Paris was Arthur Honegger. As a citizen of neutral Switzerland whose music was banned in the German Reich as 'degenerate', Honegger was in a privileged but delicate position in Paris. A number of questions present themselves. Why did Honegger decide to remain in Paris throughout the Occupation? In the earlier stages of the war at least, it would have been easy for him to return with his wife to Switzerland and to sit it out in comfort and safety, though as his biographer Harry Halbreich points out this would have meant leaving behind his former mistress, the singer Claire Croiza, and their son. Was it through a sense of solidarity with his adopted country of France? Was there an element of ambition and self-interest? It must have been gratifying to be the biggest fish in the somewhat smaller pond that Paris had become. Was he following some kind of creative imperative or was it simply as Picasso said, through inertia? Why did the Germans allow so much prominence to a composer of whom they apparently disapproved?

Honegger was astonishingly prolific during the years of the Occupation. Indeed, they may be regarded as the peak years of his career. As well as acting as music editor for the arts journal

Arthur Honegger was the most performed contemporary composer under the Occupation.

Comoedia—his reviews provide a fascinating and remarkably objective commentary on the musical life of Paris in these years—he composed incidental music for eight plays (including Claudel's *Le soulier de satin* and Giraudoux's *Sodome et Gomorrhe*), scores for ten films and three radio pieces. He also composed his second symphony (Symphony for Strings), the opera *Charles le téméraire*, and numerous lesser works. His opera *Antigone* was taken into the repertoire of the Opéra in 1943 and his orchestral works were regularly programmed, in particular by Charles Munch, the conductor of the Conservatoire Orchestra.

The climax of his wartime musical activities was a week-long festival of concerts to celebrate his fiftieth birthday in June 1942. Arthur Hoerée, his fellow critic at *Comoedia*, wrote: 'He is incontestably the most original musician and the strongest personality currently in France.'

Four major works of Honegger have become indelibly associated with the war: the cantatas *Jeanne d'Arc au bûcher* ('Joan of Arc at the Stake') and *La danse des morts*, and the Second and Third Symphonies. The first two were composed shortly before the outbreak of war. The first three of these were accorded the rare honour of wartime recordings. In particular, the 1943 recording of *Jeanne d'Arc au bûcher* made by Pathé-Marconi in Brussels ranked along with the same firm's *Pelléas*, *Damnation of Faust* and Berlioz *Requiem* as one of its four great wartime prestige projects. *Jeanne d'Arc au bûcher* had been commissioned in 1934 from Honegger and the poet and dramatist Paul Claudel by the great Russian dancer, actress and patroness Ida Rubinstein; it was she who played the title role in the world premiere in Basle in 1938 and in a number of highly successful performances in France and Belgium just before and during the early months of the war, before taking refuge in London after the fall of France.

The story of Joan of Arc who led the French to victory over the English in the Hundred Years War appealed to all shades of opinion in France in the aftermath of defeat—from those who now sided with Germany and regarded Britain, after the sinking of the French fleet at Mers el-Kébir, as France's real enemy, to those who saw Joan of Arc as a symbol of resistance against foreign and specifically German oppression. The fervour with which the piece was promoted under the new Vichy regime may be regarded as somewhat questionable. Beginning in July 1941 more than forty performances were given in towns of the southern zone of France. (The Vichy government also commissioned an oratorio on the theme of Joan of Arc from seven French composers, including Tony Aubin, Louis Beydts and André Jolivet.)

La danse des morts was written in 1938 to a text of Claudel based upon the Bible. The premiere took place in Basle in March 1940. The Paris premiere projected for June 1940 had to be postponed for obvious reasons. The apocalyptic tone of the text—'Remember, man, that thou art dust, a dust that my breath hath scattered to the four corners of Heaven'—proved uncannily apt and the piece evoked a powerful response when it was finally premiered in Paris on 26 January 1941.

Honegger's Second Symphony (Symphony for String Orchestra) was commissioned by the Swiss conductor Paul Sacher as early as 1936. After false starts it was finally composed between November 1940 and October 1941. The deep gloom of the first movement clearly reflects the mood of France and of Honegger himself at the time. The third and final movement builds to a climax of blazing optimism. It is a moment of spine-tingling excitement when the string orchestra is joined by a trumpet for an ecstatic chorale-like melody. This is usually interpreted as prophetic of French victory and liberation. It would have taken remarkable optimism or perspicacity to foresee such an outcome to the war in October 1941. However, Honegger wrote his 'Chant de libération' in the spring of 1942 when the military situation was not much better. Charles Munch, who had conducted the premiere of the Second Symphony, gave his own explanation of the work in a 1967 interview: 'It's the expression of this terrible time, and the end is just the liberation when come [sic] the American soldiers in Paris, and then this big revolt, big tumult, and finally start[s] the chorale. The victory.'[14]

The Third Symphony ('Symphonie liturgique') was composed between January 1945 and April 1946 and might be understood as a retrospective view of the war and its outcome. As Harry Halbreich puts it: 'The triumphant cry at the end of the Second symphony would never be heard again. The symphony that followed would escape despair only by taking refuge in prayer, and in the utopian vision of a better world ... the *Symphonie liturgique* tells of a future that is painful rather than pleasant. The price of victory has been too high, with all its bereavements and sufferings, leaving behind a world ravaged and desolate in which mankind has become no better than it was before.'[15]

With such high exposure during the Occupation it was inevitable that Honegger would come under suspicion after the Liberation. It seemed incomprehensible that, career-wise at least, he had managed to lead such a charmed existence through such dark times. In December he wrote ruefully to Paul Claudel: 'My situation is somewhat comical.

They don't want to bring me before a commission of purification because apparently they've got no charges against me. But one or two totally well-meaning colleagues think that in my own interest it's not a good idea for my music to be played at the moment.'[16] The most serious accusations against Honegger were that as a critic of *Comoedia* he was part of the French delegation to the Mozart celebrations in Vienna in 1941 and that he wrote reviews praising the work of living German composers such as Egk and Strauss. Honegger was bewildered at the accusations and rejected any imputation of wrongdoing. In his comprehensive biography of Honegger, Harry Halbreich puts up a passionate and, on the whole, convincing defence of the composer's comportment during the war.

A composer whose music is often associated with the Resistance is Francis Poulenc. Like Honegger, Poulenc was a former member of the group known as 'Les Six' but was a composer of a very different character—witty and playful rather than muscular and monumental. The disaster that befell France helped to encourage a more serious side of Poulenc's art that had already begun to emerge in the late 1930s.

As Poulenc was born in 1899, he was still of military age but did not receive his call-up papers till June 1940 and never saw military action. As Richard D E Burton shows in his insightful small book on Poulenc, the composer's attitudes and actions during the war were occasionally less than heroic. There were references in his correspondence in the summer of 1940 to 'the dear Maréchal'. In the words of Burton, the 1942 'Chansons villageoises' 'might be seen as a musical version of the Vichyist *retour à la terre*'[17] that is also celebrated in popular songs of the period such as 'Douce France' and 'Ça sent si bon la France'.

One of Poulenc's most delightful compositions was the song 'Les

chemins de l'amour' written in 1941 for Yvonne Printemps to sing in *Léocadia*, a play written by the very young and as yet little-known playwright Jean Anouilh. With beguiling charm the 47-year-old Printemps played the part of a teenage girl. The recording she made of the song in 1941 is, in the true sense of the word, inimitable. In Colette's famous description,

Yvonne Printemps in Jean Anouilh's Léocadia *in 1941.*

94

Yvonne Printemps does not sing but 'breathes melodiously'. It would be impossible to notate quite what she does with this song.

Poulenc engaged more directly with the idea of resistance when in 1943 he made song settings of two poems by the Communist poet Louis Aragon, 'C' and 'Fêtes Galantes', both dealing with the depressing realities of occupied France. The core of Poulenc's ballet *Les animaux modèles*, based on the *Fables* of La Fontaine, which was presented at the Opéra, made bold use of a traditional anti-German song 'Non, non, vous n'aurez pas notre Alsace-Lorraine'. The song dated back to the war of 1870 but was still ringing in the ears of the French in a recording made by Georges Thill at the beginning of the war. Intended as a private joke to be shared with French members of the audience, it is unlikely that its meaning escaped the Germans, even though Poulenc succeeds in transforming the fragment of melody into something that sounds like typical Poulenc, but his little joke must have carried a certain risk.

Poulenc's most significant contribution to the music of resistance, not heard in public till after the war, was the choral work *Figure humaine*, based on texts by the poet Paul Éluard that had been secretly circulated amongst the Resistance. The cycle culminates with a sublimely simple and beautiful setting of the poem 'Liberté', copies of which had been dropped all over occupied France by Allied aircraft.

Born nine years later than Poulenc, Olivier Messiaen had not only served in the French Army but had been interned as a prisoner of war from 1940 to 1941, during which time he wrote his 'Quatuor pour la fin du temps' ('Quartet for the end of time'). The most important work by Messiaen premiered in Paris during the Occupation was the two-piano 'Visions of Amen'. It is a dark and austere work that may reflect the mood of 1943. Messiaen was not the kind of composer to comment directly on the political situation, but to compose and perform music of such uncompromising modernity in 1943 was in itself an act of resistance. Honegger displayed both the breadth of his musical sympathies and his moral courage in praising the work warmly in an article in *Comoedia* on 1 May 1943. He described it as 'a work of great musical richness and true grandeur of conception.' Messiaen wrote to thank Honegger for the review saying 'the really great artists are simple and good. You have just proved this anew.'[18]

André Jolivet and Henri Dutilleux were both recipients of commissions from the Vichy regime, but both wrote songs that expressed their private feelings about the war and the German Occupation. Henri Dutilleux joined the anti-German 'Front national'. In conversation with Claude Glayman, he commented on the irony of being united with the musically and politically conservative Claude Delvincourt to whom he had previously been opposed. Amongst the political songs that Dutilleux wrote at this time were 'La chanson de la deportée' and 'La géole'. The latter was a setting of one of the 'Trente-trois sonnets composés en secret' written by Jean Cassou while in prison from 1941-42 and published clandestinely under the name of Jean Noir in 1944.

André Jolivet had established himself as a leading figure of the musical avant-garde in the 1930s. During the war he returned to a more conservative and populist manner, obeying perhaps the 'call to

order' that affected many artists in both world wars, rather than the dictates of Vichy. In 1940 he wrote 'Les trois complaintes du soldat', using texts he had written himself while serving as a soldier, and expressing his feelings about French defeat. The songs were received with great acclaim when first performed in a piano-accompanied version in 1941 and then again in a new orchestral version in February

The composer André Jolivet.

1943, conducted by Charles Munch and sung by the baritone Pierre Bernac. Bernac and Munch recorded the songs in late 1943 and early 1944 though publication was delayed till after the end of the war.

It might seem surprising that songs expressing agonizing despair at French defeat would be encouraged or even allowed by the German and Vichy authorities. The first song opens with the words:

> Me voici donc sans armes et nu,
> Me voici donc sans haine et muet,
> Me voici donc vide et pauvre comme des mains d'abondance
> Qui n'ont pas assez donné.
> Me voici comme une image inutile
> De la souffrance de l'homme …

(Here I am without weapons and naked,
Here I am silent and without hatred,
Here I am empty and poor like hands of abundance
That have not given enough.
Here I am like a useless image
Of the suffering of man ...)

The songs contain no element of continuing defiance or hostility towards the victorious enemy. The religious sentiment would have pleased Vichy and also the emphasis on the need to rebuild—always a great theme under Vichy. It is easy to see how Vichy and the Germans could turn the following words to their own advantage.

Et si Dieu m'a gardé la vie
C'est pour travailler et construire avec vous,
Nous tous nous avons à refaire la vie
Nous tous nous serons bâtisseurs de ce monde.
Et si je suis sans haine et muet,
Nous serons tous forts et riches
Comme des mains d'abondance qui savant tout donner.

(And if God has saved my life
It is in order to work and build with you
We all have to remake our lives.
We all have to be builders in this world.
And if I am without hate and silent
We shall all be strong and rich,
Like hands of abundance that give everything.)

Pierre Bernac, who recorded these songs, was one of the few French performing artists who declined on principle to work for German-controlled radio stations but did make a number of very lovely recordings under the Occupation, including Poulenc's 'Six chansons villageoises' and a version of Bach's cantata 'Meine Seele rühmt und preist' in charmingly French-accented German.

It is ironic that between 1942 and 1944 when America brought out no commercial recordings because of a long running musicians' strike, France continued to produce a stream of excellent records of serious music both old and new, despite worsening political and material restrictions.

In 1942 and 1943 the pianist Alfred Cortot took time off from his official duties for Vichy to record Chopin études and waltzes. His old colleague, the violinist Jacques Thibaud, recorded Mozart violin concertos and sonatas. The trio of André Navarra (cello), Joseph Benedetti (piano) and René Benedetti (violin) recorded works by Beethoven, Schubert and Ravel. The redoubtable Marguerite Long, in the studio to record Fauré on 10 May 1940 as German troops broke through towards France in the East, was back in the studio to complete a recording of Beethoven's 'Emperor' Concerto on 18 June 1944 as Allied troops poured into Normandy.

The most prolifically-recorded conductor of the period was Charles Munch with his Orchestre de la Société du Conservatoire. Apart from the Honegger and Jolivet works already mentioned, he recorded a sparkling account of Debussy's 'La mer' in 1942, Mozart's Violin Concerto No 5 K. 219, and Piano Concerto No 20 K. 466, Beethoven's 'Emperor' Concerto with Marguerite Long, Tchaikovsky's Piano Concerto No 1, several works by Ravel including an authoritative account of the Piano Concerto for the Left Hand with Jacques Février, and a number of works by contemporary French composers such as Marcel Delannoy, Gustave Samazeuilh and Louis Aubert. The lushly exotic orchestral song cycle 'Le cercle des heures sur des poèmes orientaux' by Samazeuilh, with the mezzo Eliette Schenneberg, is particularly enjoyable. Schenneberg's name crops up constantly in the cast lists of the war period. A fine singer with a highly distinctive timbre, she died too soon after the war to make much of a mark on the post-war period.

At the end of the war, Munch faced accusations of collaboration because of his uninterrupted high profile under the Occupation. His dilemma had been that of many who held posts of responsibility in the arts. To refuse would have allowed the Germans to take control of his orchestra, which risked its dissolution and even the deportation of its members as forced workers. In September 1940, Munch re-convened the orchestra, and spoke of 'the joy of working together towards a shared ideal':

> ... the enemy can ruin us materially, but it cannot take away our artistic gifts or our patrimony, if we remember to defend them. On that field of battle we are not beaten. On that field we continue to fight.[19]

Between November 1942 and June 1943 Roger Désormière recorded a series of modern French works with the newly 'Aryanised'

Orchestre Pierné. The composers included Maurice Thiriet, Claude Delvincourt, Henry Barraud and most adventurously, considering his reputation as a pioneer of the avant-garde, Olivier Messiaen. The work chosen, Messiaen's early and pious 'Les offrandes oublées', accorded well with Vichy sensibilities though the markings for the three movements—'douloureux, profondément triste', 'féroce, désesperé, haletant' and 'Avec une grande pitié et un grand amour'—could have been interpreted as provocative under the Occupation.

In October 1943 Georges Thill recorded an abridged version of Verdi's *Otello* in French, with José Beckmans as Iago. It was a role the great tenor never sang on stage, and one may speculate that the recording may have been a response to the great success enjoyed at the Opéra a few months earlier by his rival José Luccioni as Otello.

The revival and recording of early French music was another way to assert 'Frenchness' and celebrate the French patrimony. The violinist and conductor Maurice Hewitt, a former member of the Capet quartet that had famously entertained Proust with nocturnal performances in his cork-lined room, undertook the ambitious task in 1942 of recording Rameau's *Les indes galantes* with Irène Joachim and Camille Mauranne as soloists for the independent label of Les Discophiles Français. Hewitt worked for Radio Paris, something generally regarded at the end of the war as a punishable collaboration. In Hewitt's case, for a time at least, working for Radio Paris provided an effective cover for his involvement in the Resistance. In 1943 he was denounced and transported to the concentration camp of Buchenwald where he organised clandestine musical activities amongst the prisoners.

Before November 1942 French musical life continued outside Paris, particularly in the southern or so-called Free Zone. The exodus of artists from Paris in June 1940, many of whom preferred to remain in the relative safety of the

German soldiers arrive at the Marseilles Opéra for a concert given by the Berlin Philharmonic.

south, launched something of a golden age of the performing arts in Marseilles and other southern cities. Vichy, the new capital of the Free Zone, offered a brilliant programme of opera, operetta and concerts that diminished in 1944 but did not finally peter out until 22 August 1944 with a concert given by the violinist Marcel Reynal. Amongst the distinguished artists who performed in Vichy were the singers Germaine Lubin, Marcelle Bunlet, Vina Bovy and Yvonne Printemps and the instrumentalists Jacques Thibaud, Alfred Cortot, Marcel Ciampi, Jacques Février, Ginette Neveu, Marguerite Long, Jeanne-Marie Darré, the Bouillon and Vegh Quartets and the Pasquier Trio. France's two most famous opera singers, Ninon Vallin and Georges Thill, who had fallen out while recording Charpentier's *Louise* in 1935, were reunited for a gala concert at Vichy on 31 March 1941.[20]

The French National Radio Orchestra (Orchestre National de la Radiodiffusion Française) under its conductor Desiré-Émile Inghelbrecht, decamped to Marseilles and remained there till 1943. The centre of musical life in Marseilles was the opera house, a solidly handsome building, re-built in the Art Deco style after a fire in 1919 that retained only the great classical column of the façade of the eighteenth-century theatre. During the war the building housed the French National Radio as well.

Marseilles maintained an operatic tradition that was fiercely independent of Paris and metropolitan tastes. Preference was given to nineteenth-century French and Italian repertoire. Reyer's *Sigurd* was more often performed than Wagner and the powerful-voiced Corsican tenor César Vezzani, who rarely sang in Paris, was the local hero. In the 1940-41 season 125 performances were given, amongst which was a performance of Berlioz's *Damnation of Faust* with Ninon Vallin and 200 performers.

The music hall artist Josephine Baker scored a brilliant success in *La créole* by Offenbach. A fragment of film of Baker on stage in this piece leaves a vivid impression of her extraordinary energy and charisma as a performer. A certain mystery is attached to this brief triumph in Marseilles. Christophe Mirambeau, the biographer of Albert Willemetz who reworked the plot and text of this version of *La créole*, tells the following story:

> Josephine, who was involved in the Resistance from the first moments of the Occupation, in effect received an order to rejoin the Allied forces in North Africa. It was

The Berlin Philharmonic performing inside the Marseilles Opéra.

necessary however for her 'to work under cover' near to the Mediterranean and be at the right place for the moment that someone could be found to smuggle her out. To present *La créole* in Marseilles seemed the ideal solution. In 15 days, the production was mounted and the curtain rose on Josephine-Dora on Christmas Eve. The first act was a triumph but Josephine fell ill in the course of the evening. At the same moment, she received the expected order: she had to break her contract with the Marseilles opera and leave.[21]

X-rays were taken in order to give her a medical excuse to break the contract, but they showed that she was genuinely ill with shadows on the lungs. Even so, she was sued for 400,000 francs of which she ended up paying a quarter. Josephine left for North Africa accompanied by a menagerie of pets, reasoning, as her biographer Lynn Haney put it 'that the animals would help disguise her true mission. After all, how many undercover agents would travel with two monkeys, one Great Dane, two white mice and a hamster?'[22]

In the following season the locally trained 21-year-old soprano Renée Doria, later one of the best French singers of the post-war period, made her debut at the Marseilles opera as Rosine in *Le barbier de Séville*. Surviving transcripts of two operas—Lalo's *Le roi d'Ys* and Bizet's *Carmen* broadcast from Radio Marseilles in 1942 and 1943, are evidence of the high musical standards in the city. Both are conducted by Inghelbrecht. Outstanding among the uniformly fine casts of both operas are the Corsican tenor Gaston Micheletti as Mylio in *Le roi d'Ys* and Germaine Cernay as Margared and Carmen. There have been sexier and more vividly characterized Carmens than Cernay's but rarely as well sung. Altogether this *Carmen* is as good an example as one could find of a French tradition of singing that disappeared soon after the war.

This performance took place on 9 November 1942, one day after the Allied 'Torch' landings in North Africa. Radio listeners must have been anxiously awaiting the news. Two days later the Germans moved into the southern zone and the musical life of Marseilles was transformed in one fell swoop.

Under German orders *Guillaume Tell, Boris Godunov, Lakmé* and *Madame Butterfly* were dropped from the repertory of the opera house. It is obvious why the German authorities would be uncomfortable about an opera dealing with heroic resistance to a foreign oppressor *(Guillaume Tell)* or a Russian national epic *(Boris Godunov)*. *Lakmé* and *Madame Butterfly* were apparently dropped because the hero of the former wears a British army uniform and of the latter an American naval uniform—no matter that neither hero does much credit to his uniform or his country. With the American army on the offensive in North Africa, Nazi authorities must also have worried about the potential audience reaction to Pinkerton's toast 'America forever!' accompanied by the triumphant strains of 'The Star-Spangled Banner' in Act One of *Butterfly*.

After November 1942, German music and culture were forcibly introduced to a city that had previously been resistant to it. German classical music was broadcast from Radio Marseilles. The Berlin Philharmonic under Hans Knappertsbusch arrived in May 1943 and the pianist Wilhelm Kempff gave a concert in March 1944.

Before the arrival of the Germans, policies towards Jewish musicians and composers had been highly inconsistent. The music of Mendelssohn was banned in deference to the Germans but not that of Offenbach. Jewish musicians were sacked from the National Radio Orchestra but the same orchestra performed under the baton of Reynaldo Hahn and on one occasion of Maurice Rosenthal.

The Berlin Philharmonic on the road.

Various musicians who were disapproved of by Vichy and the Germans, either because they were Jewish like the pianists Youra Guller and Clara Haskil, the harpist Lily Laskine and the singer Madeleine Grey or because, like the composer Jacques Ibert, they had taken a very public stand against Fascism, were offered shelter and employment by three courageous and generous local women, Marguerite Fournier, Cécile de Valmalète and the Countess Pastré, who enriched the cultural life of Marseilles by arranging concerts. The Countess Pastré sheltered up to forty refugees in her chateau close to Marseilles, where on 27 July 1942 she sponsored a performance of *A Midsummer Night's Dream* with music by Ibert played by the National Radio Orchestra conducted by Maurice Rosenthal.[23]

On 9 May 1940, the eve of the German onslaught, Reynaldo Hahn was conducting a performance in Paris of a new authentic version of Gounod's *Mireille* that he had helped to prepare. He conducted a further performance on 14 May before retreating to Vichy and then to the south where he remained for the rest of the war, apart from a brief return to Paris in September 1940 to conduct a single performance of *Les noces de Figaro* at the Opéra Comique. The former lover of Proust must have seemed like a relic of another age. Hahn was only 65 in 1940, but the fact that he had written his most famous song, 'Si mes vers avaient des ailes', at the age of 13 and published his popular 'Chansons Grises' in 1893 must have made him seem a lot older. He was by now completely out of touch with current musical trends and continued to compose as if the First World War had never happened. But he was enjoying an Indian summer of creativity, completing a string quartet that was first performed in January 1940 and a piano quartet that would not be heard till after the war and after his own death. Hahn was much respected and in demand as a conductor, particularly of works by two composers close to his heart—Mozart and Gounod.

After the armistice of 1940, Hahn found himself, like many others, in an oddly ambiguous situation. He was a practising Catholic who was half Jewish on his father's side—enough to qualify him as a Jew in the eyes of the Nazis if not in those of Orthodox Jews. His stage works were banned in the occupied zone, but in one of those strange inconsistencies that mark Nazi cultural policies *Ciboulette* and *La colombe de Bouddha* were broadcast by the Nazi-controlled Radio Paris in the summer of 1943. His works also continued to be performed at Vichy with *Ciboulette* being presented there in July 1942 and *Mozart* in June 1943.

Until November 1942 Hahn was able to travel freely within the Free Zone conducting operas at Cannes and other towns, and accompanying singers such as Ninon Vallin in song recitals. We have a precious souvenir of Hahn's conducting in fragments of a performance that took place in the Roman theatre in Arles and was broadcast by Radio Marseilles on 11 June 1941. We also hear him saying a few words about his authentic version of *Mireille*.

After the arrival of the Germans in November 1942, Hahn was doubly menaced as a Jew and as a known homosexual, and sat out the rest of the war in increasingly straitened circumstances in Monte Carlo.

The situation of Manuel Rosenthal was a good deal more precarious, both financially and in terms of his personal safety after he failed to escape from France and was trapped in the south for the rest of the war. Often said to be the favourite pupil of Ravel, he had established a reputation in the 1930s as a composer of successful comic operas and as a stylish and capable conductor of French music. The runaway success of his brilliant arrangements of the music of Offenbach for the ballet *Gaîté parisienne* in 1938 should have ensured him security and income for life and he can hardly have imagined the state of desperation and penury that he would be reduced to during the war. Lucky to survive, he was only able to exercise his profession as a musician on two occasions between 1939 and 1944. During this dark time in his life he experienced the best and worst of human behaviour and not always from the expected quarters. The Swiss tenor Hugues Cuenod offered to support him through the war if he could get an invitation to conduct in Switzerland. The conductor Ernest Ansermet failed to provide the invitation or to respond to Rosenthal's pleas. Most surprising was a dangerously indiscrete letter from the French musician widely regarded as the arch collaborator, Alfred Cortot, in which he expressed his sympathy and support for Rosenthal and his disgust at Nazi racial policies. Rosenthal took great comfort from the letter and kept it till his return to Paris late in the war when, realising that its discovery would endanger both him and Cortot, he destroyed it. Rosenthal had, however, learned the letter by heart and was able to repeat it word for word in Cortot's defence in his post-war trial for collaboration.[24]

The last edition of *Comoedia* under the German Occupation, much reduced in size due to paper restrictions, appeared on 5 August 1944, just three weeks before the arrival in Paris of Allied troops. Most theatres and concert halls were now closed and there were no more musical events to review. Though there are generalized references to war damage and to post-war reconstruction, the military situation could not be discussed and contributors were forced to write in the most general terms about music and the arts in France. In the yellowed and fragile copy that I consulted, the only hint of the momentous events currently taking place is in the form of cryptic pencil inscriptions hastily scribbled on the margins, among which the names of cities in the war zone—St Malo and Rouen—can be deciphered.

At this point the fate of Paris was very much in the balance. Had it not been for the decision of the commanding German General von Choltitz to disobey Hitler's orders, Paris could have been as thoroughly destroyed as Warsaw was in the same month. A large part of the final wartime edition of *Comoedia* is given over to an extended interview with Georges Hilaire, 'Sécretaire Général des Beaux-arts' of the Vichy regime, in which he lays out his ideas for the future reform of arts administration in France. It must have been clear to him that these reforms would indeed take place shortly but without his own participation.

In another front-page article, entitled 'Musique française', Honegger welcomes a series of radio programmes devoted to French music, which he regards as a healthy change from 'uninterrupted multitudes of Beethoven cycles', but regrets that the series is to be devoted to composers from the past. He offers a list of living composers whom he would like to see given greater exposure—Ibert, Delvincourt, Poulenc and Messiaen: all composers who had in one way or another taken a stand against the crumbling regime.

The strange sense of dislocation from the realities of the war felt by many as they passively awaited the outcome of the Normandy landings is indicated by an attempted 'coup' by the veteran bass-baritone Vanni-Marcoux who lobbied the already paralysed Vichy administration to allow him to take control of the two Paris opera houses in July 1944. It was just as well for his subsequent reputation that events were already too far gone, as Paris was liberated the following month. Musical life resumed quickly. After a closure of just over two months, the Paris Opéra re-opened its doors for a concert featuring a work forbidden under the Occupation, Mendelssohn's Violin Concerto with Yehudi Menuhin as soloist. The concert sold out within two hours of its announcement.

Notable among the works written by French composers to celebrate the Liberation and the end of the war are Milhaud's Third

Symphony and Henri Tomasi's 'Requiem pour la paix'. Milhaud was commissioned by French Radio to write a Te Deum to celebrate the end of the war and he responded with the Third Symphony. This would seem to take off where Honegger's Second Symphony finishes in a mood of joyous triumphalism. After the sadness of the beautiful second movement with its wordless chorus, the symphony ends with what seems like a much more positive view of the post-war future than Honegger's own Third Symphony.

Henri Tomasi's 'Requiem pour la paix', subtitled 'To all the martyrs of the Resistance and to all those who died for France', premiered in April 1946. It is a straightforward setting of the Latin text of the traditional Requiem mass but without the consoling final 'In Paradisum' that is such a feature of both the Fauré and the Duruflé Requiems. Tomasi's Requiem is beautiful but conventional.

The work that most potently embodies the mood of the Liberation of Paris is Messiaen's 'Trois petites liturgies de la présence divine'. Written in 1944 when the eventual outcome of the war was no longer in doubt, it could not be more different from the bleakness of the preceding 'Visions of Amen'. Scored for the highly unusual combination of celesta, vibraphone, maracas, gong, tam-tam, piano, onde Martinot, string orchestra and women's chorus, it is an explosion of almost animalistic energy and joy.

The premiere took place on 21 April 1945 in the hall of the Old Conservatoire with the Orchestre de la Société des Concerts du Conservatoire under Roger Désormière. Hitler had just over a week to live and the war still raged in the Pacific. The great and the good of French cultural life were assembled, including Honegger, Auric, Poulenc, Sauguet, Roland-Manuel, Jolivet, Delvincourt, Irène Joachim, Georges Braque and Paul Éluard. The performance was recorded live. The rawness of the performance and even the primitive quality of the recording evoke an extraordinary sense of actuality and presence in this document of the first great cultural event to take place in Paris after the Liberation.

3 Defeated France

1   Marcel Delannoy, *Honegger*, 1953, p. 194.
2   Willem de Vries, *Sonderstab Musik*, 1996, p. 212.
3   Erna Berger, *Auf Flügeln des Gesanges*, 1988, p. 59.
4   Nicole Casanova, *Isolde 39*, 1974, p. 175.
5   Lanfranco Rasponi, *The Last Prima Donnas*, 1994, p. 92.
6   Brigitte Massin, *Les Joachim*, 1999, p. 253.
7   Ibid., p. 254.
8   Georges Van Parys, *Les Jours comme ils viennent*, 1969, p. 284.
9   Stéphane Wolff, *Un Demi-Siècle d'Opéra-Comique*, 1953.
10 *The Record Collector*, Volume 41, no. 3, pp. 191-223.
11 Serge Lifar, *Ma Vie*, 1965, p. 232.
12 Richard D E Burton, *Francis Poulenc*, p. 83.
13 Leslie Sprout, 'Les Commandes de Vichy', in *La Vie Musicale sous Vichy*, p. 159.
14 D Kern Holoman, *Charles Munch*, Oxford University Press, 2012. p. 67
15 Halbreich, p. 317.
16 Ibid., p. 180.
17 Burton, p. 83.
18 Delannoy, p. 175.
19 Holoman, p. 57.
20 Josette Alviset, 'La Programmation Musicale à Vichy', in *La vie musicale sous Vichy*, p. 399.
21 Christophe Mirambeau, *Albert Willemetz, un regard sur le siècle*, 2004, p. 313.
22 Lynn Haney, *Naked at the Feast*, 1986, p. 223.
23 Jean-Marie Jacono, 'Marseille en liberté', in *La Vie Musicale sous Vichy*, p. 385.
24 Dominique Saudinos, *Manuel Rosenthal: Une Vie*, 1992, p. 147.

Chapter 4
MUSIC IN THE GERMAN REICH

A famous photograph of Toscanini on a visit to Berlin during the Weimar period shows him surrounded by a galaxy of local conductors—Wilhelm Furtwängler, Erich Kleiber, Otto Klemperer and Bruno Walter. If Walter Legge was correct in saying that a conductor is only as great as his ego, the atmosphere must have been crackling with musical testosterone on this occasion. By 1935, Toscanini had ceased to visit Germany and Kleiber, Klemperer and Walter had all fled abroad. Only Furtwängler—after wavering for a while in 1934—decided to stay. As far as music was concerned, the triumph of Nazism was the triumph of mediocrity and a golden opportunity for the second rate.

Arturo Toscanini on a visit to Berlin surrounded by Bruno Walter, Erich Kleiber, Otto Klemperer and Wilhelm Furtwängler.

Wir von der Oper

Ein kritisches Theater-Bildbuch herausgegeben von Walter Firner

Mit Beiträgen von

Gitta Alpar	Herbert Janssen	Maria Müller	Lotte Schöne
Fritz Busch	Maria Jeritza	Sigrid Onégin	Elisabeth Schumann
Willy Domgraf-Faßbaender	Maria Ivogün	Tino Pattiera	Leo Slezak
Carl Ebert	Erich Kleiber	Alfred Piccaver	Fritz Stiedry
Irene Eisinger	Otto Klemperer	Delia Reinhardt	Richard Tauber
Hans Fidesser	Lotte Lehmann	Wilhelm Rode	Bruno Walter
Wilhelm Furtwängler	Frida Leider	Helge Roswaenge	Luise Willer
Gustaf Gründgens	Emanuel List	Theodor Scheidl	Fritz Wolff
Ludwig Hofmann	Lauritz Melchior	Josef Schmidt	

Einleitung: Oscar Bie

Mit 40 Porträtstudien in Kupfertiefdruck nach Originalaufnahmen von Walter Firner

VERLAG F. BRUCKMANN AG · MÜNCHEN 1932

Title page of Wir von der Oper, *1932.*

The title page of a book published by the Bruckmann Verlag in Munich in 1932 also illustrated the haemorrhaging of German talent after 1933. It lists thirty-five artists who had made an important contribution to opera in Germany—singers, conductors and directors including Fritz Busch, Carl Ebert, Erich Kleiber, Otto Klemperer, Lotte Lehmann, Elisabeth Schumann, Josef Schmidt, Lotte Schoene, Richard Tauber and Bruno Walter. Within a half dozen years, twenty of the thirty-five had gone abroad or ceased to perform in Germany.[1]

In no area of German cultural life were greater opportunities created for the racially acceptable and the politically pliant than in the profession of the conductor. During the Weimar period Germany had been overpopulated with talented conductors. But now, not only were the key figures at the top of the profession, such as Walter, Kleiber, Klemperer and Busch, driven out but the ranks of aspiring younger conductors were thinned with the disappearance of Jascha Horenstein, Fritz Stiedry, Fritz Reiner, George Szell, Erich Leinsdorf, and many others.

Sensing rich pickings the Austrian Clemens Krauss abandoned his position as director of the Vienna State Opera and moved to the Berlin State Opera, hoping to be in a position to replace Furtwängler at the apex of German musical life should the latter decide to emigrate. When that failed to happen, Krauss contented himself with taking over the National Theatre in Munich from another conductor who had temporarily fallen foul of the Nazis, Hans Knappertsbusch. Krauss possessed a more substantial talent than some other musical opportunists. Carl Zuckmayer was perhaps over-harsh when he dismissed Krauss as 'smooth and skilful as a musician but unimportant, earlier a kind of opposite to Kleiber and Klemperer.' Zuckmayer continued that Krauss 'apparently always had Nazi sympathies and enjoys high regard in the Third Reich'[2] but as we know from Ida Cook's memoir *We followed our Stars*, Krauss and his wife Viorica Ursuleac took considerable risks to help Jewish refugees.

Karl Böhm and Herbert von Karajan were doubly blessed by twentieth century political developments. Both owed much of their early success to opportunities created by the Nazis and both owed their rapid post-war forgiveness and brilliant international careers to the exigencies of the Cold War. In 1934 Böhm's career was boosted when he stepped into the shoes of Fritz Busch, the ousted director of the Dresden Opera. The undoubtedly brilliant Herbert von Karajan (though it might be that his genius was more managerial rather than purely musical) also benefited from his usefulness to the Nazi authorities as a pawn in their game of cat and mouse with Furtwängler. In 1939 Goebbels wrote in his diary: 'I have had a detailed talk with Furtwängler. He cannot desist from attacking everything about the young conductor Karajan ... I would like under all circumstances to help Karajan in Berlin, either alongside or behind him. Of course as an artistic figure Karajan does not bear the least comparison with Furtwängler.'[3]

In both cases the commitment of Böhm and Karajan to the Nazi movement went beyond mere opportunism. Karajan first joined the Nazi party in Austria in 1933 long before it was expedient to do so. Though Böhm was never a party member he was happy to proclaim his devotion to the Führer. In an interview published in 1938 in the book *Künstler plaudern*, Böhm spoke with emotion of his memories of Hitler's failed 1923 putsch.

> In Munich I had an unforgettable experience; it was that memorable 9 November 1923, when the brown columns of Hitler marched to the Feldherrnhalle. That morning I had an orchestral rehearsal in the foyer of the National Theatre, the windows of which look out onto the Max-Joseph-Platz, close by the Feldherrnhalle where the dramatic events took place that proved a milestone in German history. In those days there was a feverish tension in Munich and one sensed that great things were about to happen and it was not possible to maintain musical concentration. Suddenly shots burst out over the square; we rushed to the window to see the National Socialists retreating from the murderous bullets. With incredible emotion we saw the wounded carried away and the bloodshed for an idea that has since proved victorious.[4]

In his autobiography Böhm denied having said any of this on the grounds that 'it would have been so stupid that I could not possibly have said it.'[5] The tone of this book is best described by the German adjective *kleinkariert* (loosely translatable as 'small-minded'). The combination of smugness, self-importance and self-pity makes a disagreeable impression. Böhm clearly regarded the brief interruption to his career at the end of the war as a gross miscarriage of justice.

Unlike America where musical life was enormously enriched and stimulated by a wide range of new influences during the war, German musical life was diminished and doomed to provincialism throughout the Nazi regime by a policy of cultural isolationism and by official hostility to modernism and innovation. It was a policy that found its most blatant expression in the notorious 'Entartete Musik' exhibition in 1938.

Once war began the music of enemy nations was banned. Even the performance of French music was restricted and intermittently banned within the Reich. Musical exchange with Germany's Axis ally Italy was surprisingly limited. A few modern Italian operas were performed in German opera houses without notable success. German opera companies visited Italy and famed Italian singers such as Gigli were always welcome in Germany. Gigli gave a series of concert and opera performances in Berlin in April 1941, and the coloratura soprano

Margherita Carosio toured Germany in 1943. The Italians seem to have been more adventurous than the Germans as far as operatic repertoire was concerned. Strauss's then little known *Die Frau ohne Schatten* was presented in Rome and Milan. A fragment exists of what was evidently a very thrilling Milan performance, with Iva Pacetti and Benvenuto Franci. In a post-war interview, Pacetti recalled: 'The tessitura kept me on my toes—so many high C's!—but the part was spellbinding and I am sorry I never had the chance to sing it again.' Hearing this music sung in such a full-throated Italian way is nothing less than revelatory.[6]

La Scala presented the first staged performance of Carl Orff's *Carmina Burana* outside of Germany in 1942. More adventurously still, Berg's *Wozzeck*, an opera that was an anathema to the Nazis, was performed at the Rome Opera in 1942 with Tito Gobbi in the title role. It was a performance that Gobbi described as 'one of the most overwhelming experiences' of his career.[7]

During the war Germany was still open to composers from friendly neutral countries such as Sweden and Switzerland. The prestige of a German premiere still tempted composers from these countries even after the tide of war turned against Germany. The Swedish composer Kurt Atterberg premiered his Seventh Symphony in Frankfurt in February 1943.[8] Toscanini, who was normally so scrupulous in avoiding musicians who compromised with Fascism, was presumably unaware of this when he conducted Atterberg's Sixth Symphony in a broadcast performance from New York on 23 November 1943.

Two Swiss composers, Heinrich Sutermeister and Othmar Schoeck, continued to find favour in Germany. Sutermeister's opera *Die Zauberinsel* was premiered in Dresden in October 1942.[9] Schoeck's *Das Schloss Dürande*, set in a chateau during the French Revolution, was premiered in Berlin in 1943 with a magnificent cast including Peter Anders, Marta Fuchs, Willi Domgraf-Fassbaender, Maria Cebotari and Josef Greindl. The over-realistic staging of the explosion that destroys the chateau in the final scene caused panic on the first night amongst an audience that was becoming accustomed to Allied air raids. The explosion was dropped from later performances and is not evident in the surviving broadcast. Schoeck may have hoped that using a well-known Nazi sympathiser, the poet Herman Burte, as his librettist might ingratiate the opera with the German authorities but he miscalculated. Goebbels fired off an angry telegram to Heinz Tietjens, the director of the Berlin Opera saying: 'Have just read the libretto of *Schloss Dürande*. I cannot understand how the State Opera could perform this utter bullshit *(Bockmist)*. The librettist must be an absolute madman.'[10] The opera was dropped from the Berlin repertoire after four performances. To judge from the broadcast extracts, it was a sumptuously scored and highly dramatic work in a late Romantic vein. Its Berlin premiere so late in the war told against it in the post-war period and it would not be staged again for another forty years.

Two established composers of the older generation, Hans Pfitzner and Franz Schmidt, greeted the triumph of Nazism with undisguised enthusiasm. It was probably just as well that Schmidt died in February 1939 before the outbreak of war and indeed it might have been better if he had died a year earlier, before he had had a chance to start work on the cantata 'Deutsche Auferstehung' to a Nazi text celebrating the *Anschluss*. The fact that he left it unfinished at his death, having worked on other projects in the meantime, has been charitably interpreted as a lack of commitment to the Nazi cause and it may be that he was politically naïve rather than genuinely committed to Nazi ideology. The unfinished work was tidied up for a first performance in Vienna in 1940.

There is less room for doubt about the attitudes of Pfitzner, who was an outspoken nationalist and anti-Semite. Though Pfitzner's irascible character made enemies amongst the Nazi hierarchy he was one of the most honoured and frequently performed of living composers in the Nazi period, in fact second only to Strauss. The highly publicised production of his opera *Palestrina* imposed upon the Paris Opéra during the Occupation did Pfitzner's reputation more harm than good in the long run. Despite all the prizes and honours he received he complained bitterly that he was neglected under the Nazi regime and not acknowledged as 'the foremost man in the country in artistic matters'[11] that he felt himself to be. Pfitzner's paranoia may not have been entirely misplaced. On 9 June 1943 Goebbels wrote in his diary: '… the Führer is strongly against Pfitzner. He thinks he is a half-Jew, which according to the documentary evidence he is not.'[12]

Two major modernist composers with solid international reputations might have been willing to compromise with the Nazi regime had the regime itself been willing to meet them half way—Paul Hindemith and Anton Webern. Hindemith's music had been at the centre of the battles between musical modernism and Nazi ideology in the early years of the regime. It was Furtwängler's public defence of Hindemith's music that triggered the crisis in his relations with the Nazi regime in 1934.

Hindemith was willing to sign a declaration of loyalty to the regime and aspects of his musical aesthetic in the 1930s could have been accommodated by the Nazis; he was doomed by his earlier fame during the Weimar period, by his Jewish wife, and above all by the personal antipathy of Hitler. Hitler had been deeply affronted by the spectacle of a naked soprano singing in the bath on stage in Hindemith's opera *Neues vom Tage* in 1929. Hindemith's music was banned in Germany from October 1936 and when he was sacked from his teaching position at the Berlin Hochschule für Musik in September 1937 he finally went into exile.

The still more radical Anton Webern, a leading figure of the 'Second Viennese School' excoriated by the Nazis as degenerate, remained in the Reich after the *Anschluss* earning a living with such menial tasks as musical editing and proofreading. As the performance of atonal music was now banned in the Reich, Webern's most important wartime work, the Variations for Orchestra Opus 30 of 1940, was premiered in Switzerland in 1943.

Three composers working in a moderated Modernist idiom proved more acceptable to the Nazis—Werner Egk, Rudolf Wagner-Régeny and Carl Orff. The watered down influence of Stravinsky and Kurt Weill in Egk's 1938 opera *Peer Gynt* might have got him into trouble had the opera not taken the fancy of Hitler and Goebbels. After attending a performance in the company of Hitler, Goebbels wrote in his diary on 14 February 1939: 'I'm quite enthusiastic and the Führer too. A new discovery for both of us.'[13] From that moment Egk became something like the poster boy for Nazi Modernism and Egk's music was actively promoted in France under the Occupation to show that composers in the German Reich could write modern music too.

In 1941 Egk agreed to compose music for the movie *Jungens* that celebrated the courage of the Hitler Youth and which entailed writing a march titled 'The March of German Youth'. Somewhat ingenuously Egk explained his willingness to be involved in this movie as resulting from pure financial necessity. 'The film fee would mend a hole in my purse that had been torn by the wartime diminution of my opera royalties.' He dismissed the film as a harmless boy's adventure movie in which the boys happen to wear Hitler Youth uniforms in the final scene and was indignant that his music for the film might be interpreted as a sign of Nazi sympathies.[14]

Egk was a great deal less given to examining his conscience than fellow German composer Norbert Schultze with regard to the war years, but his autobiography does provide a convincing account of the hazards faced during the war even by one of the regime's most favoured artists. For Egk these hazards included spies and denunciations, a terrifying confrontation with a raging Goebbels, and towards the end the twin threats of Allied bombs and Nazi press gangs. Like Schultze, Egk was either adept or just plain lucky in avoiding conscription.

For the first two or three years of the war while Germany was still in the ascendant it was very much life as usual for Egk. After its successful premiere in January 1940, Egk's ballet *Joan von Zarissa* was performed in eighteen different theatres over the next year or so (which surely should have filled the hole in his pocket left by the lessening of interest in his operas), and his opera *Columbus,* originally written for the radio, was given its stage premiere in Frankfurt in January 1942. After the premiere of *Columbus* Strauss made the withering and, under the political circumstances, massively tactless comment that Egk 'could have been the twentieth century Meyerbeer.'[15] (Nevertheless the success of the opera was widely publicised in occupied Europe.)

Egk's success as an opera composer brought him a great many unsolicited and unwelcome proposals for new operas. These included patriotic epics celebrating Luther, Bismarck and Frederick the Great, or sentimental folkloric subjects of which he gives an example:

> The sweet blond maiden from the Rhine finds herself under an appalling suspicion; Heini (beside himself with rage) 'Tell me how many you have kissed before me?' Lore (in floods of tears) 'By the Holy Mother of God of Kevelaer, none!' He believes her because the calumny would be too great.[16]

Rudolf Wagner-Régeny first won favour with the regime in 1935 with his opera *Der Günstling*, which became one of the most performed contemporary operas under the Third Reich. He was one of several composers to accept the challenge to write incidental music for Shakespeare's *A Midsummer Night's Dream* to replace that of Mendelssohn. His opera *Johanna Balk*, which premiered in Vienna in 1942, lost Wagner-Régeny his earlier official approval both on musical grounds because of its supposed formalism, and because it depicted the resistance of an oppressed people and could have been interpreted as a veiled criticism of German policies in Eastern Europe.

In a sense it is reassuring that so much of the art and music produced under the Third Reich is so feeble. Hitler did not find a

Michelangelo or a Beethoven to serve the regime. Apart from the late works of Strauss that belong to another era and another ethos, the only piece of music from the Nazi era to have established itself in the concert repertoire is Carl Orff's *Carmina Burana*, premiered in 1937. For all its attractive, indeed irresistible qualities *Carmina Burana* is very much a product of its time and place. If the motoric, Stravinskian elements displeased some in the Nazi hierarchy others liked its earthy folkloric qualities and its brutal populism. A review in the *Völkischer Beobachter* in 1940 praised it as 'the clear, ardent and disciplined music required for our times.'

Orff's relationship with the regime is as ambiguous and contested as that of Strauss. His only wartime opera *Die Kluge*, premiered in Frankfurt in February 1943, has been interpreted as a sly mockery of tyranny. The following passage from the text certainly lends itself to such an interpretation.

> Den wer viel hat, hat auch die Macht,
> Und wer die Macht hat, hat das Recht,
> Und wer das Recht hat, beugt es auch!
> Denn über allen steht Gewalt!
>
> (So whoever has much, has power,
> And whoever has power has right.
> And whoever has right, is bowed to!
> Since might rules over everything!)

According to the composer's daughter Godela Orff, spontaneous applause after this passage during a wartime performance led to the work being declared *unerwünscht* or undesirable.[17]

Orff was friendly with Kurt Huber, one of the founders of the 'White Rose' resistance movement, but failed to use his influence to help Huber when he was arrested and executed in 1943. Orff's postwar claims to have been involved in resistance have not been believed. His daughter had few illusions about her father's moral courage or lack of it. 'After the execution of Kurt Huber in 1943 … my father "disappeared" … as I said, my father was not a hero and sought as far as possible to avoid dangerous situations; however he felt a deep aversion to the appalling ideology of the "Third Reich" and saw through it from the beginning. But he did not dare to oppose it. He kept silent.'[18]

Young composers who espoused any form of musical modernism were regarded with suspicion and always in danger of being labelled *unerwünscht*. Four such composers who continued to write 'modern' music and consequently had to wait till the end of the war to receive recognition were Boris Blacher (born 1903), Karl Amadeus Hartmann (born 1905), Wolfgang Fortner (born 1907) and Gottfried von Einem (born 1918). According to Blacher '… the situation for composers was a strange one. All the same you can say that whoever wrote modern music did so genuinely, because he needed to and could not compose in any other way. This kind of music was not in demand. On the contrary … if you were lucky you had a piece performed. If you were less lucky you had a setback. There would probably be a *Verbot* ('ban'). Or: "This composer is undesirable." When you were on the list of undesirables, that was the worst. There was no possibility of protest.'[19]

Blacher's pupil Gottfried von Einem recalled Goebbels's obsessive desire to suppress 'subversive' musical tendencies to the very end and the subterfuges necessary to protect his 'Concerto' in 1944. 'He (Goebbels) apparently had nothing more important on his mind in 1944 than examining the case of my "Concerto". Was it "cultural bolshevism" or not?'[20]

Fortner remembered performing the music of Bartók, Hindemith and Stravinsky with friends in secret, 'not only as a private protest against the reigning cultural policies, but much more from a connection with artistic values that we neither wished nor were able to relinquish.'[21]

There were always a number of hack composers prepared to serve the regime in the most abject way until the very end. To this number must be ascribed Gottfried Müller whose cantata 'Führerworte' was given on 14 April 1944, memorably described by Nicolas Slonimsky as 'dedicated to the "heroes of the German fight of destiny" to texts reverently selected from Hitler's speeches, with the Führer's applosive sentences nearly submerged in a magma of neo-gothic polyphony, with a brassy ending in the key of C major intended to symbolize the purity of Nazi ideals.'[22]

Norbert Schultze was perhaps the most faithful of all the regime's musical servants, though not without talent and, as can be discovered from his autobiography, not without insight and conscience. Schultze continued to compose marches and music for propaganda movies as and when required, while trying to maintain his career as a serious composer. His children's opera *Schwarzer Peter*, first performed in

1936, was one of the greatest operatic successes of the regime. It was followed in 1943 by the fairy-tale opera *Das kalte Herz*. Both works have considerable charm if one is able to forget the circumstances in which they were composed and performed.

Two figures at the apex of the Nazi hierarchy concerned themselves with the dissemination of classical music amongst the German populace—Robert Ley, the leader of the German Labour Front, and the all-powerful propaganda minister Joseph Goebbels. Ley's Kraft durch Freude ('Strength through Joy') organisation subsidized concert and opera visits for workers and organised concerts in factories. After the outbreak of war Kraft durch Freude took over the organisation of the Bayreuth Festivals that continued on Hitler's insistence until the summer of 1944, with the fashionable audiences of pre-war seasons replaced by munitions workers and by soldiers from the front. In 1940 and 1941 *Der fliegender Holländer* and the Ring Cycle were presented. In 1942 *Der fliegender Holländer* was again on the programme together with *Götterdämmerung* and one complete Ring Cycle exclusively for wounded soldiers. Sixteen hours of Wagner must have been quite an endurance test for exhausted soldiers from the Russian front and it was probably as well that nurses were on hand. The programmes included instructions about what to do in the event of an air attack and directions to bomb shelters. *Tristan und Isolde* had been excluded from the season because of Tristan's long Act III dying monologue that Winifred Wagner, the director of the wartime festivals, felt would be 'too much for some badly wounded onlookers to bear.'[23]

In 1943 there was a new production of *Die Meistersinger von Nürnberg* designed by the 25-year-old Wieland Wagner, grandson of the composer and heir apparent of the Bayreuth Festival. The event was milked for all it was worth in terms of publicity. There were illustrated articles about the festival in *Signal* and other magazines. At

Soldiers and nurses in front of the Bayreuth Festspielhaus in 1943. (Der Adler)

119

a press conference, invited journalists were entertained by female dancers in flimsy costumes, a spectacle that might have been more to the taste of many of the exhausted and wounded soldiers than four hours of Wagner. The depleted Bayreuth chorus was supplemented by members of the Hitler Youth and men of the SS Viking Division, taking time off from their usual murderous activities on the Eastern Front to impersonate the happy burghers of sixteenth-century Nuremberg. Sixteen performances were seen by a total of 30,000 soldiers and workers who were given lectures to prepare them for the performances and also a thick programme of explanatory essays. The booklet opens with a statement from Robert Ley in which he tells the audience: 'You now have the luck to be the guests of the Führer in Bayreuth where you may experience a performance of *Die Meistersinger von Nürnberg*, the most beautiful and deeply German opera.' This is followed by a series of mindlessly wordy nationalistic and anti-Semitic rants by various 'experts'.

A near-complete recording exists of a broadcast performance conducted by Furtwängler. His incandescent conducting fully lives up to his reputation. The singers, Jaro Prohaska as Sachs, Maria Müller as Eva and Max Lorenz as Walther, were the most admired exponents of their roles in Germany at the time. All give vivid and committed characterisations but from a purely vocal point of view

Maria Müller

The tenor Max Lorenz as Walther in Die Meistersinger.

compare unfavourably with their
equivalents in the extended excerpts
recorded by HMV a decade earlier or
in live broadcasts from the Met in New
York from the late 1930s and early
40s. Compared to Friedrich Schorr,
Jaro Prohaska makes a gruff and un-
ingratiating Hans Sachs. Maria Müller
as Eva is squally and shrill under
pressure. Lorenz, Nazi Germany's
leading Heldentenor, is explosive and
unsteady and can hardly be said to sing
at all, performing the role of Walter in a
kind of *Sprechgesang*.

*Dancers disport themselves for the
entertainment of journalists at the
Bayreuth Festival of 1943.*

It is doubtful if by this time anyone
at Bayreuth had the courage to express
political views but conversation among
the cast of *Die Meistersinger* may have
been unusually tense. Jaro Prohaska
and Maria Müller were true believers
in Nazism. Prohaska's wife was said
to faint with emotion when the Führer
entered the room and Müller travelled
in the opposite direction from many
German singers, giving up a thriving
career at the Met to return to Nazi
Germany. In *Künstler plaudern* she
gushed that the high points of her career
had been singing for the Führer. She
cherished especially warm memories of
the occasion when Hitler bought a ticket
to one of her concerts in Munich. At the
sight of the Führer sitting in the front
row, the singer and her accompanist
were both so overcome with emotion
that they launched into different songs
and had to begin again. 'The Führer
smiled in such a friendly way that the
situation was overcome.'[24]

Act III of Die Meistersinger *at
Bayreuth in 1943.*

The audience for Die Meistersinger
*is marched from the Bayreuth railway
station in 1943.*

121

Camilla Kalab, who sings Magdalena, had been one of the few members of the Dresden Opera with the courage to refuse to sign a Nazi-inspired petition against Fritz Busch. For Max Lorenz, as a known homosexual married to a Jewish woman, an awful lot rested on his—from the evidence of this performance—greatly overstretched vocal chords. Happily for Lorenz, there was a desperate shortage of *Heldentenors* in Nazi Germany and Winifred Wagner was able to plead Lorenz's cause directly with Hitler when the singer had been caught *in flagrante* with a male member of the chorus. Just how precarious the position of Lorenz and his wife was is indicated by a secret report by Nazi spies on the 1943 festival which complained 'that Kammersänger Lorenz' was in Bayreuth with his Jewish wife, and she stayed in rooms allocated to the Festival and 'enjoyed the same privileges in the Restaurant as everybody else'. This had 'incited a real outcry among all the Festival participants who know about it, and was regarded in National Socialist circles as provocative.'[25]

An audience of soldiers at the Salzburg Festival.

An audience of munitions workers at the Salzburg Festival.

The Nazis made the most of these wartime festivals in illustrated propaganda journals such as *Der Adler*, which was published in Belgium, France, Portugal and Switzerland in local languages. The edition of 24 August 1943 illustrates Wieland Wagner chatting with local Gauleiter Wächtler, his mother Winifred Wagner mingling with wounded soldiers, and a press conference for journalists. 'Thus', we are told, 'in the middle of the war Germany pursues its great work of educating the people.'

A similar article had appeared in June 1942 in *Der Adler* celebrating the Salzburg Festival of that year:

That Germany after three years of inexpiable warfare

and despite the heavy trials she had surmounted on all fronts, has succeeded in organizing this year the festivals of Bayreuth and Salzburg as though we were in times of peace is eloquent proof that Germany has an immense consciousness of the mission she must accomplish and for which she offers in sacrifice, the blood of her children on the battlefield, to save at all costs European culture from barbarism and to breathe a new conception into it. Alongside the destruction Germany has conserved her artistic and spiritual strength and the refinement of Western civilisation … Who could deny that the festival of Salzburg organised this year in honour of soldiers from the front and munitions workers, is the prelude to a true artistic renaissance?

We see pictures of Salzburg bedecked with Nazi flags and of solemn-faced soldiers and workers listening to concerts. At this date the Salzburg Festival could still attract an impressive roster of musicians that included Richard Strauss, Willem Mengelberg, Karl Böhm, Clemens Krauss, Ernest Ansermet and Edwin Fischer.

There are also images of a lavish production of Strauss's opera *Arabella*. A complete broadcast of this opera exists, Viorica Ursuleac singing the title role. She and her husband Clemens Krauss, who conducts this performance, had created the opera in Dresden in 1933. This broadcast displays Ursuleac's vocal and interpretative qualities to better effect than her commercial records do and makes it more comprehensible that she was so admired by the composer. Strauss's romantic comedy with its 'Mills and Boon' plot and its unacknowledged half-Jewish librettist Hugo von Hofmannsthal, might seem an odd choice for the entertainment of the Wehrmacht, but the audience clearly enjoyed the melodious duet of the sisters in Act One as we hear from the enthusiastic applause.

Salzburg decorated with swastikas for the festival.

Radio remained under the tight control of Joseph Goebbels as his weapon of choice, but played an enormously important role in the musical life of the Third Reich. Werner Egk was contemptuous of Goebbels's musical populism and felt that

Goebbels was responsible for the musical 'dumbing down' of the radio. 'Of classical and serious contemporary music, only what the masses had already accepted could be played. From *Tannhäuser* only "The Song to the Evening Star" could filter through and from *Lohengrin* only the Bridal March.'[26] Certainly a great deal of broadcasting time was devoted to *Unterhaltungsmusik* ('entertainment music') and Goebbels took particular interest in the popular weekly request programme 'Wunschkonzert für die Wehrmacht', which combined cheerful and sentimental songs with popular classics. The most popular star of the programme was the operatic bass Wilhelm Strienz who could turn his talents to Sarastro's arias from *Die Zauberflöte* or songs like 'Gute Nacht Mutter'.

Though adventurous modern music was avoided and was in any case banned in wartime Germany, the radio broadcast prodigious quantities of serious music including a great many operas, either complete or in extended extracts. Despite losses caused by Allied bombing and pillage by the Russians at the end of the war (1,462 magnetic tapes of classical concerts were taken by the Russians in 1945 and only returned in 1989), far more recorded classical music has survived from German radio stations than from those of any other belligerent country and in better quality sound thanks to the German invention of magnetic tape. Until theatres were closed in the late summer of 1944 opera performances might be broadcast live from opera houses, as was the case with the 1943 Bayreuth *Meistersinger*, the *Arabella* from Salzburg, a *Lohengrin* from the Berlin Staatsoper in 1942 with a cast identical to that of the 1936 Bayreuth production, and a performance of Strauss's *Ariadne auf Naxos* broadcast from the Vienna State Opera in June 1944 in honour of the composer's 80th birthday.

More often, complete operas and extracts were purpose-recorded in radio studios using conductors and singers from the local opera house. The three most important radio stations for the creation of these opera recordings were Berlin where they were usually conducted by Artur Rother or Robert Heger, Vienna where Karl Böhm was usually in charge, or Dresden with Karl Elmendorff.

French opera was represented by Bizet's *Carmen* which was simply too popular to repress, and by Auber's *Fra Diavolo* which had been adopted as quasi-German. There was also the surprising exception of Dvořák's *Die Jakobiner* that had proved popular at the Dresden Opera, but otherwise the broadcast repertoire was exclusively Austro-German and Italian with all the operas being performed in German including the Mozart-Da Ponte operas in their new 'Aryanised' translations. This was a time when the differences in national styles were very much more marked than they are today. Verdi sung in German by singers such as Helge Rosvaenge, Tiana Lemnitz, Margarete Klose and Heinrich Schlusnus sounds startlingly strange to modern ears not only because of the language but because of the singers' style and approach

to the music, which is utterly different from that of any Italian singer. This is not entirely negative and indeed these German-language, wartime recordings make one listen to familiar operas with fresh ears.

For Germans the tenor of choice in the standard Italian repertoire was the Danish Helge Rosvaenge. In his autobiography he claimed to have sung a total of 2,000 performances in four Italian operas, *Rigoletto*, *La Traviata*, *La Bohème* and *Madama Butterfly*, many of them during the war years. Rosvaenge was hardly as 'Italianate' as German critics claimed. His throaty, effortful voice production was typically German but there was certainly no doubting the genuine passion he brought to everything he sang.

The Danish tenor Helge Rosvaenge was regarded as ideal for the Italian repertoire.

Opera continued in the re-built Berlin Staatsoper even as the destruction of Berlin intensified, with performances frequently interrupted by air raids. Rosvaenge remembered a particular performance of *La Bohème*. 'We had just begun the third act. As Rodolfo, I come out of the inn and sing: "Marcello, Ah, there you are! I have to tell you it is all over …" And it really was over this time as the curtain was already descending in anticipation of other ominous sounds. The public left the auditorium quietly and crossed the street to the Humboldt University where there were bomb shelters. The staff of the opera remained in the shelter in the theatre. Used to such interruptions, the music-hungry audience were interested first and foremost in if and when the performance would continue. It continued after a good hour of interruption. As soon as everyone had taken their places, the curtain reopened, the orchestra played and I sang: "Marcello, You are there again!"'[27]

Later, after the second destruction of the Staatsoper, opera performances continued in concert form at the Schauspielhaus am Gendarmenmarkt. The costume collection of the Staatsoper had been taken to safety in Bavaria and a dozen remaining soloists, including Rosvaenge, performed—somewhat bizarrely under the circumstances—in evening dress.

Perhaps the most remarkable wartime achievement of German radio as far as classical music was concerned was a monumental project initiated by the pianist Michael Raucheisen to record a comprehensive overview of the German song repertoire from Mozart to Strauss. Continuing under ever increasing difficulties until the last weeks of the war, Raucheisen made enough of these recordings to fill sixty-six CDs on a recent re-issue. Some of the greatest interpreters of the *Lied* such as Elena Gerhardt, Lotte Lehmann, Elisabeth Schumann, Richard Tauber and Alexander Kipnis had already fled from Germany, but Raucheisen was still able to bring together an extraordinary array of talent for this project including Peter Anders, Erna Berger, Rudolph Bockelmann, Anton Dermota, Willi Domgraf-Fassbaender, Karl Erb, Hans Hotter, Margarete Klose, Frida Leider, Emmi Leisner, Tiana Lemnitz, Julius Patzak, Helge Rosvaenge, Erna Sack, Heinrich Schlusnus, Paul Schöffler, Franz Völker and Raucheisen's special protégée, Elisabeth Schwarzkopf.

Like every artistic endeavour during the Nazi period, this great project was compromised by Nazi racial policies. The songs of Mendelssohn could not be included and even more damagingly all song settings of Heine texts had to be excluded, including some of the greatest masterpieces of German song literature such as Schumann's 'Dichterliebe' and the Heine settings from Schubert's 'Schwanengesang'.

The conductor Wilhelm Furtwängler and the composer Richard Strauss were the two most esteemed musicians to remain in the Third Reich to the end of the war (or near to it in the case of Furtwängler). By remaining, they provided a fig leaf of cultural respectability to the regime. The degree of their collusion with the Nazis and their culpability is still a matter of intense debate. Though both were regarded with considerable suspicion by the regime as unreliable, the reputations of both were ruthlessly exploited for propaganda purposes. Both were the subject of laudatory articles in *Signal*, a lavish, colour-illustrated propaganda magazine that defied paper restrictions and was circulated in Belgium, Bohemia-Moravia, Bulgaria, Croatia,

Denmark, Spain, Finland, France, Greece, Hungary, Italy, Norway, the Netherlands, Portugal, Rumania, Serbia, Sweden, Switzerland, Slovakia and Turkey—a list which in itself gives some idea of Germany's cultural hegemony in 1942.

In February 1942 Strauss gave an interview to *Signal* for an article titled '"Signal" pays a visit to the great German composer.' Strauss was taciturn and clearly ill-at-ease, giving virtually nothing away about his opinions. The following month *Signal* published an article on Furtwängler entitled 'The secrets of success' that attempted to explain Furtwängler's greatness as a conductor. The author evokes the mystique of the great conductor and the aura of the demi-god or superman that surrounded Furtwängler and to which the conductor himself seems to some extent have fallen victim. In the finale of Beethoven's Fifth Symphony, we are told, the conductor has 'to take on in the eyes of the musicians, the attitude and the appearance of the hero'.

By the time the war broke out, Furtwängler had long since burnt his bridges and thrown in his lot with the regime. His attempts to maintain some kind of moral rectitude—not always successful attempts to avoid conducting in occupied countries or for the concerts to celebrate Hitler's birthday, or to give the Hitler salute or to publicly shake hands with Goebbels—were futile, as he must have known. His intercessions on the behalf of victimized colleagues such as the Russian Jewish Issay Dobrowen, who he enabled to cross the border from occupied Norway to neutral Sweden in April 1943, were laudable but a drop in the ocean of suffering caused by the regime which he now served. Travelling sometimes with the Berlin Philharmonic and sometimes on his own, Furtwängler was the Nazi regime's most effective goodwill ambassador to neutral countries such as Sweden and Portugal.

In the secret report on leading German artists and intellectuals prepared for the American government by the émigré writer Carl Zuckmayer in 1943, Furtwängler was placed in the category of 'Special cases, partly positive, partly negative—not easy to categorize'. Zuckmayer's analysis of Furtwängler's moral strengths and weaknesses is

The Berlin Philharmonic boarding a flight for a concert tour with Furtwängler.

penetrating and not without a certain sympathy for his situation. He concludes: 'It is certainly true that Furtwängler is the most "German" amongst the great conductors—but this German quality and its musical expression is not necessarily bound to the borders of the German Reich ... in any case it also lies to an extent in Furtwängler's personal character that he is very happy to be the only one in his field and in his world. The position of official conductor to the German Reich may however throw him into deep conflicts—Funeral March from *Götterdämmerung*.'[28]

The frequency with which Furtwängler is mentioned in Goebbels's diaries is an indication of just how important he was to the Nazi regime. Goebbels's entries on Furtwängler read like a series of school reports on a gifted but recalcitrant pupil. On 28 July 1942 Goebbels noted an 'improvement' in Furtwängler's attitude and that he was 'practically bursting with nationalist enthusiasm. This man has undergone a profound transformation, which it gives me great pleasure to witness. I fought for years to win him over and can now see success.'[29]

Goebbels's final assessment of Furtwängler acknowledged that he had not in fact won him over as he hoped. 'An artist like Furtwängler compels my deepest admiration ... he has never been a national socialist. Nor has he ever made any bones about it. Furtwängler, whose stance towards us has not changed in the least, showed by his conduct during the bombing of Berlin just how far he stands above the rabble.'

In the end Furtwängler was not quite as steadfast as Goebbels imagined. In the final months of the war, apparently under threat of assassination from extremist elements within the Nazi movement, the conductor abandoned the Berlin Philharmonic Orchestra to which he was supposed to be so devoted, and fled to the safety of Switzerland. The mysterious episode of Furtwängler's last minute defection is explored in depth in Audrey Roncigli's 2009 book *Le Cas Furtwängler* (The Furtwängler Case). Roncigli argues persuasively that Furtwängler was about to be arrested on suspicion of involvement with the German resistance and his connections with participants in the July 1944 bomb plot against Hitler.[30] In the final stages of the war Furtwängler was also endangered by the scorched earth policies of Goebbels and Hitler, who were disinclined to allow such an important cultural asset as Furtwängler to survive into the post-Nazi era.

The case of Richard Strauss is different from that of Furtwängler if only because he was a creative rather than an interpretative artist. The late masterpieces of Strauss are the great exception amongst the general mediocrity of most of the art produced in Germany under the Third Reich.

The belated flowering of Strauss's genius was unexpected both because it coincided exactly with the most terrible events in German history and because by the 1930s Strauss was generally regarded as a spent force. Despite the local success of *Arabella* in Germany in 1933 it failed to catch on elsewhere. In London it was dismissed by the leading critic Ernest Newman as a 'poor imitation of *Der Rosenkavalier*'.[31] The other inter-war operas did even less well and it was generally felt that Strauss's inspiration was running thin. Like other major composers of his generation Strauss was swimming against the tide of musical taste and might have been expected like Sibelius to retreat into musical silence. Though Strauss was routinely described as the world's greatest living composer, few critics believed he could still write great music. Even Stefan Zweig who collaborated with Strauss on the opera *Die Schweigsame Frau* thought: 'His technique remains intact but the dynamic isn't there.'[32]

The composer Richard Strauss in his study.

One could argue the theory that it was the isolation in which Strauss found himself under the Nazi regime, both within Germany and in the wider world, that enabled or even triggered the extraordinary outpouring of inspired and highly individual music in the last decade of his life.

From 1889 when Strauss composed the tone poem *Don Juan,* until the 1909 premiere of *Elektra,* he had been the *enfant terrible* of Western music and the cutting edge of the musical avant-garde. He had his Nietzschean moments in the 1890s with the tone poems *Ein Heldenleben* and *Also sprach Zarathrusta* but monomaniacal bombast was neither

129

an essential nor a lasting element of Strauss's musical inspiration. It might be argued that the overblown pathos and monumentalism of the Mahler symphonies would have been far more in keeping with the Nazi ethos if Mahler had not the misfortune from the Nazi point of view to be a Jew. Works such as *Salome* and *Elektra* represented everything the Nazis most detested in what they deemed to be degenerate art, with the added disadvantage that the libretto of the former was by a homosexual and the latter by a Jew. Though Thomas Mann found it astonishing that Beethoven's *Fidelio* could be performed under the Nazi regime, it is rather more surprising that *Salome* and *Elektra* continued to be tolerated. There is a spectacularly gloomy and chilling performance of *Elektra* broadcast from Hamburg in 1944 that can have done little for the morale of that bomb-ravaged city.

In the interview that the tight-lipped Strauss gave to *Signal* in 1942, almost the only remark that could be elicited from him about his own work was: 'You find in my *Salome* firstly an example of atonality.' It was hardly a remark calculated to curry favour with a regime that had banned atonal music.

Though Strauss, like Furtwängler, worshipped the Austro-German musical tradition he remained sublimely indifferent to nationalism or indeed to any kind of patriotism in both world wars. During the First World War Strauss wrote to Hofmannsthal: 'It is sickening to read in the papers about the regeneration of German art … or to read how young Germany is to emerge cleansed and purified from this "glorious war" when in fact one must be thankful if the poor blighters are at least cleansed of their lice and bed-bugs and cured of their infections and once more weaned from murder.' This attitude was completely unchanged in the Second World War when he outraged Nazi officials by refusing to take in wounded soldiers to his spacious villa in Garmisch on the grounds that nobody needed to get wounded on his behalf.[33]

Strauss's behaviour under the Third Reich was far from glorious. It was shameful that he was prepared to curry favour with the regime by dedicating a song to Goebbels entitled 'Das Bächlein' ('the brooklet') which ended with the flattering words:

Der mich gerufen aus dem Stein
Der, denk ich, wird mein Führer sein.

(He who summoned me from the stone
Will, I think, be my guide.)[34]

Strauss's brief honeymoon with the Nazi regime was abruptly ended in 1935 by the interception of a letter he wrote to his Jewish librettist Stefan Zweig, who had told Strauss he could no longer work with him under the political circumstances. Though this letter is well known, it is worth repeating. Rarely can any creative artist have revealed himself so completely in both his idealism and his egotism.

> Dear Herr Zweig,
> Your letter of the 15th is driving me to distraction! This Jewish obstinacy! Enough to make an anti-semite of a man! This pride of race, this feeling of solidarity! Do you believe that I am ever, in any of my actions, guided by the thought that I am 'German' (perhaps, *qui le sait*)? Do you believe that Mozart composed as an 'Aryan'? I know of only two types of people: those with and those without talent. 'Das Volk' exists for me only at the moment it becomes the audience. Whether they are Chinese, Bavarians, New Zealanders, or Berliners leaves me cold. What matters is that they pay full price for admission.[35]

The letter made it clear to the Nazis that Strauss's core beliefs about culture were diametrically opposed to their own. Strauss was forced to resign from his official positions and was henceforth regarded with suspicion and distaste by Goebbels and Hitler, though he continued to benefit from the protection of two high-ranking Nazis, the Gauleiter of Vienna Baldur von Schirach, and the Governor General of Poland Hans Frank. Strauss's continuing naivety in believing that he was somehow above the politics of the time is illustrated by a story told by his Jewish daughter-in-law Alice Strauss:

> During the war Papa travelled from Vienna to Dresden. He stopped in Theresienstadt and wanted to visit my grandmother. He went to the camp gate and said 'My name is Richard Strauss, I want to see Frau Neumann.' The SS Guards thought he was a lunatic and sent him packing.[36]

The ultimate humiliation for Strauss was when Goebbels summoned him for a dressing-down in front of other German composers. Werner Egk described how Goebbels screamed at Strauss, reducing the venerable composer to tears: 'Be quiet! You have no idea of who you are, or of who I am. You dare to refer to Lehar as a street musician. Lehar has the masses and you haven't. Stop your rubbish about the importance of serious music, once and for all. You, Herr Strauss, belong to yesterday.'[37]

Strauss's official commissions during the Nazi period were carried out with a minimum of engagement and enthusiasm and it shows in the wretched quality of the music. The hymn composed for the opening of the 1936 Olympics was broadcast around the world and must have convinced many that the composer's genius was finally extinguished. The 'Japanische Festmusik' commissioned in 1939 to celebrate the 2,600th anniversary of the monarchy of Germany's ally Japan, displays Strauss's customary skill in orchestration, but is little more than fourteen minutes of note-spinning.

It is in the final scene of the opera *Daphne* premiered in Dresden on 1 October 1938, less than a month before *Kristallnacht* and at a time when it was impossible to ignore that Europe's most 'civilised' nation had plunged into barbarism, that we first hear intimations of Strauss's late style in the ecstatically soaring vocal line.

Shortly after the outbreak of war in the autumn of 1939 Strauss got down to work on his final opera *Capriccio*. The idea for this

Strauss delivers the Japanische Festmusik to the Japanese Ambassador.

opera, concerning a debate amongst a group of artists and aristocrats in a country house, about the primacy of words or music in opera, had first come from Stefan Zweig a few years earlier. With Zweig no longer available Strauss worked on the libretto himself with the help of the conductor Clemens Krauss. Strauss described the work as 'a dainty morsel for cultured gourmets', which is not to suggest that he did not take it seriously. Strauss regarded *Capriccio* as his artistic testament and made it clear that there would be no more operas from his pen. It is significant that just after Germany found herself at war with France for the second time in the twentieth century, Strauss insisted on changing the setting from a German Schloss in the Romantic period to a French chateau in the eighteenth century, specifically to avoid the possibility that the opera might be given a nationalistic or patriotic interpretation.

Whilst Strauss worked imperturbably on this exquisitely serene score, Poland was crushed, Rotterdam and the British cities were blitzed, and Germany launched her attack on Russia. Between the completion of the score in August 1941 and its first performance just over a year later the Wannsee Conference initiated the industrial slaughter of European Jewry. The premiere took place on 28 October 1942 as the decisive battles of the Second World War raged in Stalingrad and at El Alamein.

Strauss's post-war reputation was irretrievably damaged by an interview he gave unsuspectingly to Thomas Mann's son Klaus, posing as an American journalist. There can be little doubt that Strauss made the insensitive remarks that Klaus Mann attributes to him. He had a lifelong history of making similarly clumsy and naïve comments on a variety of subjects. But it is also possible that Klaus Mann's portrait of Strauss as a selfish old man without moral scruple was coloured by his own state of mind, and the bitterness and disillusion that led him to suicide soon after. Mann is even more damning in his judgment of the composer's Jewish daughter-in-law Alice, who complained of the petty restrictions and humiliations she suffered while millions of her fellow Jews went to the gas chambers.

After Czechoslovakia was invaded and dismembered in 1939, the 'Protectorate of Bohemia and Moravia' effectively became part of the greater German Reich. The Nazis aimed to promote Prague as a bastion of German culture. The Czechs, of course, had an incomparably rich musical tradition of their own. As early as the nineteenth century there had been tensions between German- and Czech-speaking inhabitants of Prague, with rival Czech and German opera houses. These tensions were greatly exacerbated by the German occupation as is clearly audible in remarkable and moving recordings of two concerts given in Prague in June 1939 by the Czech Philharmonic under Václav Talich. The concerts were broadcast in several European countries and preserved in the archives of the Norwegian radio. The first concert on June 5 consisted of Smetana's epic tone poem Ma Vlast (My country) and the second on June 13 of Dvořák's Slavonic Dances (Second Series)—music that expresses the irrepressible spirit of a people too often oppressed by over-mighty neighbours. The shared emotion of musicians and audience is palpable and the frenzied applause between movements evidently a political protest.

An objective view of musical life in Prague in the early years of the occupation is provided by the newspaper reviews and by the autobiography of the German critic Hans Heinz Stuckenschmidt. As an outspoken opponent of Fascism and an advocate of modern musical tendencies, Stuckenschmidt had been forced to leave Germany for Prague, and in 1937 he took up the role of music critic for the German language *Prager Tagblatt*. Surprisingly given his known views, he was able to continue as critic for the Nazi-controlled *Der neue Tag* until 1942. Stuckenschmidt and his wife were acutely conscious of their equivocal position in Prague. 'We had come to Prague as half-immigrants and now we were, so to speak, taken back through the occupation of Czechoslovakia. In Prague we were mistrusted by both sides.'[38]

As in Paris at the same time, there was a constant stream of visiting German musicians. Stuckenschmidt noted: 'Berlin sent many of the best musicians to the new part of the "Greater German Reich" ... we heard Walter Gieseking, the violinist Georg Gulenkampf, the chamber orchestra of Hans von Benda and other excellent things, besides the Nazi artists such as the conductor Otto Wartisch and similar figures'.[39]

Relations between native and visiting artists were not always cordial. Stuckenschmidt remembered trying to introduce Joseph Keilberth, the conductor of the German Philharmonic Orchestra in Prague to Václav Talich, the chief conductor of the Czech Philharmonic and the National Theatre. Despite the fact that both men admired each other's work, 'the greeting was icy from both sides'.[40]

Talich went a step further than Furtwängler in the strategic use of illness in order to avoid conducting on Hitler's birthday. Rather than conduct a celebratory *Lohengrin* at the National Theater in 1940, he checked himself into a hospital for an entirely unnecessary operation.[41]

Because of Mozart's many and happy associations with Prague, the city was chosen as one of the principal centres for the Mozart celebrations of 1941. However, no opportunity was lost to humiliate the Czechs and to assert German cultural hegemony. A prestigiouslycast performance of *Don Giovanni*, staged in the exquisite neo-classical Estates Theater on 29 October 1941 to commemorate the 154th anniversary of its premiere in the same theatre, was reserved for Nazi party members, the Wehrmacht and state officials. Needless to say it was given in German translation rather than in the Czech vernacular or the original Italian. In an elaborate ceremony a new statue of Mozart was unveiled on Smetana Square in front of the Rudolfinum concert hall and the square itself renamed Mozartplatz.[42]

In April 1945 it was the music of Anton Bruckner that revealed the death of Adolf Hitler to the allies. The great Viennese art historian Ernst Gombrich was working for the BBC as a de-coder and translator. When an important announcement on the German radio was prefaced by Bruckner's Seventh Symphony, which had been written to commemorate the death of Wagner, he realised that it meant that the Führer must be dead and communicated the fact immediately to Churchill before it was actually announced over the radio.

After the fall of Berlin at the end of the war, the Russians used music to lure fearful Berliners from their hiding places among the ruins. Loudspeaker vans travelled the city playing the song 'Das gibt's nur einmal' by Werner Richard Heymann from the immensely popular 1932 movie *Der Kongress tanzt*. This heart-warming and catchy melody by a composer who had spent the Nazi years in exile in Paris and Hollywood was a clever choice. Not only did it remind Germans of what they had been missing under Nazi rule, but there can hardly have been a more effective way to intimate that a return to normality and decency was now possible after the nightmare years.

In his book *The Theatre at War* Basil Dean, in giving an account of some of the first performances of opera that took place in Hamburg under British occupation at the end of the war, betrays a grudging admiration of the German passion for music.

> The Opera House had been unlucky: twice blasted during the raids, once by fire. The second attack destroyed the front of the building, including the auditorium. So a temporary one was built upon the original stage, the huge scene-dock in the rear being converted into the new stage. Here we saw a performance of *The Marriage of Figaro*, done with enforced simplicity, but great taste. Owing to underfeeding, neither singers nor orchestra could sustain the whole evening; by

the time the last act was reached both music and voices became deplorably flat. The auditorium was packed: seemingly neither war nor hunger can quell the German passion for opera. Both the audience and those behind the scenes used the original lavatories intended for the artistes. It was strange to see performers in their costumes joining the queues waiting to relieve themselves, but the incongruity was accepted by everyone. 'Figaro' taking his place beside me, begged in broken English for a cigarette, explaining that it helped to stave off the hunger.[43]

4 Music in the German Reich

1 Oscar Bie, *Wir von der Oper*, 1932.

2 Carl Zuckmayer, *Geheimreport*, 2004, p. 170.

3 Fred K. Prieberg, *Trial of Strength*, 1991 p. 264.

4 H E Weinschenk, *Künstler plaudern*, 1938 p. 48.

5 Karl Böhm, *Ma Vie*,1980, p. 136.

6 Lanfranco Rasponi, *The Last Prima Donnas*, 1984, p. 202.

7 Tito Gobbi, *My life*, 1979, p. 49.

8 Nicolas Slonimsky, *Music since 1900*, p. 766.

9 Ibid., p. 760.

10 Chris Walton, Othmar Schoeck. *Eine Biographie*, 1994, pp. 243-4.

11 Claire Taylor-Jay, *The artist-operas of Pfitzner, Krenek and Hindemith. Politics and the ideology of the artist*, 2003, p. 69.

12 Ernst Klee, *Kulturleben zum Dritten Reich*, 2009, p. 413.

13 Ibid., p. 115.

14 Werner Egk, *Die Zeit wartet nicht*,1981, p. 333.

15 Michael Kennedy, *Richard Strauss*, Cambridge, 1999, p. 342.

16 Egk, p. 330.

17 Godela Orff, *Mein Vater Carl Orff und ich*, 2008, p. 56.

18 Ibid., p. 56.

19 Joseph Müller-Marein and Hannes Reinhardt, *Das musikalische Selbstportrait*, 1962, p. 41.

20 Ibid., p. 86

21 Ibid., p. 392.

22 Slonimsky, p. 784.

23 Brigitte Hamann, p. 347.

24 *Künstler plaudern*, p. 224.

25 Hamann, p. 369.

26 Egk, p. 350.

27 Helge Rosvaenge, *Mach es besser mein Sohn*, 1963, p. 141.

28 Zuckmayer, p. 135.

29 Prieberg, p. 290.

30 Audrey Roncigli, *Le Cas Furtwängler*, 2009, pp. 170-192.

31 Harold Rosenthal, *Two Centuries of Opera at Covent Garden*, 1958, p. 490.

32 Kennedy, p. 302.

33 Matthew Boyden, *Richard Strauss*, 1999, p. 347.

34 Ibid., pp. 316-17.

35 Norman Del Mar, *Richard Strauss*, Volume III, 1972, p. 162.

36 Kennedy, p. 339.

37 Egk, p. 343.

38 Hans Heinz Stuckenschmidt, *Zum Hören geboren*, 1979, p. 49.

39 Ibid., p. 163.

40 Ibid., p. 167.

41 Ibid.

42 Erik Levi, *Mozart and the Nazis*, 2010, p. 205.

43 Basil Dean, *The Theatre at War*, 1956, p. 481.

Chapter 5
USA

On the afternoon of Saturday 6 December 1941, a few hours before Japanese bombers set off for Pearl Harbor, the Metropolitan Opera in New York presented a very fine performance of Wagner's *Die Walküre*. It was conducted by a 29-year-old Austrian Jewish émigré, Erich Leinsdorf, who had recently taken over the German wing of the Metropolitan after the death of Artur Bodanzky. The announced cast was one of the most brilliant ever brought together for this opera. The Wotan of Friedrich Schorr, the Siegmund of Lauritz Melchior, the Sieglinde of Lotte Lehmann and the Hunding of Alexander Kipnis are generally regarded as having been unsurpassed. The Fricka of the stately Swedish mezzo Kirsten Thorborg was also greatly admired and the American soprano Helen Traubel, who was essaying her first Brünnhilde in place of the recently departed Kirsten Flagstad, possessed a voice of extraordinary power and splendour.

Friedrich Schorr had sung Wotan in the first Ring Cycle that Hitler had attended at Bayreuth in 1925. Hitler had been outraged to find a Hungarian Jew in the role of the Teutonic god. Schorr was consequently one of the first singers to be forced to leave Germany when the Nazis took power. Disgracefully, he was also dropped by the management of the Royal Opera House in London who wished to avoid offending the Nazi regime.[1] Europe's loss was New York's gain and Schorr was central to the great Wagnerian casts assembled in New York between the wars. Over a period of eighteen years, he chalked up 250 Wotans and more than 200 performances of Hans Sachs.[2] By 1941 Schorr was nearing the end of his career and no longer in his vocal prime but still capable of noble and beautiful singing, as we can hear from the broadcast of the 6 December performance.

Fifteen years at the Met and hundreds of performances as Tristan and Siegfried had done nothing to tarnish the trumpet-like tones of Lauritz Melchior. His stentorian cries of 'Wälse! Wälse!' at the end of Act I are each held for more than ten seconds while the presumably intimidated young Leinsdorf was forced to fold his arms and wait for the tenor to run out of breath.

With the exception of Traubel, all of these artists had once graced the stages of Berlin and Vienna. Kipnis and Thorborg had represented the Vienna Opera in the performance of the Mozart *Requiem* conducted by Bruno Walter in Paris during the 1937 World Exposition. By 1941 it was impossible to find Wagnerian singers of such calibre in the length and breadth of the Reich. If Hitler had wanted to hear Wagner sung by the optimum casts he would have had to travel to New York for the purpose.

In New York this astonishing cast was routine. What was not routine about the 6 December performance was that the great Lotte Lehmann fell ill the day before and the Met management was forced to entrust the role to a twenty-three-year-old girl who had never before set foot on stage professionally. The debutante Sieglinde was an American of Swedish-Hungarian origin called Astrid Varnay. In her autobiography Varnay wrote: 'And so I would be making my debut in one of the most prestigious opera houses in the world, in a difficult principal role in one of the longest operas in the repertoire, with one of the biggest

orchestras, sharing the stage with a virtual *Almanach de Gotha* of Wagner singers, each one twice my age or more, despite the fact that I had never once set foot on stage or ever rehearsed the work with any of the people involved.'[3] As we hear from the broadcast, Varnay gave a performance of resplendent beauty and astonishing confidence and maturity that fully lived up to her great colleagues. The critic of *The New York Times* wrote that she 'acted with a skill and grace only possible to those with an inborn talent for the theatre. In fact,

Astrid Varnay as Sieglinde.

140

Sieglinde in Miss Varnay's hands was one of the most satisfying and convincing portrayals the season has brought forth.'[4] Sadly, Varnay was upstaged by history. Her glowing reviews the following day were buried behind the front page news of the Japanese attack.

After German troops entered Paris in June 1940, the New York critic Harold Rosenberg proclaimed portentously in an article in the *Partisan Review* (Nov./Dec. 1940), 'The laboratory of the twentieth century has been shut down.' As we have seen, Nazi repression did not in fact stifle the creativity of Paris and may in some ways even have stimulated it. But it was certainly true that around that time New York took over the role of Paris as cultural capital of the Western world. New York in the 1940s must have been a very exciting place to be. It was cosmopolitan and culturally 'hot' in a way that Berlin had been in the 1920s and Paris in the 1930s.

The United States was evidently the destination of choice for the vast majority of European refugees, with South America serving as a possible alternative and Shanghai for the desperate. An intriguing exception was the case of the German composer Manfred Gurlitt, who emigrated to Japan in 1939. Gurlitt had been a prominent figure in the musical life of Weimar Germany, though it was his misfortune that the texts of his two best operas, *Wozzeck* (1926) and *Soldaten* (1939), were both set independently by better known composers (Alban Berg and Bernd Alois Zimmermann). Gurlitt survived the war despite Japan's alliance with Nazi Germany. He apparently assimilated into Japan rather better than many Europeans in the United States; having married a local woman, he remained in Japan after the war.

The steady flow of European artists and intellectuals from the old world to the new that had been gathering pace in the 1930s became a flood after the fall of Paris. The 'Emergency Rescue Committee', based in Marseilles, played an important role in this. The journalist Varian Fry, assisted by a rogue American diplomat, Hiram Bingham IV, the Vice-Consul in Marseilles, issued more than 2,000 visas to allow artists and intellectuals to escape. Amongst those saved were Hannah Arendt, Jean Arp and Sophie Taeuber, Hans Bellmer, Victor Brauner, Marc Chagall, Oscar Dominguez, Marcel Duchamp, Max Ernst, Lion Feuchtwanger, Wanda Landowska, Jacques Lipchitz, Alma Mahler and Franz Werfel (carrying a suitcase full of Mahler and Bruckner scores), Heinrich Mann, André Masson and Max Ophüls. Precedence was given to writers and painters; musical performers would often have to find their own way to America. Amongst the European composers who spent the war in America were Igor Stravinsky, Arnold Schoenberg, Darius Milhaud, Bohuslav Martinů, Alexandre Tansman, Ernst Krenek, Ernst Toch, Vittorio Rieti, Mario Castelnuovo-Tedesco, Kurt Weill, Hanns Eisler, Alexander Zemlinsky, Paul Hindemith, Jaromir Weinberger, Erich Zeisl, Emmerich Kálmán, Oscar Straus, Ralph Benatzky, Robert Stolz, Friedrich Hollaender and Werner Richard Heymann.

For most émigrés the first sight of the Manhattan skyline on the horizon, like some magical Xanadu, was an unforgettable experience, after which the reality of life in America would often prove a disappointment. Some thrived, like the abstract painter Piet Mondrian who delighted in American popular music and the view from his Manhattan apartment, and found new stimulus in American life. Stravinsky, who had complained to his German publishers about Nazi disapproval of his music and assured them of his 'negative attitude— to use no stronger expression—to Communism and Jewry', evidently accommodated himself to working with Jews and pursued his career very successfully in America. Arriving in New York on 30 September 1939, Stravinsky went straight to Cambridge, Massachusetts, to deliver six Charles Eliot Norton lectures in French on the poetics of music. His prestige as a leader of musical modernism brought him major commissions such as the Symphony in Three Movements for the New York Philharmonic Society.

Stravinsky was sufficiently famous in America to have made it into the text of Richard Rodgers and Lorenz Hart's *Pal Joey* ('I've interviewed Pablo Picasso and a countess named Di Frasso. I've interviewed the great Stravinsky …'). He was even able to meet popular American musical culture halfway with his 1945 *Ebony Concerto*, composed for the jazz clarinettist Woody Herman: the marriage of his Neo-Classical style with a refined jazz idiom was a natural one. But the prickly composer may have been taken aback by an arrangement of music from his ballet *Firebird*, made in the big band style by David Rose in 1942 for broadcast on American radio stations. The result is unexpectedly delightful and conjures up images of GIs, and girls with their hair piled high, dancing cheek to cheek and jitterbugging to music that had originally showcased the choreographic and balletic talents of Fokine and Karsavina.

Kurt Weill successfully transformed himself from a Berliner into a New Yorker, but for many other European composers life in the New World was a less happy experience. Composers with great European reputations such as Schoenberg and Bartók struggled to earn a living, and even Stravinsky was forced to accept some off-beat commissions, such as the 'Circus Polka' for dancing elephants in the Barnum and Bailey Circus in 1942. Apparently the piece was better liked in the concert hall than it was at the circus. According to the bandmaster, the elephants listened to the music 'with growing distaste and uneasiness' and Sir Osbert Sitwell quipped that they 'turned up their trunks'.[5]

For some composers, the experience of being cut off from the European wellsprings of their inspiration was tragic. Finding no interest in his life's work and reduced to the indignity of writing popular songs to stave off hunger, Zemlinsky discussed the option of suicide with his wife. One winter's day while walking down Broadway, Zemlinsky turned to his wife and said bitterly: 'I wouldn't even want to be buried here.'[6] Zemlinsky died impoverished and utterly forgotten in Larchmont, New York on 15 March 1942. The fate of the Czech composer Jaromir Weinberger was possibly even sadder because it was more drawn out. Weinberger's opera *Schwanda*, premiered in Prague in 1927, brought him world fame and had reached the Met. But after he arrived in America works with titles such as 'Prelude and Fugue on Dixie' (1940), 'Mississippi Rhapsody' (1940) and 'The Lincoln Symphony' (1941) failed to find him a new audience and he eventually committed suicide in 1967.

The bitterness of living in a country where they were neither understood nor appreciated was expressed by Bertolt Brecht and Hanns Eisler in the *Hollywood Songbook* and in particular in the song 'Die Stadt Hollywood hat mich belehrt.'

> Die Stadt Hollywood hat mich belehrt
> Paradies und Hölle können eine Stadt sein
> Für die Mittellosen
> Ist das Paradies die Hölle.
>
> (The town of Hollywood has made me realise
> Paradise and hell are the same city.
> For the unsuccessful
> Paradise itself is hell.)

The same message comes across in the diary of the operetta composer Ralph Benatzky for the years 1940 to 1945. Benatzky was lucky in being able to get away from Europe as late as May 1940 and in not having to take the perilous route across the Pyrenees and the Iberian Peninsula. He arrived in New York in luxury aboard the *Ile de France* on 28 May. On 7 July after playing golf at a country club he wrote 'Ein anderes Leben! Sehr "lovely" und ganz "wonderful"' ('Another life! Very lovely and quite wonderful'). Matters deteriorated rapidly. On 9 September he wrote despairingly: 'I believe that I will not be able to achieve the slightest thing', and contemplated the eventuality of suicide. Suicide becomes a recurrent theme. On 5 December 1942 he wrote: 'I was alone in the apartment this afternoon, often tempted to throw myself off the balcony. It will come sooner or later.' Earlier in the same year in March, he wrote: 'Nothing written for a long time! Outside spring seems to have come. But not in our hearts! The same lack of hope, comfort or future!' [7]

Benatzky attempted to learn English and peppered his diary entries with newly learned English words but his circle of friends and acquaintances in New York was restricted almost entirely to Austro-German émigrés. As they appear in his diary, their names are a roll call of pre-war European cultural life—Max Reinhardt, Erwin Piscator, Kurt Weill, Lotte Lenya, Franz Werfel, Alma Mahler, Carl Zuckmayer, Fritzi Massary, Oskar Karlweis, Bertolt Brecht, Helene Thimig and Elisabeth Bergner.

In his frustration Benatzky lashed out in every direction. New York theatrical producers are gangsters, the New York art world is 'hundertprozentig verjudet' ('hundred percent Jew-dominated')—an odd complaint from someone who has just escaped from Nazi persecution. Lotte Lehmann is boring. Marlene Dietrich is 'an appalling, mock unpretentious, arrogant stupid cow. The old-fashioned whore type with pretend "Look how simple I am."' Leonard Bernstein is 'a second rate amateur'. The work of George S Kaufman, Irving Berlin and Cole Porter is 'mediocre entertainment—(but not entertaining) mass production, without charm or wit, larded with crude barrack-room, vulgar obscenities.' Benatzky reserves the full force of his scorn for every aspect of the culture of the country that had given him shelter. On 16 January 1941 he tells us: 'The level of the local American theatre is a) twenty-five years behind the times b) culturally the very bottom c) as a base of comparison, because of its crudeness, cheap effects and commercialism, completely unusable.' [8]

While Benatzky was trying in vain to sell his operetta *Bezauberndes Fräulein* ('Enchanting Lady') to the 'hundred percent Jewish dominated' New York, it was being used to entertain the SS troops

144

inside Auschwitz. One wonders whether Benatzky himself knew this when shortly after the war he came up with the bizarre idea of writing an ironic sequel to *The White Horse Inn* set in the final days of the war, in which Hitler takes refuge in the White Horse Inn and sings 'Ich habe nur das Beste gewollt!' ('I only wanted the best!') Alas, more than two decades before *The Producers* and 'Springtime for Hitler' there was little prospect of such a project being realized.[9]

Benatzky's fellow Central European operetta composers Robert Stolz, Oscar Straus and Emmerich Kálmán suffered similar disappointments during their wartime American exile. The bitter truth soon dawned on all of them that popular American taste (always excepting the indestructible *Merry Widow)* had turned against their type of musical theatre and, so far away from their homelands, their melodic inspiration dried up.

Robert Stolz was discouraged to be warned by friends that 'Viennese music is box office poison in America.'[10] Earlier, as one of the few successful 'Aryan' operetta composers in the German-speaking world, Stolz had been courted by the Nazi hierarchy. At a film premiere in Berlin he had been told by Hermann Goering: 'I am aware that you have outspoken opinions against the Reich—but you are all the same one of Germany's strongest weapons … German films with your music have been like a military campaign through the entire world—and you have been victorious everywhere.'[11]

Stolz arrived in New York on April Fools' Day 1940 aboard the SS *Washington*. His initial euphoria at discovering that his lover (later his fifth wife) Yvonne Louise Ulrich ('Einzi') had reached New York the same day by a different route soon gave way to depression as he discovered that his name meant a great deal less to Americans than it did to Hermann Goering. Though a number of his songs, notably the four that had been inserted into Benatzky's *White Horse Inn,* had been popular in America there was no name recognition to go with that popularity. This was brought home to Stolz forcibly when, by bizarre coincidence, he encountered a Hungarian lion tamer on a New York street desperate to find the sheet music for Stolz's song 'Du sollst der Kaiser meiner Seele sein' ('You shall be the Emperor of my soul'). The lion tamer needed the music for a circus act with six dancing lions but believed the song was by Franz Lehar.

Robert Stolz's most successful operetta in the 1930s had been *Venus in Seide*, loosely adapted from Count Sacher-Masoch's erotic novella *Venus in Furs* (title song: 'Venus in Seide, du lachst wenn ich leide'—

'Venus in silk, you laugh while I suffer'). A musical on the theme of sado-masochism was never likely to appeal at that time to Middle America; but Stolz's more wholesome *Frühjahrsparade* ('Spring Parade') was successfully adapted as a movie vehicle for that most wholesome of Hollywood stars, Deanna Durbin, in 1941. After this initial success, Stolz worked occasionally for the movies—his song 'Waltzing in the Clouds' was nominated for an Oscar in 1941—but he survived by working as a conductor rather than as a composer. Stolz's breakthrough as a conductor in America was the result of another encounter on a New York Street. This time he bumped into an old acquaintance who was now in the violin section of the New York Philharmonic. The violinist told him that the orchestra was due to perform a concert of Johann Strauss at Carnegie Hall that night but the conductor Bruno Walter had fallen ill. Stolz stepped in and scored a great success. From that moment, as he put it, he acted as a 'musical ambassador' for Austria, conducting hugely popular concerts of Viennese music all over America at a time when Austria and America were at war.

Both Kálmán and Straus, who had enjoyed huge international reputations between the wars, arrived in New York to considerable fanfares. Straus's adventurous escape from German-occupied France had been aided by the personal interventions of Marshal Pétain and General Franco, and he was met in New York by journalists and press photographers.[12] Kálmán, who had declined the tainted offer of honorary Aryan status, arrived in New York aboard the luxury liner *Il Conte di Savoia* with 60 suitcases and $100,000 in his luggage, paid by the Hollywood studio MGM for the rights for a movie version of his operetta *Countess Maritza*—a movie that would never be made. Despite all the brouhaha surrounding their arrival, Straus and Kálmán soon found themselves forgotten and ignored. Kálmán's attempt to write a new operetta entitled 'Miss Underground' with Lorenz Hart was abandoned after the latter's death in 1943.

In 1941 Oscar Straus had the satisfaction of seeing his most popular operetta, *The Chocolate Soldier*, filmed in a glossy new version by MGM with Nelson Eddy and Risë Stevens, but it was not a success.

Like Robert Stolz, Oscar Straus had a name recognition problem in America, albeit of a slightly different nature. Straus's legendary good humour must have been tested to the limits by the constant confusion caused by his name. At a Hollywood party in 1941 during the filming of *The Chocolate Soldier*, Straus was asked by a film executive to play 'The Blue Danube'.

> Oscar played and the producer seemed very enthusiastic.
> 'Sure is a fine tune, Mr. Straus!'
> 'Yes, isn't it?' agreed Oscar. 'Such a pity it's not mine.'
> 'Not yours?' The film king was slightly disconcerted. 'Oh, I see, there are so many of you Strausses, aren't there? Then play the "Radetzky March".'
> Oscar played, and the producer listened patiently. 'Quite something that,' he commented at the end. 'You must be mighty proud of having written it.'
> 'I wish I had,' said Oscar, 'but alas I didn't.'
> The great man was at first rather baffled, but he soon recovered. 'Ah, yes, now I know who you are. Play your great hit—you know …' And he hummed the first few bars of the *Rosenkavalier* waltz.
> Oscar was quite enjoying the situation. He played again, and then said regretfully: 'Now please don't be angry with me, but I must confess I didn't write that one either.'
> This was too much for the high-powered executive. 'What the hell do you mean—you didn't write that one either? Are you the great Strauss, or aren't you?'
> Oscar paused for a second, and then began quietly: 'I am not *the* great Strauss, my dear sir, but perhaps I am *one* of the great Strausses. I did not write "The Blue Danube", but I did write this.'—He started playing 'A Waltz Dream'.[13]

Both Kálmán and Straus took American nationality during the war, but not surprisingly they did not wish to stay, and returned to Europe after the war at the first opportunity.

Whatever disappointments and humiliations were heaped upon Straus and Kálmán in America, their fate was benign compared to that of two other celebrated musical theatre composers of the Weimar period—Paul Abraham and Richard Fall. Abraham was best known for the operattas *Viktoria und ihr Husar* and *Blume von Hawaii*. After fleeing Berlin in 1933 he took the usual route via Vienna and Paris. He eked out a living for a while as a bar pianist in Cuba before ending in penury in New York, where he sank into mental illness and was institutionalized after blocking traffic on Madison Avenue while he conducted an imaginary orchestra.[14]

Richard Fall was the younger brother of the more famous operetta composer Leo Fall. Richard Fall also wrote operettas but was chiefly known for his humorous songs such as the sexually subversive 'Was hast Du für Gefühle, Moritz?' There was no scope for such daring songs in America. Mysteriously, and one can only speculate that he found America unbearable, in the middle of the war Richard Fall returned to Europe where he was picked up by the Gestapo and dispatched to Auschwitz.[15]

Even less embittered composers than Benatzky and Richard Fall could be consumed with homesickness. Shortly before he died the Hungarian composer Béla Bartók wrote: 'But I would like to go home—forever.' Bartók was not Jewish but was forced to flee from Nazi-dominated Europe both because of the radicalism of his music and because of his uncompromising stand against Fascism. His final years in America were difficult for him but he was helped by the devoted support of fellow musicians such as the violinist Joseph Szigeti and the conductor Serge Koussevitzky, who eased his financial problems by organising commissions (notably the 'Concerto for Orchestra' for Boston) and as long as he was well enough to play, concert engagements. The American Society of Composers, Authors and Publishers (ASCAP) did great credit to itself by financing expensive medical treatment for Bartók when he fell ill in 1942. A commission from the jazz clarinettist Benny Goodman resulted in a particularly happy fusion of Old and New World idioms in the chamber piece 'Contrasts', recorded in May 1940 by Goodman and Szigeti with the composer at the piano.

Schoenberg, one of the giants of twentieth century music, found himself in the odd position of being revered and ignored at the same time. America's most successful composer, George Gershwin, paid Schoenberg the honour of expressing an interest in taking lessons from him and offered the older composer the use of his tennis court. There is an amusing description of the two playing tennis together, by another émigré musician, Albert Heink Sendrey. 'There they were, separated by a mere net, perhaps the two greatest and certainly the most discussed musicians of this decade. On one side the younger one who had succeeded in making a respectable woman out of that little hussy, jazz, on the other side of that separating net the older man, agile, small of stature but immense of mind, who is beating new paths for music through the wilderness of the unknown, over which we are as yet unable to follow him. There they were, those two contrasting giants of modern music, George Gershwin and Arnold Schoenberg, united in one common thought to make a little ball scale the top of the net, as though nothing else mattered.'[16]

In one of the more bizarre meetings of Old and New World, Irving Thalberg, the 'boy wonder' of MGM, approached Schoenberg with an invitation to write music for the movie *The Good Earth*. Thalberg had been impressed by Leopold Stokowski's performance of Schoenberg's lush pre-First World War score 'Gurrelieder', little comprehending that Schoenberg's musical idiom had moved on. Negotiations foundered on Schoenberg's insistence that his music should take precedence and not be altered in any way with the actors having to accommodate the music, rather than the other way round.[17]

The Czech Bohuslav Martinů was another European composer who was plagued with longing for Europe during his wartime stay in America. He fled Paris in June 1940, leaving his manuscripts and possessions. His last work to be premiered, on 9 February 1940, before his flight, was the Double Concerto for Two String Orchestras, Piano and Timpani. It is a dark and agitated work that reflects his fears for his country. He wrote: 'With anguish we listened every day to the news bulletins on the radio … During this time I was at work on the Double Concerto; but all my thoughts and longings were constantly with my endangered country … It is a composition written under terrible circumstances, but the emotions it voices are not those of despair, but rather of revolt, courage and unshakable faith in the future[18] … the foreboding of approaching tragedy anticipated the character of the whole work, like a warning against unleashed destructive elements, as if it were in my power to hold them back.'[19]

After prolonged misadventures Martinů arrived in New York with his wife on 31 March 1941. At this point the composer was little known in America and it was once again Koussevitzky who came to the rescue with a commission for the first of five symphonies that Martinů would write between 1942 and 1946. The First Symphony is permeated with musical references to his homeland; but his only wartime work directly and specifically inspired by political events was the sombre and powerful orchestral piece entitled 'Memorial to Lidice', first performed in Carnegie Hall on 28 March 1943 by the New York Philharmonic under Artur Rodzínski. Though tragic and contemplative in mood the discreet use at the climax of the four-note 'V' for Victory motif from the opening of Beethoven's Fifth Symphony expresses faith in the ultimate victory of the Allies.

The Nazi massacres at the village of Lidice in June 1942, in retaliation for the assassination by Czech partisans of Reichsprotektor Reinhard Heydrich, were widely publicised, initially by the Germans themselves, making the wider world aware of the lengths of brutality to which the Nazis were prepared to go. Two other famous Czech refugees, the soprano Jarmila Novotná and the politician Jan Masaryk, who was a gifted amateur pianist, recorded a set of Czech folk songs that were published under the title 'Songs of Lidice' as a memorial to the victims. The songs were in fact recorded on 6 May 1942 and acquired an altogether new resonance with news of the massacre a month later. Jan Masaryk explained: 'The ordinary but unforgettable people of that unfortunate village [Lidice] used to sing all these songs and I and Jarmila have decided to dedicate them in tribute to them, to the American public with their name.'[20]

Of all the émigré composers who spent time in America during the war, the one for whom it was the happiest experience was probably Darius Milhaud, perhaps because he was anyway an essentially happy man—his autobiography was entitled *Ma vie heureuse* ('My Happy Life'). Not that Milhaud was impervious to the unfolding tragedy of the war and its effects upon his own country. Describing his transatlantic voyage, he wrote: 'That was a gloomy crossing. There were a few Frenchmen on board, Robert de Saint-Jean, Levy-Strauss, the Duviviers and that American writer who is such a Frenchman at heart, Julian Green. Like ourselves, all were filled with inconsolable grief. I remember now, the desperate, profound sadness that fell upon us on that 14th July 1940 when we foregathered in my cabin …'[21]

As with all these European émigrés, this journey was a great leap into the unknown for Milhaud. However, a telegram received on board with an offer to teach at Mills College in California at least assured him his material existence. Always a prolific composer, Milhaud was not struck down by the creative block that afflicted so many of his refugee colleagues and he produced a prodigious amount of new music during his American years. This was partly in response to the fact that very few of his earlier scores were available in America for performance purposes.

Milhaud was exceptionally open to new experience. He described his long journey across America in a car to California and his life when he got there with heart-warming delight, but he added: 'We lived in this garden of enchantment, but with our ears glued to the radio, for our hearts remained attached to our native shores, and our thoughts were ever with those who had to live in the midst of the tragedy that had engulfed our world.'[22] Milhaud expressed his gratitude to the nation that had given him refuge in his symphonic work 'Opus Americanum' premiered by the San Francisco Symphony Orchestra under Pierre Monteux on 6 December 1943.

Like Milhaud, the Viennese composer Ernst Krenek was seduced by California. At first sight he knew 'with absolute certainty' that 'This is the land where I want to live!' Krenek had achieved international fame in the late 1920s with his controversial 'jazz opera', *Jonny spielt auf*. He had been invited to attend the New York premiere in 1929 but declined because Prohibition was in force and he did not want to forego the pleasure of wine. Though *Jonny spielt auf* celebrates a fantasy of American life that was common to many European intellectuals in the 1920s, Krenek admitted: 'I didn't have the slightest idea about America. I only knew that there were gangsters and Prohibition and neither was to my taste.'[23]

Krenek had a second opportunity to travel to America in 1937 with the Salzburg Opera Guild and a few months later found himself stranded as a refugee after the *Anschluss*. He wrote: 'Of course Prohibition was happily over, and my other prejudices proved unjustified; however, there were other aspects of which I would never have dreamt in my romantic view of America. I spoke very little English, and had a strong prejudice against the language, which in my head I had decided not to learn.' This attitude changed rapidly when Krenek was invited to give a lecture in English at Princeton. He embraced teaching and academic life as a means of avoiding the indignity of earning a living through writing film music.

Just how undignified that could be and how crass Hollywood moguls were towards pretentious European composers is illustrated by an amusing (though possibly embellished) account given by Krenek's friend George Antheil of an encounter with the film producer Sam Goldwyn.

> When Ernst Krenek, the composer, came to town, Ben [Hecht] and I decided that Sam Goldwyn would have to hire him to write the score of a picture which Sam was then planning, one with a Czech background. As Krenek was Czech, had just arrived from Europe 'where he had been persecuted by the Nazis', because he was an old and very good friend of mine, and finally because he was out of a job, Ben and I

immediately went to Sam and started screaming at him that the greatest composer in the world was in town.

'Is that so?' said Goldwyn, without falling off his chair. 'What's his name?'

'Krenek, Ernst Krenek!'

'Never heard of him! What has he written?'

'What's he written, what's he written?' screamed Ben. 'Listen to that!'

'Well, what *has* he written? I never heard tell of the guy before.'

'You tell him, Georgie,' said Ben. I took over.

'He wrote one of the world's most successful operas, *Jonny Spielt auf*. It made over a million in Germany before Hitler came in.'

'Never heard of it.'

'Well," I said, reaching, 'He wrote "Threepenny Opera." (Actually, Kurt Weill wrote it, and I knew it, but all of Krenek's operas, symphonies, and other pieces seemed so feeble now.)

'Never heard of it.'

'And "Rosenkavalier," interrupted Ben. 'He wrote "Rosenkavalier." It grossed over two million dollars last on the Continent.'

Goldwyn brightened up a bit. He thought he might have heard of "Rosenkavalier".

'And "Faust" too; Krenek wrote that.'

'No kiddin'!' said Goldwyn speculatively. I could see Krenek was going to get the job.

'And "La Traviata" too,' said Ben, to clinch it.

'So he wrote "La Traviata" did he!' Goldwyn's smiling face suddenly turned black. 'Just bring that guy around here so's I can get my hands on him. Why, his publishers almost ruined me with a suit just because we used a few bars of that lousy opera. We had to retake half of the picture for a few lousy bars.'

As we quickly withdrew from his wrath, both Ben and I sadly realized that we oversold our product.[24]

Krenek was probably relieved to have lost the job and missed out on Hollywood servitude. Instead he delighted in the research opportunities offered by American universities and in particular in the wealth of early music scores on microfilm at the Library of Congress in Washington. He commented: 'Yes, there was a certain paradox in coming to America in order to study European treasures.' Krenek was able to join his newfound interest in early European music with his American experience in 1945 when he set the Santa Fé railway timetable for an 'A Capella chorus' in a work inspired by the medieval composer Josquin des Prez.[25]

Another great musical educator who spent the war years in America was Nadia Boulanger. In the company of the Polish pianist Paderewski, Boulanger travelled from Lisbon to New York in December 1940 on the SS *Excambion*, the very same ship that had carried Milhaud a few weeks earlier. Boulanger had already made an important contribution to twentieth-century American music by teaching Aaron Copland, Walter Piston, George Antheil, Roy Harris and Virgil Thomson at the American conservatory at Fontainebleau between the wars. Once in America she continued this work by teaching at Wellesley College, Radcliffe College and the Juilliard School during the war.[26]

As elsewhere in the world, there was a greatly increased appetite for classical music in America during the Second World War and the émigré performers had it relatively easy compared to their composer colleagues. There can never have been a time or a place with such a constellation of conducting talent as in the United States during the war. At the pinnacle of the conducting confraternity was Arturo Toscanini. A notorious tyrant in the rehearsal room and the concert hall, Toscanini was given to terrifying rages. The cynical might think that Italy had been too small to contain the egos of Toscanini and Mussolini. But with his steadfast opposition to Fascism and support for his persecuted colleagues Toscanini had established a position of unimpeachable moral authority.

The NBC (National Broadcasting Company) Symphony Orchestra had been specially formed for Toscanini in 1937 and it was his orchestra throughout the war, though shared with Stokowski from 1941 to 1944. Numerous concerts, broadcast from NBC Studio 8-H with its notoriously dry acoustic, have survived. The repertoire was largely conservative and dominated by Verdi and the Austro-German classics with the odd 'bleeding chunk' of Wagner thrown in.

On 1 November 1942, in a concession to wartime patriotism, the normally unbending Toscanini gave his first ever all-American concert with Gershwin's 'Rhapsody in Blue' as a highlight, with Benny Goodman and Earl Wild as clarinet and piano soloists. 'The question

-PERE EST LE PLUS GRAND MUSICIEN DU MONDE

Arturo Toscanini, 'the world's greatest musician', with his granddaughter.

that agitated the curious music-lovers of the nation, not only symphonists but jitterbugs and musical American-first-ers, was what the distinguished maestro would do with the popular strains of the famous piece in indigo. To abate this burning curiosity at the earliest possible moment, it may be said that the piece was played magnifico and also con amore, and that the maestro might have spent his life with the denizens of Tin Pan Alley for any backwardness that he showed in his comprehension of an apparent enthusiasm for the American idiom,' wrote Olin Downes, the critic of *The New York Times*[27] with a lack of 'comprehension of an apparent enthusiasm' for the English language. Despite Downes's endorsement, Toscanini's performance is uncomfortably stiff and shows a remarkable lack of empathy for the jazz idiom of the 'Rhapsody in Blue'.

Another notable Toscanini broadcast took place on 23 July 1943. The concert was entirely devoted to Verdi. The first half of the concert ended appropriately enough with the aria 'Pace, pace, mio Dio' from *La Forza del Destino*. At the end of the interval the announcer breaks in to say: 'We delay returning to the symphonic program for this brief round out of the important developments in Italy. Rome Radio announces premier Mussolini has resigned. King Victor Emmanuel has assumed command of the Italian armed forces.' According to Harvey Sachs, Toscanini's biographer, the conductor leapt back on the stage wringing his hands and gazing heavenwards in gratitude while the audience cheered and wept.[28]

Only slightly less revered than Toscanini were Leopold Stokowski and Serge Koussevitzky. Though born and brought up in St John's Wood, London, Stokowski affected a wonderfully amorphous middle European accent at this time. Either side of his stint with the NBC Symphony Orchestra, Stokowski created two new orchestras, the All-

American Youth Orchestra in 1940 and the New York City Symphony Orchestra in 1944. The first, which auditioned nationwide for players of between 18 and 25, was intended to be a democratic riposte to widely publicised Fascist youth organisations. With the blessing of the US State Department Stokowski took the orchestra on a goodwill tour of South America in order to counter the dominant musical influence of Germany and Italy. The All-American Youth Orchestra ran for two years with new players being auditioned in 1941, but was disbanded in 1942 after America's entry into the war and conscription was introduced.

Between 1941 and 1944 Stokowski gave an extraordinary number of performances of new works including Prokofiev's 'Alexander Nevsky Suite' in its American premiere and works by Schoenberg, Stravinsky, Hindemith, Milhaud and several American composers. Works such as Robert Kelly's 'Sunset Reflections from the Adirondack Suite' broadcast on 18 November 1941, Roy Harris's 'Folk Rhythms of Today' broadcast on 19 December 1943 and Efrem Zimbalist's 'American Rhapsody', reflect the wartime mood of patriotism. The bombastic Symphony No 4 '1942' by George Antheil was premiered by Stokowski on 14 February 1944. Antheil had been a luminary of the American avant-garde in the 1920s but by the 1940s was reduced to peonage to Hollywood. According to the composer the symphony was intended to express his 'tense and troubled state of mind' in reaction to the events of 1942. It would have been more truthful to say that it expressed the tense and troubled state of Shostakovich's mind, as the piece is heavily indebted to Shostakovich's blockbuster Leningrad Symphony of the previous year. In Stokowski's wizard hands, as we hear from a live recording of the premiere, the piece was not without its attractions and excitements, but Antheil's joint invention together with the glamorous film star Hedy Lamarr of an anti-submarine device was probably a more significant wartime contribution.

Stokowski did his bit for Anglo-American relations by programming a number of British works for wartime concerts, including Holst's 'The Planets' on 14 February 1943, Vaughan-Williams Symphony No 4 on 14 March 1943 and George Butterworth's poignant 'A Shropshire Lad' on 13 February 1944.

The greatest champion of new music and especially of new American music was undoubtedly Serge Koussevitzky. Koussevitzky had led the Boston Symphony Orchestra since 1924 but only took American citizenship in 1941. Throughout the war he continued to commission and premiere new works, including Martinů's First Symphony on 15 October 1942, Roy Harris's Symphony No 5 on 26 February 1943, Samuel Barber's Symphony No 2 on 3 March 1944, Roy Harris's Symphony No 6 (Gettysburg Address Symphony) on 14 March 1944, Bartók's Concerto for Orchestra on 15 December 1944, and Virgil Thomson's 'Testament of Freedom' on 6 April 1945.[29]

Another great European conductor whose career was established in America long before the advent of fascism was the Frenchman Pierre Monteux. After conducting the world premiere of Stravinsky's *Petroushka* and *Sacre du printemps*, Debussy's 'Jeux' and Ravel's 'Daphnis et Chloe', he came to America in 1917. From 1935 he was based in San Francisco where he remained through the war years. The Hungarian Fritz Reiner, conductor of the Pittsburgh Symphony Orchestra from 1938-48, had arrived in the USA in 1922 and had been a naturalized citizen since 1928; the Polish Artur Rodzínski, who was with the Cleveland Orchestra from 1933 to 1943 and the New York Philharmonic Orchestra from 1943 to 1947, had also arrived as early as 1925.

But it was the darkening situation in Europe from 1933 onwards that brought an extraordinarily rich crop of conducting talent, transforming orchestral standards throughout the country. The Greek Dimitri Mitropoulos arrived via Germany in 1936 and took control of the Minneapolis Symphony Orchestra from 1937 to 1949. Fritz Busch, forced out of his directorship of the Dresden Opera, added lustre to the German repertoire at the Met. Efrem Kurtz, dropped from the Stuttgart Philharmonic in 1933, took over the Kansas City Philharmonic the same year. Maurice Abravanel came from Berlin to the Met in 1936 before working on Broadway and eventually taking over the Utah Symphony Orchestra. William Steinberg came from the Frankfurt Opera via Palestine to the NBC Symphony Orchestra as assistant conductor before moving on to the orchestras in Buffalo and Pittsburgh. Otto Klemperer went from the Kroll Opera in Berlin to the Los Angeles Philharmonic in 1933. George Szell—on a return journey from Australia to Europe in 1939—stopped and remained in America, conducting performances at the Met before rejuvenating the fortunes of the Cleveland Orchestra.

The most highly reputed of all the refugee conductors was Bruno Walter. By the time he settled in America Walter had had a long and distinguished career behind him in Vienna, Munich, London, Berlin and Salzburg as well as previous successful visits to America. Walter arrived in December 1939, devastated not only by the loss of his European career but also by the murder of his daughter Gretel at the hands of her jealous husband after she had had an affair with the great Italian bass Ezio Pinza.[30] Walter divided his wartime career between Los Angeles where he preferred to live, and New York. In New York Walter did particular service to three great composers—Bach, Mozart and Mahler. Now that all three are so central to the standard repertoire it seems strange that these composers needed the help of a conductor however distinguished. Walter's performances of *Don Giovanni, Le Nozze di Figaro* and *The Magic Flute* (the last performed in English, and all incidentally with Ezio Pinza) were regarded by the New York critics as revelatory and setting a new standard. Surviving broadcast performances of *Don Giovanni* are indeed thrilling but sound rough and ready by the post-war standards of Mozart performances.

Walter's annual performances of the complete Bach *St Matthew Passion* in New York were dubbed 'a noble experiment' by Olin Downes. In performing the work without cuts and in attempting a more sober and objective approach, Walter was indeed ahead of his time. To modern ears though, the performance of 1 April 1945 falls badly between two stools. Without the Romantic sweep of Mengelberg or Furtwängler, the slow tempi and heavy orchestration sound stodgy and dull. If Walter somehow fails to convey the emotion of Bach's Passion, it was not because he did not feel it. The cellist Leonard Rose was repelled by the emotion that Walter displayed during rehearsals. 'It always galled me that Bruno Walter, who was born a Jew, found it necessary to be so moved that when the text of the *St Matthew Passion* got the roughest—for example, in the text when they sing "They put a crown of thorns upon his head"—Bruno Walter used to cry the hardest.'[31] It may be that like the painter Marc Chagall, Walter found a metaphor for the sufferings of the Jews in the passion and crucifixion of Christ.

Walter's first operatic performances in New York in February 1941 were of Beethoven's *Fidelio*. The broadcast performance on 22 February 1941 is powerful and moving. Some of the intensity may be due to the fact that all of the main participants had direct and personal experience of tyranny. The conductor himself, the bass Alexander Kipnis as Rocco and the baritone Herbert Janssen as Don Fernando had all fled from Germany. The Belgian René Maison as Florestan and the Norwegian Kirsten Flagstad as Leonora were citizens of countries that had been overrun by the Nazis. Even the normally placid Flagstad sounds deeply moved in the Dungeon Scene. Shortly after the performance Flagstad would make the very Leonora-like decision to give up her career and return to occupied Norway to be with her husband. Walter's comment to a journalist before the first of his *Fidelio* performances was: 'Somehow this music tells us that happiness is deeper than unhappiness.'[32]

One of Walter's most remembered wartime concerts was one that in the end he did not conduct himself. When he was taken ill with flu and had to drop out of a broadcast concert on 14 November 1943, the young Leonard Bernstein scored a sensational success that helped to launch his career as the first American-born conductor with a world reputation. Bernstein later gratefully acknowledged the generous help Walter had given him in preparing the concert, despite his illness.

Three British conductors, though not refugees, should be mentioned as contributing to American musical life during the war: Eugene Goossens, with the Cincinnati Symphony Orchestra from 1931 to 1946, John Barbirolli doing his bit for English music and fighting a losing battle against hostile New York critics as Toscanini's successor at the New York Philharmonic Orchestra, and Sir Thomas Beecham.

Before the outbreak of war Beecham had announced that he was planning a temporary retirement from musical life. After the brief interruption of concert life in London at the outbreak of war Beecham reappeared, conducting the London Philharmonic at the Queen's Hall on 29 October 1939. When asked what had prompted this unexpected return to the podium Beecham replied waggishly: 'My dear fellow, we were given to understand that the country was in a state of emergency, and so I emerged.'[33] But it was not to be for long as far as London was concerned. In May 1940 he set off for a lengthy tour of Australia. He arrived in America in November 1940 on the way back from an Australian tour and found himself stranded, or perhaps chose to stay for the next four years. During this time, Beecham conducted many orchestras in many American cities and was appointed principal conductor of the Seattle Symphony Orchestra for two seasons. His greatest American success was in conducting mainly French repertoire at the Met for which he garnered rave reviews from the New York critics. In October 1941 Toscanini wrote a letter to the critic Olin Downes in which he referred to Beecham as 'that Nazi sympathiser man' and expressed indignation that he 'lives here, in

America protected, adulated and honoured by critics and American people.'[34] Beecham's biographer John Lucas dismisses these comments as libellous and attributes them to jealousy on the part of Toscanini. In view of Beecham's coquetting with the Nazis in 1937, Toscanini was not so wide of the mark and as someone who had taken such a firm moral stand against performing in Nazi Germany he had every right to be critical of Beecham.

Beecham cut a colourful figure in wartime America. Trailing his mistresses, the singer Dora Labbette, Lady Cunard and the pianist Betty Humby (who would become the second Lady Beecham), Beecham always provided good copy for the press. When not making music he exercised his other great talent for ruffling feathers and generating newspaper headlines with tactless and insulting comments about his hosts. Beecham had a nice line in invective. One American critic who annoyed him was described as having the 'literary approach of a street Arab, the monumental vanity of the high school magazine editor, the range of knowledge of a stevedore and the vocabulary of a baboon.' Beecham's flippant remarks about the war caused alarm in diplomatic circles. When asked by a journalist what he felt about the bombing of London he answered: 'There are a number of buildings there—including Covent Garden and that huge object of terror, the Royal Albert Hall—that have long wanted destruction.'[35] A file was kept on Sir Thomas at the Foreign Office in London in which an official wrote: 'Such remarks as those which are attributed to Sir Thomas are much more than foolish; in these times they are positively mischievous.'

Luckily, despite headlines such as 'Beecham Blast at America Brings Storm of Protest Here', in *The Los Angeles Times*, Americans proved remarkably tolerant of Sir Thomas. He was honoured with a *Time Magazine* cover and a four-page profile in which he was described as a 'treasured and crusty feature on the musical landscape of democratic America'.[36] Beecham even made enough of an impression on American consciousness to be affectionately caricatured by the film director Preston Sturges as the anti-hero of the brilliant black comedy *Unfaithfully Yours*.

As far as solo instrumentalists and singers were concerned the transformation wrought by the influx of refugees was not as marked as with the conductors. Certainly a number of celebrated instrumentalists formerly based in Europe, such as the pianists Arthur Rubinstein and Robert and Gaby Casadesus, the violinists

Bronislaw Huberman and Joseph Szigeti and the cellists Emmanuel Feuermann and Gregor Piatigorsky, and the Kolisch, Pro Arte and Budapest Quartets moved to America, but great instrumental soloists are the most peripatetic of musicians and most had been there before. Standards of solo instrumental playing had already been galvanised by an earlier musical diaspora triggered by the Russian Revolution that had brought Rachmaninov, Jascha Heifetz, Vladimir Horowitz and many other musicians who continued to enrich concert life in wartime America.

Amongst vocal artists the Trapp family, later celebrated in the Rodgers and Hammerstein musical *The Sound of Music*, formed a rather special case. They arrived in New York in November 1938 having fled their native Austria shortly after the *Anschluss* earlier that year. Having adjusted to American tastes by agreeing to include more 'light, happy music' in their concerts, to smile on stage and even to wear a minimum of make-up (though not to wear high-heeled shoes) they toured the United States throughout the war years as the 'Trapp Family Singers' becoming one of the most successful and popular acts of the period.[37]

The practice of giving public recitals of *Lieder* and art songs was still a relatively new one in the 1940s. Here America did benefit during the war from the presence of two of the greatest mistresses of the art form—Lotte Lehmann and Elisabeth Schumann, both of whom had been forced to choose between their Austro-German careers and their Jewish husbands.

The greatest of all twentieth-century German sopranos, Lehmann had been something of a national treasure. Many years later she wrote an amusing but possibly not entirely accurate account of the desperate Nazi attempts to woo her for their cause in an article entitled 'Göring, the Lioness and I'.[38] She was honest enough to admit that when she entered into negotiations with the Nazi regime 'not for one moment did I realize that it meant the beginning of a world-shattering struggle between good and evil.'

Lehmann's defection to America was undoubtedly a loss to German musical life and a consequent gain for America. The final years of her operatic career were spent at the Met with occasional forays to San Francisco, and we are lucky to have a number of broadcasts of live performances in which we can hear her passionate interpretations of Elsa, Sieglinde and the Marschallin. But it was primarily as a recitalist that Lehmann made a major contribution to American musical life.

Her recitals in New York were always regarded as important events. In addition to her regular accompanist Paul Ulanowsky, she could always count on the service of Bruno Walter both for recitals and recordings. In 1942 they recorded complete versions of the Schumann song cycles 'Dichterliebe' and 'Frauenliebe und Leben'.

Between 1 October and 24 December 1941, just before and after America's entry into the war, Lehmann recorded a series of radio programmes of German songs. Her spoken introduction to the first programme is hilariously condescending towards her American listeners and shameless in its attempt to sell her records.

The great German soprano Lotte Lehmann sings over the radio in America.

> Good evening. I'm so glad to be with you all. There's always something particularly heart-warming for me in singing over the radio. I think of all those people who cannot go to concerts, the sick and the old and those who live in lonely places. I think of all those people into whose lives the radio and the phonograph have brought music and it makes me happy to know that you may repeat for yourself on records whatever gives you pleasure in these broadcasts. Now please, think of yourselves in my home—in my own living room ...

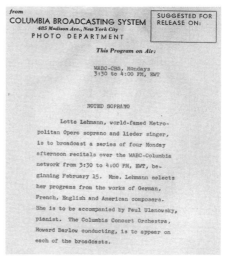

Publicity release for Lotte Lehmann's radio concerts.

The concert broadcast on 3 December, just four days before the attack on Pearl Harbor, was devoted to Richard Strauss, and that of 10 December, three days after the attack, to Mozart. A requests programme on 17 December 1941 when the United States had been at war with Germany for over a week still consisted entirely of German songs.

There seems to have been remarkably little resistance to the performance of the German song repertoire. On 2 December 1944 Elisabeth Schumann gave a concert at the New York Town Hall in which she sang 'Mit deinen blauen Augen' by Richard Strauss. In the programme it was noted that she was performing it 'in honour of the 80th birthday of the composer'. That Strauss was a citizen of a country with which the United States was at war does not seem to have bothered the New York critics who praised the concert warmly. However, a Christmas programme consisting of German songs broadcast by the Columbia Broadcasting Corporation shortly afterwards did elicit one letter of protest:

> Gentlemen,
> I would like most emphatically to protest about the Christmas programme sung by Elisabeth Schumann at 10.30. To think of a Christmas programme in America being sung entirely in German, while the German soldiers are mowing down our captured and disarmed boys is just more than I can stand. Can you for one moment imagine such a performance in Germany in English?
> Yours in disgust
> Leah G H Buss
> (Mrs Raymond Buss)[39]

Perhaps the most remarkable song recital to take place in New York during the war was given by Florence Foster Jenkins at Carnegie Hall on 25 October 1944. Foster Jenkins was an aging socialite who decided to launch herself as a coloratura soprano. Her annual by-invitation concerts in the ballroom of the Ritz Carlton Hotel had become a social fixture and her unique ability to sing an aria without a single note in tune had become legendary. The sold-out Carnegie Hall was the only public concert she ever gave and the only opportunity New Yorkers had to find out what the fuss was about. They were not disappointed. By all accounts it was a joyous occasion. Foster Jenkins's recording of the Queen of the Night's aria made shortly afterwards is a memento of that occasion and continues to give unalloyed delight.

At the Metropolitan Opera House, repertoire was largely unaffected by America's entry into the war. The one conspicuous casualty was Puccini's *Madama Butterfly,* dropped from the repertoire until the end of the war. The spectacle of a Japanese woman being mistreated by a uniformed American was felt to be inappropriate.

Wagner, on the other hand, continued to thrive at the Met and over the airwaves in the regular Saturday afternoon Met broadcasts. Started in 1931, these broadcasts became a great American cultural institution. By 1935 it was estimated that the broadcast reached nine million listeners. Between the fateful *Walküre* of 6 December 1941 and the final opera broadcast of the war—*Il Trovatore* on 31 March 1945—there were eighty broadcasts in the series. Of these, 36 were devoted to Italian opera, 18 to French, 15 to German, 5 to Mozart (with *The Magic Flute* given in English), 3 to Russian—proportions that remained unchanged from the pre-war period. It might seem strange that three-quarters of the operas broadcast from the Met during the war were by composers from countries with which America was at war. Richard Strauss, one of only two living composers performed in this period, was represented by a single broadcast on 19 February 1944.[40] In January 1942 *Time* announced that the Met was dropping plans to present *Salome*, 'partly because it involves heavy royalties to the nazified composer (although now he could not collect them)'. In fact, the Met did go ahead and stage *Salome*. While America was at war with Germany *Salome* was staged four times and *Der Rosenkavalier* eight times and presumably Strauss or his estate eventually collected the royalties.[41]

It may be significant that Wagner's *Die Meistersinger*, promoted as the great national opera in Germany at this time, received only one broadcast, after having been broadcast several times before the war. The only part of that opera that might have offended wartime audiences—Hans Sachs's patriotic peroration in Act III—was routinely cut at the Met on the grounds of length.

Several eagerly anticipated European singers, notably the German Tiana Lemnitz and the French Germaine Lubin, failed to arrive. Mussolini had already cut off the supply of leading Italian singers some time before America's entry into the war. The Italian basso Ezio Pinza was detained on Ellis Island as an enemy alien at the outbreak of war but soon released to continue as an indispensable member of the company. Pinza believed that he had been denounced by a jealous colleague. One can only wonder which other bass on the Met roster could have had the chutzpah to imagine that he could step into the shoes of the glorious Pinza. The suspicions of the FBI agents sent to search Pinza's house were aroused by a framed autograph letter of Verdi hanging on the wall. It is an indication of the hysteria to which the Americans had succumbed that the most serious charge against Pinza was that he had sent 'coded messages from the stage of the Metropolitan Opera House during the Saturday matinee radio broadcasts. The code was allegedly based on a system of changed tempi in my singing.'[42] Pinza's singing in a concert on the behalf of the International Ladies Garment Worker's Union—cited as evidence of his anti-Fascist leanings—was something that could easily have got him into political trouble of a different kind at a later date when 'premature anti-Fascism' was deemed un-American.

The war years saw a far higher proportion of American singers taking on leading roles at the Met. This was only partly due to the impossibility of importing new singers from Europe. It was also the continuation of a policy instituted in the 1930s. The price of financial aid from the Juilliard Foundation to see the Met through the financial crises of the Depression was that greater opportunities should be given to American born and trained singers. Amongst the American singers who debuted at the Met during the war were Astrid Varnay, Eleanor Steber, Regina Resnik, Jan Peerce (Jan Perelmuth) and Richard Tucker (Reuben Ticker)—the last two making it apparent that even while America was fighting Hitler it was not yet possible to have an operatic career in New York with an obviously Jewish name.

American composers were not given the same kind of opportunities at the Met as the singers. It seems quite extraordinary that in the three and half years America was at war only one opera by an American composer was performed at the Met. This was *The Island God* by the Italian-born Gian Carlo Menotti, who was not strictly speaking American as he still retained his Italian citizenship. Nicolas Slonimsky describes the libretto written by the composer himself as 'dealing with a married couple marooned on a Mediterranean island during the Second World War and a young fisherman who seduces his wife, starting a tumult and rousing an obsolescent Greek god from his musty antiquity in a ruined temple, who hurls an Olympian thunderbolt at the offenders, but loses so much electric potential by this violent discharge that he lapses into an ontologically primordial nihility.'[43] *The Island God* failed to please either critics or public despite a strong cast, and disappeared after four performances.

American composers fared much better in the concert hall with many commissions for patriotic and uplifting works arising from the war. A plethora of new works inspired by Abraham Lincoln and the Gettysburg Address included Roy Harris's Symphony No 6, subtitled 'Gettysburg Address Symphony', and Aaron Copland's 'Lincoln Symphony'.

Other works inspired by the war included Roy Harris's Symphony No 5, dedicated to 'the heroic and freedom-loving people of our great ally the Union of Soviet Socialist Republics'; Walter Damrosch's 'Dunkirk', a cantata for solo baritone, chorus and chamber orchestra dedicated to the heroes of the Dunkirk evacuation; 'Freedom Morning' for orchestra and a chorus of enlisted black men and the 'Airborne Symphony' by the socially conscious Marc Blitzstein; the symphonic suite 'The Four Freedoms' by Robert Russell Bennett inspired by the well-known speech of Franklin Roosevelt, Randall Thompson's 'Testament of Freedom', Bernard Hermann's orchestral piece 'For the Fallen', described by him as a 'berceuse for those who lie asleep on the many alien battlefields', and William Grant Still's 'In Memoriam: The Colored Soldiers Who Died for Democracy.'[44] Few of these works were ever heard again after they had fulfilled their wartime purpose. Randall Thompson's 'Testament of Freedom', a choral setting of the words of Thomas Jefferson in four movements, is a work of singular dreariness, as we can hear from a recording made by the Harvard Glee Club and the Boston Symphony Orchestra conducted by Koussevitzky in April 1945.

In the summer of 1942 Eugene Goossens, the conductor of the Cincinnati Symphony Orchestra, commissioned a series of fanfares from nine composers—eight American and one French—Paul Creston, Morton Gould, Howard Hanson, Henry Cowell, Walter Piston, Virgil Thomson, Roy Harris and Aaron Copland and the French Darius Milhaud. He wrote to Copland: 'It was my idea to make these fanfares stirring and significant contributions to the war effort, so I suggest that you give your fanfare a title, as for instance "A Fanfare for Soldiers" or "A Fanfare for Airmen" or some such heading.' Virgil Thomson titled his 'Fanfare for France'. Paul Creston's was 'A Fanfare for Paratroopers', Morton Gould's a 'Fanfare for Freedom' and Milhaud's contribution was 'Fanfare de la Liberté'. The most enduring has been Copland's 'Fanfare for the Common Man'—a striking title that reflects Copland's left-wing political ideals, but not arrived at without a fair amount of agonizing. Amongst the rejected titles were 'Fanfare for a Solemn Ceremony in which Man's Spirit is Re-dedicated to the Proposition of a Better World', 'Fanfare for the spirit of democracy' and 'Fanfare for the Rebirth of Lidice.'[45]

The three American composers who were most inspired by the events of the war were Samuel Barber, Roy Harris and Aaron Copland. The 33-year-old Samuel Barber was still of military age and was conscripted into the American Air Force in 1943. Most of his time seems to have been spent on the ground engaged in musical rather than military assignments.

In an interview shortly after the war he said: 'Well, my first musical assignment, which lasted some months, was moving pianos and very heavy radios that had been given to the army—you know, those awfully heavy old radios that don't work anymore.' Barber's first military composition was the 'Commando March' originally scored for military band and premiered in an orchestrated version by Serge Koussevitzky on 29 March 1943. His most important wartime commission was from the Air Force itself, for his Second Symphony, again premiered in Boston by Koussevitzky on 19 March 1944. Barber wrote the piece under what seems to have been rather loose military supervision. He recalled: 'I had to report every two weeks and play what I had written to a colonel. As it was one of my most complicated works, I had no idea what he expected to hear. I rather thought it might be something like "You're in the army now." So I was a little nervous when I reported to play for him on a battered-up piano in the back of an army theater. All he said was: "Well, corporal, it's not quite what we expected from you. Since the air force uses all sorts of the most technical devices, I hope you'll write this symphony in quarter tones. But do what you can, do what you can, Corporal."'[46]

If it did not actually use 'quarter tones', the Second Symphony turned out to be one of Barber's toughest and most complex pieces. It is a powerful and exciting work. Motoric rhythms, stabbing dissonances, floating melodic line and vivid orchestration combine to convey sensations of flight and combat. Despite being broadcast across the world on short-wave radio, the symphony failed to catch on. Always insecure and hypersensitive, Barber withdrew the work, and destroyed the original score and such printed scores as he could find. He reworked the haunting second movement and published it under the title of 'Night Flight'. The original full version of the symphony has luckily been re-discovered and re-established.

Roy Harris's Fifth and Sixth symphonies were both written in very direct response to wartime events. Composed in 1942 and premiered in Boston on 26 February 1943 less than a month after Russia's decisive victory at Stalingrad, the Fifth was dedicated to 'the heroic and freedom-loving people of our great ally, the Union of Soviet Socialist Republics, as a tribute to their strength in war, their staunch idealism for world peace, their ability to cope with stark materialistic problems of world order without losing a passionate belief in the fundamental importance of the arts'. The Symphony No 6 (Gettysburg) was again premiered by Koussevitzky in Boston in April 1944 and was dedicated 'to the Armed Forces of Our Nation'.

Aaron Copland's wartime compositions were not just a patriotic response to finding his country at war, but the logical outcome of long-held political convictions. The outbreak of war confirmed the direction he had been taking in the 1930s towards a more populist style. In an article published in 1941 Copland wrote: 'The new musical audience will have to have music which it can understand. That is axiomatic. It must therefore be simple and direct … It is not a time for poignantly subjective lieder, but a time for large mass choral singing. It is the composer who must embody new communal ideals in a new communal music.'[47]

Copland was given an opportunity to put these ideas into practice days after the attack on Pearl Harbor when the conductor André Kostelanetz commissioned Copland, Virgil Thomson and Jerome Kern each to write a musical portrait of a great American. Thomson chose the then mayor of New York Fiorello La Guardia, Jerome Kern chose Mark Twain and, after initially choosing Walt Whitman, Copland fixed upon Abraham Lincoln. The three-movement work begins with solemn and portentous music followed by a lively central movement that incorporates traditional American songs. In the final section, words chosen from Lincoln's letters and speeches that held a special resonance for America in the Second World War are recited by a narrator: 'Fellow citizens, we cannot escape history. We of this congress and this administration will be remembered in spite of ourselves. No personal significance or insignificance can spare one or another of us. The fiery trail through which we pass will light us down in honour or disdain to the latest generation. We, even we here hold the power and have the responsibility.'

In contrast to the grandiloquence of the 'Lincoln Portrait', the gentle and sentimental orchestral piece 'Letter from home' was meant in the words of Copland 'to convey the emotion that might naturally be awakened in the recipient by reading a letter from home'— a sentiment evoked in many popular songs of the period.[48]

Despite the low opinion of Ralph Benatzky, musical theatre in New York underwent a renaissance in the war years. At this moment the Broadway musical reached full maturity as an art form, leaving behind the inconsequential silliness of pre-war musicals like Benatzky's *White Horse Inn*, striving for more adult subject matter and a more coherent integration of plot, text and music. Rodgers and Hart led the way with the gritty urban atmosphere, cynical tone and flawed characters of *Pal Joey*, which premiered on 25 December 1940. Though it achieved a respectable run of 374 performances it was not universally appreciated. According to Rodgers himself, 'approximately one half of the first-night audience applauded wildly while the other half sat there in stunned silence.'[49] The critic Brooks Atkinson famously asked: 'Can one draw sweet water from a foul well?'[50]

Another major step towards a more grown-up type of musical theatre was taken a month later when *Lady in the Dark* was premiered on 25 January 1941. *Lady in the Dark* combined the talents of Moss Hart for the book, Ira Gershwin for the razor sharp lyrics with the music of the now thoroughly Americanized Kurt Weill, and starred the dazzling Gertrude Lawrence and Danny Kaye. It dealt with the ambitious and unlikely topic of psychoanalysis, albeit in a rather simplistic, cod-Freudian way. It would seem that the circumstances of war and the influx of European intellectuals enabled New Yorkers to take on board an altogether more sophisticated form of musical entertainment.[51]

It is generally acknowledged that this development of the American musical came to full fruition with Rodgers and Hammerstein's *Oklahoma!* which reached the stage on 31 March 1943. This was the Broadway musical as a full-blown music drama, or even, taking into account Agnes de Mille's fully integrated dance sequences, a form of *Gesamtkunstwerk*. The record-breaking initial run outlasted the war itself. The rural mid-Western setting of *Oklahoma!* was far-removed from the war, but it presented a picture of an America that many in the audience would have felt was worth fighting for. 'Oh, What a Beautiful Morning' became one of the great hits of the end of the war, sounding equally well in the middle-European accent of Richard Tauber in a delightful version recorded in England as it does in the Mid-Western accent of the original Curly, Alfred Drake.

The Broadway musical would not be ready to tackle the more tragic aspects of war until Rodgers and Hammerstein's *South Pacific* in 1949, though Hammerstein reworked Bizet's *Carmen* in 1943 in an all-black version that updated the action to the Second World War. Leonard Bernstein's *On the Town*, premiered on 28 December 1944, presented the highly topical subject of American servicemen on leave in New York. The pungent dissonance of certain moments in the score shows that not only Bernstein himself but his New York audiences had fully absorbed the lessons of Stravinsky.

There were those among the émigrés who chose the West Coast in preference to the East. The father of the composer and conductor André Previn, picked California after being struck by a particular scene in an early Technicolor movie of *Ramona*. '"Imagine," he told us, "the whole family had breakfast on a veranda outdoors. Red strawberries! White milk! Bright sunshine! Green lawns! Let's try to emigrate to California."'[52]

Previn makes light of the difficulties they had in achieving this goal. There were six months of what must have been an agonizing wait for a visa in Paris where the Previns lived in a hotel 'much more accustomed to renting rooms by the hour than housing refugee families', and the young Previn was able to enroll in the classes of the distinguished organist and composer Marcel Dupré at the Conservatoire. Once in California, Previn's father, a formerly prosperous lawyer, had to support his family by working as a neighbourhood piano teacher. For a precociously gifted boy like Previn, there were golden opportunities in Hollywood, with the film industry booming and a lot of the slightly older competition conscripted into the armed forces. Previn gained his first job at MGM in the last year of the war at the age of 16.

Many émigré musicians found the climate and laid back atmosphere of California more congenial than the East Coast. Igor Stravinsky, Arnold Schoenberg, Sergei Rachmaninov, Ernst Toch, Mario Castelnuovo-Tedesco, Ernst Krenek, Otto Klemperer and Bruno Walter all lived in the Los Angeles area—not to mention the composers involved in the film industry, such as Erich Korngold, Franz Waxman, Friedrich Hollaender, Werner Richard Heymann and Erich Zeisl. Exile made strange bedfellows. Musicians who had little in common such as Stravinsky and Rachmaninov, or who had been bitter enemies such as Korngold and Schoenberg, drew comfort from one another's company. Exiled artists tended to socialize in cliques. There was scarcely a need to learn English. Gottfried Reinhardt, the son of the theatre director Max Reinhardt, remembered an occasion when the film producer and director Otto Preminger, becoming furious with Hungarians who insisted on speaking their native language, shouted. 'Goddamnit, guys, you're in America! Speak German!'[53]

The most important musical venue in Los Angeles during the war years was the Hollywood Bowl, a vast Art Deco, covered stage and open amphitheatre that could accommodate an audience of well over 20,000. For security reasons, during the war the audience was limited to 10,000, but the concerts were kept going as a morale booster, a means of offering entertainment to the military on their way to the Pacific War and as a useful venue for selling war bonds. Popular and high culture did not always rub shoulders comfortably. When an announcement was made at the end of Bruno Walter's final concert of the 1943 season that the next concert would feature Frank Sinatra accompanied by the Los Angeles Philharmonic, there was a 'noticeable gasp from the audience and then shocked silence'. An article in *The Los Angeles Times* was headlined 'Cash to Be Crooned into Coffers of Bowl'. In fact, Sinatra's sell-out concert helped to subsidize the classical concerts. During the war the Hollywood Bowl benefited from the best that America had to offer: the conductors Otto Klemperer, Bruno Walter, George Szell, Leopold Stokowski, Eugene Ormandy, Artur Rodzínski, Sir Thomas Beecham, William Steinberg and John Barbirolli and soloists Arthur Rubinstein, Yehudi Menuhin, Jascha Heifetz, Vladimir Horowitz and Rudolf Serkin.[54]

Musical life in America had been radically and permanently changed for the better by the influx of European refugees. However much the refugees themselves may have complained about life in their new homeland, most were deeply grateful for having been taken in, in their hour of need. Asked at a press conference in Vienna after the war, whether he had suffered from homesickness in America, the actor Hans Jaray answered tartly, 'One doesn't feel homesickness for a concentration camp'.[55] For Robert Stolz, who returned to Europe with substantial, if hard won successes under his belt, New York 'was always an exciting and happy town. Like Berlin in the 1920s, New York was also a place in which a talented artist, as long as he did not lose courage or fall into the hands of unscrupulous agents and managers, could always find work. It might take a while and there would certainly be thin times but finally, and this soon became clear to me, for everyone of exceptional talent, there was a potential public in a land of the size of the United States.'[56]

On the eve of his return to Europe in 1946 even the grouchy Ralph Benatzky reviewed his American sojourn more benignly. On 26 November of that year he wrote in his diary: 'If I had only had the possibility of making a "living" [he uses the English word "living" in his German text] I would not have gone away … I was not bothered by the skyscrapers or the weather. And if I am going there remains a feeling: Despite all the disappointments, bitternesses, humiliations etc.—I thank you, America!'[57]

1   Harold Rosenthal, *Two Centuries of Opera at Covent Garden*, p. 487.
2   *The New York Times*, November 2, 1942, p. 16.
3   Astrid Varnay, with Donald Arthur, *55 Years in Five Acts*, p. 4.
4   *The New York Times*, December 7, 1941, p. 72.
5   Neil Tierney, *The unknown country: a life of Igor Stravinsky*, p. 234.
6   www. arcensemble.com/pdf/ Music%20in%20Exile%20London.pdf: accessed 7 December 2011.
7   Ralph Benatzky, *Triumph und Tristesse, aus dem Tagebüchern von 1919 bis 1946*, p. 353.
8   Ibid., p. 324.
9   Robert Dachs, *Sag beim Abschied*, p. 172.
10 Robert and Einzi Stolz, *Servus Du*, p. 405.
11 Ibid., p. 356.
12 Bernard Grun, *Prince of Vienna*, p. 173.
13 Ibid., pp. 181-2.
14 Dachs, pp. 137-142.
15 Ibid., p. 157.
16 Rodney Greenburg, *George Gershwin*, p. 202.
17 Malcolm MacDonald, *Schoenberg*, p. 78.
18 Miloš Šafránek, *Bohuslav Martinů, His Life and Works*, p. 180.
19 Ibid., p. 184.
20 Jan Kralik: notes for a CD of Jarmila Novotná, published by Supraphone in 1992.
21 Darius Milhaud, *Ma vie heureuse*, p. 220.
22 Ibid., p. 224.
23 Joseph Milller-Marein and Harms Reinhardt, *Das musicalische Selbstportrait*, pp. 176-192.
24 George Antheil, *Bad Boy of Music*, pp. 312-313.
25 Müller-Marein and Reinhardt.
26 Jérôme Spycket, *Nadia Boulanger*, 1987.
27 *The New York Times*, November 2, 1942, p. 16.
28 Harvey Sachs, *Toscanini*, p. 385.
29 Slonimsky, *Music since 1900*.

30 Ryding and Pechefsky, p. 289.
31 Ibid., p. 276.
32 Geissmar, p. 365.
33 John Lucas, *Thomas Beecham*, p. 266.
34 Ibid., p. 258.
35 Ibid., p. 293.
36 *Time Magazine*, 5 April 1943.
37 Agathe von Trapp, *Memories before and after the Sound of Music*.
38 Lone Lehmann, 'Göring, the Lioness and I', in *Opera 66*, 1966.
39 Gerd Puritz, *Elisabeth Schumann*, p. 254.
40 *The Metropolitan Opera: The Radio and Television Legacy*.
41 *The Metropolitan Opera Annuals*, 1947.
42 Ezio Pinza, with Robert Magidoff, *Ezio Pinza, an autobiography*, p. 216.
43 Slonimsky, p. 748.
44 Ibid.
45 Elizabeth B Crist, *Music for the Common Man*, p. 183.
46 Peter Dickinson, *Samuel Barber Remembered. A Centenary Tribute*, p. 36.
47 Aaron Copland, 'The Musical Scene Changes', *Twice a Year* 6-6 (1940-41) p. 343.
48 Crist, pp. 163-4.
49 Meryle Secrest, *Somewhere for me*, p. 217.
50 *The New York Times*, December 26, 1940, p. 22.
51 Bruce D McClung, *Lady in the Dark, biography of a musical*.
52 Andre Previn, *No minor chords*, p. 22.
53 Gottfried Reinhardt, *The Genius*, p. 304.
54 Ryding and Pechefsky, p. 290.
55 Dachs, p. 48.
56 Stoltz, p. 371.
57 Bentazky, p. 416.

Chapter 6
RUSSIA

A minor unforeseen consequence of Hitler's attack on the Soviet Union in June 1941 was that it changed the concert programmes for the entire world for the remainder of the war. Throughout the 1930s Soviet Russia and Nazi Germany had been locked in mutual hostility and recrimination. This found its most striking visual manifestation in the architectural face-off between the Nazi and Soviet pavilions in the 1937 Paris World Exposition. When the non-aggression pact between the great musical nations of Russia and Germany was signed by Molotov and Ribbentrop on 23 August 1939, it required symbolic musical gestures on both sides. The implicitly anti-German film *Alexander Nevsky*, with its superb score by Prokofiev, was withdrawn. Prokofiev's opera *Semyon Kotko*, which dealt with resistance to a German invasion of Russia after the Revolution, was another victim of the Molotov-Ribbentrop pact. The opera reached the stage in June 1940 but was rapidly dropped from the repertoire. It was a disastrous piece of timing. A year later *Semyon Kotko* would have been all too apt.

The director of *Alexander Nevsky*, Sergei Eisenstein, was consoled with a commission to stage a prestigious new production of Wagner's *Die Walküre*, that was intended to curry favour with Russia's new ally (and starring Stalin's mistress, the soprano Natalia Shpiller, as Sieglinde). The gambit misfired. The avant-garde production reminded the Nazis of what they regarded as the worst excesses of the Weimar years and they took the fact that Eisenstein was a Jew as an insult.

With suspicious prescience the most lavish and important German film production of 1939 was *Es war ein rauschende Ballnacht*, released on 15 August 1939 exactly one week before the signing of the non-aggression pact; the film glorified the life of Russia's most popular

Stalin's mistress, the soprano Natalia Shpiller, sang the role of Sieglinde in a production of Die Walküre *that failed to please the Nazis.*

composer Tchaikovsky. This splendidly over-the-top and improbable movie starred Zarah Leander as the great love of Tchaikovsky's life. A production on this scale with the German film industry's biggest star would have needed the approval and close involvement of Joseph Goebbels, suggesting that the new alliance had not been unforeseen on the German side. Less than two years later, when German propaganda was promoting the idea that Russia was a barbarous nation without culture and it was no longer convenient to acknowledge the genius of Tchaikovsky, the composer's house at Klin, near Moscow, was desecrated by invading German troops. Shortly after, when Klin was re-captured by the Russians, *Izvestia* reported indignantly:

A pack of mad swine could not have befouled the house of Tchaikovsky as much as the Germans did. They tore off the wall panels and used them for fuel, even though there was plenty of wood in the backyard. Fortunately, Tchaikovsky's manuscripts, his library, his favourite piano, his writing desk, all had been previously evacuated. I saw with my own eyes a Beethoven portrait torn down from the wall and carelessly thrown on a chair. Near this chair the German soldiers excreted on the floor. The German army men made a latrine next to an excellent portrait of Beethoven![1]

This, from the self-proclaimed guardians of Western culture and civilisation, seemed almost worse than the atrocities committed against the Russian population.

After the outbreak of war between Germany and Russia, the performance of Russian music was banned in the German Reich, while that of Sibelius, the national composer of Russia's enemy Finland, which had never been as popular in Germany as it was in Britain and America, was now encouraged. A German Sibelius society was set up early in 1942 on the initiative of Goebbels.[2]

The fate of Russia's greatest opera, Mussorgsky's *Boris Godunov*, also reflected the changing political situation. Inevitably *persona non grata* in the Reich, *Boris Godunov* was also forcibly dropped from the repertoire of the Marseilles Opéra after the Germans occupied the city in November 1942. However, it was welcomed back at the Met in New York the following month after its three-year absence since 1939. The first of the 1942 performances were given in Italian with Ezio Pinza in the title role, but in February 1943 a Boris was found who could sing the role in Russian. This was the great Ukrainian bass Alexander Kipnis, who had become familiar to New Yorkers as a Wagnerian. The other members of the cast continued to sing their roles in Italian, eliciting the comment from *The New York Times*: 'To those who understood neither language it was not a ludicrous procedure, though it was certainly a convincing argument for opera in English.'[3]

The 1942-43 performances were given in the Rimsky-Korsakov version made familiar in the West by Chaliapin. But on 23 July 1944, in a striking example of the close musical co-operation of Russia and America at this time, Kipnis sang in the world premiere of three scenes from a new version of Mussorgsky's masterpiece prepared by Shostakovich. Radio broadcasts preserve Kipnis's histrionic interpretation of the role in both versions.

In wartime Britain, an opera as demanding as *Boris Godunov* would have been impossible to mount in any language. The British public had to content itself with a touring production of Mussorgsky's lighter-weight *Sorochinski Fair* by the so-called Russian Opera Company. The British public certainly had plenty of other opportunities to enjoy Russian music during the war. From 1942, the percentage of Russian works presented at the Proms rose steeply. Over the 1942 and 1943 Prom seasons there were no less than five concerts entirely devoted to Russian music. Tchaikovsky and Rachmaninov continued to be the most frequently performed composers, as they had been before the war, but a number of recent works were presented as well in deference to the new alliance with the Soviets. The British premiere of Shostakovich's Leningrad Symphony took place on 29 June 1942

175

Aram Kachaturian, whose 'Ode to Stalin' was performed in London in July 1943.

under the baton of Sir Henry Wood, three weeks ahead of its American premiere under Toscanini. Aram Khachaturian's 'Ode to Stalin' was performed on 1 July 1943.[4]

The most elaborate pro-Soviet cultural event of the war in London was the 'Salute to the Red Army' organised and staged by Basil Dean before an invited audience in the Albert Hall on 21 February 1943. Drawing upon the resources of ENSA, Dean managed to assemble 2,000 performers including the London Philharmonic Orchestra, augmented by members of the BBC Symphony Orchestra and the Royal Choral Society conducted by Sir Malcolm Sargent, and a bevy of distinguished actors including Laurence Olivier, John Gielgud, Marius Goring, Ralph Richardson, and Sybil Thorndike. Joan Hammond, accompanied by a women's chorus all dressed in white, sang Elgar's 'To Women' from 'The Spirit of England' (a left-over from the previous world war). Fanfares were commissioned from William Walton, Arnold Bax and Alan Rawsthorne. In Britain, publicity for the event was suppressed in the interest of security. Dean commented ruefully: 'Certainly a 1,000 pound bomb dropped on the Albert Hall during the performance would have destroyed a great number of key people. In spite of this precaution I was told subsequently that the programme had been announced by Moscow Radio over short wave, even naming the Albert Hall and some of the important personages who were to be present!!!'[5]

It took a little while for the importance that music could play in the war effort to sink in for the Soviets, though according to historian Rodric Braithwaite, more than a hundred new patriotic songs were composed in the first days of the war. Levan Atovmyan, the Director and Deputy Chairman of Muzfond, the financial division of the Union of Soviet Composers, recalled that almost as soon as the war broke

176

out 'the decision was made to mobilize all composers for the creation of anti-fascist songs.' 'Arise, O Mighty Country' with words by Vasili Lebedev-Kumach and music by Alexander Aleksandrov, after being played daily on the radio became, according to Rodric Braithwaite, 'one of the defining theme songs of the war.'[6]

In Russia as in the West, sentimental songs and dance music of this period, such as Lydia Ruslanova's records of 'Katyusha' and 'Valenki' and the swing-inflected music of Alexander Tsfasman's band, came to evoke the intense emotions and experiences of the war, even when they were not directly inspired by it. As in every other combatant nation, young people threw themselves into dancing as though their lives depended on it. The American war correspondent Larry Lesueur, in his book *12 Months that Changed the World*, published in 1943, described how the restaurant of the Metropole Hotel in Moscow was transformed into a dance hall with a ten-piece orchestra that played Russian waltzes and American jazz. He thought the Russian girls displayed a better sense of rhythm than most Europeans, and was astonished to see them dancing the jitterbug.[7]

Musicians, artists and writers were swept up into the first desperate attempts to defend Russia against the Nazi onslaught. Two hundred and fifty musicians from amongst the staff and students of the Moscow Conservatoire, including the pianists Emil Gilels and Abram Diakov and the violinist David Oistrakh, were taken into the 8th (Krasnaya Presnya) Volunteer Division. Gilels and Oistrakh were returned to musical life before the serious fighting began but Diakov and an unknown number of young musicians, who might have become household names in the post-war period, died when the division was encircled and annihilated in October 1941.[8]

ЛАУРЕАТ МЕЖДУНАРОДНЫХ КОНКУРСОВ
ПРОФЕССОР ОРДЕНОНОСЕЦ
Д.Ф ОЙСТРАХ

The violinist David Oistrakh served briefly in the "8th Volunteer Division" before returning to musical life.

177

Once the value of music in boosting morale and flying the flag for the Soviet Union internationally was recognised, elaborate steps were taken to ensure the safety of leading composers and performers. As the German army approached Moscow in October 1941 and the fall of the city seemed imminent, 40 train carriages and 35 goods wagons rolled eastwards carrying several theatre companies, including the Bolshoi, and the composers Shostakovich (already rescued once from Leningrad), Khachaturian, Kabalevski, Glière and Shebalin.[9] Larry Lesueur gives a vivid account of one of the early improvisatory performances given by the Bolshoi in the city of Kuibyshev:

> It was a pocket edition of *Aida*, interspersed with variety dancing and solo singing [perhaps Lesueur did not realize that *Aida* is always interspersed with variety dancing and solo singing]. The audience was variously composed of intellectuals and factory workers. No one looked very dapper, because Kuibyshev was certainly a one-dress city. Few refugees had been lucky enough to bring more than a limited amount of clothes when they left Moscow or the conquered west. The orchestra members were as poorly provided. Some wore leather windbreakers. Others wore striped morning suits. Some violinists wore tuxedos. But the music was first-rate. The cast of *Aida* had no costumes, nor were there any settings. There hadn't been time to move stage sets from Moscow, in the face of more important traffic. The hundred or so people in the cast, including a large women's chorus, were bearing up in spite of the fact that they all lived together in an overcrowded dormitory. Despite some noticeable coughs, they all looked fairly healthy. Although they were dressed in street clothes, their characters were transformed once they began to sing in Russian. They were transfigured refugees singing to a refugee audience. I forgot that there were no stage sets.[10]

Russia developed its own equivalent of ENSA, with performers of all kinds—from classical ballet dancers and opera singers and Shakespearean actors to folk singers and popular dance band musicians—organised into brigades that travelled to entertain troops at the front. The young operatic bass Ivan Petrov sang at the front line in dugouts as the German army approached Moscow. On one occasion he sang within hearing distance of the Germans who responded with mortar fire, and on another 'a sergeant left the bunker halfway through the concert with a few soldiers and returned almost immediately with a German prisoner. The sergeant offered the prisoner to Petrov as a present, saying that they had no other way of expressing their appreciation for his singing.'[11] The 1942 documentary film *A Day at War* shows the young Emil Gilels sending pilots off to battle with a fiery rendition of the famous 'C Sharp Minor Prelude' by the exiled Rachmaninov, a composer formerly denounced as reactionary but rehabilitated now that Russians and Americans were comrades in arms.

Even after the massed departure of the artists, cultural life continued in Moscow throughout the desperate winter of 1940-41. The Stanislavski Theatre re-opened with the cheerful and tuneful French operetta *Les Cloches de Corneville* and continued with a mixture of popular operas and operettas.[12]

There were sufficient singers and dancers still in Moscow for performances to resume at the Bolshoi. The golden-voiced tenor Sergei Lemeshev, chief rival of the great Ivan Kozlovsky, had been left behind, having overslept and missed the train that carried his colleagues to safety. On 18 November 1941 as the battle for Moscow was entering its most

The bass Ivan Petrov was rewarded for a concert at the front by being given a captured German soldier.

The tenor Sergei Lemeshev who was left behind in Moscow.

179

desperate phase, the mixed bill that included songs, operatic arias and ballet divertissements was interrupted three times by bombing attacks.

Musical life continued under the grimmest of circumstances in the besieged city of Leningrad as well. On 9 December 1941 a new version of Tchaikovsky's 1812 Overture, banned since the Revolution because of its use of the Tsarist national anthem at the climax, was presented in the city. Prepared by Vissarion Shebalin, it substituted the people's chorus from Glinka's *Ivan Susanin* for the offending Tsarist anthem. Even after the highly publicised rescue of Shostakovich with the score of his unfinished Seventh Symphony, other composers remained behind, such as Orest Yevlakhov and Yuri Kochurov who wrote patriotic and encouraging songs for the front line defenders of the city with titles such as 'Our girls', 'The song of the anti-aircraft', 'Our ancestors' and the 'Artillery Regiment Song'.

For Russia as for Germany, music played an extremely important role in the nation's self-image. Stalin was perhaps even more successful than Hitler in mobilizing contemporary composers and harnessing their talents to the war effort. Throughout the war, resources were made available to ensure that there was a constant stream of premieres of important works by Russia's leading composers, many of which were of an overtly patriotic or propagandistic character.

With remarkable speed, a number of operas were created that dealt with the events of the war itself and that were often based on actual incidents of resistance to the invader. Only six months after the German attack, the one-act opera *Blood of the People* by Ivan Dzerzhinsky, honouring the heroism of a Soviet girl guerrilla, was performed by the evacuated Leningrad Opera at Tchkalor in the Urals. On the 7 November 1942, two operas were premiered chronicling a war that had begun less than 18 months earlier—Dmitri Kabalevsky's *At the approaches of Moscow* about the defence of Moscow only months before, staged in Moscow itself, and Nazib Zhiganov's *Ildar*, premiered in Kazan, that in the words of Nicolas Slonimsky dealt with the 'earnest love pact between a tractor driver and a collective farm milkmaid in the midst of Nazi war.' On 28 December 1942 it was the turn of Victor Voloshinov's *Stronger than Death* 'depicting the heroism of Soviet men and women in a Nazi-occupied village', and on 8 September 1943 the opera *Nadezhda Svetlova* by Ivan Dzerzhinsky based on events in the still besieged city of Leningrad. On 18 April 1944 Yury Shaparin's

6 Russia

cantata in twelve scenes, 'Tale of the Battle for the Russian Land', narrated events from the invasion of 1941 through to the turning point of 1943. Evgeny Tirotsky's opera *Alessia*, celebrating Byelorussian resistance, was premiered in Minsk in December 1944 shortly after the Germans had been ejected from the region. On 8 May 1945, the day of Germany's unconditional surrender, the four act opera *Veten (Fatherland)* by the Azerbaijan composers Dzhevdet Gadzhiev and Kara Karaev, dealing with the German invasion of Azerbaijan, was given in Baku.[13]

There were also plenty of symphonic and choral works with programmatic or narrative content concerning the war. Nikolai Myaskovsky's 22nd Symphony, written as a direct response to the German invasion, was first performed on 12 January 1942 in the Caucasian city of Tbilisi to which the composer had been evacuated. It was initially entitled 'Ballad Symphony of the Great Patriotic War'. When the work was performed in Moscow the following April, Myaskovsky dropped the descriptive title, feeling that the work should be able to speak for itself. 'Of course, there is no particular plot there—but can't you hear a

The mezzo Sophia Preobrazhensakaya still looking gaunt after the siege of Leningrad.

menace, against the background of the first movement's calm narrative (beginning), and isn't the second movement a nightmare of aggression and horrors like that? Can't you hear the struggle for liberation in the finale?'[14]

Yuri Kochurov's 'Heroic Aria for Mezzo-Soprano with Orchestra', written in Leningrad in 1942 and fulsomely dedicated to the famous operatic mezzo Sophia Preobrazhenskaya for her 'outstanding and extraordinary talent of a Russian singer' and for 'her behaviour and attitudes in life manifesting her steadfast and staunch traits of a true Russian woman', exhorted the starving citizens of Leningrad:

181

Be strong in the time
of ordeals.
Be sharp-sighted in the dark of the night.
And struggle! That's what our city orders us,
And it foresees the enemy's death.[15]

The powerful-voiced Preobrazhenskaya remained behind in besieged Leningrad after the Kirov ensemble was evacuated to safety in the Ural mountains. She became particularly associated with the role of Joan of Arc in Tchaikovsky's opera *The Maid of Orleans*. The theme of inspired resistance to a foreign invader accorded well with Russia's situation, and Preobrazhenskaya performed excerpts from the opera for troops at the front and aboard battleships.

Tikon Khrennikov's Second Symphony in C minor, premiered in Moscow on 10 January 1943, is described by Nicolas Slonimsky as 'depicting in its four movements the purposeful Socialist labour of the Soviet man, a lament for the victims of Nazi aggression, the undaunted spirit of young Soviet soldiers and the victorious military impetus, culminating in a triumph, in gloriously shining C major, over the Nazi war machine.'[16]

Musically speaking, the Soviet Union's greatest international asset during the war was the reputation of Prokofiev and Shostakovich. In

A rare photograph of Prokofiev in the 1940s.

January 1943 both were accorded the quite extraordinary honour of being elected members of the American Academy of Arts and Letters.

Between 1918 and 1936 Prokofiev had led a high profile if only intermittently successful international career alternating between France and America. His return to the Soviet Union in 1936, just before that country entered its darkest time with the great Stalin purges and the trauma of German invasion, is a matter of mystery and speculation but may be attributed to a simple case of bad timing. Prokofiev's most important work of the war years was his opera *War and Peace* based on Tolstoy's novel. It had been envisaged early in 1941 as an intimate opera, concentrating on the personal relationships of the protagonists. The outbreak of war prompted Prokofiev to expand and transform the opera into a historical and patriotic epic in the tradition of Glinka's *A Life for the Tsar* (*Ivan Susanin*) and Mussorgsky's *Boris Godunov*. The final choral peroration, 'Our Field Marshal led us onward, led us rightly into battle for our country', may be interpreted as a celebration of the wartime leadership of Stalin.

Prokofiev engaged more directly with the war with patriotic songs (and a failed attempt to compose a new national anthem), with the orchestral suite 'The Year 1941' and the cantata 'Ballad of an unknown boy' which fits into the pattern of the many wartime Soviet propaganda operas and cantatas. Prokofiev explained that it was 'a story about a boy whose mother and sister were killed by fascists, eradicating his happy childhood. The shock to his spirit matures him, and readiness for action ripens within him. During the German retreat from his hometown, the boy detonates a car containing fascist commanding officers with a grenade. The boy's name and fate remain unknown, but word of his brave deed spreads from the rear to the front and beckons forward.'[17] In a misguided and ultimately unsuccessful attempt to regain official favour after he had fallen victim to the post-war crackdown on Soviet composers, Prokofiev returned to Second

An extremely rare programme for the world premiere of Shostakovich's Seventh Symphony (not yet nicknamed 'Leningrad') on 5 March 1942.

World War subject matter for his final opera *The Story of a Real Man*, which celebrated the heroism of the pilot Alexey Meres'gev.[18]

The composer who excited more international interest than any other during the war was Dimitri Shostakovich. Much of this interest was generated by the dramatic circumstances of the composition and early performances of his Seventh Symphony.

In 1936 the brutal realism and explicit depiction of sex in Shostakovich's opera *Lady Macbeth of the Mtsensk District* had shocked the oversensitive Stalin, rather as Hindemith's opera *Neues vom Tage* had shocked Hitler in 1929. Shostakovich was attacked for the 'formalism' and 'bourgeois decadence' of his music. The following year he managed to re-establish himself in precarious official favour with his Fifth Symphony, widely touted as 'a Soviet artist's reply to just criticism', and in 1940 he received the Stalin Prize for his popular Piano Quintet.

This new-found security was shattered by the outbreak of war with Germany. The 34-year-old composer's immediate response was to offer himself for military service. 'I am going to defend my country and am prepared, sparing neither life nor strength, to carry out any mission I am assigned.'[19] After helping to dig defensive ditches around Leningrad, Shostakovich was transferred to fire brigade duty on the roof of the Leningrad Conservatory. Even here though, his colleagues, understanding his importance for the cultural life of Russia, conspired to keep him out of danger.

On 19 July 1941, less than a month after the German attack, Shostakovich began work on the Seventh Symphony. In his autobiography he recalled 'I wrote my Seventh Symphony, the *Leningrad*, quickly. I couldn't not write it. War was all around. I had to be together with the people. I wanted to create the image of our embattled country, to engrave it in music.'[20] The Soviet authorities were quick to appreciate the publicity value of this symphony being written under such dramatic and tragic circumstances in the besieged city. On 17 September, soon after the Germans had consolidated their grip on the city, Shostakovich was heard over the radio saying: 'An hour ago I finished the score of two movements of a large symphonic composition. If I succeed in carrying it off, if I manage to complete the third and fourth movements, then perhaps I'll be able to call it my Seventh Symphony. Why am I telling this? So that the radio listeners who are listening to me now will know that life in our city is proceeding normally.'[21]

On 1 October the reluctant composer was flown out of the stricken city with his wife and children and the unfinished score of the symphony, but leaving behind his mother and sister. Two weeks later he was evacuated yet again from Moscow, at one point briefly mislaying the precious score in the chaos of the crowded train. He ended up in the city of Kuibyshev where he completed the last movement on 27 December 1941. The world premiere followed just over two months later on 5 March 1942 in Kuibyshev, broadcast to the rest of Russia and around the world. Shostakovich explained his intentions with the symphony in an article in *Pravda*:

> The war we are fighting against Hitler is an eminently just war. We are defending the freedom, honour, and independence of our Motherland. We are struggling for the highest human ideals in history. We are battling for our culture, for science, for art, for everything we have created and built. And the Soviet artist will never stand aside from that historical confrontation now taking place between reason and obscurantism, between culture and barbarity, between light and darkness … I dedicate my Seventh Symphony to our struggle with fascism, to our coming victory over the enemy, and to my native city, Leningrad.[22]

The idea of the war being a struggle between 'culture and barbarity, between light and darkness' would have been familiar to Germans. Indeed, the very same words could have been used by Goebbels. Shostakovich later told a friend that the symphony was 'not only about fascism but about our system, in general about any totalitarianism.'

In his controversial autobiography *Testimony*, Shostakovich went further in insisting that the symphony was not solely or even primarily about the Nazi invasion.

> The Seventh Symphony had been planned before the war and consequently, it cannot be seen as a reaction to Hitler's attack. The 'invasion theme' has nothing to do with the attack. I was thinking of other enemies of humanity when I composed the theme … Actually, I have nothing against calling the Seventh the 'Leningrad' Symphony, but it's not about Leningrad under siege, it's about the Leningrad that Stalin destroyed and that Hitler merely finished off.[23]

A photograph of Shostakovich taken in 1942.

If Shostakovich later wanted to distance his symphony from specific historical events, it was not so at the time. In an interview he gave to the American correspondent Larry Lesueur in October 1942, he claimed that the finale of the symphony was directly inspired by what was going on around him in besieged Leningrad: '... I just could not hear the finale. It just wouldn't come. Then one day I heard shouting in the streets. When I looked out, I saw a surging crowd around a group of German prisoners. Some of the wolves had been caught and they were being marched under guard through Leningrad. From that cry of triumphant anger that rose from the throats of the crowd came the music I had searched for in vain.'[24]

The Moscow premiere of the 'Leningrad' Symphony took place on 29 March 1942, but the most extraordinary Russian premiere was the one that took place in Leningrad itself on 9 August 1942 after the score had been flown back into the besieged city. The performance of this vast and complex work by an orchestra and for an audience on the verge of death by starvation was in itself an act of heroic defiance. The concert was broadcast across the city and beyond to the encircling German army, briefly pacified by intense Russian artillery bombardment in preparation for the performance.[25]

The story of how the symphony reached the rest of the world is equally remarkable. The score was flown to Tehran on microfilm and from thence to Cairo and on to London and New York. In London the first non-Russian performance was given in a Prom concert on the 29 June 1942 by Sir Henry Wood and the London Philharmonic Orchestra.

When the score crossed the Atlantic it opened up a new war front between rival American conductors contending for the honour

of giving the first American performances. In the running were
Serge Koussevitsky, Leopold Stokowski, Arturo Toscanini and Artur
Rodzínski. The Russian-born and recently American-naturalized
Koussevitsky had the best track record as a proponent of Russian
and of contemporary music. He had commissioned major works by
Stravinsky and Prokofiev and had worked tirelessly on behalf of both
Russian and American music. Koussevitsky secured the rights for the
American concert premiere, which he gave on 14 August 1942. But it
was the broadcast premiere that proved the chief bone of contention.

Stokowski had persuaded NBC to acquire the broadcasting rights
and he assumed that the honour of the first broadcast performance
would be his, only to find that he had been outflanked by the wily and
ruthless Toscanini. Stokowski tried in vain to appeal to Toscanini's
better nature—not something that was ever much in evidence in his
dealings with rival conductors. Stokowski wrote to Toscanini:

> About 10 years ago, when I was in Russia and Shostakovich
> was comparatively unknown, it was I who perceived his
> great gifts, believed in him, and against much opposition
> was the first to play his music in the United States. At that
> time I became friends with Shostakovich, and since then
> we have been in correspondence. I have a most tremendous
> love and enthusiasm for his music … That is why last
> December I requested NBC to obtain broadcasting rights for
> Shostakovich's Seventh Symphony.
>
> Now that you know all the facts, I feel confident you will
> wish me to broadcast this symphony, and that it will be
> with your approval and in harmony with the agreement we
> made together … [26]

Toscanini was having none of this and played on his own
anti-Fascist credentials in his reply.

> Don't you think, my dear Stokowski, it would be very
> interesting for everybody, and yourself, too, to hear the old
> Italian conductor (one of the first artists who strenuously
> fought against Fascism) to play this work of a young Russian
> anti-Nazi composer?[27]

In this letter the 'old Italian conductor' assumed a mask of friendly
jocularity to hide the deep loathing he really felt for Stokowski. This

was revealed in a letter that he had written a few months earlier in October 1941 but wisely never sent, in which he even managed to misspell Stokowski's name.

> My dear Stokowsky, this afternoon you have vitrolized Franck's Symphony. Never in my long life I have heard such a brutal, bestial, ignobil [sic] unmusical performance like yours—not even from you.
> The Divine Art of Music too, has its own gansters [sic] like Hitler and Mussolini ... Believe me, you are ready for madhouse or for jail ... Hurry up!!!
> Toscanini.[28]

Stokowski fired a final and futile salvo questioning Toscanini's commitment to new music and to America.

> If I am an acceptable American conductor who enjoys bringing music of American composers to the American public, it would seem fair that I should have the same consideration as a conductor who has not made himself an American citizen and who very seldom plays American music and who ignores the inventions and new methods of broadcasting which have mainly developed in the United States.[29]

Toscanini's performance over the airwaves on 19 July 1942 is one of blistering intensity that emphasizes the more brutal aspects of the work. After just three performances Toscanini cast the symphony aside like a child bored with a new toy, leaving it to Stokowski and other American conductors who gave more than 60 performances of the work in the 1942-43 season. Later, Toscanini was dismissive of the Leningrad Symphony and wondered why he had ever bothered with it.

Shostakovich had sent a stiffly worded endorsement of Toscanini that was read over the radio before the first performance. 'I am confident that with your consummate inherent talent and superlative skill you will convey to the public of democratic America the concepts I have endeavoured to embody in this work.'[30] Privately, Shostakovich expressed his true feelings about Toscanini with a venom that would have done credit to the old Maestro himself.

I hate Toscanini. I've never heard him in a concert hall, but I've heard enough of his recordings. What he does to music is terrible in my opinion. He chops it up into a hash and then pours a disgusting sauce over it. Toscanini 'honoured' me by conducting my symphonies. I heard those records, too and they're worthless ...

Toscanini sent me his recording of my Seventh Symphony and hearing it made me very angry. Everything is wrong. The spirit and the character and the tempi. It's a sloppy hack job.[31]

1 Nicolas Slonimsky, *Music since 1900*, 1972, p. 744.
2 Andrew Barnett, *Sibelius*, 2007, p. 344.
3 *The New York Times*, February 14, 1943, p. 50.
4 BBC Proms Archives.
5 Basil Dean, *The Theatre at War*, 1956, p. 302.
6 Rodric Braithwaite, *Moscow 1941*, p. 90.
7 Larry Lesueur, *12 Months that Changed the World*, pp. 123-124.
8 Braithwaite, pp. 109-10.
9 Laurel E Fay, *Shostakovich: a Life*, 2000, p. 126.
10 Lesueur, p. 71.
11 Braithwaite, p. 122-3.
12 Ibid., p. 273.
13 *Music since 1900*, p. 800.
14 Losif Ryskin, Sleeve note for CD: *Wartime Music*, Volume I, in the series *Northern Flowers*, 2009.
15 Sleeve note for CD: *Wartime Music*, Volume II, *Northern Flowers*, 2009.
16 Slonimsky, p. 764.
17 Simon Morrison, *The People's Artist*, 2009, pp. 204-5.
18 Ibid., pp. 315-16.
19 Fay, p. 123.
20 Ibid., p. 124.
21 Ibid., p. 125.
22 Ibid., p. 131.
23 Dmitri Shostakovich, *Testimony*, 1979, p. 118.
24 Lesueur, p. 331.
25 Michael Jones, *Leningrad*, 1988, pp. 256-61.
26 Joseph Horowitz. *Understanding Toscanini*, 1994, p. 175.
27 Ibid., 175.
28 Harvey Sachs, *The Letters of Toscanini*, 2002, p. 382.
29 Horowitz, p. 176.
30 From the essay by John W Freeman, in the booklet accompanying RCA's CD issue of the 'Leningrad' Symphony, GD60293.
31 Shostakovich, p. 17.

Chapter 7
MUSICAL LIFE IN BRITAIN

Both sides in the Second World War claimed to be defending civilisation, but the British placed far less emphasis than the Germans on 'high culture'. Nowhere was this difference more clearly defined than in their policies on that most elitist of art forms, opera. Germany maintained state-subsidized opera companies in all its major cities up until and sometimes beyond the destruction of the opera houses in Allied bombing raids. In Berlin there were no less than three opera houses operational throughout most of the war: the Staatsoper in its handsome eighteenth century theatre, which was rapidly rebuilt after its initial destruction on 9 April 1941 and reopened on 7 December of the following year; the Deutsche Opera (formerly Städtische Oper); and the more down-market and populist Grosse Volksoper.

Britain had no state-subsidized opera houses and only two more or less permanent houses, the Royal Opera, Covent Garden, and the Sadler's Wells Theatre, both in London. At the outbreak of war both closed for opera and did not re-open till 1945, the Covent Garden theatre escaping unscathed and the Sadler's Wells sustaining only minor damage. The Royal Opera House suffered the ignominious fate of being leased to Mecca Cafés as a dance hall, and Sadler's Wells became a refuge for the homeless of Islington during the Blitz. As Covent Garden depended almost entirely on imported talent it was perhaps inevitable that it should cease its operatic activities.

After the initial panic, the Sadler's Wells Company, which used local talent and presented opera in English, continued much as usual during the Phoney War with performances of *Faust* (the first on 29 September 1939 sponsored by a private donor), *Carmen*, *La Traviata*, and even a new production of *Otello* in December 1939. While touring the Netherlands, the Sadler's Wells ballet company was caught on the hop in May 1940 by the German invasion. The dancers and company personnel made an adventurous, last minute escape, leaving behind most of their costumes and scenery to the Germans. For the opera division of the company it was business as usual until 7 September 1940 when the first night of the London Blitz coincided with another performance of Gounod's *Faust*. According to Tyrone Guthrie, staff went up onto the roof of the theatre where they counted 'seventeen conflagrations turning the night sky to crimson, while from below the 'Jewel Song' from *Faust* incongruously tinkled.'[1] After this there was a gap until a touring company was able to resume performances on a much-reduced scale in various temporary locations. It was financially supported by CEMA thus giving the idea of state sponsorship of the arts a toehold in Britain.

In typically blunt fashion, Sir Thomas Beecham berated the British for their lack of support for music in a fundraising speech for the London Philharmonic Orchestra in the interval of a concert he conducted on 14 January 1940.

> You, of course, are the élite of London musical society. Don't feel too encouraged—it is not much to be proud of. But if there is in this Metropolis a modicum of interest in this art of music—and there is very little—I think most of it is centred within these walls this afternoon ... In every country in the world but this, musical institutions are of a permanent character ... There is nothing here corresponding to that which we see in New York, Philadelphia, Boston, Chicago and—ahem! Berlin or Vienna, and so on.[2]

Under the direction of Tyrone Guthrie, the Sadler's Wells company presented a repertoire of seven operas—*The Beggar's Opera, Dido and Aeneas, The Magic Flute, Thomas and Sally, The Marriage of Figaro, La Traviata* and *Madame Butterfly*. In his introduction to the programme Tyrone Guthrie wrote: 'This season makes no pretence to being Grand Opera. For a time opera cannot be grand. To survive it must at present be shorn of much; the Sadler's Wells Orchestra and Chorus are reduced in numbers; the repertoire is drastically curtailed and the scenery has to be arranged for condition of wartime touring.' For the remainder of the war, shortages of materials required considerable resourcefulness. For the production of *La Traviata* sumptuous crinolines were contrived from netting, which unlike other materials was not rationed. Joan Cross, who took over direction of the opera company, was forced to appeal to the Metropolitan Opera in New York for a 'Bundle for Britain' consisting of hard-to-come-by 'tights, shoes, stockings, gloves'.[3]

In a post-war history of the company, Michael Stapleton recalled: 'When the company set out on the first tour the orchestra consisted of four pieces and a piano, from which Lawrence Collingwood conducted. The scenery amounted to little more than a few screens and a sofa or two. The "chorus", consisting of two men and two women had a great deal to do apart from singing. The entire company, including stage hands, totalled twenty when they opened their first tour at Buxton.'[4] In an article in the *Record Collector* Robert Bunyard gives further details of this touring company. 'Guthrie arranged for Lawrence Collingwood and Sumner Austin to head a twenty-strong troupe made up of Joan Cross, Edith Coates, Ruth Naylor, Henry Wendon, Powell Lloyd and John Hargreaves, a chorus of four singers and a five-piece pit band, with Collingwood conducting from the piano.'[5] For security reasons there was no advance publicity and the company travelled to areas most affected by the bombing. An entry in Joan Cross's diary gives a vivid impression of the conditions under which the company performed:

> 12th May 1941 Hull
> A rather quiet company is in the train on the way to Llandudno. Miraculously we have escaped intact having been through a night when it seemed impossible any single person would escape destruction. The blitz on Hull was terrifying, bombers dropped incendiaries until the early hours, everything seemed to be on fire; our hotel was the only building in that part of the town that wasn't a mass of flames but a violent explosion broke all the windows, the curtains flared up and we cowered in the basement.[6]

As both the company and the theatre had survived the ordeal, the performance went ahead as planned the following afternoon before an audience of two hundred.

The contrast is striking between these modest performances and the extraordinarily lavish production of *Die Fledermaus* taken to Paris by Berlin's second company, the Deutsche Oper, four months later in September 1941.

It is interesting to note *Madame Butterfly* in the reduced repertoire of the Sadler's Wells Company. Puccini's Japanese opera was dropped by the Met in New York after Pearl Harbor and by the Marseilles Opéra after the Germans took control in November 1942, but the British remained devoted to the opera throughout the war, as did the Germans who enjoyed performances with the Romanian soprano Maria Cebotari. Joan Cross and later Victoria Sladen sang the title role for Sadler's Wells though neither can have been very convincing as a 15-year-old geisha; the still more powerfully-built Australian soprano Joan Hammond scored a great success as Butterfly for the Carl Rosa touring company despite having the shoulders of a champion golfer. Though Britain was also at war with Japan, the British public seemed to have no problem with the Japanese heroine. Joan Hammond encountered hostile or maybe just astonished glances when she had to rush from a performance in Glasgow to the main station, still dressed in her kimono in order to catch the last train back to London where she was due to sing the next day.[7]

The Carl Rosa Company, the only other organisation to provide opera on a regular basis in Britain during the Second World War, had been founded by the German conductor and impresario Karl Rose in 1875 and survived as a commercial venture by satisfying the need left by the absence of provincial opera companies in Britain. During the war, the company not only toured the provinces but also appeared in various theatres in London. For these wartime performances, it brought together an impressive roster of singers, including Dora Labbette, Gwen Catley, Heddle Nash, Tudor Davies, Norman Allin, and Otakar Kraus.

The Australian soprano Joan Hammond endeared herself to audiences in wartime Britain.

The redoubtable prima donna of the company was Joan Hammond. Aged 27 in 1939, Hammond possessed the most impressive soprano voice to be heard in Britain, apart perhaps from that of the veteran Eva Turner. Hammond had signed a two-year contract with the Volksoper in Vienna in 1938 and after a promising debut there had been invited to sing at the more prestigious Vienna State Opera and at La Scala in Milan. The outbreak of war robbed

Hammond of the major international career that she might have had. Instead, she forged a special bond with British audiences during the war, not only through her Butterflys and her Violettas with the Carl Rosa Company but also through appearances at the Proms, on the radio and above all through her best-selling records.

Probably the most successful British-made operatic record of the war years was Hammond's 'O my beloved father' ('O mio babbino caro') from Puccini's *Gianni Schicchi*. Hammond had insisted—against the wishes of the record producer Walter Legge—on recording this still little-known aria as the 'B' side of her 'Love and Music' ('Vissi d'arte'), and the record became a surprise runaway success. By the end of the decade it was to be found in just about every music-loving middle-class household in Britain, including that of my grandparents. A copy of Hammond's 1943 recording of the love duet from *Madame Butterfly*, 'Ah! Love me a little!' with Webster Booth, inscribed 'with love from Bill', was offered to my mother as a delicate token of affection by a member of the Royal Army Service Corps she had met on board a ship returning from Egypt in 1944.

Another private venture that attempted to fill the operatic void in wartime Britain was the 'Russian Opera Company' formed in 1941. It was the brainchild of the conductor Anatole Fistoulari, the entrepreneur Eugene Iskoldoff and the designer George Kirsta, and was financed by another Russian émigré, Jay Pomeroy. According to the (historically somewhat inaccurate) account by the soprano Kyra Vayne, who sang with the company: 'The USSR had recently reneged on Germany to join Britain in the war against Hitler and everything Russian must therefore be of great interest, so why not put on a Russian opera?'[8]

The production of Mussorgsky's *Sorotchintsi Fair* proved to be one of the musical highlights of the war years with a sold-out three week run at the Savoy Theatre in London,

The Anglo-Russian soprano Kyra Vayne.

195

Sorotchintsi Fair

Comic Opera in Three Acts by MODESTE MUSSORGSKY
Orchestrated by N. TCHEREPNINE

Characters in Opera :

Khivria...	ODA SLOBODSKAYA / KYRA VAYNE / EUGENE SAFONOVA
Tcherevick	ARSENE KIRILLOFF / LEO HOCHLOFF / OTAKAR KRAUS
Parassia	DARIA BAYAN / KYRA VAYNE
Gritsko	EDWARD BOLESLAWSKI / JOHN DOLINGER
Old Crony	OTAKAR KRAUS / LEO HOCHLOFF
Popovitch	ERMO SIMBERG / PAUL ANDRE
A Gypsy	MARIAN NOWAKOWSKI
The Red Devil	AUDREY SEED
1st Guest	BASIL YAKOUSHEFF
2nd Guest	WILLIAM BRUCKNER
3rd Guest	ERMO RICH

Peasants, Vendors, etc. : Anne Ashley, Francis Mellor, George Gorst, Walter Gruner, Jenny Hanoff, Alice Hellerova, Max Kowalski, Mary Joseph, Alfred Lewis, Ray Lubicz, Carlotte Makins, Bruna McClean, Helen May, Basil Klon, Olga Orlova, Evelyn Rouse, Erika Storm, Betty Saville, Maisie Simpson, Mary Johnson, Liesel Goldsmith.

SCENE............ The Village of Sorotchinsti, in Ukraine

Finale : Ballet " GOPAK " by full Ballet Company

NOTE.—The names of the artistes taking the parts of Khivria, Tcherevick, Parassia, Gritsko and Old Crony at this performance are shown on the notice board in the main vestibule.

THE BALLET IN THE THIRD ACT—
"THE NIGHT ON THE BARE MOUNTAIN"

Libretto by GEORGE KIRSTA   Choreography by CATHERINE DEVILLIER

Characters in the Ballet :

The Red Cost Devil	AUDREY SEED
Venus of the Inferno	DIANA GOULD
Popovitch	TOM LINDEN
The Young Cossack	LOU VAN YCK
The " Khivria " Witch	BARBARA JDANOVA
The Drowned Maid	IRINA VINOGRADOVA
The " Tcherevick " Ghost	NADYA RADOWITZ
Witches	UNITY GRANTHAM, DAPHNE ANDERSON, OLGA SAVILLE
Devils	BETTY OGLETHORPE, IRENE MOYES, DIANA MOYES, TANIA DURAY, FRANCES MELLOR, GLADYS WALTON, KATRINA TAMAROVA

LONDON SYMPHONY ORCHESTRA
Leader : GEORGE STRATTON

Musical Director and Conductor ... ANATOLE FISTOULARI
Choreography ... CATHERINE DEVILLIER

Scenery by Brunskill & Loveday. Costumes by Helen Norman, Mme. Germaine, and Alec Shanks. Shoes by Anello & Davide. Wigs by Gustave. Head-dresses by Olga Allan.

General Manager		CHAS. MOOS
Manager	For	OSCAR POMEROY
Stage Manager	JAY POMEROY	HAMISH WILSON
Press Representative		STAR TREADAWAY
Manager ...	For ADELPHI THEATRE	A. E. WARREN

Box Office (P. F. PIDGEON) Open 10 a.m. to 7 p.m. TEM 7611

The Management reserve the right to refuse admission, also to make any alteration in the cast which may be rendered necessary by illness or other unavoidable causes.

Chocolates and Cigarettes are sold at standard prices. Any complaints should be addressed to the Management.

Programme for Mussorgsky's Sorotchinski Fair *given by the Russian Opera Company.*

followed by a lengthy provincial tour and a second London run at the Adelphi Theatre. Three fine émigré conductors took part in the run— Fistoulari, Walter Süsskind and the composer Berthold Goldschmidt. Kyra Vayne alternated with the revered Russian soprano Oda Slobodskaya in the role of Khivria and with Daria Bayan in the other soprano role of Parassia. In her autobiography Vayne wrote a sublimely vitriolic account of the run that included prostitution, sado-masochistic sex and gangsterism in addition to the usual backstage intrigues and bitchiness, and left no reputation unscathed. Daria Bayan flaunted her illicit relationship with the impresario Jay Pomeroy by 'very tactlessly arriving in a new outfit every day at a time when clothes were scarce and clothing coupons even scarcer ... The vocal warming up of Slobodskaya and (Herman) Simberg were positively awe-inspiring. Oda would bark like a seal in distress ... and Simberg would saunter up and down the corridors singing his scales to the words *Alles ist beschissen* [loosely translatable as 'Everything is fucked']—his personal mantra—in various tonalities.' Vayne rid herself of a rival soprano who invaded her dressing room by 'accidentally' dropping a fish behind the radiator over a weekend and accusing the hapless soprano of being the cause of the smell.[9]

Oda Slobodskaya did not deign to mention Kyra Vayne by name but had her own stories to tell of rivalries and cruel jokes during the run of *Sorotchintsi Fair*. One thing she had in common with Vayne was a deep resentment of the fact that the less talented Daria Bayan had been given the plum role of Parassia. Slobodskaya had made a superb recording of Parassia's aria ten years earlier and was deeply aggrieved to find herself relegated to the secondary role of Khivria.[10]

Once the worst of the Blitz was over in May 1941, London's musical life continued unabated throughout the war, if without the cosmopolitan glamour of New York in the same period. My aunt Nell Crombie studied for her LRAM at the Royal College of Music and wrote humorous poems about the college illustrated with caricatures of her fellow music students. She kept a record of London concert life in these years in the form of an autograph book illustrated with portraits and caricatures of her favourite musicians, which she asked them to sign. Amongst the luminaries of wartime musical life that she caught up with were the conductors Anatole Fistoulari, Henry Wood, Malcolm Sargent, Adrian Boult, Basil Cameron, the pianists Solomon, Benno Moiseiwitsch, Lev Pouishnoff, Eileen Joyce, Mark Hambourg and Myra Hess, the violinists

Nell Crombie. Sketch of fellow students at the Royal Academy of Music.

Nell Crombie. Flautist in uniform at the Royal Academy of Music.

Jean Pougnet and Yehudi Menuhin, the singers Richard Tauber, Dennis Noble, Frank Titterton and Derek Oldham, and the composer Howard Ferguson.

Two official organisations promoted the performance of classical music in wartime Britain: CEMA and ENSA. CEMA was the direct antecedent of the post-war Arts Council. According to an official report published in 1943, 'it had been founded by the Pilgrim Trust and Lord De La Warr, the president of the Board of Education, as a private committee to meet an immediate, wartime problem; the sudden isolation of country places during the first winter blackout, the concentration of workers in new centres, and the collapse of all ordinary sources of theatre and music.'[11]

At the beginning of 1942, the government took over full responsibility for financing the activities of CEMA and on 1 April 1942 John Maynard Keynes became chairman of the committee. This was subdivided into separate committees for drama, the visual arts under Sir Kenneth Clark, director of the National Gallery, and music under Sir Stanley Marchant, principal of the Royal Academy of Music. The music committee consisted of the composers Arthur Bliss and Constant Lambert, the musicologists Ferruccio Bonavia and Dr Thomas Wood, and the pianist Dame Myra Hess. Between January and December 1943, CEMA sponsored concerts by the Bournemouth Philharmonic, the Hallé, the Liverpool Philharmonic, the London Philharmonic, London Symphony, Northern Philharmonic and Scottish Symphony orchestras, a total of 286 concerts heard by an overall audience of 345,682. In addition there were smaller scale concerts given by chamber and string ensembles; 1,065 concerts were given in villages and small towns and 2,429 concerts in factories usually with just three or four musicians.[12] Concerts were also given for special groups such as the Women's Land Army and in YMCA canteens. During the Blitz numerous concerts were given in shelters and for the homeless after air raids.

ENSA was the brainchild of the theatrical impresario Basil Dean. With remarkable prescience Dean envisaged as early as the Munich crisis in 1938 the need for organised entertainment in the coming war. In the opening paragraph of his book *The Theatre at War*, he described the birth of the idea:

> Have you ever watched children throwing stones into a pond and wanted to join in hunting for larger and larger stones to fling, until the widening ripples cover the whole surface and melt away against the further bank? ENSA began rather like that when four theatre men sat down together on a Sunday morning in the summer of 1938 in a charming little Regency house in St John's Wood, home of Leslie Henson, to ask themselves the question 'What shall the Theatre do if there is a second world war?' The other three were Owen Nares, Godfrey Tearle and myself. A desperate fellow named Hitler was throwing stones into the ocean of world politics. We wanted to throw stones too, so as to stir the theatre world into preparation for what was to come.[13]

Though ENSA was popularly known as 'Every night something awful', Dean could proudly and justifiably boast that 'Such a mobilisation of entertainment had never been seen before and never will be again.' ENSA largely concerned itself with straight theatre and light entertainment but also sponsored a fair amount of serious music. Among the classical musicians who performed under the aegis of ENSA were John Barbirolli, Adrian Boult, Albert Coates, Constant Lambert, Malcolm Sargent and Sir Henry Wood, the pianists Harriet Cohen, Eileen Joyce, Denis Matthews, Benno Moiseiwitsch, Phyllis Sellick, Cyril Smith and Solomon, and the singers Joan Cross, Nancy Evans, Joan Hammond, Parry Jones, Miriam Licette, John McCormack, Walter Midgley, Frank Mullings, Denis Noble, Gladys Ripley, Elisabeth Schumann, Richard Tauber, Maggie Teyte and Eva Turner. The singers and instrumentalists needed piano accompanists and Britain's two leading accompanists, Gerald Moore and Ivor

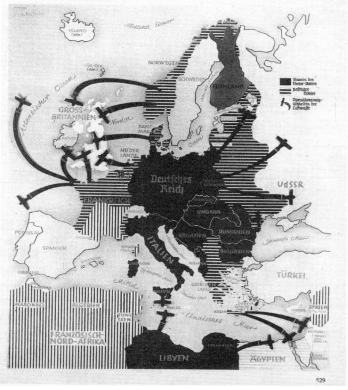

The desperate situation of Britain in 1941 as depicted in the German propaganda magazine Der Adler.

Newton, spent a very busy war. When Ivor Newton arrived back in London after a tour of Australia soon after the outbreak of war, he bumped into Gerald Moore and asked: 'Tell me, is there any work to be had in this town?' Moore answered: 'If you're lucky you may be able to pick up the occasional guinea.' Moore joined the Home Guard but Newton soon discovered:

> Musicians were finding new audiences and new, totally unconventional places in which to perform; when the Blitz started I found that concerts in air-raid shelters as well as factories were always exciting and rewarding in spite of the commonly held view that a taste for music is necessarily the prerogative of a select minority. [The Blitz and music in combination helped to break down old class divisions.] The musician set forth in the black-out—itself an ordeal—to find no buses running and taxis very rare. He walked uncertainly in the darkness to the nearest Underground station and embarked for a rendez-vous, usually Holborn Station, from which to find a way to a shelter in the battered East End, where most of our work was done. Sometimes we found ourselves hopelessly lost in such parts of London or Silvertown, where most of us had never before had any reason to go ... Artists accustomed to footlights, boiled shirts and comfortable concert halls, found themselves in conditions whose difficulty could hardly be overestimated—bare walls, men and women lying on mattresses, scattered newspapers and litter of all descriptions, small children running about almost between one's legs as one tried to concentrate on what one was playing, and the overpowering smell of humanity in the shelters that had become vast overcrowded dormitories.[14]

During the Blitz and later on in Germany under Allied bombing raids, artists displayed remarkable sang-froid in conditions of real danger. Ivor Newton recalled a concert in a factory with the ample-voiced soprano Lelia Finneberg that was interrupted by a bombing raid. 'Lelia Finneberg had not finished her first song when the audience began to pour in an orderly fashion out of the improvised concert hall. She turned to me in consternation. "What on earth is the matter?" she asked. "The red light has gone on, there's an air-raid warning," I replied. "Oh, what a relief," she said. "I thought my singing was driving them out."'[15]

Oda Slobodskaya was engaged to give concerts by both CEMA and ENSA. She sang in shelters, hospitals and camps at a fee of thirty shillings (£1.50) 'plus transport and tea. I was more than grateful.' Like Ivor Newton she had many stories to tell.

> If there was no proper hall then I sang for the people in the middle of the street and, more than once, pieces of shrapnel landed within a few feet of me. I didn't stop or even move, I just kept on singing … I once sang in a hospital for mental diseases and my high notes caused a strange reaction in a woman patient, who couldn't take them and collapsed, unconscious, falling under the piano. Two attendants came and took her away but I continued with my aria the whole time.
> Another time I was singing for the blind and the guide dogs started howling but I carried on.
> Often the warning system sounded, indicating bombers overhead, but I did not interrupt my song.[16]

This combination of stiff upper lip and musical dedication was typical of the many performers who provided music for the war effort. The pianist Marguerite Wolff gave more than a thousand concerts for the entertainment of troops during the war, often continuing in the midst of air raids. 'The conditions we were playing in were sometimes dreadful,' she commented, 'but we were making music, and the only thing that really mattered was a wrong note.'[17]

In Britain as in America there was a great revival of interest in the intimate art form of the song, giving plenty of employment opportunities to both Gerald Moore and Ivor Newton. Moore noted that in contrast to the First World War, the *Lieder* of Schubert, Schumann, and Brahms could be sung in the original German rather than always in translation. There was some apprehension when Elena Gerhardt, regarded as the 'high priestess' of the German *Lied*, first presented a programme of German songs accompanied by Myra Hess at the National Gallery. Far from protesting, the audience met singer and accompanist with 'a demonstration of such overwhelming enthusiasm and affection that both artists were too moved to be able to begin for some seconds.' Moore took this not only as a tribute to two great artists but also as evidence of a 'loyal, sensitive and discriminating public.'[18]

The tolerance of enemy languages did not extend to the recording industry. Isobel Baillie and even the great Austrian tenor Richard Tauber recorded their Schubert in English and Joan Hammond recorded her Italian repertoire in English as well. Happily, the foreign language ban did not extend to French and the great Maggie Teyte was able to continue recording her Debussy, Fauré and Reynaldo Hahn songs in the language for which they were composed. The outbreak of war ended Maggie Teyte's long career in opera but helped her develop a new career as a specialist in the French art song in which she attained her greatest glory. During the Phoney War this diminutive and no longer youthful soprano drove an army truck, but was eventually persuaded by the Francophile music critic Felix Aprahamian that 'singing Debussy was just as laudable a gesture of hostility to the Germans.'[19]

With disastrous timing an Anglo-French music festival was planned to take place in London in June 1940 to celebrate the renewal of the two countries' military alliance. The collapse of France prevented the arrival of most of the French artists, but on 21 June 1940, the eve of the French surrender, Teyte sang Berlioz's 'Nuits d'été' and Duparc songs in what must have been an emotionally charged concert at the National Gallery, with the London Philharmonic under Constant Lambert.[20] Later she sang in numerous concerts sponsored by the French Committee of National Liberation as well as touring the provinces for ENSA. For the latter she had to extend her rather specialized repertoire of French art songs. 'I sang during the bombings and strafings, during hot weather and cold, sang the classics and some popular songs, even a rendition of Porter's "Begin the Beguine".'[21]

Another much loved British singer of the war years was Isobel Baillie, the quintessential Anglo-Saxon soprano with a vibrato-less voice, pure as driven snow. Baillie sang in factory canteens around the country, on one occasion inspiring the headline: 'Roast beef, two veg and Isobel Baillie.' She declined to sing down to her audiences. 'For the most part I sang my usual repertoire saving, perhaps, a few lighter songs for a happy conclusion. As the audience appeared to enjoy what they were offered, I saw no point in changing the contents or giving them watered-down fare.'[22]

Isobel Baillie had been established in the affections of the British public well before the war. During the war she encountered and frequently worked with a young singer who was to become the most loved British classical singer of her generation—Kathleen Ferrier. They first sang together in a *Messiah* in December 1941 at Lytham St Annes. Baillie recalled: 'We shared a dressing room and when we came off the platform Kathleen put down her score and said in a triumphant yet relieved tone, "Well, Isobel, that's my first *real Messiah!*" My reply did not require any degree of foresight. "Well dear, you had better start counting for it certainly won't be your last!"'[23] Isobel Baillie's prediction proved accurate. Ferrier sang twelve *Messiahs* between 23 November 1943 and 2 January 1944, seventeen between 2 December 1944 and 9 January 1945, and 20 over the same period in the following year, illustrating the insatiable appetite of the British public for Handel's masterpiece.[24]

Thanks to CEMA, Ferrier underwent a gruelling but valuable apprenticeship, concertizing around the country for the remaining war years. Early highlights in her career were her debut in one of Myra Hess's National Gallery concerts and another *Messiah* with Isobel Baillie, this time at Westminster Abbey, conducted by Ralph Vaughan Williams. In a letter of 9 January 1943, Ferrier described her London debut at the National Gallery: 'I made my London debut a week last Monday at the National Gallery and oh boy! Did my knees knock! But I got through without running off in the middle or swallowing in the wrong place. Myra Hess, the boss of the concerts, was very nice and encouraging. There was a huge crowd and it was a bit of a facer, so I was glad when it was safely over.'[25]

One of ENSA's most important musical collaborations was with the re-born Hallé Orchestra and its conductor John Barbirolli. Barbirolli's return from New York at the height of the war and his re-creation of the moribund Hallé Orchestra and his own career at the same time, is one of the great redemptive stories of the war. Founded in 1857 by Carl Hallé (later Sir Charles Hallé) in Manchester when that city was one of the richest and most dynamic in the world, the Hallé was yet another German gift to British musical life. Under Sir Hamilton Harty it had probably been the finest British provincial orchestra in the interwar period.

Barbirolli had been languishing in New York as the chief conductor of the New York Philharmonic, with his self-confidence and his career withering under the attacks of the New York critics who regarded him as an unworthy successor to Toscanini. In 1942, when his contract with the New York Philharmonic was up, Barbirolli declined an invitation to take over the Los Angeles Philharmonic and made the brave decision to cross the Atlantic at the height of the U-boat danger to give a series of concerts in Britain. Only 32 of the 75 ships in his convoy survived the 23-day crossing to Liverpool. After ten weeks of concerts with the London Symphony Orchestra and the London Philharmonic, Barbirolli returned to the USA.

The following year he responded to the challenge to take up the baton of the Hallé, a provincial orchestra on the verge of dissolution in a city ruined by German bombs. Though the Battle of the Atlantic was now past its peak, this second journey was not without its dangers. Barbirolli survived the second leg of the journey from Lisbon to London only because he had agreed to swop places with the film star Leslie Howard for a seat on a plane that was shot down by the Germans. Barbirolli arrived in Manchester in June 1943 to discover that the BBC had poached the best players from the Hallé. He had just over a month in which to audition, recruit, and rehearse what was an almost entirely new orchestra—a daunting task made all the more difficult by the fact that most able-bodied musicians had been conscripted. As Barbirolli himself put it: 'I had to find the "slightly maimed"; it didn't matter if they had flat feet as long as they had straight fingers.'[26]

The first concert, in the Prince's Theatre in Bradford on 5 July 1943, consisted of the Overture to *Die Meistersinger*, Delius's 'A Song of Sunrise', Tchaikovsky's Fantasy Overture 'Romeo and Juliet' and Brahms's Second Symphony. It was a resounding success and from there the Hallé went from triumph to triumph. For Barbirolli's biographer Michael Kennedy 'the whole Hallé adventure was a symbol, in artistic terms, of the feeling in Britain, once the tide of war had turned at El Alamein in 1942, that music and the other arts would matter more than they had when peace returned.'[27]

There was an element of missionary zeal in the way that Barbirolli and the Hallé took music to the people. On one occasion, Michael Kennedy tells us, Barbirolli 'sensed a frigidity in the applause' after he had conducted Strauss's 'Bourgeois Gentilhomme Suite' in Sheffield. It is not clear whether the frigidity was due to the unfamiliarity of the music or the fact that Strauss was a citizen of Nazi Germany, but Barbirolli 'told the audience a little of the work's history and what Strauss's writing for the orchestra meant to him, and he played it all again.'[28]

On 11 October 1943 Barbirolli and the Hallé gave the first in a series of concerts organized by Basil Dean under the title of ENSA Symphony Concerts for War-Workers, marking the beginning of a fruitful collaboration between the two organisations. Echoing the words of Churchill, Barbirolli described the Hallé's ENSA-sponsored tour to entertain the Allied troops in Belgium and the Netherlands at the end of 1944 as the orchestra's 'finest hour'. It was the orchestra's first-ever foreign venture and it was no small feat to transport and house its 87 members under wartime conditions. In Brussels they performed Mendelssohn's Violin Concerto, the first time that music by a Jewish composer had been performed in the city since the German Occupation.

Soon after, the orchestra found itself caught up in and nearly overrun by the Battle of the Bulge, the last great German offensive of the war. Throughout the crisis the Hallé gave two full symphony concerts a day. According to Basil Dean: 'The enemy provided frequent reminders of the dangers outside, machine-gunning the players from the air on one occasion as they were getting on a coach; upon another, just after the *Fledermaus* overture had been broadcast in a Forces Programme, shooting down seven or eight soldiers waiting in a queue outside: poor return for an admirable performance of some of their own music.'[29]

The concert on New Year's Eve was a particularly memorable and emotional occasion. 'At the end there was a wild rush for the platform, because every member of the audience was led to shake Barbirolli by the hand. These young men had undergone an experience that might never be repeated. Undefined, unspoken was a prophetic sense of the brevity of life, brought into focus under the spiritual illumination of the music.'[30]

The conductor who most impressed himself on the British imagination during the war, becoming virtually synonymous with the art of conducting, was Malcolm Sargent. This was as much due to his dapper appearance and his popular touch as to his musical abilities, great though these were. Sargent led the way early in the war in taking symphonic music to the people. In a tour organised by the dance band leader Jack Hylton, Sargent took the London Philharmonic to ten cities—Glasgow, Manchester, Liverpool, Birmingham, Coventry, Newcastle, Leeds, Bradford, Edinburgh and Sheffield, playing in theatres and music halls. Beginning at the height of the Battle of Britain on 10 August 1940 and continuing for 14 weeks,

Malcolm Sargent caricatured by Nell Crombie.

Flyer for the popular symphony concerts conducted by Malcolm Sargent.

the concerts were soon dubbed the 'Blitz tour'. Sargent was delighted to be told that his only rival in popular esteem was George Formby and exulted: 'For the first time hundreds of humble gallerites [sic] normally entertained by conjurers, contortionists and red-nosed comedians will listen for an hour to heaven-sent music.' Not everyone reacted with enthusiasm and in Edinburgh an old woman was ejected from a concert after shouting 'Play something cheery!' in the midst of the slow movement of Dvořák's 'New World' Symphony.[31]

In the absence of Beecham in America, Sargent was the best that Britain could muster to counter the impact in neutral countries of the musical goodwill trips of Furtwängler and the Berlin Philharmonic. Sargent travelled twice to Sweden in 1942 and 1943, and in Portugal in 1943 actually overlapped with Furtwängler. Sargent's biographer Charles Reid tells us that during the rehearsal for the final concert in Portugal 'the big swagger of trombones in the *Cockaigne Overture* (Elgar) … the players began surreptitiously giving Britain's V for Victory sign with forked fingers while he returned the compliment with his left hand.'[32]

For those with a missionary turn of mind, the war was an opportunity to bring classical music to the people or vice versa. In 1944 the beer manufacturers 'Messrs Tennant of Sheffield' funded a series of concerts in drinking venues prompting a tongue in cheek article in the magazine *Parade* entitled 'Beer and Bach'. 'If there is one word likely to throw the drinking world into a panic it is "culture".' But the writer goes on to express surprise and satisfaction that a pub full of drinkers had managed to sit through 27 minutes of Schumann 'not only without batting an eyelid but with obvious and undisguised pleasure.'[33]

The two great institutions of London's musical life that stand out in the collective memory of the Second World War were the Prom concerts of Sir Henry Wood and the National Gallery concerts of Dame Myra Hess. Sir Henry Wood's summer season of 'Promenade' concerts in the Queen's Hall had been central to British musical life since 1895. Sir Henry was perhaps less glamorous than some of his contemporary conductors but greatly respected. Recorded excerpts from a rehearsal for a Prom concert on 21 June 1942 reveal a vigorous and authoritative approach to the music but also a rapport with the orchestra that is comradely rather than dictatorial.

The 1939 Prom season was in mid-flow when Hitler invaded Poland on 1 September 1939. The concert of that evening was abruptly terminated at the interval after Harriet Cohen had performed Beethoven's Second Piano Concerto, and the remaining concerts of the season abandoned. However, the 1940 season went ahead more or less as planned. In the words of the pianist Gerald Moore:

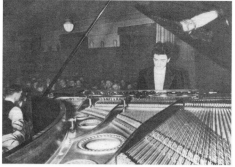

Beer and Bach. Concerts in pubs in 1944.

The conductor Sir Henry Wood who presided over the Proms until 1944.

It was not to be expected that Sir Henry Wood would call off a Promenade Season because of a mere war. At first all

207

went merrily; the audience willingly resigned to a struggle home in a blackout. Then one Saturday afternoon the enemy decided to give us our baptism of bombs.

As I changed into evening dress at my club overlooking St James's Park, I saw a mile away to the eastward huge columns of black smoke. But, nothing daunted, the gallant Sir Henry, carnation in buttonhole as usual, strode jauntily through his orchestra at ten seconds before eight to start his concert. The Queen's Hall Promenades were going on, come what may.[34]

The 1940 season started somewhat late on Saturday 10 August. As a concession to age rather than to Hitler, Sir Henry lightened his conducting load by taking on Basil Cameron as his assistant, but otherwise the season proceeded as usual through the Battle of Britain.

The first wartime Prom was not notably patriotic in tone. Though it included works by Elgar and Sullivan it also included Verdi and Liszt, and Wagner's *Tannhäuser* Overture. Only one item might have been chosen with reference to the war, the march from Arthur Bliss's score for the film *Things to Come*, which ironically had done so much to convince Londoners that their city would be reduced to rubble within hours of the declaration of war.

The second concert given on Monday 12 August was largely given over to Wagner with the huge-voiced Eva Turner singing the Immolation Scene from *Götterdämmerung* (apparently in German, as it is listed in the programme as 'Starke Scheite'), and William Walton's jaunty Suite No I from *Façade* sandwiched bizarrely between the Prelude to Act III of *Lohengrin* and *Aida*'s 'Ritorna vincitor' and Honegger's cacophonous *Pacific 231*, and still more bizarrely two Schumann *Lieder* sung by Astra Desmond with Gerald Moore at the piano.

The programming of the wartime Proms strikes the modern concertgoer as oddly incoherent and heterogeneous but in fact it followed a fairly regular pattern. The choice of works was conservative and popular, with most drawn from the standard repertoire, though there is the occasional surprise such as Aleksandr Mosolov's 'Foundry' played on 17 August 1940, well before Soviet Russia's entry into the war, or the Overture to Hindemith's *Neues vom Tage*, the opera that so outraged Hitler in 1929, played on 20 August 1940. The wartime Proms repertoire was littered with the names of British composers rarely encountered today—Hamilton Harty, Walford Davies, Granville

Bantock, Rutland Boughton and Joseph Holbrooke. Dame Ethel Smythe's Overture to *The Wreckers* seems to have been a particular favourite. There are premieres of works that have since disappeared without trace: Ruth Gipps's 'A Knight in armour' presented on 22 August 1942 and Montague Phillips's 'Festival Overture: In praise of my country' on 26 June 1944. Numerous American and Russian works were given British premieres after those countries entered the war.

Inevitably, the organisers of the Proms were forced to rely upon a limited pool of soloists and the same names crop up on the concert programmes with regularity. This pool was, however, a remarkably rich one. Given the wartime propensity for Romantic piano concertos it is not surprising that pianists figure prominently; these included Lev Pouishnoff, Benno Moiseivitsch, Frederic Lamond, Mark Hambourg, Clifford Curzon, Irene Scharrer, Myra Hess, Maurice Cole, Solomon, Harriet Cohen, Cyril Smith, Phyllis Sellick and Louis Kentner. The most prolific of these were Clifford Curzon with 16 concerts, Myra Hess with 14, Benno Moiseivitsch with 13 and Cyril Smith and Moura Lympany with 11 each. By far the most frequently heard violinist was Ida Haendel with 12 concerts.[35] A quite extraordinarily high proportion of these instrumentalists were Jewish and one would hope that this was duly noted by those from King George VI downwards who had so ungenerously opposed the acceptance of European Jewish refugees in the pre-war period.

Amongst the singers, the most hard-working was Eva Turner who appeared in 16 concerts, mostly singing Wagner, an aspect of her repertoire that is sadly under-represented in her recorded output. Other popular singers at the Proms, in descending order of their number of appearances, were Frank Titterton, Parry Jones, Astra

The soprano Eva Turner frequently sang Wagner at the Proms.

Part I conducted by Sir Henry Wood

OVERTURE Egmont		*Beethoven*
VIOLIN CONCERTO in D		*Beethoven*
SYMPHONY No. 5, in C minor		*Beethoven*

Part II conducted by Basil Cameron

SYMPHONY in C		*Alan Bush*
(First performance)		
(Conducted by the Composer)		
OVERTURE The Boatswain's Mate		*Ethel Smyth*
Solo Violin IDA HAENDEL		

The concert will end at 8.50 approximately

Friday night was always Beethoven night at the Proms.

Desmond, Lilian Styles-Allen, Isobel Baillie, Joan Hammond, Roy Henderson and Mary Jarred.

Gerald Moore described the impact of the first major bombing raids on the Prom audiences: 'Everybody was advised when the programme was over that they would be safer to remain in their places. Half the audience preferred to return to their homes ... but for those who did not budge something had to be done. Basil Cameron, Sir Henry's assistant conductor, some of the orchestra, and I at the piano, led the audience in community singing; this was alternated by solo pieces from members of the orchestra and even by some of the audience contributing solos until our dispersal, hours later, when the "all clear" sounded.'[36]

On 26 August 1940 after a concert devoted to Wagner extracts and Strauss's tone poem *Till Eulenspiegel*, a large part of the audience was trapped in the Queen's Hall overnight by a severe bombing raid. The orchestra re-assembled and a resourceful member of the violin section announced as 'a famous British conductor now in Australia' appeared on stage in a perfect impersonation of Sir Thomas Beecham with all his ticks and mannerisms and conducted a very convincing overture to *The Marriage of Figaro*.[37] Presumably the orchestra had performed this piece so often under the baton of Sir Thomas that they could now do his interpretation without him. The 1940 Prom season was eventually abandoned after a concert on 7 September because of the intensification of the bombing raids on central London.

From the summer of 1941 the Proms took place in the vast and monstrous Albert Hall (that Sir Thomas Beecham had so casually invited German bombers to destroy in an American newspaper interview). The reason for this was the destruction of the old Queen's Hall in a particularly severe raid on 10 May 1940 that also destroyed the House of Commons and damaged Westminster Abbey. With its superb acoustic and its central position, the Queen's Hall was never to be replaced in the hearts of London's music lovers. More immediately disastrous than the destruction of the building was the loss of the instruments of the London Philharmonic Orchestra. They had been stored in the building overnight after an afternoon performance of Elgar's *Dream of Gerontius* and in anticipation of a rehearsal the following morning. The orchestra's administrator Bertha Geissmar came to survey the ruins of the building and the sad attempts to retrieve the charred remains of the instruments, and was taken aback by the calm reaction of the manager of the concert hall. 'We shook hands, and though deeply moved, like a true Britisher he did not reveal what this sight must have meant to him personally. He just said: "It looks a bit untidy, doesn't it?"'[38] Just as the public had come to the rescue of the orchestra at the beginning of the war through their financial donations, they once again came to its rescue by donating musical instruments so that it could continue performing.

The fifth and final Prom season of the war in 1944 began on 10 June 1944. The renewed German bombing in the early months of 1944, known as the 'Baby Blitz', had petered out in May and victory now seemed assured. The onset of the V1 rocket attacks on London only a few days later seemed to provoke more fear than the far more destructive area bombing of the Blitz in the winter of 1940-41, and the 1944 season was curtailed after only 17 concerts at the end of June.

If one person could be deemed to represent the musical life of London during the war, it would have to be the pianist Myra Hess. She had made her debut at the age of 17 in 1907, playing Beethoven's Fourth Piano Concerto at the Queen's Hall under the baton of Sir Thomas Beecham. By the outbreak of war Myra Hess was established as one of the most respected pianists of her time, admired in particular for the seriousness of her musicianship even in America where the dazzling virtuosity of pianists such as Joseph Hofmann and Vladimir Horowitz was in vogue.

Myra Hess was held in affection by audiences and by her younger colleagues alike. She was happy to be addressed as 'Auntie' by members of the Griller Quartet and in turn wrote to them as her 'dear nephews'. Despite her serene and dignified platform manner, she had an earthy sense of humour that

Myra Hess drawn by Nell Crombie and autographed by Myra Hess.

would occasionally break out in mid-concert. She was well known amongst friends for a hilarious impersonation of Queen Victoria for which by 1940 she had the *physique du rôle*. Hess was legendary for her kindness and generosity towards fellow musicians. Joyce Grenfell recalled her attempt to help a newly arrived refugee musician from central Europe whose name had unfortunate connotations for Anglo-Saxon ears. Grenfell was too coy to let us know what the name was, but we may guess. Myra Hess gently advised the man to change his name, which he duly did, but had visiting cards printed proudly bearing the new name and the old one in brackets.

When the war broke out Hess had just signed the most lucrative contract of her career for a seven-month tour of America and Australia to start in November 1939. She could easily have followed the example of Sir Thomas Beecham and sat out the war in the comfort and safety of the United States. Instead she chose to break her contract and remain in London. It was a courageous decision. Not only did she elect to share the dangers of her fellow Londoners during the Blitz, but as a Jew she knew that in the not unlikely eventuality of a German victory she would have faced a terrible fate.

Hess was dismayed at the lack of music available to the British public in the first fortnight of the war and on 16 September 1939 she wrote pleadingly and admonishingly to the BBC: 'Since the outbreak of the war, the whole world has been listening in to England, and the entire nation has been waiting in vain for programmes of good music befitting the dignity and seriousness of the present situation.'[39] Receiving no response Hess discussed with her friends ways in which she could make a difference to wartime British musical life and came up with the idea of approaching the director of the National Gallery, Sir Kenneth Clark, with a request to use the Trafalgar Square building, newly emptied of its pictures, as a venue for the occasional concert. Enthused by the idea Sir Kenneth answered: 'Why not give one *every day?*' Permission was needed (and gained with remarkable speed) from the trustees of the National Gallery, and from the Home Office and the Ministry of Works in view of the ban on public gatherings in the first month or so of the war.

The first concert took place on 10 October 1939 and was given by Myra Hess herself 'in case the whole thing is a flop.' She need not have worried. Despite a Home Office directive that no more than 200 should be admitted, around a thousand were squeezed in with many more disappointed music-lovers left out on the street. That first concert consisted of two Scarlatti sonatas, two Bach preludes and fugues, Beethoven's 'Appassionata' Sonata, a group of Schubert dances, two pieces by Chopin, three of the Opus 119 Intermezzi by Brahms, and ended with the piece most popularly associated with Myra Hess—her own arrangement of Bach's chorale, 'Jesu Joy of Man's Desiring'. (My own first encounter with the name of Myra Hess was as a small child when I bought a copy of the best-selling 7-inch 78 rpm plum-label record of this piece in a church bazaar.)

Sir Kenneth Clark was present at the first concert and described its impact. 'I do not think that anyone who was present at the first concert will forget it … I stood behind one of the curtains, and looked at the packed audience. They had come with anxious, hungry faces, but as they listened to the music and looked at Myra's rapt expression, they lost the thought of their private worries. I had never seen faces so transformed and I said to myself this is how men and women must have looked at the great preachers who gave them back their courage and their faith.'[40]

It was to be the first of 1,698 concerts that continued until 10 April 1946. The composer Howard Ferguson, who acted as assistant to Myra Hess, calculated that '238 pianists, 236 string players, 64 wind players, 157 singers, 24 string quartets and 56 other ensembles, besides 13 orchestras, 15 choirs, and 24 conductors'[41] took part in the series and all for minimal fees. Myra Hess took nothing for the 146 concerts in which she appeared, nor for tireless work in organising the whole series.

The repertoire continued very much as it had begun, dominated by the Austro-German classical tradition, particularly when Myra Hess herself was playing. Bach, Mozart, Beethoven, Schubert, Schumann and Brahms took the lion's share of the programmes.

One of the advantages of the National Gallery building was that it possessed some of the sturdiest cellars in Central London that made very effective bomb shelters. During the worst period of the Blitz from September 1940 to June 1941 the concerts descended into these cellars, where audiences endured freezing cold, stifling heat and leaking roofs. Some physical comfort was brought by the setting up of a canteen that served the best sandwiches to be had in wartime London. Though the National Gallery was hit by bombs on several occasions and severely damaged, there was only one occasion, on 1 October 1940, when an unexploded bomb caused the concert to migrate to neighbouring South Africa House. On 23 October of the same year a concert continued while a bomb disposal team attempted to deal with a thousand pound unexploded bomb in another part of the building. The bomb exploded of its own accord in the middle of the Scherzo of Beethoven's 'Razumovsky' Quartet, happily while the bomb disposal team were taking their lunch break.

In addition to her onerous duties at the National Gallery, Myra Hess played in fourteen wartime Proms, concertized around the country, was summoned to Buckingham Palace to distract Queen Elizabeth while she posed for a portrait by Augustus John, and found time to go to Bletchley Park to entertain an audience of codebreakers. Hess became a national figure whose fame spread beyond the restricted world of classical music. In June 1941, in recognition of her role in boosting the morale of the nation, she was made 'Dame Commander of the British Empire'. A rather shy woman, she had to accustom herself to public speaking. The price of persuading a military brass band to move on from Trafalgar Square during her concerts was that she had to climb onto the wings of a B36 bomber in the square and make a public appeal for war savings.

The Crown Film Unit took Myra Hess's music making to a wider audience than could come to the National Gallery, by filming her performing the first movement of Beethoven's 'Appassionata'. It is music that exemplifies those qualities of heroic struggle that gave Beethoven such universal appeal during the war. Dame Myra's hair tied up in a style dating from the Edwardian era gives her a reassuringly old-fashioned air. She plays with un-showy concentration against the background of the vast empty frame of Pollaiuolo's *Martyrdom of St Sebastian*. We get even more of a sense of what a National Gallery concert was like from a brief excerpt of a Mozart piano concerto included in Humphrey Jennings' famous wordless documentary *Listen to Britain*. Here, Dame Myra is accompanied by the uniformed orchestra of the Central Band of HM Royal Air Force. The camera homes in on leaking ceilings, sandbags, fire buckets, sandwiches and tea, and rapt faces. We glimpse the Queen in the audience wearing her customary regal smile and seated beside the gallery's grinning director, Sir Kenneth Clark.

The BBC recruited Dame Myra to make a broadcast with the actor Marius Goring, intended to refute the repeated claims made over the German radio that Britain was 'Das Land ohne Musik' and had no culture. It was billed as 'Britain's reply to Goebbels by Hess and Goring'.[42]

Clearly Goebbels had touched a sensitive point. A wartime statement of policy by the BBC asserted: '... the BBC regards it as a matter of first importance to develop a strong sense of pride in British music in order to exorcise the long-standing national sense of inferiority in music and to rid music of its status as a foreign art.'[43] In fact, a great deal of music of lasting value was written by British composers during the war, rather more than by German composers if one removes the special case of Richard Strauss from the equation.

Amongst the British composers who emerged from the war with reputations enhanced was Ralph Vaughan Williams. Sixty-seven years old when war broke out, Vaughan Williams had already inherited the mantle of Elgar as the 'Grand Old Man' of British music. Like Maggie Teyte, Gerald Moore, Joan Hammond and even Myra Hess for a very short time, Vaughan Williams initially busied himself with non-musical matters before coming to the conclusion that he could best serve his country through music. At the end of September 1939 he wrote to his future wife Ursula Wood: 'Is it Herbert Fisher's *History of Europe* you are reading?—magnificent book—depressing—all good things men try to do perish ... but nothing can destroy music— (a platitude).'[44]

Vaughan Williams worked on two of his greatest symphonies during the war—the serene Fifth Symphony (1938-43) and the desolate and turbulent Sixth Symphony (1944-47). Though the composer denied programmatic intent, it was inevitable that the Fifth Symphony would be interpreted as a vision of post-war peace and the Sixth Symphony as a reflection on the tragedy of war. The Fifth Symphony was performed to great acclaim in a Prom concert on 24 June 1943 with the composer conducting and received its first commercial recording a few months later with the Hallé under Barbirolli.

Vaughan Williams also wrote a quantity of music more directly connected with the war, including a number of film scores for propaganda and documentary films, and the cantata 'Thanksgiving for Victory', commissioned somewhat prematurely by the BBC in 1943. Composed to texts taken from the Bible, Shakespeare and Rudyard Kipling, it was recorded on 5 November 1944, so as to be ready for broadcasting at the imminently-expected end of the war.

By 1939 William Walton had moved on from the cheeky insouciance of *Façade*, his setting of the Surrealist poems of Edith Sitwell, to become a composer of considerable *gravitas* and of large-scale symphonic and choral works. In an essay of 1946 which displays a disapproval of 1920s experimentalism that could hardly have been outdone by a Nazi musicologist, A L Bacharach commented: 'Then as now, Walton was a man of the moment, the fashionable composer of the intelligentsia.'[45] The 37-year-old composer was saved from military service by the intervention of the director of the films division of the Ministry of Information. His career was thus deflected away from the concert hall and towards the writing of film music for the next five years. Some of this film music was good enough to survive independently and to make its way into the concert hall. The 'Prelude and Fugue: the Spitfire', composed for the film *The First of the Few*, with a fine pastiche Elgar opening section, was first performed as a concert piece by the Liverpool Philharmonic conducted by the composer on 2 January 1943. Walton's music played such an important role in Laurence Olivier's patriotic film of *Henry V* that certain scenes were filmed to fit the music rather than the other way round. Walton's reputation was such that the British Council commissioned a recording of his stirring pre-war choral masterpiece *Belshazzar's Feast* to be distributed abroad as cultural propaganda.[46]

Another composer whose music was deflected along different paths by the war was the 36-year-old Lennox Berkeley. Berkeley spent most of the war working for the BBC in various capacities and also writing music for both feature and documentary propaganda films. He found time to write plenty of independent music and, according to his biographer Tony Scotland, believed that: 'Music can play such a role in this war as few people dream.'[47] Nevertheless, most of what he wrote at this time has no obvious connection with the war.

A work that caught the fancy of the British public was Julius Harrison's 'Bredon Hill, Rhapsody for Violin and Orchestra'. Belonging to the same generation as Vaughan Williams, Harrison was an intensely conservative composer; 'Bredon Hill' has more than a whiff of the First World War about it, and of those works written just before and just after that war that were imbued with the nostalgic yearnings of A E Housman's *A Shropshire Lad*. 'Bredon Hill' was first performed in a concert broadcast to the British Empire on 29 August 1941 and later re-broadcast to America. It may have dampened the eyes of British expatriates but was unlikely to have had the same effect on Americans. In an introductory talk it was explained that the piece was a 'witness to the eternal spirit of England'. An example of what is sometimes dubbed the 'English cow-pat' school of music, it is the

Tiefland. *Cover of score.*

The Paris Exposition of 1937 by night. (L'Illustration. Album. *1937)*

Tout va très bien Madame la Marquise.

Paris under allied bombardment June 1944.(L'Illustration June 1944)

'Academie Nightmare' by Nell Crombie.

Raymond Legrand on the cover of a fan magazine.

*The first edition of the radio magazine on 27 April 1941
featuring the operetta star Yvonne Printemps.*

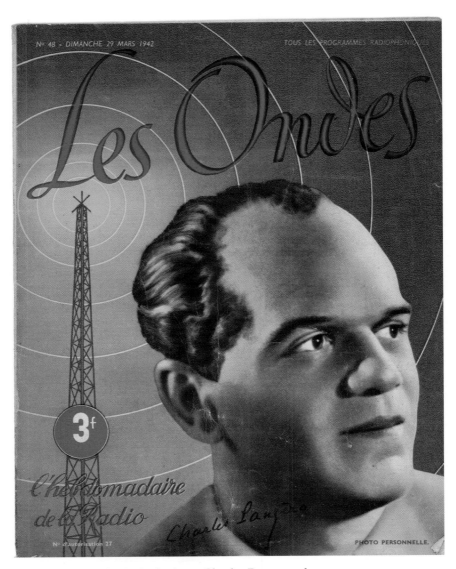

*The Swiss baritone Charles Panzera who was one
of the finest interpreters of the French art song.*

Popular film star Ginette Leclerc.

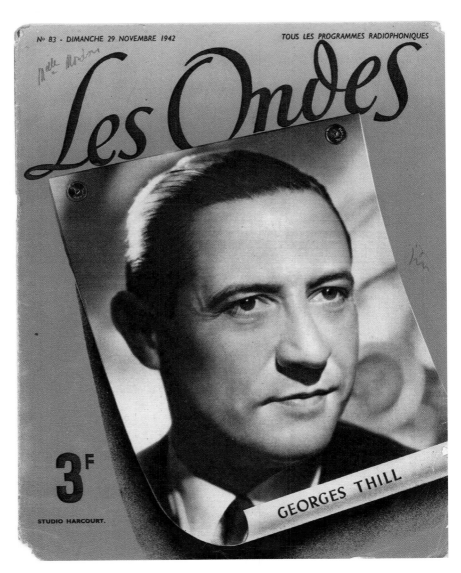

Georges Thill, the most admired French operatic tenor of his period.

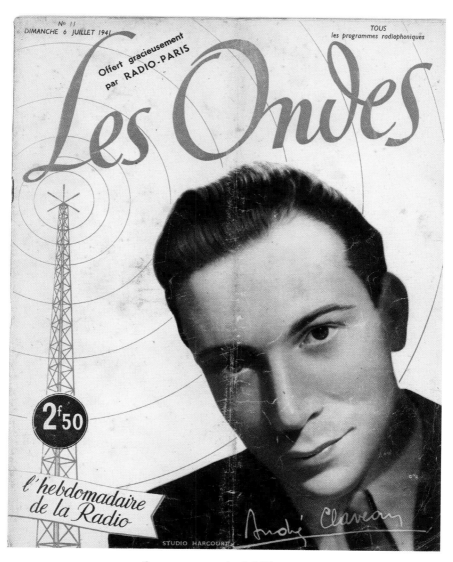

Suave crooner André Claveau.

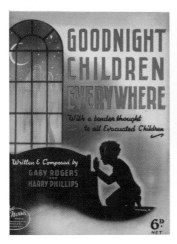

'The stars will remember'. Music sheet.

'Goodnight children everywhere'. Music sheet.

'Somewhere in France with you'. Music sheet.

'Wish me luck
as you wave
me goodbye'.
Music sheet.

'When the lights
go on again'.
Sheet music.

'Good Night'.
Sheet music.

'Till the lights
of London
shine again'.
Sheet music'.

'Le Vagabond'.
Song sheet.

'The White Cliffs
of Dover'.
Sheet music.

'Un bruit de sabots'.
Song sheet.

'Un avion tout blanc'.
Song sheet.

'Ça sent si
bon la France'.
Song sheet'.

'We're gonna hang out the washing on the Siegfried Line' represented the bluster and false optimism of the Phoney War.

musical equivalent of the posters of idyllic rural England bearing the slogan: 'This is your England—fight for it!'

Three important young British composers declared themselves to be pacifists and conscientious objectors, with varying consequences. Alan Bush's pacifism stemmed from his left-wing political convictions. His support of the 'People's Convention' in 1940 led to a ban on the broadcast of his music. Bush wrote a scathing letter of protest to the magazine *Picture Post*:

> Last week, the two Governors of the B.B.C. drove that institution one more step along the totalitarian path. I had a meeting with two B.B.C. officials from whom I learned that it is proposed to ban not only the microphone appearance of all People's Convention signatories, but their compositions also. I asked why the B.B.C. proposed to ban my works and yet broadcast those of Richard Strauss, who occupies a leading official position in Nazi Germany (though I agree Strauss's works should not be banned). The B.B.C.'s answer was that Strauss does not derive financial benefit! Further, they declared that if I stated in writing that I no longer supported the People's Convention, now or at any time in the future, I should be readmitted to broadcasting. This sounded to me like a palpable attempt to threaten or bribe me to change my political opinions. But the B.B.C. denied this was their intention. 'Democracy is fighting for its life,' said Mr. Ogilvie in last week's *Picture Post*. I wonder what he means by democracy.[48]

Bush was bravely supported by Vaughan Williams who, while disassociating himself from Bush's political views, withdrew a choral song that had been commissioned from him by the BBC in protest at the corporation's treatment of the younger composer.[49]

For Michael Tippett the consequences of his pacifism and his refusal to undertake agricultural or other war work were more severe. In 1943 he was sentenced to three months' imprisonment in Wormwood Scrubs. Harsh though this may seem, it was undoubtedly less draconian than the treatment of would-be conscientious objectors in Nazi Germany where in 1942 suicide was the only alternative to military service for the composer Hugo Distler.

Tippett had reacted to the outbreak of war with the naïve egotism typical of many artists on both sides in the conflict. 'My self-assurance as a composer and my technical skills meant that I could now stand by anything I had written ... I was currently beginning to get a few professional performances of my work and there were signs that the music might be published and recorded. At the very least, the war was a damned nuisance.' It was all the more of a nuisance because Tippett had just received an offer of a contract from the German music publisher Schott. The implications of working with a publisher in Nazi Germany do not seem to have occurred to Tippett, even by the time he wrote his autobiography in 1991: 'In the event, I had to wait until the war ended for anything significant to come of it. What mattered was that I had received a first hint that I could belong to the European musical scene.'[50]

In October 1940 Tippett took on responsibility for re-organising the music department of Morley College after it had been bombed. There he worked with a number of émigré musicians including the composers Walter Goehr and Matyas Seiber and the string players Norbert Brainin, Peter Schidlof and Siegmund Nissel, bringing a much needed stimulus to London's wartime musical life. Tippett's pacifism was genuine enough. '... although I agreed that Nazism was evil, I thought war was the wrong means for defeating it. I couldn't accept that Hitler's evil acts justified the gratuitous slaughter unleashed by Stalin, Churchill or the Allies. After all, it is the innocents who suffer most on either side—the mothers and children of Dresden, of Coventry or wherever.'[51]

In fact it was not Tippett's pacifism that earned him a prison sentence but his refusal to do any kind of war work or even what was termed 'approved cultural activity'. Once again Vaughan Williams attempted to come to the rescue, testifying at his tribunal: 'I think Tippett's pacifist views entirely wrong, but I respect him very much for holding them so firmly. I think his compositions are very remarkable and form a distinct national asset and will increase the prestige of this country in the world. His teaching at Morley College is distinctly work of national importance to create a musical atmosphere at the college and elsewhere.'[52]

In prison Tippett was allowed a copy of Bach's 'The Art of Fugue', which he used to improve his sight-reading, and he asked to organise a prison orchestra. By a strange coincidence, he was reunited with his friends and fellow conscientious objectors Benjamin Britten and Peter Pears, who had been asked to give a prison concert. 'Ben and Peter brought along with them John Amis to act as page-turner, but

I had protested to the authorities that the music was so complicated that the recital would be impossible unless I also turned the pages for the pianist. This was allowed, though it was touch and go: at the last moment I stepped out of the ranks of prisoners and sat down unexpectedly on the platform beside Ben. It was a strange moment for both of us.'[53]

On the day that Tippett was released from prison, his Second String Quartet was performed at the Wigmore Hall. His comment was: 'England was a very curious, tolerant country then.'[54] That tolerance did not extend to nudity and Tippett nearly found himself back in prison a few days later when he was spotted by a coast guard, bathing nude with three friends.

Tippett's most important wartime composition and perhaps his most significant work altogether was the cantata *A Child of Our Time*. This piece was inspired by the story of Herschel Grynszpan, a 17-year-old Polish Jewish boy who assassinated a German diplomat in Paris on 7 November 1938, triggering the notorious anti-Semitic riots of *Kristallnacht*. In Tippett's own words: '*A Child of Our Time* arose out of the general situation in Europe before the Second World War. But a Europe, for me, stretching out through its torments towards Russia in the East and even America in the West. So that though, after much searching, the final jolt into composition came from a particular political event, I knew from the first that this work itself had to be anonymous and general, in order to reach down to the deeper levels of our common humanity.'[55]

Tippett began work on the day war was declared against Germany, 3 September 1939, and completed it in 1941. *A Child of Our Time* had to wait until 19 March 1944 for its first public performance under the émigré conductor Walter Goehr and with Joan Cross and Peter Pears among the soloists. The cantata made an immediate and deep impact. A L Bacharach wrote: 'Such universality of address as Tippett achieves in *A Child of Our Time* exalts the work into a realm infinitely removed from controversy about the text. He has written, indeed, what may prove to be the most important oratorio by a British composer since Elgar's *Dream of Gerontius*.'[56] A remarkable wartime document of Tippett's work is the recording made in 1941 of his 'Fantasy Sonata' No. 1 by the pianist Phyllis Sellick.

Both Britten and Pears were conscientious objectors and though Britten, like Tippett, had refused to do alternative war work he had been treated more leniently. However, the pacifism and the homosexuality of Britten and Pears engendered a great deal of hostility. In particular, their absence in America in the early part of war was viewed by many with resentment. An enthusiastic review of the premiere of Britten's Violin Concerto by Ernest Newman, the doyen of British music critics, in *The Sunday Times* in April 1941 while Britten was still in America, triggered an acerbic correspondence that Newman dubbed 'The Battle of Britten'. It spilled over into the pages of the specialist journal *Musical Times* with the composer E J Moeran coming to Britten's defence:

> It seems to be assumed that Mr Britten went to America at the beginning of the war ... In fairness to Mr Britten I would point out that he left this country many weeks earlier, and that at the time of the outbreak he was already fulfilling engagements in the USA.
> Provided that he keeps valid his artistic integrity, I consider that he is doing his duty in remaining where he is.
> The death of Butterworth in 1915 was a tragedy, the nature of which no country with any pretensions to the preservation of culture and a respect for art can afford a recurrence.[57]

The war years coincided with a fruition of Britten's genius and the freshest phase of his musical inspiration. The song cycle 'Les Illuminations' was completed in October 1939 and premiered in London on 30 June 1940. At the end of 1939 Britten, Strauss and Ibert amongst other Western composers were commissioned to write works to celebrate the 2600th anniversary of the Japanese Empire. Britten offered the Sinfonia da Requiem. This was followed by another of his finest works, the song cycle 'The Seven Sonnets of Michelangelo'.

If Britten felt any moral qualms about accepting a hefty fee from the war-mongering Japanese, he comforted himself with the thought that the work was intended to express his 'anti-war convictions'. It was just as well for Britten's reputation that the Japanese, having paid him, did not include his work in their festival because of its Christian character. Britten blithely explained to his friend Ralph Hawks that the Japanese would not be able to reclaim the money from him because he had already spent it on a second-hand Model T Ford.

Remarkably, we can hear 'Les illuminations', the Sinfonia da Requiem and the 'Seven Sonnets of Michelangelo' in performances close in time to their creation—'Les illuminations' in a radio broadcast of the first American performance on 18 May 1941 with Peter Pears singing and Britten conducting. Of the Sinfonia da Requiem we have the second performance given at Carnegie Hall on 30 March 1941 under Barbirolli. The 'Seven Sonnets' exist in a private recording made by Pears and Britten in America, prior to the official premiere in Britain in 1942.

Britain and Pears made it back to Britain across the U-boat infested Atlantic in April 1942. During the torturously long voyage Britten had time to compose the 'Hymn to St Cecilia' and to sketch the first version of 'A Ceremony of Carols'.

Returning to Britain as conscientious objectors meant facing a tribunal. Britten was lucky in having the powerful backing of the BBC (even though there were many within the organisation who continued to regard Britten and Pears with distaste and suspicion). The corporation provided the following testimonial: 'This is to bring to the notice of the tribunal considering the case of Mr Britten that Mr Britten has been commissioned by us to write music for a series of important broadcast programmes designed to explain this country to listeners in America, and we hope to be able to use Mr Britten's services for musical compositions in connection with a large number of similar programmes.'[58]

These musical duties allowed Britten to complete another work which did much to consolidate his reputation and fulfil the high expectations of him—the 'Serenade for Tenor, Horn and Strings', which was premiered at the Wigmore Hall on 15 October 1943 with Pears and Dennis Brain as soloists.

The trigger for Britten's return to his native country and ultimately for his operatic masterpiece *Peter Grimes* was his chance reading of the 29 May 1941 issue of the BBC magazine *The Listener*. Britten and Pears were in California at the time, intending to cross the Mexican border in order to re-enter the United States on the 'labour quota' and remain permanently. This particular issue of *The Listener* contained an article by E M Forster on the eighteenth-century poet George Crabbe, who was, like Britten, a native of Suffolk and who celebrated the people and landscape of the Suffolk coast in his poetry.

Britten found a copy of *The Poetical Works of the Rev. George Crabbe* in a Los Angeles bookshop and was struck by the tale of the violent and alienated fisherman Peter Grimes in Crabbe's narrative poem 'The Borough'. Many years later he explained: 'In a flash I realized two things: that I must write an opera, and where I belonged.'[59]

Though the eighteenth-century plot of *Peter Grimes* had nothing to do with the war, the opera was very much a product of its time and of Britten's particular circumstances. As conscientious objectors and homosexuals, Britten and Pears identified with Grimes, who excited the suspicion and hostility of his fellow citizens.

Britten explained: 'A central feeling for us was that of the individual against the crowd, with ironic overtures for our own situation. As conscientious objectors we were out of it. We couldn't say that we suffered physically, but naturally we experienced tremendous tension. I think it was partly this feeling which led us to make Grimes a character of vision and conflict, the tortured idealist he is, rather than the villain he was in Crabbe.'[60]

Before Britten left America he had a firm commission from the conductor Serge Koussevitsky for the opera. It was intended that *Peter Grimes* should be premiered at the Berkshire Music Festival in Massachusetts in the summer of 1944. Due to wartime exigencies the Festival was cancelled. Koussevitsky generously gave permission for a British premiere. After several delays the premiere took place on 8 June 1945, exactly one month after the end of the war in Europe, as the first post-war performance in the re-opened Sadler's Wells Theatre. Despite a poisonous backstage atmosphere during rehearsals that must have reinforced Britten and Pears's identification with the protagonist of the opera, the premiere was a sensational success and *Peter Grimes* hailed as the greatest English opera since Purcell's *Dido and Aeneas* in the seventeenth century. Hopes were expressed that *Peter Grimes* heralded a golden age of British opera and the renewal of the art form itself. This was not to be. *Peter Grimes* is a swan song, not a new beginning. It was the unique product of its wartime circumstances and its powerful impact could never be replicated, even by Britten himself.

1 Susie Gilbert, *Opera for Everybody*, 2009, p. 71.
2 Bertha Geissmar, *The baton and the jackboot*, p. 366.
3 Gilbert, p. 79.
4 Michael Stapleton, *The Sadler's Wells Opera*, 1954, p. 10.
5 Robert Bunyard, 'Joan Cross and Edith Coates. Pioneers of Opera in England', *The Record Collector*, March 2011, pp. 32-78.
6 Ibid., p. 49.
7 Sarah Hardy, *Dame Joan Hammond*, 2010, p. 118.
8 Kyra Vane, *A Voice Reborn*, 1999, p.175.
9 Ibid., p. 52.
10 Maurice Leonard, *Slobodskaya*, 1979.
11 C.E.M.A., *The Arts in Wartime*, 1943, p. 3.
12 Ibid., p. 3.
13 Basil Dean, *The Theatre at War*, 1956, p. 21.
14 Ivor Newton, *At the Piano*, 1966, p. 122.
15 Newton, p. 224.
16 Leonard, p. 91.
17 *The Times*, Obituary, June 24, 2011, p. 64.
18 Gerald Moore, *Am I too loud?*, 1962, p. 120.
19 Garry O'Connor, *The Pursuit of Perfection*, 1979, p. 187.
20 Ibid., p. 186.
21 Ibid., p. 189.
22 Isobel Baillie, *Never sing louder than lovely*, 1982, p. 130.
23 Ibid., p. 64.
24 Christopher Fifield, *Letters and diaries of Kathleen Ferrier*. 2011, p. 21.
25 Ibid., p. 26.
26 Michael Kennedy, *Barbirolli*, London: Hart Dairs MacGibbon, 1971.
27 Ibid., p. 173.
28 Ibid., p. 176.
29 Dean, p. 420.
30 Ibid., p. 421.
31 Charles Reid, *Malcolm Sargent*, 1968, p. 275.
32 Reid, p. 295.
33 *Parade*, Vol.17, no. 22, November 4, 1944, p. 14.
34 Moore, p. 123.
35 BBC Proms Archive.
36 Moore, p. 124.
37 Geissmar, p. 377.
38 Ibid., p. 389.
39 Marian C McKenna, *Myra Hess: a portrait,* London: Hamilton, 1976, p. 140.
40 *Myra Hess. By her friends.* 1966, p. 99.
41 Ibid.
42 McKenna, p. 149.
43 Lewis Foreman, *From Parry to Britten*, 1987, pp. 273-4.
44 Ursula Vaughan Williams, *RVW. A biography of Ralph Vaughan Williams*, 1964, p. 230.
45 A L Bacharach, *British Music of Our Time*, 1946, p. 137.
46 Neil Tierney, *William Walton*, 1984, p. 104.

47 Tony Scotland, *Lennox and Frida*, 2010, p. 326.

48 Lewis Foreman, *From Parry to Britten*, 1987, p. 239.

49 Ibid., pp. 239-240.

50 Michael Tippett, *Those Twentieth Century Blues*, 1991, p. 114.

51 Ibid., p. 121.

52 Ursula Vaughan Williams, p. 255.

53 Michael Tippett, p. 145.

54 Vaughan Williams, p. 255.

55 Michael Tippett, *A passion that asks questions*, 1965, p. 6.

56 Bacharach, p. 234.

57 Foreman, p. 242.

58 Ibid., p. 242.

59 Humphrey Carpenter, *Benjamin Britten*, 1992, p. 156.

60 Ibid., p. 203.

Chapter 8
EAST WEST MUSICAL ENCOUNTERS:
NORTH AFRICA AND THE MIDDLE EAST

North Africa was one of the principal theatres of war between 1940 and 1943. The Allied victories at El Alamein and Stalingrad thwarted a pincer movement of German armies with an intended meeting point in the Middle East. Though the Middle East itself remained a military backwater, apart from skirmishes between French factions in Syria and manoeuvres by the British in Iraq, it remained an area of vital strategic importance. The Suez Canal was Britain's lifeline to its empire, and the oil fields of the Middle East were one of the keys to ultimate victory. Throughout the war the Middle East was densely manned with military personnel, for whom musical entertainment was provided by ENSA and other organisations.

Along the fault line between Western and Islamic cultures from Lebanon to Morocco, Europeans and Arabs were introduced to one another's musical traditions during the war. However, music often proved to be a dividing rather than a uniting factor. With increasing numbers of European refugees arriving in Palestine in the 1930s, the Jewish community in Palestine became an important outpost of Western musical culture. In the 1930s, the rise of Nazism and of anti-Semitism in other Eastern and Central European countries triggered a huge rise in the rate of Jewish immigration to Palestine. 175,000 refugees arrived between 1932 and 1939. These were very different from earlier pioneers of the Zionist movement. Many were cultivated and thoroughly assimilated Europeans. They were not necessarily motivated by the Zionist ideal and came to Palestine because there was nowhere else to go. Their devotion to European ways of living and dressing earned them the derisive nickname of Yecke ('jackets'). They remained equally wedded to the musical traditions of the countries from which they came. These musical traditions would presumably have meant as little to the descendents of the Jews who had lived in the Holy Land since the Middle Ages as they did to Palestinian Arabs or the Oriental Jews who arrived after the creation of the state of Israel. Significantly 'Hatikvah', the anthem of the local Zionist movement that was later adopted as the Israeli national anthem, was set to music in 1888 by an immigrant from Bessarabia called Samuel Cohen, who borrowed a traditional European melody, most famously used by Smetana in his patriotic tone poem 'Ma Vlast'. The melody of this unusually melancholic national anthem is more redolent of the rivers and forests of Middle

Clash of cultures in the Middle East.

Europe than it is of the River Jordan and the deserts of the Middle East.

The most conspicuous and remarkable fruit of the transposition of Middle European musical culture into the Middle East was the creation in 1936 of the Palestine Symphony Orchestra. This was largely due to the heroic efforts of the great Polish violinist Bronislav Huberman. From the first, Huberman had taken a principled and very public stand against Nazi policies. In an open letter to Furtwängler he explained why he could not accept an invitation to perform in Germany in the 1934 season. The organisation of an orchestra in Palestine was an attempt to mitigate the situation of persecuted German Jewish musicians. The enterprise was blessed and validated by the generous offer of Arturo Toscanini to conduct the inaugural concerts free of charge. Toscanini's action should be interpreted as a gesture of solidarity with Germany's Jews rather than as an endorsement of a nascent Jewish state in the Middle East. Despite mounting Arab hostility to Jewish immigration, the attitudes of Arabs and Jews were far from being as polarised as they were to become, and it is interesting to note that after completing the initial run of concerts in Palestine, the conductor went on to Egypt where he repeated the same concerts in Cairo and Alexandria.

226

Le porte-avion « Italie »

Italy as an aircraft carrier; the war in the Mediterranean as seen from the Axis point of view.

The marathon programme of the inaugural concert consisted almost entirely of music from the Austro-German classical tradition. The exception was Rossini's *La scala di seta* overture which began the concert; it was followed by Schubert's 'Unfinished' Symphony, Brahms Symphony No 4, excerpts from Mendelssohn's 'A Midsummer Night's Dream' and Weber's *Oberon* Overture. A second concert programme consisted entirely of Beethoven. Throughout the early years of the orchestra, Austrian and German composers continued to dominate the repertoire. As late as 1938, when Toscanini returned for a second series of concerts, Wagner (whose music would later be banned for public performance in the state of Israel) was still considered acceptable, and Toscanini included the Preludes to Acts 1 and 3 of *Lohengrin* alongside the music of Schubert, Beethoven, Mendelssohn, Saint-Saens, Tchaikovsky, and the contemporary Italian Jewish composer Leone Sinigaglia.

Huberman proudly noted how well these concerts were supported by the local Jewish community and claimed that out of a population of 280,000, 8,000 were regular concertgoers. Later on during the war, a British army officer called Major C E Law, who had attended the Palestine Symphony Orchestra concerts, recalled: 'I don't think that I saw an empty seat … The Jews are, of course, an extremely musical race, but I was glad to notice so many non-Jewish folk in the audience—officers and men of the British, Greek, Czech and Polish armies.'[1] Apparently he did not notice any Arabs among the non-Jewish members of the audience.

One of the more colourful musical visitors to Palestine in the run-up to the Second World War was the strikingly beautiful British pianist Harriet Cohen. While she was on holiday in Egypt in the spring of

1939 she received a telegram from the Palestine Symphony Orchestra asking if she could replace the renowned cellist Emanuel Feuermann, who was unable to make the crossing from America to fulfil an engagement with the orchestra. The experience of playing in Palestine for a Jewish audience put her in touch with her own Jewish roots and politicized her. She became a passionate and very vocal advocate of Zionism. She even offered her services to the Foreign Office as a secret agent. From a report written by a Foreign Office official at the time, it would seem that she was not taken all that seriously.

> Miss Cohen talks so continuously and so vivaciously that the auditor is apt to lapse into a sort of coma, but I did gather that she had had some dealings with the New Zionist Organisation, and particularly with Jabotinsky ... Miss Cohen then asked whether she could be of any service to the British Government, suggesting that she might be sent on a mission to Palestine ... Miss Cohen talked about a good many other matters relating neither to Palestine nor Zionism, and finally departed saying that in her view we could not do better at this stage than let a Jewish army invade and occupy Lebanon![2]

The outbreak of the war interrupted the flow of distinguished conductors and soloists who frequently, like Toscanini, offered their services gratis or at reduced rates to the Palestine Orchestra. Huberman succeeded in returning in 1940 for a series of concerts in which he played the Mendelssohn and Brahms violin concertos. Huberman's last appearance with the orchestra that owed him so much was in Cairo on 20 February 1940. Once again he played the Mendelssohn and Brahms concertos, in a concert for the benefit of the Red Crescent Society under the patronage of King Farouk. The circumstances of this concert underline the noble ideals of Huberman and his desire to serve all of humanity. Toscanini's concerts with the Palestine Orchestra sparked intense interest and comment around the globe and were an undoubted fillip to Jewish aspirations in the Middle East. In so far as they were aware of this, Arab Palestinians may have perceived the creation of a first-class European orchestra in their midst as a threat rather than as an exercise in cultural bridge-building.

For many German Jewish orchestral players and jobbing musicians, the Palestine Orchestra must have seemed a god-sent lifeline. A more exceptional talent as a soloist was the best possible passport to safety elsewhere. Distinguished Jewish instrumentalists and singers still at the height of their powers usually chose to go to the Americas rather than to Palestine. Even William Steinberg, the first musical director of the Palestine Orchestra, moved on to America when the opportunity arose in 1938. The only locally-born opera singer of international reputation, the baritone Vittorio Weinberg (familiar to record collectors as an exceptionally sympathetic Sharpless in a complete recording of *Madama Butterfly*), chose to emigrate to America in 1939 to become cantor of the Beth Shalom synagogue in San Francisco and to sing occasional roles with the San Francisco Opera.

For Jewish singers at the end of their careers, Palestine was sometimes the only alternative to death in a cattle truck or a gas chamber. This was undoubtedly the case with the great Latvian tenor Hermann Jadlowker. Jadlowker had been a star of the Berlin Court Opera and of the Metropolitan Opera in New York before the First World War. At a gala performance of *Lohengrin* in Berlin, Kaiser Wilhelm II and Tsar Nicholas II had both laid claim to the Latvian-born tenor as 'their' Lohengrin. Though he specialized in heroic roles

such as Florestan and Otello, he is chiefly remembered today for a virtuosity in florid music that remains unmatched by any other tenor on record. In 1929 he retired from the stage and took up a post as chief cantor of the synagogue in Riga. Wisely, he chose to emigrate to Palestine in 1938 and remained there until his death in 1953. He gave occasional concerts during the war years and even a performance in his old starring role of Otello, but earned a living as a *Gesangpädagoge* (a term for which 'singing teacher' is a rather inadequate translation).[3]

The tenor Hermann Jadlowker, a nice Jewish boy from Riga who became the favourite Lohengrin of Kaiser Wilhelm II and Tsar Nicholas II, and ended up in Tel Aviv.

Anyone seeking musical training of the highest order in Palestine during the war years would have found it cheaply and easily. The author's mother Josephine Crombie, who had aspired to a singing career before the outbreak of war and who found herself in Palestine in 1944 serving with the British navy, took the opportunity to continue her training with a German Jewish émigré she knew as Mrs Weiss. In a letter of 17 April 1944 to her parents she explained how she made the contact. 'This afternoon I went to the music shop to ask if they had anywhere for me to play the piano, with no luck. However, they gave me the address of a man here who was the conductor of some opera house in Berlin. I'm very tempted

Josephine Crombie as a Wren stationed in Palestine.

to get in touch with him as he has two pianos, and with a woman who taught singing in Berlin as I admire the German way of singing. Of course they will be Jewish refugees and as such probably far more clever than a pure German.'

A great European opera singer who gave singing lessons towards the end of the war in Palestine was the Hungarian soprano Rose Pauly. After being forced to leave Germany, Pauly travelled the world—Vienna, London, New York, San Francisco and Buenos Aires, always singing the role with which she most closely identified—Elektra—in the opera by Richard Strauss. Her most successful pupil in Palestine was the soprano Hilde Zadek, also a refugee from Nazi Germany. Zadek described her teacher as a 'wild beast' and tormented soul who hardly needed to act the part of Elektra.[4] Zadek's career opportunities in Palestine as a dramatic soprano were extremely limited and at the end of the war, at the first opportunity, she returned to Europe and a brilliant career at the Vienna Opera.

If Ashkenazi immigrants in Palestine looked backwards to Europe, musically speaking, Palestinian Arabs and Jews of Levantine origin looked to Egypt. Cairo was the capital of the Arab film and entertainment industries and acted as a magnet for talent from all over the Arab world. The greatest stars of the period included Umm

Kulthum, Muhammad Abd al-Wahhab, Leila Mourad, Farid Al Atrash and his beautiful sister Asmahan. Arab traditions of music-making remained strong, though it was around this time that Western musical instruments and practices began to be incorporated into popular Arab music. Interestingly, being Jewish seems to have been no impediment to popularity in the Arab world, until the creation of the state of Israel. Several of the leading female singers of the period were of Jewish origin including Leila Mourad (who converted to Islam), the superb Algerian singer Reinette l'Oranaise, and Habiba Msika, who was the most popular singer in Tunisia until her brutal murder by a jealous lover.

The British attempted to hold themselves aloof from both Arabs and Jews to whom they had made conflicting promises during the First World War, with the result that they found themselves painted into a very awkward corner during the Second World War. There was always the chance that, resentful of increasing Jewish immigration and broken British promises, the Arabs might rise up to throw off the British yoke, as indeed the Grand Mufti of Jerusalem Mohammad Amin al-Husayni urged them to do in propaganda broadcasts from Nazi Germany. Perversely, there were extremist elements within the Zionist movement prepared to intrigue against the British with the Italians and even with the Germans in their determination to create a Jewish state. While still fighting Hitler, the British faced a mounting campaign of Jewish terrorism. At this point musical contacts between the British and Arabs and Jews were curtailed by strict instructions to military personnel not to fraternize with either. Josephine Crombie was obliged to turn down an invitation to sing for a local Jewish radio station for this reason.

Clumsy attempts by the British to placate Arab opinion by stemming the flow of Jewish refugees ended in tragedy and were in any case completely in vain. It is estimated that a further 50,000 Jewish refugees arrived in Palestine during the war. On one occasion at least, in a twist worthy of a movie plot, the British

The Grand Mufti of Jerusalem with Adolf Hitler.

were able to turn this disastrous situation to their own advantage, as recounted by Basil Dean, the head of ENSA. Henry Caldwell, the officer in charge of theatre shows in Cairo, was sent to investigate the arrival in Haifa of a ship loaded with illegal refugees and 'reported the presence of a number of Hungarian artistes of undoubted ability. From their number he created two complete variety entertainments ... one of them being given the title of "Café Continentale". This was the origin of the BBC television feature.'[5]

On the whole, the British rulers of Palestine preferred to act the role of musical philistines. Neither the Middle European 'high culture' of the Jews nor the indigenous musical culture of the Arabs was much to their taste. They preferred regimental bands, amateur performances of Gilbert and Sullivan, travelling productions of *No, No, Nanette* and the musical offerings of ENSA, such as Joyce Grenfell who could stretch to the Bach/Gounod 'Ave Maria', and her accompanist Viola Tunnard, who attempted to soothe her sometimes restive audiences with Chopin and Rachmaninov and encores of the 'Warsaw Concerto'.

In North Africa the earliest wartime attempts to entertain troops came from within the army itself. Travelling shows with names such as 'The Muddle Easters', 'Nomads of the Nile' and 'Middle East Varieties' were made up from military personnel. Towards the end of 1941 ENSA brought out the 'Hello Happiness' and 'Spotlights' entertainment companies. There were bitter complaints from the troops and caustic comments from Noel Coward and Joyce Grenfell about the dire quality of some of the ENSA entertainments. General Montgomery caused problems by adamantly refusing to allow female entertainers near the front—not because he feared for their safety but because he disliked women and thought they undermined the morale of his men.

Later, ENSA redeemed its reputation by sending companies with genuine star talent. The 'Fol-de Rols' brought Geraldo and his band, George Formby, Noel Coward, Florence Desmond and Gracie Fields. The 'Spring Company' included Vivien Leigh who recited scenes from *Gone with the Wind*, Dorothy Dickson, famous for her rendition of Jerome Kern's 'Look for the Silver Lining,' and Beatrice Lillie. Though grieving for her son who had been declared 'missing presumed dead', Bea Lillie maintained her reputation as the funniest woman on the planet. Even Noel Coward was impressed. 'Beatrice Lillie gave the most spectacularly brilliant performance I have ever seen her give. She never condescended or overplayed, she looked enchanting and sang with attack, ineffable humour and charm. It seemed to me that her always assured technique had gained a little extra magic; she played to those men with good will and a shining heart and, I need hardly add, absolutely tore the place up.'[6]

The most hard-working musical star in the North African theatre of war was the French singer Alice Delysia. With her well-trained soprano voice, her charming French accent and a nice line in *risqué double entendre*, Delysia had been a major star of the London stage since the First World War. By this time Delysia was well into her fifties and must have seemed like a relic from another age to troops weaned on Judy Garland and Vera Lynn. But as reported by Noel Coward she gave good value. 'She looked perfectly delightful and as young as ever. For two solid years she has been back and forth across the desert, tirelessly and uncomplainingly entertaining the troops, frequently under conditions that would send many temperamental leading ladies into screaming hysterics. She has bounced about in lorries and trucks and been under fire and lost in sandstorms and the net result of it all is that she looks happier and gayer and more vital than I have ever seen her.'[7]

The French and Italian settlers in North Africa must have been puzzled by Anglo-Saxon ideas of cultural entertainment. On 27 September 1943 in his *Middle East Diary* Noel Coward described a performance by the Royal Artillery Band in the opera house in Tripoli. 'It really was rather a peculiar performance. The RA Band played well but the high-voiced, twittering French social audience seemed a trifle bewildered by the whole thing.'[8]

In those areas of North Africa and the Middle East that had been dominated by the French and Italians, 'high culture' in the form of opera had been second only to Christianity as a means of imposing European cultural dominance. Wherever the French colonized, from Hanoi to Algiers, they built splendid opera houses. On the central avenue of colonial Tunis, a charming icing-sugar-white Art Nouveau opera house had been built opposite the Catholic cathedral, the façade of which was provocatively adorned with sculptures representing the triumph of Ecclesia over Synagogue. French opera companies featuring stars drawn from the Paris Opéra and the Opéra Comique travelled along the North African coast from Casablanca to Algiers, Oran and Tunis and various smaller towns with municipal theatres, presenting a nineteenth-century French repertoire with the odd Italian pot-boiler thrown in. Although Algeria gave France two remarkable opera singers, the baritone Dinh Gilly and the coloratura soprano Leila Ben Sedira, opera failed to put down deep local roots and when the French settlers eventually departed in the 1950s, opera left with them, and the splendid opera houses remained as relics of an unfulfilled dream of French cultural hegemony. When Noel Coward arrived in Oran in 1943 he discovered 'in the centre of the town of course, that inevitable, imperishable monument to French provincialism, a Municipal opera house. This one looked a bit decayed, its façade was battered, either by bombardment or climate, and a lot of its plaster work was cracking, but there was still a weary old playbill of *La Bohème* pasted on to one of its columns.' Coward saw it as a sign of the changing times that there

The splendid opera house in Oran was, according to Noel Coward, ' an imperishable monument to French provincialism'.

was also a poster announcing: 'To-Nite! Bing Crosby and Dorothy Lamour', adding: 'I really felt quite sorry for the poor old Municipal Opera House.'[9]

Up until the Allied landings in November 1942 it had been business as usual for these municipal opera houses. In the final months of 1939 during the *drôle de guerre*, the exquisite lyric soprano Germaine Féraldy sang in performances of *Manon*, *Le Barbier de Séville*, *Faust* and *Mireille* in the opera houses of Algiers and Tunis. In Tunis the tenor scheduled to sing Almaviva fell sick. As substitute Rossini tenors were not to be found in wartime Tunisia, the redoubtable Féraldy donned male costume and sang the tenor role opposite the soprano Lucienne Tragin.[10] For the many refugees from metropolitan France in wartime Algiers, the frequent appearances at the opera of the clarion-voiced Corsican tenor César Vezzani must have been a particular pleasure.

The collapse of metropolitan France brought to music lovers among the *pieds noirs* the unexpected windfall of visits by France's two most celebrated opera singers—the tenor Georges Thill and the soprano Ninon Vallin. In February 1941 Thill sang in performances of *Carmen* at the Algiers Opéra, *Samson et Dalila* and *I Pagliacci* at Tunis, and *I Pagliacci* at Constantine, as well as giving concerts at

Sétif, Bône, Oran, Rabat, Meknès and Sidi-Bel-Abbès.[11] Vallin, fearful of crossing the Atlantic to return to South America where she had been the most idolized soprano of the interwar period after Claudia Muzio, chose instead to go to North Africa, only to find her boat under fire from the Italian navy on the way. She appeared in concerts in Rabat, Fez and Tunis.[12]

Although the war in North Africa went badly for the Italians from the first, they maintained opera performances in Libya for as long as they could. As late as 1941 the celebrated Catalan soprano Mercedes Capsir gave guest performances in Tripoli and Bengazi.[13] After the Germans arrived in 1942, they too were keen to establish an operatic as well as a military presence and while they were briefly in control of Tunis in 1943 a certain Lieutenant Pfeiffer, former director of the German Opera in Moscow, staged a season of operas in the Tunis Opera House.

Further along the North African coast, the most venerable and prestigious of all North African opera houses was in Cairo, built in 1869 to celebrate the opening of the Suez Canal. In contrast with the French colonies, the taste for opera had penetrated more deeply into at least the upper strata of Egyptian society. Though Egypt was under the effective control of the British, the Cairo Opera was an Italian fiefdom. Italian impresarios and Italian stars dominated the Opera in the years before the war and for a short time after as well. Early in 1939 the Cairo Opera presented a season with the Italian tenor Aureliano Pertile. Though records from this time show that he was a little past his best, it must have been a thrill for Cairo audiences to hear one of the century's greatest tenors in four of his most famous roles: Otello, Manrico in *Il Trovatore*, Rhadames in the inevitable *Aida*, and Wagner's *Lohengrin* sung in Italian.[14] After the war there were operatic thrills of a different kind when the baritones Tito Gobbi and Gino Becchi battled it out for the favour of the Cairo audiences with enough intrigue and dirty tricks to furnish an opera plot.[15]

If Cairo ceased to be an operatic centre under British control and in the absence of the Italians, it gained in other ways. Like Lisbon, Marseilles before November 1942, and above all New York, the city became a buzzing cosmopolitan cultural centre as a result of the war. Cairo possessed its own symphony orchestra, which though it did not have the prestige of the Palestine Orchestra, achieved a respectable level.

Sunday night concerts under the baton of Hugo Rignold were sold out.

It was Rignold who, in October 1944, conducted the Cairo premiere of the 'El Alamein Concerto' for piano and orchestra by Albert Arlen. Born Albert Aarons, Arlen was an Australian of Turkish Jewish ancestry who was serving as an officer in the

The Cairo Opera House was used for many purposes other than opera during the war.

Royal Air Force. The piece is attractive in a cinematic way, a delightful rag-bag of musical clichés including a piano evocation of a bugle call, calculated to appeal to the broadest musical tastes. It was used in a wartime documentary film about the decisive battle of El Alamein. The seven-minute mini-concerto is a blatant imitation of Richard Addinsell's 'Warsaw Concerto', that was itself a blatant imitation of Rachmaninov's Second Piano Concerto. If anyone had stopped to think about it at the time, it should have seemed odd that a piece of music inspired by a British victory in North Africa was couched in a pastiche late Romantic Russian idiom borrowed from a film about Poland (*Dangerous Moonlight*) and that Arlen's Turkish background did not give him an ear for local colour and local musical idioms. Instead, the 'El Alamein Concerto' evokes incongruous images of dinner jackets amongst the sand dunes.

The famous Cairo Opera House was put to a variety of non-operatic uses. On 31 March 1944 Joyce Grenfell went there to watch a performance of the play *Night Must Fall* featuring its author Emlyn Williams and Adrienne Allen. It also hosted a long-running production of *The Merry Widow* with sets borrowed from a London production, and starring the Australian husband and wife team of Madge Elliott and Cyril Ritchard and the ballerina Diana Gould (later Mrs Yehudi Menuhin). While it is strange that the British would perform music in Cairo by an Austrian composer who was under the direct protection of Goebbels, it would seem that Hanna Glawari, like Lili Marleen, was a lady capable of crossing enemy lines.

The Cairo Opera was used for occasional concerts by local and visiting artists but Egyptian opera lovers had to content themselves with concert performances of extracts. As part of a Middle Eastern tour in 1943 the singers Miriam Licette, Nancy Evans, Walter Widdop and Dennis Noble, accompanied by the violinist Alfred Cave and the pianist Ivor Newton, gave a week of concerts in the Cairo Opera House. This was a fine line-up of the best singers that Britain had to offer, though the Egyptians, used to the high voltage performances of Pertile and other Italian singers of the time, may have found the more restrained British offerings, particularly the Anglo-Saxon virginal sounds of Miriam Licette, a little on the anaemic side. In fact Walter Widdop was one of the more red-blooded British tenors of the period. Ivor Newton relates how he was persuaded to give a full-throated account of Rhadames' aria 'Celeste Aida' on a moonlit visit to the pyramids.[16]

They all belonged to what Walter Legge, who was in charge of the classical music division of ENSA, called the 'Good Music' party. Basil Dean was agreeably surprised to hear of the 'fantastic success of the "Good Music" party as it flew over the desert wastes with its mini-piano, fiddle and glorious talent.' He was impressed by the musical tastes of the audiences. 'At Sharjah, a lonely RAF station on the Persian Gulf, reached after considerable delays caused by persistent sandstorms, the party decided upon a plebiscite concert—all requests to be sent in writing to the orderly room by 1 pm. The only concession to popular taste was the *Warsaw Concerto,* the remaining items, selected by majority vote, being as follows: the duet from the first scene of *Madam Butterfly* (Miriam Licette and Nancy Evans); Mendelssohn's Violin Concerto (Alfred Cave): excerpts from *Carmen;* two Beethoven sonatas (Ivor Newton); various operatic arias (Dennis Noble and Walter Widdop); Gounod's 'Ave Maria', and 'One fine day' from *Madam Butterfly* (Miriam Licette).'[17]

After the final defeat of the Axis powers in North Africa, Bea Lillie, George Formby, Joyce Grenfell, Noel Coward and a number of dance bands arrived to entertain the troops. Grenfell and Coward both left diaries of their North African and Middle Eastern experiences. Coward's was published to general derision and indignation in 1944. His account of sunbathing, gin-slings at the mess and ogling handsome young sailors went down badly in war-weary Britain, as did his self-important name dropping: 'At ten o'clock I went to call on General Eisenhower armed with a letter from Dickie [Admiral Lord Mountbatten].'[18]

Grenfell's far more perceptive and better-written diary (strictly forbidden as she was travelling with ENSA which banned the keeping of diaries) was first published many years later after her

death. For all her powers of
observation and the high literary
quality of the diaries, they also
exhibit the limitations of her
background and her period. There
is an unattractively snobbish
preoccupation with the vowel
sounds of every British person she
meets though this could be put
down perhaps to the professional
interest of a monologist. She
seems to be obsessed by personal
hygiene. We get detailed accounts
of almost every bath she took
over a period of months. What is
lacking from both these diaries is
any sense that the writers were

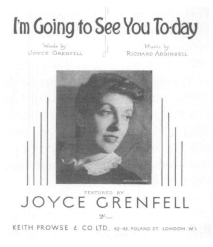

Joyce Grenfell was a sharp-eyed observer of North Africa and the Middle East.

able to engage with the local cultures of the places they visited. The
diaries suggest that the wartime collision of Arab and European
cultures brought very little interaction or mutual understanding.

In April 1944 Grenfell arrived at a military camp in Iraq to find
a British officer 'about to give a gramophone recital of Stainer's
Crucifixion to an audience of soldiers and a few English residents.' It
is unlikely that the officer was interested in edifying the natives but if
any had strayed in out of curiosity on a 'hottish and rather sultry' day,
the chances were that they would have been put off Western music
for life.[19]

In Cairo on 31 March 1944 Grenfell reported that her accompanist
Viola Tunnard had been 'taken to a Moslem wedding by two ADCs
and loved it, though they said it was disappointing. She said it was
very Birmingham and no one *talked*. They just waited, covered with
ill-set diamonds, for something to happen, and a mezzo-soprano
costing £150 a night sang with a range of six notes for well on an
hour!'[20] Though the singer is not identified, she could easily have been
Umm Kulthum, who frequently sang at weddings. The dark colour of
her voice and its relatively low range could be described in Western
parlance as 'Mezzo' and she would have been one of the few Egyptian
singers who could have commanded such an astronomical fee. The
greatness of Umm Kulthum's art, especially in live performances, lay
in her ability to improvise over lengthy periods of time with infinitely

varied nuances of expression. This aspect of Arab singing was clearly not appreciated by Viola Tunnard and her friends and is indeed difficult for any listener to appreciate who cannot follow the meaning of the text. The beauties of Arab music were and remain a closed book to many westerners.

In 1932 the art lover and musicologist Baron Rodolphe d'Erlanger, as the culmination of a life devoted to the study of Islamic art, had organised a musical conference in Cairo intended to demonstrate and preserve the great variety of Arab music. The conference was attended by such important Western musical figures as Béla Bartók, Paul Hindemith, Alois Haba, Egon Wellesz and Henri Rabaud, but it is not evident that any of them were significantly influenced by the experience. It would be interesting to know how Rabaud, who was best known for the decorative orientalism of his popular opera *Marouf*, reacted to hearing real Arab music. Another French composer of the same generation, Jean Cras, who died prematurely in the year of the conference, showed in his evocation of Arab music in his piano quintet, how Western musicians tend to hear Arab music as atmospheric sound rather than as structured music.

If the British authorities in Egypt failed to appreciate the subtleties of Umm Kulthum's art, they certainly understood the power of her hold over the hearts of millions of Arabs at a time when there was increasing resentment of the British domination of the region and when Arab support in the struggle against Hitler was far from guaranteed. Umm Kulthum was the first Arab artist to fully exploit the possibilities of the new media of records, radio and film to increase her fame.

Her concerts on the first Thursday of the month, beginning in the 1930s and continuing until her death in 1975, became a national institution and were listened to devoutly by millions of Egyptians in the war years.[21] Though overtly political songs would not have been tolerated by the British administrators of the Egyptian radio, the move away from romantic escapism in Umm Kulthum's repertoire towards a more populist style had a political dimension. It coincided with a rise in national consciousness that would eventually be fatal to British domination of the Middle East. At this point though, Umm Kulthum's ability to attract so many listeners to a radio station that was relatively friendly to British interests was in itself a huge asset to the Allied war effort and all the more important because in the early phase of the war, it was generally considered that the BBC Arabic Service came off worst in its propaganda duel with its German equivalent, which benefited from the services of a charismatic Iraqi announcer called Yunis al-Bahri.[22]

Nowhere in the world was radio more crucial to the outcome of the war than in the Middle East. The Italians were first in the field in the mid-1930s at the time of their Abyssinian adventure, with Arab language broadcasts from Bari aimed at disgruntled Palestinians and Egyptians. According to Andrew Walker in his history of the BBC World Service: 'Radio sets locked to Italian stations were reported to be distributed free or at very low cost to cafes and other places where Arabs congregated in large numbers'.[23] The Germans and the British followed from 1938. The British shot themselves in the foot with their very first Arabic broadcast on 3 January 1938, containing a news item about a Palestinian executed for the crime of owning a rifle: this caused outrage throughout the Arab world.[24]

The Iraqi radio announcer Yunis al-Bahri broadcasts to the Arab world from Germany.

Tensions between the British and the Egyptians were ratcheted up in February 1942 when British troops surrounded the Royal Palace and forced King Farouk to accept a pro-British government. The troops showed open disrespect to the Egyptian monarch by singing ribald words to the Egyptian national anthem:

> Up your pipe, King Farouk,
> Hang your bullock on a hook, etc. [25]

With the defeat of the Axis forces at El Alamein, Arabs tuned into British radio broadcasts with greater frequency. The BBC even began to support its broadcasts with a fortnightly publication entitled the *Arab Listener.* The BBC was no doubt gratified to receive the following letter from one particular Arab listener:

> Behold! Your weekly programme schedule reaches me regularly—except when it is delayed in the post owing to the present war crisis brought about by that insubordinate house-painter, that insatiable and low-born tyrant, that

John Bade who served with the Green Howards in North Africa and Palestine.

manslayer, Hitler, may Allah destroy him and his adherents and grant humanity rest from his evil craft—a task easy unto Allah! Behold us here, constant auditors of your broadcasts, which are the greatest, the best arranged, the most intelligible in language of all Arabic emissions!"[26]

Or do we detect a hint of public school humour here? Perhaps this happy Arab, so satisfied with the services of the BBC was merely another invention of British propaganda.[27]

Like all radio stations during the war, the BBC needed to offer music in order to attract listeners to its Arabic service. The fees commanded by the top Arab singers Umm Kulthum, Asmahan and Muhammad Abdul Wehab were so high that the BBC could rarely afford to broadcast them live and instead relied heavily on commercial recordings.[28]

Egyptians could be forgiven for their lack of enthusiasm for a European war that seemed to offer them little but hardship. Many Egyptians were more pre-occupied with another kind of war that was going on between Umm Kulthum and her greatest rival Asmahan. The two could not have been more different in every way. Asmahan was born a princess whereas Umm Kulthum for all her great earning power prided herself on being a woman of the people. In her movies she played humble slave girls. Asmahan's stunning beauty contrasted with the more homely appeal of Umm Kulthum. Umm Kulthum stood for traditional values and virtues whereas Asmahan was notorious for her scandalous private life. With her higher-placed and more wide-ranging voice, Asmahan was also more open to Western influences and innovations. Her record 'Ya habibi taala' ('My love, come quickly') made in 1944, the year of her death, presents a delightful and surprising fusion of Western and Eastern elements. A vocal line full of typically Arabic inflections is accompanied by piano, accordion, wailing saxophones and Latin American syncopated rhythms. This is a record that Westerners could have danced to. Other records show her attempting to incorporate operatic elements, such as high-lying coloratura, rather less successfully.

The rivalry between the two became so intense in the early 1940s, with their most successful films appearing simultaneously, that when Asmahan's chauffeur-driven car fell into the river Nile and she was drowned, many believed that Umm Kulthum had given orders for her death. In fact, if Asmahan's death was not a freak accident, it was almost certainly the British secret services who were responsible. In the early stages of the war, during the struggle for control of Syria between the Vichy French and the Allies, Asmahan had worked for the Allied cause. It seems that when promises of Syrian independence were not kept, Asmahan attempted to make contact with the Germans and may have paid for this with her life.[29]

After the Torch landings in November 1942, it was the turn of the Americans to provide entertainment for the troops in North Africa and they did not stint themselves. Amongst the stars who came over were Bob Hope, Jack Benny, Irving Berlin, Larry Adler

The Egyptian singer Umm Kulthum was adored throughout the Arab world.

Umm Kulthum's rival, the beautiful Asmahan, died in mysterious circumstances.

and, as a gesture towards 'high culture', the great violinist Jascha Heifetz. One star who came with the Americans eclipsed all the others and created one of the enduring legends of the Second World War. That was Marlene Dietrich.

In the late 1930s, Dietrich's American film career had been in the doldrums. She had been dubbed 'box office poison' and made no films between 1937 and 1939. It took considerable moral conviction for her to turn down the blandishments of Goebbels, who was prepared to offer virtually anything to win her return to the German film industry. Soon after the outbreak of war in Europe the huge success of the film

Destry Rides Again gave a second wind to Dietrich's career, but after America's entry into the war at the end of 1941 she gave up filmmaking in order to devote herself to entertaining Allied troops. She made her North African debut on 11 April 1943 in the Algiers Opera House before an audience of GIs, performing a tantalising striptease on stage by changing out of her military uniform into a revealing sequined costume. Her performance on a musical saw propped between her thighs and with the sequined skirts raised high was more notable for drawing attention to the famous legs than for its musical qualities.[30]

It was during this trip that Dietrich became identified with 'Lily Marlene', a song that could have been written for her and that many people believed actually was. Her identification with the song lasted for the rest of her life and she invariably sang it in her later concerts. Dietrich had made her own translation of the lyrics, but her biographer Steven Bach describes how on one occasion when broadcasting to American troops Dietrich spontaneously reverted into German to address her fellow Germans: 'Jungs! Opfert euch nicht! Der Krieg ist doch Scheisse, Hitler ist ein Idiot!' ('Boys! Don't sacrifice yourselves! The war is really shit, Hitler is an idiot!') before launching into the original German text of the song.[31]

Another legendary performer, the Afro-American Josephine Baker, had been a refugee in North Africa for some time. Initially she

had worked as a spy for the Allies, travelling back and forth between North Africa and Spain and gleaning useful titbits of information as she rubbed shoulders with diplomats and other notables. This activity was ended by a lengthy and severe illness. The Torch landings coincided with her recovery and brought her back to the role she had undertaken so successfully during the *drôle de guerre* as entertainer and morale booster. Eight days after the end of the Allied Casablanca Conference in January 1942 Baker returned to the stage to do her bit for the war effort. She inaugurated a service club for black GIs, after which she attended

Josephine Baker in her glory days at the Folies Bergère.

an official reception given by an American general. Typically for Baker this was not just about defeating Hitler's Germany. It was about defeating racism in all its forms. In her autobiography she wrote: 'In order to present a united front to the enemy we would have to be *true* allies, oblivious of colours and origins.'[32]

Baker, who had converted to Judaism when she married her second husband Jean Lion, said: 'I want to show that Arabs, blacks and whites can meet as brothers.'[33] She tried to do this by performing all the way along the North African coast from Casablanca to Cairo and up to Tel Aviv and Beirut.

Josephine Baker with Charles Trenet in Casablanca at the time she was working as a secret agent.

For soldiers stationed in the remoter parts of Iraq, their best chance of hearing a concert would have been with the intrepid Joyce Grenfell accompanied by a rickety piano. But while they were stationed in the Middle East, tens of thousands of soldiers from Middle England and Middle America had the opportunity of hearing Umm Kulthum, Jascha Heifetz, Noel Coward, Marlene Dietrich and Josephine Baker. Sadly though, it would seem that Arabs, Jews and Europeans, Westerners and Easterners, were not listening to each other's music.

1   A J Sherman, *Mandate Days*, 1997, p. 167.
2   Helen Fry, *Music and Men. The Life and Loves of Harriet Cohen*, 2008, p. 252.
3   KJ Kutsch and Leo Riemens, *Grosses Sängerlexikon*, 1987.
4   In conversation with the author.
5   Basil Dean, *The Theatre at War*, p. 431.
6   Noel Coward, *Middle East Diary*, 1944, p. 13.
7   Ibid., p. 74.
8   Ibid., p. 109.
9   Ibid., p. 19.
10   *The Record Collector*, Vol. 41 #3, pp. 191-223.
11   Georges Thill, *L'Avant Scène*, September 1984.
12   Robert de Fragny, *Ninon Vallin*, p. 136.
13   Maria Lluisa Tanzi Capsir, *Merce Capsir*, 2002, p. 75.
14   Bruno Tosi, *Pertile. Una voce, un mito*, 1985, p. 281.
15   Tito Gobbi, *My Life*, 1979, pp. 84-5.
16   Ivor Newton, *At the Piano*, 1966, p. 230.
17   Dean, p. 432.
18   Coward, p. 24.
19   Joyce Grenfell, *The Time of my Life*, 1989, p. 88.
20   Ibid., p. 80.
21   Virginia Danielson, *The Voice of Egypt*, 1997.
22   Peter Partner, *Arab Voices*, 1988, p. 35.
23   Andrew Walker, *A Skyful of Freedom*, London 1992, p. 29.
24   Ibid., p. 32.
25   An alternative version sung to me by my mother ran 'King Farouk, King Farouk, hang your balls upon a hook.'
26   Walker, p. 660.
27   Ibid., p. 660.
28   Peter Partner, *Arab Voices*, 1988, p. 76.
29   Sherifa Zuhur, *Asmahan's Secrets*, 2000.
30   Steven Bach, *Marlene Dietrich*, 1993, p. 291.
31   Ibid., p. 292.
32   Josephine Baker and Jo Bouillon, *Josephine*, 1977, p. 130.
33   Ibid., p. 132.

Chapter 9
MUSIC IN CAMPS

No previous war in history had seen so many men and women locked up for such long periods. Tens of millions found themselves in internment camps, prisoner of war camps, concentration camps and extermination camps. There was music in all of them.

French prisoners of war were exceptionally lucky in having entertainment provided by top French musical stars, including

Maurice Chevalier, Edith Piaf, Lys Gauty, Irène de Trébert, Fréhel and various popular dance bands. Lys Gauty recalled that her audience of soldiers cried when she sang the song 'Revenir'. These tours of German prison camps by French artists were exploited by the Germans for propaganda purposes and at the end of the war participation in the tours was regarded as a form of collaboration. Both Piaf and Fréhel claimed that they helped prisoners to escape. Fréhel said: 'We were received with touching joy. In advance of the tour I bought detailed maps of the Reich, which I gave discretely to the prisoners along with compasses. I hope they were useful to a number of them.'[1] Piaf had herself photographed with prisoners and the resulting photographs were used to create false documents to facilitate escape.

Usually it was the prisoners themselves who made the music. The British internment camps on the Isle of Man, the transit camp at Westerbork in Holland, and the concentration camp of Theresienstadt or Terezín stand out as centres of cultural activity during the war years.

It is astonishing how much music was composed in captivity. The richest legacy is undoubtedly that of Terezín. Ever since the first post-war performances of Viktor Ullmann's masterpiece *Der Kaiser von Atlantis* in the 1970s, much of this music has been rediscovered and become familiar. In the 1990s the remarkable recording project of 'Entartete Musik', undertaken by Decca under the direction of Michael Haas, did much to consolidate the reputations of the Theresienstadt composers Ullmann, Pavel Haas and Hans Krasa. More recently the Italian pianist and musicologist Francesco Lotorio has cast his net wider to research, perform and record works of all musical and political tendencies produced in camps on both sides in the war.

Of course not all prisoners were capable of making, let alone composing, music. For some, when the means were available, records and a wind-up gramophone satisfied their craving for music. At the end of the war the husband and wife piano duo, Cyril Smith and Phyllis Sellick, played the Brahms 'Variations on a theme of Haydn' in its two-piano version, for an audience of British soldiers who had recently been released from Japanese prison camps. They were astonished when an officer came up to them at the end of the concert and asked why they had omitted the repeat of the seventh variation. 'The colonel told us how he knew about it, and it was a strange story. In his camp a few prisoners shared an ancient gramophone, a few worn records and two or three gramophone needles. There was no hope of replacing these treasures, and the men's greatest fear was that the needles would not last out. It was not uncommon for one of the prisoners to spend the best part of a day sharpening a single needle on a stone, the only crude tool available, simply in order to hear a little music. And one of the records in this tiny tattered collection was the *Haydn-Brahms Variations*, which the colonel had played over so many times that every note of it was fixed in his memory.'[2]

In Britain, invasion hysteria after the fall of France and Churchill's notorious 'Collar the lot' led to the rounding up of over 70,000 enemy aliens and other suspects, many of whom were refugees from Nazi Germany.

PRIVATE HENRY WALLWORK,
ROYAL ARMY SERVICE CORPS.

A British prisoner of war in Germany.

On the Isle of Man distinguished academics gave each other lectures and musicians played chamber music together and gave concerts. Also there were those like the author's aunt, Edith Bade, a simple midwife born and bred in Middlesbrough, who would have had little to offer Hitler by way of information had she wanted to. It was enough to have had a German grandfather and surname and some malicious neighbours.

The happiest outcome of this rather shabby episode in British history was the bringing together of the string players Norbert Brainin, Siegmund Nissel and Peter Schidlof who would later form three-quarters of the famous Amadeus Quartet. Schidlof, who was only seventeen at the time of his arrest and internment, gave concerts, practised sonatas with his pianist friend Ferdinand Rauter, took lessons in music theory and harmony, and attended lectures. He later claimed that his education as a musician had been completed on the Isle of Man.[3]

The German composer and conductor Peter Gellhorn, later best known as a distinguished vocal coach at Covent Garden and Glyndebourne, was interned on the Isle of Man from 1939 to 1941. While there he took advantage of the string talent to compose his

The now delapidated PoW camp for Germans at Harperley, Durham.

virtuoso 'Two studies for violin'. The Austrian composer Hans Gál wrote the charming and cheerful 'Huyton Suite' for the unusual combination of flute and two violins (presumably the instruments available to him at the time) in the Huyton transit camp before being sent to the Isle of Man.

The defeat of the Axis armies in North Africa in the winter of 1942-3 brought increasing numbers of Italian and German prisoners to Britain. In the prisoner-of-war camp at Harperley, near Durham, a miniature theatre was built, used not only for the inmates but also for the surrounding British populace. Traditional gilt and plush was simulated with paint, papier-mâché and sackcloth, and there was an orchestra pit large enough to accommodate eight to twelve musicians. Operettas—for which printed programmes still exist—were devised by a German prisoner called Helmut Entz.

After the debacle of 1940, a number of French composers were taken into captivity, including Jean Martinon (who composed his setting of 'Psalm 136, Opus 33' and 'Absolve Domine' for male chorus), Maurice Thiriet and Emile Goué. Goué organised courses on harmony and counterpoint for his fellow prisoners and composed prolifically throughout his lengthy captivity, including the poignant song 'Nuits d'exile', full of nostalgia and anguish, in 1940.

Also amongst the French prisoners of war was the 31-year-old French composer Olivier Messiaen, who had been caught up in the debacle. Though Messiaen was as yet relatively unknown he had already composed a number of impressive works including 'Le banquet céleste' for organ, the orchestral pieces 'Les offrandes oubliées' and 'L'ascension', and the song cycle 'Poèmes pour Mi'. In Stalag VIIIA, a prisoner of war camp in Silesia, Messiaen composed during the winter of 1940-41 one of the most profound and moving works of the twentieth century, 'The Quartet for the End of Time', utilizing instrumentalists who were fellow prisoners: the clarinettist Henri Akoka, the violinist Jean le Boulaire, and the cellist Etienne Pasquier who had been Messiaen's superior in the medical corps, with Messiaen himself at the piano.

Messiaen recalled: 'I immediately wrote for them an unpretentious little trio, which they played to me in the lavatories, for the clarinettist had kept his instrument with him and someone had given the cellist a cello with three strings. Emboldened by these first sounds, I retained this little piece under the name of "Intermède" and gradually added to it the seven pieces which surround it, thus taking to eight the total number of movements in my "Quatuor pour le fin du temps".'⁴ A German officer gave Messiaen music paper, pencils and erasers, all of which were hard to come by, even for many non-imprisoned composers during the war.

The score is inscribed 'In homage to the Angel of the Apocalypse, who raises a hand towards Heaven saying: "There shall be time no longer".' In an explanatory lecture given to the first audience of prisoners, Messiaen insisted that 'this quartet was written for the end of time, not as a play on words about the time of captivity, but for the ending of the concepts of past and future: that is, for the beginning of eternity, and that in this I relied on the magnificent text of the Revelation ...'⁵

The first performance was given on 15 January 1941, before a motley audience of captured soldiers of many nationalities. Messiaen wrote 'After [my] lecture, they brought in an upright piano, very out of tune, and whose key action only worked intermittently. It was on this piano, with my three fellow musicians, dressed very strangely, myself clothed in the bottle-green uniform of a Czech officer, badly torn, and wearing wooden clogs ... that I was to play my *Quatuor pour la fin du temps*, in front of an audience of five thousand, among which were gathered all the different classes of society: peasants, labourers, intellectuals, career soldiers, medics, priests ...'⁶

The French singer Georges Brassens who spent time in a German forced labour camp.

It is difficult to imagine what this vast audience of cold and hungry men could have made of this lengthy and difficult piece of music. According to Messiaen he had never been listened to with 'such consideration and understanding'.[7] The musicologist Anthony Pople comments that 'One can be fairly sure that many of his fellow prisoners, listening to a work about the day of judgement, would have allowed their thoughts to alight on their future deliverance, and on their captors being brought to account before the Almighty.'[8] Messiaen himself was lucky enough to be delivered from captivity soon after and to return to his life as professor of harmony at the Paris Conservatoire.

In return for releasing military prisoners, the Germans demanded volunteer workers from France. The failure of this system resulted in February 1943 in the introduction of a form of conscription with the 'Service de Travail Obligatoire'. Among the young Frenchmen who found themselves in a labour camp at Basdorf, not far from Berlin, in harsh conditions hardly better than prison, was the 22-year-old singer and songwriter Georges Brassens, still nearly a decade away from success and fame. Brassens quickly became the leader of a tightknit group of young men who called themselves 'les Pafs'. He lifted the spirits of his companions with newly composed songs that were smutty, sentimental or slightly subversive. According to Pierre Onténéniente, who became a lifelong friend, 'It was in the toilets that he practised his art.'[9] One wonders just how much French music of this period was conceived in German toilets—'The bosses of the factory having had the idea to separate the Germans from others, there were WCs *Nur fur Ausländer* ('reserved for foreigners'). We spent most of our time there until they came to turn us out with a big fuss.'[10]

The schoolboy smuttiness that is such a disarming feature of many of Brassens's post-war songs evidently had its origin in the endless discussions about sex between the frustrated young men in the camp. Brassens's most subversive song, 'La ligne brisée', mocking the German passion for order and symmetry, was adopted by the group as their anthem. It is no coincidence perhaps, that this song was sung to the same melody as the anti-authoritarian song 'Le gorille', which after the war helped to establish Brassens's notoriety. In it, a judge cries out for his mother, just like the criminals he has condemned to death, as he is buggered in the undergrowth by a sex-starved gorilla that has escaped from the zoo.

Sentimental and nostalgic feelings were expressed in the song 'Maman, Papa' that later became one of Brassens's most popular. Another companion of his time at Basdorf, René Iskin wrote: 'I was the first to hear it ... and the first to cry.'[11]

Musical life continued even in the worst of the Nazi death camps. At Auschwitz there were several orchestras, all male except for that in the women's camp at Birkenau. These orchestras had a variety of functions, from improving the marching discipline of the slave workers on their journey to and from work, providing relaxation and entertainment for the SS, and most horrifically to soothe and deceive victims as they entered the gas chambers.

The entry of 20 September 1942 from the diary of Johannes Kremer, the camp doctor of Auschwitz, reveals a chillingly casual attitude to the musicians. In between other entries on executions, punishments and experiments on live prisoners Kremer notes: 'Today, Sunday, in the afternoon heard a concert between 3-6 o'clock in the prisoners' chapel in wonderful sunshine. The conductor was the director of the Warsaw State Opera. 80 musicians. For lunch there was roast pork, in the evening baked tench.'[12] This contrasts with a recollection by the French singer and pianist Fania Fénelon of a concert performed by the women's orchestra, which had given particular satisfaction and after which the entire orchestra was rewarded with a single rotten egg to share between them.

One of the most surprising musical creations to come out of a camp was the 'opérette-revue' devised by Germaine Tillion, a Frenchwoman deported to Ravensbrück, the notorious Nazi prison, because of her resistance activities. She quickly concluded that irony and humour were the keys to survival. Using her skills as a professional ethnologist she depicted the artificial society created by the Nazis within the camp, in verses that were sung to the melodies of popular songs and arias from operettas and operas that would have been familiar to her fellow French prisoners. Her title 'Le Verfügbar aux enfers', (`the available in hell') referred jokingly both to Offenbach's *Orphée aux Enfers*, and to the prisoners who refused to work for the Nazi war effort, and who were then designated *Verfügbar*: available for general tasks for the SS. Tillion survived Ravensbrück and lived to the age of 101.

Though the women's orchestra of Birkenau was neither the largest nor the most professional of the orchestras at Auschwitz, it is the story of that orchestra that has most captured the public imagination in later years. This is due to the fame and tragic destiny of its leader Alma Rosé and to the extraordinarily vivid memoirs of one of its members, Fania Fénelon. Fénelon's book, *The Musicians of Auschwitz* (also known as *Playing for Time*) is controversial. Aspects of her account—such as her description of the character and behaviour of Alma Rosé—have been disputed by the cellist Anita Lasker-Wallfisch, amongst others. The calm dignity and sober objectivity of Anita Lasker-Wallfisch puts the veracity of her own version of events beyond doubt. However, the passionate subjectivity of Fénelon has its own authenticity and her book is a uniquely valuable witness account.

The women's orchestra consisted of an odd combination of instruments. It was Fania Fénelon's duty to re-orchestrate familiar pieces for this combination. 'I had at my disposal ten violins, a flute, reed pipes, two accordions, three guitars, five mandolins, drums and some cymbals. No composer had ever envisaged such a combination! I read the top part carefully, and everything fell into place. I would replace the high instruments—sax, clarinet, and so on—with my first violin and my flutes. The guitars and mandolins would be the accompaniment. The accordions would bring the whole thing together and support it with their bass chords; the percussion would steady the beat.'[13]

Repertoire was extremely eclectic. It took in violin concertos to show the skills of Alma Rosé, and symphonies, arias and duets from opera, operetta, marches by Souza and overtures by Suppé, as well as popular pieces like Peter Kreuder's 'Twelve Minutes'. This last, which Fénelon described as 'an adorable pot-pourri, particularly light and tuneful', was a selection of the hit songs of Kreuder, including the surreally inconsequential 'Ich wollt ich wär' ein Huhn' originally sung by Willy Fritsch and Lillian Harvey in the 1936 movie *Glückskinder*.

The lyrics ran: 'Ich wollt ich wär' ein Huhn, ich hätt' nicht viel zu tun ...' ('I wish I were a chicken. I wouldn't have much to do. I would lay an egg every day and sometimes two on Sunday').

For the high-minded Anita Lasker-Wallfisch, much of what they had to play was 'rubbish'. Though Fania Fénelon had studied at the Paris Conservatoire where she had been a pupil of the respected concert singer Germaine Martinelli, she had also performed in cabaret and had more inclusive musical tastes. She owed her life to the fact that the infamous Maria Mandel who ran the women's camp had a soft spot for Puccini's *Madama Butterfly*. Fénelon had to perform the aria 'Un bel di' and the 'Flower duet' so often that she doubted that she would ever be able to hear Puccini again. It has been estimated that Mandel may have been responsible for the deaths of over 500,000 women and children, and yet she was strangely touched by Puccini's sentimental story of an abandoned girl and her illegitimate child. 'Could it be that she regarded herself as a sentimental geisha?' Fénelon asked. 'I hated myself at the thought of giving her pleasure.'[14] It was perhaps sympathy with Puccini's victim heroine and her child that led Mandel to briefly adopt and protect a small Polish boy before casually sending him to the gas chambers. There are other, equally grotesque, musical juxtapositions: the monstrous camp commander Joseph Kramer, moist-eyed with emotion as he listened to Schumann's sentimental 'Rêverie' while relaxing from the labour of slaughtering Jews and gypsies, Lehar's *Merry Widow* performed for Reichsführer Heinrich Himmler on a flying visit to the camp.

If making music involved an involuntary collaboration with the evil purpose of Auschwitz, it also allowed for secret gestures of defiance. Alma Rosé and her orchestra delighted in presenting the violin concerto of the forbidden Mendelssohn for the delectation of the SS who were too ignorant to recognise the composer. For Fania Fénelon, re-arranging the first movement of Beethoven's Fifth Symphony became an act of defiance. 'Alma wanted some Beethoven. I'd claimed that all I could remember was the first movement of the 5th Symphony and I suggested that she put it on the programme; a rare pleasure for me. She didn't see any malice in it, nor did the SS. They saw no connection with the signature of the Free French broadcasts on the BBC. For them it was Beethoven, a god, a monument to German music and they listened to it in respectful rapture. Their lack of a sense of humour was almost touching. There was intense jubilation when our orchestra played the piece. It was one of my most perfect moments.'[15]

Elsewhere in the camp amongst the slave workers, music occasionally allowed such defiant gestures. Trude Levi, who came from an intensely musical Hungarian family recalled: 'In the munitions factory, where during the first few days I worked on the conveyor belt, we worked with German women. The foreman ordered us to sing. On the second day I began to sing the 'Lorelei' and the Germans all joined in. I was pleased because I knew that the song was banned in Germany, the words being by Heine, the music by Mendelssohn, both of whom were of Jewish origin. The foreman ordered us to stop singing the song. We obeyed, but I had achieved a moment's triumph.'[16]

As she accompanied their daily procession to work, Fania Fénelon frequently wondered what the women workers thought of the orchestra and its music, fearing that they were resented and hated. If this was not exactly the case, the sound of music could certainly arouse suspicion and anxiety. We get a glimpse of the other side from Trude Levi.

> One day I heard music, Mozart's 'Eine kleine Nachtmusik'. Was I hallucinating? Here, in this barren wasteland, the strains of Mozart! Women started to run, all in one direction. I followed and the music was a small women's orchestra playing. I began to cry—such music in this hell! What torture was this going to bring us? What devilish tricks were they playing on us now?[17]

The story of the Auschwitz orchestras is grotesque and horrific enough, but it was the musical life of Terezín and Westerbork camps, inspiring and heroic though it was in some ways, that revealed Nazi ideology at its most perverted.

Westerbork was a transit camp intended as a staging post for Dutch Jewry on its way to extermination in the East. For the brief time that most inmates spent there conditions were less harsh than in other German camps. The cultural life in Westerbork included the performance of Shakespeare plays and symphony concerts, but it was for cabaret that Westerbork was most remarkable. Several members of the elite of Berlin cabaret in the Weimar period, including the singer and actress Dora Gerson, the comic Max Ehrlich, the composer Willy Rosen, the pianist Erich Ziegler and the versatile Kurt Gerron, had sought refuge in Holland as one of the few countries where they could find an audience sympathetic to their particular art form. Trapped by the

German invasion and finding themselves together in Westerbork they put on performances of great brilliance for their German persecutors as well as for their fellow inmates, many of whom enjoyed an evening of laughter before being transported to their deaths the following day.

In July 1943 on the eve of a major transportation the inmate Etty Hillesum reported in a letter to a friend that when Max Ehrlich, Chaja Goldstein and Willy Rosen performed 'the hall was full to bursting. One laughed till one cried, yes, till one cried.'[18] Hillesum's disgust with the proceedings is made still more clear in a letter of the following month in which she describes a concert with 'the comic Max Ehrlich and the popular composer Willy Rosen, who looks like a walking corpse … a little while ago he was on a list for transport, but he sang his lungs out for a few nights in a row for an enchanted audience including the Commandant, who has a fine artistic sense and was delighted and Willy Rosen was spared … and over there this other court jester: Erich Ziegler, the favourite pianist of the Commander. There is a story that he can even play Beethoven's 9th as a jazz piece, what about that?'[19]

In addition to the German cabaret artists there were two young Dutchmen, 'Johnny and Jones', who had been carried to fame on the wave of enthusiasm for swing just before the war. They even had the opportunity on a day out of the camp to go to Amsterdam and record a jaunty song called 'The Westerbork Serenade' before their own transportation to the East.

Amongst the more pious in the camp were those who were shocked that the stage for the cabaret was constructed with timbers pillaged from a nearby synagogue. Etty Hillesum reported that the carpenter exclaimed: 'What would God say if he could see his synagogue in Assen used for such profane purposes?'[20]

It would seem that religious life and music continued privately in Westerbork. John Fransman, who was four years old when he was imprisoned there, recalled: 'Many years after the war when I heard the singing of Moaz Tzur during the Chanukah celebration, I was aware that I knew the music. I realised that I could only have heard and learned this song in camp Westerbork during the Chanukah of 1943.'[21]

From November 1941, the eighteenth-century Habsburg fortress of Terezín, or Theresienstadt in the present-day Czech Republic, was used by the Nazis to house deported Jews, and soon after as part of an elaborate subterfuge to disguise the systematic genocide of Jews and convince an all too gullible world that they were being treated humanely. The subterfuge worked sufficiently well to convince the composer Richard Strauss who arrived there to visit the grandmother of his daughter-in-law and was surprised to be turned away. It is more surprising that the Danish Red Cross who inspected Terezín on 23 June 1944 were so easily taken in.

Terezín was a transit camp rather than an industrial death camp like Auschwitz. Despite the impressive efficiency of German record-keeping, reliable figures are hard to come by. However, it is believed that of the approximately 150,000 prisoners who passed through Terezín in a period of four and a half years, around 33,000 died there, with the great majority taken to their deaths in other camps. These included 15,000 children of whom barely one hundred survived. The Jewish cultural elite of Central Europe was brought to Terezín. Many came from Prague, which was already full of refugees from Hitler, but many also came from further afield—from Poland, Hungary, Denmark and the Netherlands.

The multi-talented Kurt Gerron—actor, cabaret artist and film-director, and one of the luminaries of Weimar Berlin—was seized in the Netherlands after proudly declining an invitation to work in Hollywood because he had only been offered second-class tickets to cross the Atlantic. Gerron agreed to make a propaganda film for the Nazis, depicting Terezín as an idyllic refuge for Jews—*Theresienstadt. Ein Dokumentar Film aus dem jüdischen Siedlungsgebiet* ('Terezín. A Documentary Film of the Jewish Resettlement'), also known as 'The Führer gives a village to the Jews'. Gerron hoped in vain that this collaboration would save his life, but it may also have been that, like Alma Rosé, he chose work as a means of escaping from the horror of reality.

Terezín was a place of surreal contradictions. Initially, before the Nazis decided to turn it into a cultural showplace it was forbidden for prisoners to whistle or sing in the streets or to possess a musical instrument. Though there was a school for Jewish children they were forbidden to receive instruction in reading or writing but allowed cultural activities such as drama, music and drawing. When Nazi officials snooped on the school the children would break into song to cover their other academic activities.

The cultural life of Terezín was extraordinary, with plays, cabaret, classical concerts (many given by the pianist Alice Herz-Sommers) and fully staged operas. The conductor Rafael Schächter undertook the Herculean task of performing Verdi's monumental *Requiem* thirteen times, recreating the huge chorus three times over as its members were deported to the death camps.

There were four outstanding young composers in Terezín—Hans Krasa, Pavel Haas, Viktor Ullmann and Gideon Klein. All four should have been leading figures of post-war European musical life. Instead, the works they wrote in Terezín proved to be their swan song. The ability to write great music under sentence of death and in such circumstances seems little less than miraculous, as is the surprising survival of so much of the music they wrote in the camp.

The Czech conductor Vilem Tausky, who had known and worked with these musicians, made no mention of them in his autobiography, *Vilem Tausky Tells His Story*, published in 1979. When he was asked about this in a public interview at the London Jewish Cultural Centre not long before his death in 2004, he answered quite simply that he had thought that the composers were forgotten and their music lost, and never imagined that there would be interest in them. As late as 1980 the comprehensive 20-volume *New Grove Dictionary of Music* devoted a mere 27 lines to Ullmann, 21 to Haas and 15 to Krasa.

In fact, the tide had begun to turn in 1975 when Ullmann's opera *Der Kaiser von Atlantis* was first performed in Amsterdam and then telecast around the world, generating a revival of interest in the Terezín composers. This led in turn to a pioneering series of recordings produced by Michael Haas for Decca, revealing such extraordinary masterpieces as Hans Krasa's *Verlobung im Traum* and Pavel Haas's *The Charlatan*. These two operas both met with brilliant success when first performed—*Verlobung im Traum* in Prague in 1933 and *The Charlatan* in Brno in 1938. These operatic successes should have established the international careers of both composers but it was too late. The route to international recognition via the German theatres, taken by earlier Czech composers such as Smetana, Dvořák, Janáček and Weinberger, was now closed. After the Nazi seizure of Bohemia and the outbreak of war, Krasa and Haas as well as Ullmann and Klein were trapped and eventually transported to Terezín. Haas adapted least well to the harsh conditions and found it difficult to compose. Of the handful of works that he wrote there and that survive, the 'Four Songs on Chinese Poetry' and the lovely 'Study for String Orchestra' are outstanding. The latter was reconstructed after the war from the instrumental parts by Karl Ancerl, who had conducted the first performance in Terezín in 1943.

Apart from Ullmann's *Der Kaiser von Atlantis*, Hans Krasa's children's opera *Brundibar* is the work most frequently associated with Terezín, but was in fact composed well before Krasa arrived in the camp. It was written in 1938 as an entry for a competition for a children's opera, sponsored by the Czech Ministry of Education. Music dramas for children were in vogue at the time across the political spectrum. *Brundibar* may be compared with Norbert Schultze's *Der Schwarze Peter* and Prokofiev's *Peter and the Wolf*, both dating from 1936. The German occupation of Bohemia aborted the competition. Instead, Krasa hoped to have it performed in a Jewish children's home.

In 1942, the performance went ahead on a modest scale with piano and just three performers but Krasa was not there to see it. By this time he was already interned in Terezín. Soon after, the director of the children's home and his son arrived in Terezín bringing Krasa's score with them. The first performance in Terezín with orchestration proscribed by the available instruments took place on 23 September 1943. There would be more than 50 further performances, with the chorus constantly needing to be replenished as the children were taken to their deaths. Amongst the works that Krasa wrote in the camp is the brief string trio 'Tanec' ('Dance'). Most chamber works written in Terezín were created for specific combinations of musicians who were available as they arrived and before they went to their deaths, but there is no record of 'Tanec' actually being performed in the camp. With its vigorous folkloric rhythms and its moments of wistfulness 'Tanec' is both exhilarating and heart-rending.

Much the most prolific of the Terezín composers was Viktor Ullmann. Between September 1942 when he arrived and October 1944 when he was transported to Auschwitz, Ullmann wrote a total of twenty works including three piano sonatas, a string quartet, several song cycles and his masterpiece, the chamber opera *Der Kaiser von Atlantis*. Ironically, most of Ullmann's Terezín works survive whereas most of his pre-war compositions do not. Ullmann arrived in Terezín together with his first wife and his third wife to find his second wife Martha already there, but not for long. Martha was transported to Treblinka a month later and gassed.

It was shortly before Ullmann's arrival that the Nazis had come round to the idea of promoting Terezín as a cultural and musical centre. Ullmann must have been surprised to find himself organising concerts and writing reviews for a local news-sheet and with the time and opportunity to compose, though he seems to have had few illusions about his ultimate fate. The title page of his seventh and final piano sonata bears the date 22 August 1944 and the heavily ironic inscription 'Performance rights for the composer during his lifetime.'[22]

Though rehearsals for *Der Kaiser von Atlantis* reached an advanced stage, the production was halted by the Nazis before the premiere. The satire of Hitler and his war was so pointed that it is astonishing that the production got as far as it did. But it may just have been that by the autumn of 1944 with the Russians approaching there was no reason to maintain the pretence of Terezín, and the Nazis were anxious to exterminate as many Jews as they could in the short time left to them.

From 1943 Ullmann worked on the libretto with the artist and writer Peter Kien, who played an important role in the general cultural life of Terezín and drew poignant images of its inmates. The plot concerns the Emperor of Atlantis (clearly based on Hitler) who attempts to conquer the world through universal war. Eventually Death goes on strike, and only agrees to resume his work if the Emperor will offer himself as the first victim.

In twenty short scenes, *Der Kaiser von Atlantis* is composed in an eclectic style that owes a great deal to the Berlin stage works of Kurt Weill. The final chorale 'Komm Tod, du unser werter Gast' ('Come death, our honoured guest') is a poignant parody of the Lutheran hymn 'Ein feste Burg ist unser Gott' ('Our God is a mighty fortress') that had the status of a national anthem for German Protestants and which had already been used by Bach for his most monumental cantata (BWV 80. Ein feste Burg), as well as by three German Jewish composers of widely differing character—Mendelssohn in his 'Reformation' Symphony, Meyerbeer in *Les Huguenots* and Offenbach in his operetta *Ba-ta-clan*.

In performance, *Der Kaiser von Atlantis* never fails to pull an emotional punch though it is hard to determine how much of that is due to the intrinsic merits of the piece and how much to the audience's knowledge of the ultimate fate of the composer and librettist.

1   Nicole and Alain Lacombe, *Fréhel*, 1990, p. 267.

2   Cyril Smith, *Duet for Three Hands*, 1958, p. 122.

3   Connery Chappell, *Island of Barbed Wire*, 1984.

4   Antony Pople, *Quatuor pour la fin du temps*, 1998, p. 7-8.

5   Ibid., p. 13.

6   Ibid., p. 15.

7   Ibid., p. 16.

8   Ibid., p. 15.

9   René Iskin, *Dans un camp. Basdorf 1943*, 2005, p. 8.

10 Ibid.

11 Ibid., p. 165.

12 *Diary of Dr Johannes Paul Kremer*, 2011, p. 35.

13 Fania Fénelon, *The Musicians of Auschwitz*, 1976, p. 54.

14 Ibid., p. 69.

15 Ibid., p. 112.

16 Trude Levi, *A Cat called Adolf*, 1995, p. 8.

17 Ibid., p. 13.

18 Etty Hillesum, *Une vie bouleversée*, 1988, p. 287.

19 Ibid., p. 333.

20 Ibid., p. 342.

21 John Fransman, *A Jewish child survivor's recollection of the Holocaust. From Zachor*, 2011.

22 Viktor Ullmann, *Komponieren in verlorener Zeit*, 2002.

Chapter 10
OPERETTA AND SWING

Two musical genres were common currency across the Western world during the war: Swing appealed primarily to the young or at least to those who were young enough to dance. Operetta had a more universal appeal. Though a handful of the more famous operettas continue to be presented by opera houses today, operetta has become virtually extinct as a form of popular entertainment partly because in the post-war period it became identified with bourgeois and reactionary attitudes. It takes an effort of imagination to envisage just how widely performed and enjoyed it was during the war years.

The entry of the United States into the war at the end of 1941 coincided with a change in the tastes of American movie-goers: this saw the end of the craze for filmed operettas that had peaked in the late 1930s with the hugely profitable films of Jeanette MacDonald and Nelson Eddy; Jeanette MacDonald's contract with MGM was terminated in 1942. On the other side of the continent, staged operettas continued to pack the East Coast theatres throughout the war. These were revivals rather than new works, despite the fact that many of Europe's best operetta composers had arrived in America as refugees. In 1942 Broadway saw productions of Offenbach's *La Vie Parisienne*, Lehar's *Merry Widow*, Sigmund Romberg's *New Moon*, and *Iolanthe*, *The Gondoliers* and *The Pirates of Penzance* by Gilbert and Sullivan. There was no let-up in the constant stream of operetta productions during the remaining war seasons, and Robert Stolz in particular promoted Viennese operetta with missionary zeal in New York productions of *Die Fledermaus*, *Der Zigeunerbaron*, and *Der Bettelstudent*.

In 1943 the Polish tenor Jan Kiepura gave up his operatic career to devote himself to operetta, together with his wife Marta Eggerth.

The Viennese tenor Richard Tauber was an indefatigable performer of operetta in wartime Britain.

They leased the Majestic Theater on Broadway and presented a highly successful new production of Lehar's *Merry Widow*. Viennese authenticity was ensured by the musical direction of Stolz, who had conducted the first run of the operetta in 1905-6. Kiepura's *Merry Widow* travelled to other American cities in the remaining war years.

The appetite for operetta was just as great in Russia where even the high-minded Shostakovich did not disdain to arrange, re-orchestrate and even write operettas. The German invasion of 1941 brought a shift from Viennese to Parisian operettas. Over the desperate winter of 1941-42 Moscovites were cheered by a production of Planquette's *Les Cloches de Corneville*.[1]

Britain benefited from the presence of the greatest operetta tenor of the century, Richard Tauber, who decided to take his chances there, rather than seeking the greater comfort and safety of the United States. Tauber was rewarded with the devotion of the British public, as anyone can tell who has visited the Brompton Cemetery on his birthday (16 May) and witnessed the piles of letters and flowers left by elderly admirers. According to Tauber's wife Diana Napier, the no longer young tenor sang almost every night of the war.[2] He was also one of the busiest recording artists of the war years, making hundreds of records in quaintly accented English of material ranging from Schubert, through Lehar and Ivor Novello, to Irving Berlin. In addition to all of this, Tauber toured the country tirelessly in a morale-boosting production of Lehar's *Land of Smiles*, and prepared and conducted an English language version of *Die Fledermaus* under the title of *Gay Rosalinda*. Somehow, he also found time to compose his own operetta *Old Chelsea*, which ran for over two years.

That operetta was not considered to be the prerogative of the middle-aged and middle class is shown by its use in entertaining

British and Commonwealth troops. The production of *The Merry Widow* that toured North Africa and the Middle East was one of ENSA's greatest successes. Tauber's *Old Chelsea* was specially recorded in order to be circulated among troops stationed abroad.

Britain had a successful home-grown operetta composer in the Welsh playwright and former matinee idol Ivor Novello. Like Irving Berlin in America, Novello cheered his nation with songs in both wars, having written the ever-popular 'Keep the home fires burning' during the First World War. Novello's musical plays offered an escape into Ruritanian romance that appealed to wartime audiences but also contained a certain topicality. *The Dancing Years,* which premiered in March 1939 before the outbreak of war, referred to the rise of Nazism and the *Anschluss.* It toured the British provinces in the early part of the war before returning to London in 1942 for another lengthy run at the Adelphi Theatre. *The Dancing Years* was followed in 1943 by *Arc de Triomphe,* set in France during the previous world war, and containing a mini-opera about Joan of Arc; and the celebratory *Perchance to Dream* opened in April 1945.[3]

Ivor Novello's The Dancing Years *continued to entertain London audiences through the early years of the war.*

Ivor Novello as Rudi Kleiber interrogated by the Nazis.

Music Wars

The widespread affection in which Ivor Novello was held by civilian and military public as a musical veteran of the previous war was unaffected by a bizarre incident in 1944 when he was sent to prison for a month for the infringement of petrol restrictions. A week after his release from prison in June 1944, he received an ovation from the public when he returned to the cast of *The Dancing Years*, and in August he was entertaining troops on the front in Normandy on a makeshift stage in an orchard 'to the distant boom of artillery fire and the nearer rattle of the Bofors gun'.[4] According to Basil Dean: 'It required moral courage of a high order to go out and face the troops so soon after his release from prison ... in doing so he gained the regard of the invasion troops as well of the public at home ... The hit number of his forthcoming success ("When the Lilacs bloom again" [sic] in *Perchance to Dream*) was composed while in Normandy, and sung in public for the first time after the play at the Garrison Theatre, Bayeux, the composer going down into the orchestra pit and playing it on the little piano there.'[5]

Several Parisian theatres were devoted almost entirely to operetta throughout the Occupation, in keeping with Nazi policies that the city should provide entertainment and relaxation for the Wehrmacht. The huge Théâtre du Châtelet mounted a spectacular production of *Valses de Vienne* utilising music by Johann Strauss, father and son, and later of *Valses de France*, a pot-pourri of melodies by various French composers. The Mogador specialised in lavishly-presented productions of operetta standards including *La veuve joyeuse* ('Merry Widow'), *Véronique*, *La mascotte* and *La fille de Madame Angot*. There were also a number of new French operettas such as *La course à l'amour* by Guy Laforge at the Théâtre des Nouveautés and *Une femme par jour* by Georges Van Parys at the Théâtre des Capucines.[6] The journals of the period contain advertisements for operetta recitals by Fanély Revoil, who had taken over as the most popular operetta diva in Paris after the half-Jewish Edmée Favart had retired to the relative safety of the south of France.

For the Nazis, operetta presented a quandary. It was an art form that was highly esteemed by Hitler and Goebbels but no other musical or theatrical genre was so completely dominated by Jews. Operetta had been invented and developed in mid-nineteenth century Paris by the German Jew Jacques Offenbach, whose works were, needless to say, banned in the Third Reich. Johann Strauss Jnr, the father of Viennese operetta, was even more problematic. His music was simply

266

too popular to ban and the Nazis went to considerable trouble to cover up his Jewish ancestry. The identity of Lehar's various Jewish librettists needed to be suppressed. A two page article in the magazine *Vedettes* in April 1941 about the filmed version of the operetta *Les Trois Valses*, starring Yvonne Printemps and Pierre Fresnay, fails to mention either the composer Oscar Straus or the director Ludwig Berger, as both were Jewish and, by then, in exile.

Apart from Franz Lehar, who wrote nothing of significance after 1934, the leading operetta composers of the Austro-German tradition were mostly Jewish or part Jewish. Amongst those who fled were Oscar Straus, Emmerich Kálmán, Paul Abraham, Ralph Benatzky—whose wife was Jewish, and Robert Stolz, who possessed the needed certificate of Aryan ancestry but was unable to accept the nazification of his native Austria. Edmund Eysler presumably meant what he said when he declared in a 1934 interview that it was 'better to die in Vienna than to live in Australia.' Despite the banning of his music and the constant danger of being deported to a death camp Eysler remained in Vienna and astonishingly survived the war.[7]

Valses de France *was typical of the lavish productions mounted at the vast Châtelet theatre.*

The Théâtre Mogador *revived old favourites such as* La Fille de Madame Angot.

The German operetta composer Eduard Künnecke remained popular despite being compromised in the eyes of the Nazis by his Jewish wife.

Paul Lincke profited from the fact that he was the only major German operetta composer who was untainted by Jewish connections.

Franz Lehar, whose Merry Widow continued to delight audiences on both sides in the war.

Paul Lincke and Eduard Künneke were the only operetta composers of any stature remaining in Germany. Künnecke had a gift for expansive melody that was relished by some of the finest singers of the day, including Helge Rosvaenge and Tiana Lemnitz, who premiered his operetta *Die grosse Sünderin* at the Berlin Staatsoper in 1935. But Künnecke also had a Jewish wife and was for various other reasons a suspect figure with the Nazi hierarchy. A leftover whiff of Weimar and his occasional indulgence in saxophones and syncopation was not to the liking of Nazi noses. This left Paul Lincke as the remaining moderately talented operetta composer who was not tainted by Jewish blood or associations. He found himself promoted rather beyond his true abilities as the leading operetta composer of the Reich, dubbed by Goebbels 'Marschall der deutschen Unterhaltungskunst'. The renewed interest in his work stimulated Lincke to compose a new operetta after a gap of more than twenty years. *Ein Liebestraum* was premiered in Hamburg in October 1940.

Franz Lehar's *Die lustige Witwe* ('The Merry Widow') was the most frequently performed operetta in the Reich, as it was elsewhere in the world, even though it presented the problem that both its co-librettists, Leo Stein and Victor Léon, were Jews. Though no longer productive as a composer, Lehar enjoyed the special protection of Goebbels, who enabled him to save his Jewish wife who was threatened at one point with arrest and deportation. Lehar was unable, however, to save Fritz Löhner-Beda, co-librettist of Lehar's most successful post-*Merry Widow* operetta *Das Land des Lächelns* ('The Land of Smiles') and who had penned the lyrics of the immortal 'Du bist mein ganzes Herz' ('You are my heart's delight'). Reports of Löhner-Beda's 'suicide' were carried in the French press as early as 1939 but according to Ernst Klee's *Kulturlexikon zum Dritten Reich* he was beaten to death in Auschwitz in December 1942.[8]

L'auteur du spectacle, Dr Loehner Beda, s'est « suicidé » dans le camp de concentration de Buchenwald où il était depuis dix-huit mois.

In 1939 the French magazine Match *carried a premature report of the suicide of Lehar's librettist Fritz Löhner-Beda.*

The craze for swing that swept the world in the years immediately prior to the outbreak of World War II was so inexorable that even the totalitarian regimes of Nazi Germany, Stalinist Russia and Vichy France—essentially disapproving of jazz in all its forms—were powerless to suppress it. All combatant nations in the Second World War attempted to harness the energy generated by this exuberant music.

Jazz and dance band musicians tended to be young and eligible for conscription. Britain and the USA got round this problem by forming jazz and dance bands within the military. In Britain the Royal Air Force went out of its way to recruit musicians from the best pre-war bands. Eight members of the Ambrose Orchestra joined up together and formed the backbone of the RAF band The Squadronaires, who, throughout the war, produced slickly professional dance records in the American big band style for the commercial label of Decca, as well as recording programmes through ENSA for the entertainment of troops.

Jazz had been born at the beginning of the twentieth century through a collision of Afro-American and European musical traditions.

It entered popular American culture largely through the agency of musicians of Russian Jewish ancestry, a fact that did not pass unnoticed by the Nazis and other racist commentators of the 1930s.

The world-wide popularity of Irving Berlin's 'Alexander's Ragtime Band' from 1911, with its elements of syncopation, opened up the way for the triumph of American popular music as well as for the acceptance of more genuine forms of ragtime and jazz, during and after the First World War. Afro-American popular music infiltrated Europe in the form of popular dances like the Charleston and the Foxtrot, but also found acceptance in more sophisticated musical circles. Stravinsky led the way in 1919 with his 'Piano Ragtime Music', followed by Darius Milhaud in 1923 with his score for the ballet *La Création du Monde*, inspired by the experience of hearing black musicians in Harlem. At the avant-garde Parisian nightclub Le Boeuf sur le Toit, frequented by Jean Cocteau and members of 'Les Six', musical entertainment was provided by the pianist Jean Wiener who alternated Ragtime with Bach. From 1934 the Quintette du Hot Club de France, that included the guitarist Django Reinhardt and the violinist Stéphane Grappelli, made the first truly original European contribution to the development of jazz.

Afro-American music triumphed in Berlin with highly successful visits by Sam Gooding and his Chocolate Kiddies in 1925 and 1926, and by Josephine Baker in 1926 and 1928. In the late 1920s Kurt Weill and Mischa Spoliansky presided over a shift towards more jazz-inflected music in the theatre. In 1927 Spoliansky made the first German recording of Gershwin's 'Rhapsody in Blue' and the following year Gershwin himself arrived in Berlin to a warm reception. The triumphant progress from 1927 of Ernst Krenek's jazz opera *Jonny spielt auf* generated fierce debate and Nazi protests against the 'desecration' by jazz of German opera houses. In the early thirties the most popular German vocal group included American jazz favourites such as Duke Ellington's 'Creole Love Song' in their varied repertoire.

Even in culturally conservative England, jazz was given intellectual respectability by Constant Lambert's 1934 essay 'The Spirit of Jazz', in which he compared the music of Duke Ellington favourably with that of Stravinsky and Ravel. For all its brilliant insights, Lambert's 'The Spirit of Jazz' has become a period piece in bizarrely unpleasant ways. Even his unstinting praise of Ellington is couched in language that seems patronising and racist. Lambert's frank anti-Semitism chimes with contemporary Nazi ideology: 'The importance of the Jewish element in jazz cannot be too strongly emphasized, and the fact that at least ninety percent of jazz tunes are written by Jews undoubtedly goes far to account for the curiously sagging quality—so typical of Jewish art—the almost masochistic melancholy of the average foxtrot.'[9]

The spread of radio from 1922, the introduction of the microphone and electric recording, the consolidation of the great Hollywood film studios in the mid-twenties and the advent of sound in the movies from 1927, all conspired to give American popular culture an unprecedented world dominance that was deplored by conservatives all over Europe and deeply feared and envied by the Nazis in particular.

Swing came along at exactly the right moment to take advantage of these technological developments, emerging from black into mainstream American popular culture in the mid-1930s through popular dance bands such as those of Benny Goodman, the Dorsey Brothers, Count Basie and Glenn Miller, and crossing the Atlantic towards the end of the decade. The triumph of swing presented the Nazis with a dilemma. As far as jazz in all its forms was concerned, they had come close to painting themselves into a corner. Saxophones and syncopation represented all that they most hated about Weimar Berlin culture. From the first, Nazi officials denounced jazz in the most strident language and intermittently attempted to ban it altogether. In an article entitled 'Der Jazzbazillus' in the *Zeitschift für Musik*, Hans Petsch described jazz as 'a cancerous growth that has to be removed from Germany at all costs.'[10] The travelling exhibition of 'Entartete Musik' in 1938 excoriated jazz alongside atonalism, and the cover of the catalogue bore a caricature image of a black saxophonist wearing a badge with the Star of David. Even before the Nazis had taken power nationally, the locally elected Nazi party in Thuringia banned the performance of jazz in that province from 1930. From 1935, officially at least, all jazz was banned from the German airwaves. The programme director of the RRG, the German Broadcasting company, announced: 'We mean to eradicate every trace of putrefying elements that remain in our light entertainment and dance music. As of today, Nigger Jazz is finally switched off on the German radio.'

As Erik Levi has demonstrated in his book *Music in the Third Reich*, jazz continued to be performed under certain restrictions and in various forms until the end of the Reich. Though the names of 'non-Aryan' composers had disappeared from the airwaves, concert programmes and record catalogues by 1938, this did not mean that their music or its influence had disappeared with them. In 1937 the Peter Kreuder Orchestra recorded a recently composed piece by Duke Ellington for Deutsche Grammophon, but without acknowledgement of the identity of the composer. Foreign dance bands such as those of Henry Hall and Jack Hylton were still welcomed in Germany in the late thirties as long as they dropped their Jewish personnel. The Swedish Arne Hülphers Band, reckoned to be the most up-to-date in Scandinavia, appeared in Berlin as late as 1942, no doubt facilitated by the fact that Arne Hülphers himself was a member of the quasi-Nazi Nysvenska movement.

Even the most traditional German dance bands—such as that of the violinist George Boulanger—could assume a veneer of jazzy sophistication with blue notes, saxophones and syncopation for numbers that required it, just as they might make use of the cimbalom and 'gypsy' harmonic modulations for a romantic number.

More hard-edged American-style bands, such as that of Kurt Widmann at the Imperator Hotel, played a game of cat and mouse with Nazi officials on the lookout for signs of *Kulturbolshevismus*, and risked being banned. But most survived, and despite his run-ins with officialdom Widmann found himself entertaining troops after the outbreak of war.

It was propaganda minister Joseph Goebbels himself who took a more pragmatic view of American-style entertainment and dance music, and overruled his more zealous Nazi colleagues. After the outbreak of war, and still more after the war had turned against Germany in 1943, Goebbels advocated the use of popular dance music as necessary for maintaining public and military morale.

The debate over what was and what was not desirable and permissible in popular music raged on unresolved until the end of the war. In an article of 1942 entitled 'Jazz on the radio', Goebbels attempted to draw up guidelines, but his arguments are vague and contradictory and cannot have been much use to either musicians or programmers. As to whether jazz was appropriate on the radio, he writes:

> The answer to this question has to be negative if by jazz we mean a form of music that totally ignores melody, indeed even makes fun of it, and is based on rhythm alone, rhythm that manifests itself principally in a cacophonous instrumental squawk that offends the ear. This alleged music

is revolting, being in reality not music at all, but talentless and unimaginative juggling with notes. On the other, it must not be suggested that our grandparents' waltzes were the apex of musical development, and that nothing since then has been any good. Rhythm is fundamental to music. We are not living in the Biedermeier period, but in a century that takes its tunes from the thousandfold humming of machines and the roar of motors. Our war songs today are set to a different tempo from even the First World War ... we have ... a duty to respond to the justifiable demands of our fighting and toiling people in this respect.[11]

Apart from the question of melody versus rhythm, which is touched upon by Goebbels and was much discussed, the debate revolved around instrumentation and whether strings or wind and percussion should be dominant. Commercial dance records made between 1941 and 1943 by the bands of Arne Hülphers, Heinz Burzynski, Fud Candrix, Ernst Van T'Hoff, Willy Berking, Lutz Templin and Michael Jarry, in which violins are foregone altogether, suggest that these bandleaders were allowed considerable latitude and simply ignored much of the debate amongst Nazi theorists. Rhythm predominates and saxophones are clustered in close harmony or used in unison in the manner of Glenn Miller and other contemporary American bands. Presumably the arrangers for these bands had access to supplies of— by then—illicit American records or they may have listened secretly to the still-more-illicit Allied radio stations.

In wartime France both the Vichy and the German authorities pursued a similar policy of reluctant acceptance of jazz and swing. An article in the collaborationist journal *La Gerbe* of 25 April 1942 called for the banning of music that might infect French culture with the 'poison of Americanism'.[12] The Vichy regime with its conservative moral values and its devotion to *Travail, Famille, Patrie*, disapproved of public dancing altogether as likely to cause moral turpitude. Just as the Nazis associated jazz with the undermining of German culture in the Weimar period, right-wing elements in France believed that the pre-war craze for jazz and swing was a symptom of a moral collapse that preceded the military collapse of 1940. Despite minor restrictions and the persecution of Jewish musicians, pragmatic voices prevailed: jazz and swing were never banned and, as Ludovic Tournès has shown, they thrived in wartime France.[13]

The period between 1938, when French popular music was galvanised by the arrival of swing from America, and the fall of France in June 1940, was a brief golden age for French dance bands. Among the best were those of Jo Bouillon, Jacques Hélian, Fred Adison, Raymond Legrand and Wal-Berg. Probably the most popular of all were the quirky and humorous Ray Ventura et ses Collegiens, the band that had made the two records most associated with the pre-war and Phoney War periods: 'Tout va très bien, Madame la Marquise' and 'On ira pendre notre linge sur la ligne Siegfried'. Because of their Jewish origin, Ray Ventura and Wal-Berg disappeared from the Paris scene. After the German invasion Ray Ventura performed initially in the unoccupied zone, later fleeing to South America, but not before participating in the most notorious of all collaborationist records—André Dassary's version of 'Maréchal, nous voilà!', a rousing declaration of loyalty to Maréchal Petain that became the unofficial anthem of the Vichy regime.

Despite lingering official disapproval, the early years of the Occupation saw a remarkable proliferation of jazz concerts. Ludovic Tournès has argued that it was precisely in these years that jazz was fully assimilated into French popular culture. The activities of the Hot Club de France, which promoted jazz events, increased, only to diminish after 1943 when German policies of forced labour made it too dangerous for young people to gather together. The Quintette of the Hot Club of France, without the violinist Stéphane Grappelli—who had remained in Britain after the outbreak of war, continued its hugely successful progress; surprisingly, its most famous member, the guitarist Django Reinhardt, pursued a very public career apparently unmolested despite his gypsy ancestry.

Jazz and swing took up a lot of time on the French airwaves as well. In August 1942 the Paris radio station 'Radiodiffusion française' put out a series of programmes on great American jazz musicians, including Louis Armstrong, Duke Ellington and Bix Beiderbecke, when America had already been in the war for nine months. The German-controlled radio station Radio Paris, notorious for its propaganda, employed the Raymond Legrand band, sending out 520 broadcasts of jazz and dance music between 1940 and 1942, for which Legrand would receive a six-month ban at the end of the war.

The jazz-loving Frank Ténot, still a schoolboy under the Occupation, recalled that in addition to Radio Paris there were plenty of other radio stations offering syncopated rhythms during the war years. Swiss radio, particularly valued in France because of the objectivity of its news coverage (reports on the progress of the Battle of Stalingrad followed information on the price of milk and public transport in Swiss cantons), offered Duke Ellington, Count Basie and Fats Waller as well. Radio Andorra and Radio Monte Carlo were also listened to by jazz lovers, and on short wave radio even New York could be picked up by those craving authentic American jazz and swing. Ténot was particularly thrilled to hear the exiled Stéphane Grappelli broadcast by the BBC on 14 March 1942.[14]

The widespread interest in jazz in wartime France is also attested to by the publication of books on the subject at a time when it was not easy to gain either permission or the materials for new books. It was a sign of the times, though, that André Coeuroy's 1942 *Histoire générale du Jazz* opened with a lengthy debate entitled 'Pour et contre le Jazz'. This included the somewhat tendentious argument that the melodic component in jazz was inherently more French than 'Saxon' because jazz was born in a part of the United States that had previously been ruled by the French.[15]

The following year Hugues Panassié published *La Musique de Jazz et le Swing* which was hailed by Pierre Mariel in the radio magazine *Les Ondes* as 'the most interesting and complete book on the subject.' For Panassié swing was a means of releasing 'a pure, natural and vital instinct devoid of all thought and calculation.' Mariel agreed but wondered whether this was such a good thing. 'We believe that jazz animates the lowest levels of our psyche that take us back to the primitivism of the African jungle.' Mariel compares the effect of swing to that of alcoholic intoxication but concedes that like a glass of alcohol a dose of jazz can deliver a healthy *coup de fouet* ('whip-lash').[16] This accords with Goebbels's view that jazz was a necessary evil that needed to be controlled and exploited.

There were a number of gifted French and Belgian jazz instrumentalists active under the Occupation including Alix Combelle, Gus Viseur, André Ekyon, Hubert Rostaing, and Fud Candrix. Undoubtedly the most celebrated was the guitarist Django Reinhardt. That Reinhardt, despite his well-known gypsy ancestry, was able to maintain such a high profile—even having his photograph illustrated in the collaborationist radio magazine *Les Ondes* in October 1941 and survive the Occupation unscathed, seems to have been down to the protection of jazz-loving German military personnel including Dietrich Schulz-Koehn, dubbed 'Doktor Jazz'.[17]

Gypsy orchestras continued to be popular in
occupied Europe as long as they contained
no gypsies.

Swiss singer Johnny Hess enjoyed
a youth cult following.

The Gypsy guitarist Django Reinhardt
survived the war unscathed.

In the same month of October 1941, as the Austrian gypsies were
being deported to the Lodz Ghetto, Pierre Hani celebrated Reinhardt
in an article in *Vedettes* that purported to tell his 'astonishing story':
'Django, gypsy by nature and temperament, though French, was
born not only with inherent rhythm but also with exceptional
"musical imagination".'

Though the Roma and Sinti, like the Jews, were destined for
extermination under the new Nazi order, their music unlike that of
Jews was tolerated and enjoyed as long as it was not actually performed
by gypsies. In August 1943 the author of an article in *Les Ondes* about
the 'Gypsy Orchestra' of Raymond Verney, currently performing for
Radio Paris, was at pains to explain to readers that there were no
gypsies in the orchestra and only one Romanian. Like Beethoven,

The Merry Widow and swing, 'gypsy' music was enjoyed by all sides in the war and too popular to be suppressed even by Hitler and Stalin.

The craze for swing, which had climaxed in 1939, continued unabated through the war. The Swiss singer and songwriter Johnny Hess achieved the kind of teen-idol status that we associate more with the post-war period. The officially sanctioned apotheosis of swing came in 1942 with the production of the film *Mademoiselle Swing* starring Irène de Trebert, accompanied by the band of her husband Raymond Legrand.

Many wartime French songs continued to celebrate the international vogue for swing.

Swing had a highly ambiguous status in Germany and France throughout the war. It was grudgingly endorsed and exploited by both the Nazi and the Vichy regimes but in Germany the very use of the word 'swing' was disapproved of or even banned. There has been a debate about the extent to which the wartime enthusiasm for jazz in France represented some form of cultural resistance. A review of concerts given in Paris in January 1942 by the Belgian jazz band of Fud Cantrix, by the critic Pierre Hani in the magazine *Vedette*, is illuminating. Without mentioning the Germans, Hani refers discretely to the period of the Occupation: 'It is absolutely undeniable that for the past 18 months, the vogue for jazz in Paris has

Irène de Trébert starred in the movie Mademoiselle Swing.

only grown and become more splendid. The Parisian public has never rushed as enthusiastically to concerts of swing and every time the Salle Pleyel has proved too small for the crowds of lovers of syncopated music.' Hani may have been pushing his luck with the ever-vigilant Nazi censors with the ringing declaration with which he ends his

The jazz-loving Zazous adopted a distinctive mode of dress.

review: 'And let us rejoice in the arrival in France of these foreign artists and friends: clear proof of the vitality of this "artistic life" that will never die.'[18]

Swing became associated with a very special kind of resistance amongst the youth of both France and Germany. This has been interpreted as an early manifestation of the kind of youth rebellion more associated with the post-war period, rather than as a sophisticated critique of Fascism. The phenomenon was not confined to countries under totalitarian rule: the 1940 Swedish film *Swing it, Master!* concerns conflict between an authoritarian older generation and a freedom-loving younger generation addicted to swing.

In France the swing rebels were known as 'Zazous', a term ultimately derived from the scatting of the black American performer Cab Calloway, and first used by Johnny Hess in the refrain of his 1938 song 'Je suis Swing!'

> La musiqu' nègre et le jazz hot
> Sont déja de viell's machin's
> Maintenant pour être dans la note
> Il faut du swing.
> Le swing n'est pas un' mélodie
> Le swing n'est pas un' maladie
> Mais aussitot qu'il vous a plu
> Il vous prend et n'vous lâch' plus
>
> Je suis swing
> Je suis swing
> Zazou, zazous
> Zazou, Zazouzé

Apart from their passion for swing, the Zazous were characterized (like many other rebellious youth groups) by distinctive and eccentric clothing. The boys and girls wore baggy and wide-shouldered jackets in defiance of wartime cloth restrictions and the girls outraged the *petit bourgeois* morality of Vichy with their short skirts. The boys provoked with their lengthy greased-up hair, and both sexes sported loud checked materials and carried umbrellas as a fashion accessory.

The idiosyncrasies of the Zazous were mocked affectionately in popular songs such as Johnny Hess's 'Ils sont Zazous!' of 1942 and 'Y a des Zazous' recorded by Andrex in

Nazi-inspired propaganda mocked the boastfulness of 'We're gonna hang out the washing on the Siegfried Line'.

January 1944, and less affectionately in caricatures in right-wing journals that implied that they were feckless and decadent. By 1943 Zazous who appeared on the streets risked being beaten up and having their hair forcibly cut by Fascist youths or being rounded up for forced labour in Germany.

Their German equivalents, the so-called 'Swingjugend', risked a far worse fate—the concentration camp or execution. The need for access to forbidden gramophone records and for some knowledge of English tended to restrict the Swingjugend to an urban elite. They shared a number of characteristics with their French cousins, particularly a partiality for baggy jackets, long hair and the carrying of umbrellas, and they adopted the provocative greeting of 'Swing Heil!' From 1941 the repression by the Nazi authorities of dissident youth groups was increasingly brutal, with raids on their clubs and the arrest and deportation of ringleaders.

Perhaps the most bizarre use of music during the Second World War involved the creation by the Nazis for propaganda purposes of a swing band made up of excellent jazz musicians drawn from all over Europe. This band went by the English name of 'Charlie and his Orchestra.' 'Charlie' was one Karl Schwedler, the son of a plumber, who affected the manners and lifestyle of a wealthy playboy, wearing an Old Etonian tie and milking to the full his privileged status as a valuable tool of Nazi propaganda. According to Friedrich Meyer who arranged some of the songs for the band, Schwedler was 'just happy to get exemption and not to have to go and play soldiers.' Schwedler possessed a reasonably pleasant crooning voice and serviceable if noticeably accented English. His English was good enough to enable him to devise lyrics for the songs, though they are often clumsy and unidiomatic. Friedrich Meyer recalled 'the lyrics were quite good and we had a good laugh at the time.'[19] It is doubtful whether English-speaking listeners would have found much to laugh at in these amateurish texts, even disregarding their objectionable content.

The musical leader of the band was the respected tenor-saxophonist Lutz Templin. Schwedler and Templin, once established, were constant but other members of the band came and went according to the fortunes of war. Germans were increasingly replaced by foreigners when required for military service. By the time the singer Evelyn Künnecke (daughter of the successful operetta composer Eduard Künnecke) came to work with the band in the final months of the war, it was made up almost entirely of non-Germans:

Evelyn Künneke was saved from death row to sing American hits on German radio.

The special orchestra, that worked for this purpose in a big bunker in the Masurenallee consisted largely of Italian, Belgian and Czech musicians. There were also half-Jews and gypsies, freemasons, Bible students, homos and communists—people who would not otherwise have sat down to play skat with the Nazis. But as their work was regarded as important for the war effort, they were sitting behind music stands and not behind barbed wire, and playing swing.[20]

As Evelyn Künnecke suggests, few of the musicians involved in these recording sessions would have had any sympathy with their ultimate aim. Even the leader of the band, Lutz Templin, was not a Nazi party member, a significant omission that would have put any professional under serious disadvantage at the time.

For Evelyn Künnecke, collaboration with Charlie's Orchestra was a matter of life and death. In January 1945 she was in prison under likely death sentence for the crime of 'defeatism', having made some casual drunken remarks about a probable Russian victory. She was rescued from this situation by two SS officers, one of whom communicated the mysterious message 'Ella lässt schön grüssen' ('Ella sends her best'). Künnecke was required to record a copy of one of Ella Fitzgerald's current hits to be used to entice Allied troops to listen to German radio. This was in any case unlikely to have made much difference in February 1945.[21]

The bulk of the songs chosen for the addition of propaganda texts were drawn from pre-war Broadway shows or Hollywood musicals. The most represented composer, unsurprisingly, was the prolific and popular Irving Berlin. (One wonders if his plagiarisers knew of the famous headline when Irving Berlin joined up in the First World War: 'American Army takes Berlin'). Among the Irving Berlin numbers used were: 'I'm Putting All My Eggs in One Basket', 'Slumming on Park Avenue' (used twice), 'Change Partners', 'Alexander's Ragtime Band' and 'But Where Are You?' The Gershwins were represented by 'They All Laughed', Rodgers and Hart by 'Blue Moon', Cole Porter by 'You're the Top', Harold Arlen by 'Stormy Weather', Walter Donaldson by 'You're Driving Me Crazy' and 'Why'd ya make me fall in love?' The 1937 Disney movie *Snow White and the Seven Dwarfs* provided 'Whistle While You Work' (Frank Churchill), and 'Alone' (Nacio Herb Brown and Arthur Freed) came from the 1935 Marx Brother's film *A Night at the Opera*.

In this context the Nazis clearly had no inhibitions about using the work of Jewish composers. At least two Yiddish songs were used: 'Bei mir bist du schön' and 'Who'll buy my Bublitchky?' 'Makin' Whoopee', the signature song of the Jewish comedian Eddie Cantor, was used for a particularly crass attack on the Jews.

> Another war, another profit
> Another Jewish business trick!

Another season
Another reason for makin' whoopee!

We throw our German names away
We are the kikes of USA
You are the goys, folks,
We are the boys, folks
We're makin' whoopee!

'We're gonna hang our washing on the Siegfried Line' was parodied almost as soon as it came out and before its boasting was proved hollow by the fall of France. Vera Lynn's great success 'We'll meet again' was reproduced straight without propaganda added and was presumably transcribed from British radio broadcasts rather than from sheet music, as the record label calls the song 'Will meet again'.

The chief criterion for the choice of songs seems to have been familiarity with British and American audiences. There are many standard favourites from earlier years. From the 1920s we find Rudolf Friml's 'Indian Love Call' and 'Tea for Two' by Vincent Youmans. From the First World War period there is 'It's a long way to Tipperary', and the musical favourite 'Daisy, Daisy, give me your answer do' dates back to the 1890s.

The very first propaganda parody, recorded on 11 October 1939 before the involvement of Templin or Schwedler, was a version of the popular hymn 'Onward Christian Soldiers':

Onward conscript army
You have naught to fear.
Isaac Hore-Beisha
Will lead you from the rear.
Clad by Monty Burton,
Fed on Lyons pies,
Fight for Yiddish conquest
While the Briton dies.
Onward conscript army, marching on to war,
Fight and die for Jewry,
As we did before.
…
Driven to the shambles
Like a flock of sheep
By lying propaganda
By their plans laid deep.

So for Israel Moses Sieff
You must fight and die,
That Marks and Spencer's neon signs
May still light up our sky.
Forward, on to Poland.
Then million men shall fall
That Judah's reign of terror
May hold us all in thrall.

The detailed knowledge of British life and the idiomatic use of language set this text apart from those of Schwedler and suggest that it was written by a native English speaker. The authors of the book *Hitler's Airwaves*, Horst J P Bergmeier and Rainer E Lotz, believe that the text may already have been in use before the war amongst British Fascists.

Another text that betrays a more competent use of English than most, and a clever if warped sense of humour, is the one added to Cole Porter's 'You're the Top'. This is the only set of lyrics that would be likely to raise a smile for an English-speaking listener if only for the surreal incongruities that would suit it for inclusion in Mel Brooks's parody Nazi musical 'Springtime for Hitler':

You're the top—
You're a German flyer.
You're the top—
You're machine gun fire,
You're a U-Boat chap
With a lot of pep.
You're grand—
You're a German Blitz,
The Paris Ritz
An army van.

You're the Nile,
An attack by Rommel.
You're the mile
That I'd walk for a Camel, etc.

Certain themes of the propaganda songs are constant—anti-Semitism and the abuse of Churchill and later of Roosevelt. Other songs follow the unfolding events of the war. Several songs refer gloatingly to the destruction of British cities in the Blitz and others the impending loss of the British Empire. The 'St Louis Blues' begins with the announcement 'A Negro from the London docks sings the Black-Out Blues':

> I hate to see the evenin' sun go down
> Hate to see the evenin' sun go down
> 'cause the German, he done bombed this town.

The propaganda version of 'Bye, Bye, Blackbird' runs:

> I never cared for you before,
> Hong Kong, Burma, Singapore-
> Bye, bye Empire!
> India, I may lose, too
> Then I only have the London Zoo—
> Bye, bye, Empire.

Other songs refer more specifically to recent events. The parody of 'Slumming on Park Avenue' recorded in late 1940, contains the lines:

> Let's go bombing, oh, let's go bombing
> Just like good old British airmen do.
> Let us bomb the Frenchmen, who were once our allies!

referring to the destruction of the French fleet at Mers el-Kébir by the British on 3 July. The new text of 'Auf Wiedersehn, my dear' celebrates the defeat of British and Commonwealth forces in Greece in April 1941. The Germans were not alone in using the tactic of broadcasting light music with propaganda lyrics. The BBC Foreign Section did the same, with the advantage that it had plenty of talented refugee German speakers at its disposal. One of these was the composer of sophisticated Berlin cabaret songs, Mischa Spoliansky. Writing propaganda songs can hardly have been a congenial task for this most gentle and urbane of musicians, but Spoliansky may have been grateful for employment by the Foreign Section at a time when his music was banned on the mainstream BBC programmes because he was classified as an enemy alien and a member of the Italian Performing Rights Society. Spoliansky's songs were performed by Martin Miller, Albert Lieven, Walter Rilla, Peter Illing, Lucie Mannheim and occasionally by Spoliansky himself (certainly a much more subtle and accomplished performer than Karl Schwedler).

Three recordings of Spoliansky's broadcast propaganda songs survive, though unfortunately not those sung by him. The musical idiom is conservative with none of the jazzy infections typical of Charlie and his Orchestra, although Spoliansky could certainly do 'jazzy' when required. In a song aimed at German bomber pilots, entitled 'Wir fliegen England entgegen', whirring strings accompany a jaunty tune in a major key with the words:

> Wir fliegen England entgegen
> Gefährlich rauchet die Nacht
> Wir fliegen dem Tode entgegen
> O Deutschland Gute Nacht
>
> Viel Tausend Deutsche Piloten
> Die sturzten zum Ozean ab
> O England dass wir bedrohten
> Du bist unser Massengrab
>
> (We fly towards England.
> The night looms dangerously.
> We are flying towards death
> O Germany good night
>
> Many thousands of German pilots
> Crashed down into the ocean.
> O England that we threatened,
> You are our mass grave.)

Broadcasting this song on 26 June 1941 was a case of shutting the door too late. The Blitz had been over for a month. Operation Barbarossa had been launched against the Soviet Union three days earlier, and mass bombings of British cities by manned aircraft would never resume.

One has to ask whether any of these propaganda songs had the effect intended or if they just antagonized listeners. Despite her own experience as a victim of Nazi brutality, Evelyn Künnecke remembered with considerable distaste the parody version of 'Lili Marleen' by the refugee actress Lucie Mannheim that was broadcast by the BBC.

Probably more effective was the gentler approach taken towards the end of the war in the broadcasts of Glenn Miller's band, in which the music is allowed to speak for itself and of a life far removed from that in Germany towards the end of the Nazi regime.

Until his unexplained but probably accidental death, Glenn Miller was a powerful propaganda weapon for the Allies.

In October and November 1944, six programmes aimed at the German Wehrmacht were recorded by Glenn Miller and the band of the American Expeditionary Force at HMV's Abbey Road studios in London. With the end of the war clearly in sight, the tone of these programmes was relaxed and reassuring rather than mocking and menacing. There is no overt propaganda though Miller dedicates a swing version of the 'Song of the Volga Boatmen' 'as a tribute to our fighting Russian Allies'. The song 'Great Day' is dedicated to the day of 'victory and peace' without labouring the point although everyone must have realised by then that it could not be far off. Miller is introduced in German 'by Ilse' [Weinberger]. A great deal of heavy-handed humour is squeezed out of Miller's inept attempts to speak German (surely somewhat exaggerated). Several American songs are given in German translations but sung by American vocalists (including Johnny Desmond who had his own radio show with the BBC) with marked American accents. This was clearly a conscious choice, and at one point 'Ilse' comments on Miller's 'romantic' American accent in German.

Though these thoroughly bland broadcasts may not have persuaded many German soldiers to drop their guns, they may well have reinforced the widespread belief towards the end of the war that it might be better to move west and surrender to the Americans rather than to wait for the Russians.

1   Rodric Braithwaite, *Moscow 1941*, 2007, p. 300.
2   Diana Napier-Tauber, *Richard Tauber*, 1949, p. 220.
3   Paul Webb, *Ivor Novello, A Portrait of a Star*, 1999.
4   Sandy Wilson, *Ivor*, 1975, pp. 236-9.
5   Basil Dean, *The Theatre at War*, 1956, p. 404.
6   Florian Bruyas, *Histoire de l'opérette en France*, 1974.
7   Robert Dachs, *Sag beim Abschied*, p. 132.
8   Ernst Klee, *Kulturlexikon zum Dritten Reich*, 2009, p. 339.
9   Constant Lambert, *Music Ho!*, 1985, p. 185.
10 Horst J. P. Bergmeier and Rainer E. Lotz., *Hitler's Airwaves*, p. 144.
11 Erik Levi, *Music in the Third Reich*, 1994, p. 121.
12 Ludovic Tournès, 'Le Jazz: un espace de liberte', in *La Vie musicale sous Vichy*. p. 329.
13 Ibid.
14 Frank Ténot, *Celui qui aimait le jazz*, 2009.
15 André Coeuroy, *Histoire générale de Jazz*, 1942, pp. 7-30.
16 *Les Ondes*, 19 October 1943.
17 Alain Antonietto and Francois Billard, *Django Reinhardt*, 2004, p. 262.
18 *Vedette*, January 1942.
19 Horst J P Bergmeier and Rainer E Lotz, p. 153.
20 Evelyn Künneke, *Sing Evelyn Sing*, 1982, p. 75.
21 Ibid., p. 76.

Chapter 11
MODERN MEDIA:
RADIO, FILM AND THE GRAMOPHONE

Radio had already proved its value for purely military purposes in the First World War. In the Second, radio became the single most important weapon of propaganda. Goebbels's understanding and exploitation of the mass media of radio and film amounted to something close to genius and Germany led the way in these matters. 'Volksemfänger'— cheap radios with the reception range deliberately limited to prevent the German people listening to foreign radio stations—were mass-produced. As early as 28 January 1939, eight months before the outbreak of war, Goebbels noted that radio was now regarded as *kriegswichtig* ('important for war') and was already being put on a war footing, adding tersely: 'More good music. Less foreign works.'[1] Ultimately Goebbels's attempts to monopolize the use of radio as a weapon were frustrated despite mass confiscations of radios in occupied countries and draconian punishments for those caught listening to foreign radio stations; the British in particular turned the tables on the Axis powers, using radio to great effect against them. The constant references to radio in the diary of Anne Frank show how the BBC became a lifeline to the oppressed peoples of Europe.

It is worth pausing here to consider the French radio magazine *Les Ondes*, which appeared between 1941 and 1944. *Les Ondes* was the house journal of the collaborationist Radio Paris. As a valued tool of German propaganda in France, *Les Ondes* enjoyed a privileged position. By wartime standards it was lavishly produced. Until its final months it had attractive coloured covers and plentiful illustrations.

The first edition, which appeared on 21 April 1941, was adorned with a smiling portrait of the operetta star Yvonne Printemps. Over the next three years the covers depicted a wide range of popular and

State of the art technology at an Italian radio station in 1940.

serious musical stars, evidence of the high quality of the programming
and of a catholicity of musical taste. A statement of intent in the first
edition informed the readers that *Les Ondes* would be more than just
a listing of programmes. '*Les Ondes* will be a journal for the family,
for the wife and the child. It will advise and entertain. It will help
readers to overcome the little difficulties of everyday life.' It also
invited readers to explore the *coulisses* of the radio through its pages

*A porter listens to a Furtwängler
concert over a 'Volksemfänger'.
(Der Adler, 21 October 1941)*

as they might explore the backstage area
of a theatre. There were also informative
and educational articles about music
and the theatre, reviews, and interviews
with leading artists, such as the sultry
chanteuse Suzy Solidor and the great
operatic bass Vanni-Marcoux.

The propaganda element was
blatant, with a declaration on the
second page that the Axis was invincible
'because of its material strength and
still more because of the spirit that

moves it … To harm Germany, to oppose its new social strength out of fear, had led us to where we are today. We agree, do we not, on this historical point? So, let us make a gesture, a single one, let us respond to her advances and march together at her side towards a future that her strength, her victories have henceforth made inevitable.'

At the end of the war, working for Radio Paris was made a punishable offence. Many musicians and actors must have breathed a sigh of relief when the premises of Radio Paris and its archives were torched during the Liberation. On leafing through the pages of *Les Ondes* it becomes clear that very few prominent musical and theatrical performers managed to stay entirely aloof from Radio Paris. However, it should be pointed out that among the names we see in the pages of *Les Ondes* are several who proved to be determined and heroic opponents of Nazism, such as the cabaret singer Eva Busch and the violinist Maurice Hewitt.

Les Ondes provided listings not only for Radio Paris but also for the quasi-independent French National Radio (programmes ending every night with the 'Marseillaise') and other French radio stations such as Paris-Mondial and Rennes-Bretagne, as well as radio stations in the German Reich.

The attempts of German and French radio stations to attract listeners with high culture were duplicated in other countries. Between Italy's declaration of war on 10 June 1940 and the abrupt cessation of all such activities in September 1943, days after the Allied landings on the Italian mainland, the Italian state radio EIAR recorded and broadcast 128 complete operas.[2] As in Germany, these operas were sung entirely in the vernacular. The repertoire was almost exclusively Italian and with a strong predominance of *verismo* and post-*verismo* operas. This may well have reflected current Italian musical taste as much as any political directive from above. Of the 128 operas, just 8 were German (3 Wagner, 2 Strauss, 2 Mozart and one Gluck) and 2 French (the inevitable *Faust* and *Carmen*). There was one Russian opera, *Boris Godunov*, broadcast on 14 June 1941, suggesting that the Italian radio authorities had no inkling of the German invasion of the Soviet Union that would take place a week later.

For opera lovers, the casting of many of these broadcasts is mouth-watering—Mascagni's *Isabeau* and *Lodoletta* with Beniamino Gigli, *La Traviata* with Magda Olivero—these are recordings every collector would love to have. Also tantalising are the names of singers with legendary reputations who are barely represented by commercial recordings,

Radio advertisement in the propaganda magazine Signal.

Shortwave radio broadcasts from Germany.

such as Giuseppina Cobelli and Iris Adami-Corradetti. It is known that radio archives in Turin were destroyed by Allied bombing, but it is nevertheless a mystery that these Italian wartime broadcasts seem to have disappeared so comprehensively.

In Britain the BBC not only mastered the arts of propaganda, but in addition gained an international reputation for relatively truthful news reportage; at the same time it offered a crop of domestic programmes that amounted to a golden age of radio entertainment.

Most popular of all was the morale-boosting humour of ITMA ('It's that man again'—referring to Hitler) that added a rich array of catch-phrases ('Don't mind if I do', 'Happy as a sandbag') and stock characters (Mrs Mopp) to the British popular imagination.[3] Music programmes such as 'Worker's Playtime' and 'Music While You Work' made their contribution to the war effort. On 29 January 1942 the BBC launched its longest-lasting radio programme, 'Desert Island Discs', with Vic Oliver, the Austrian-born comedian and musician, and son-in-law of Winston Churchill. Oliver requested a Chopin étude played by Alfred Cortot, a notorious official of the Vichy regime, the nostalgic First World War song 'Roses of Picardy', Tchaikovsky's 'Marche Slav', 'The parade of the tin soldiers' and ended with Wagner's 'Ride of the Valkyries'.[4]

In 1941 movies made in both Britain and Germany reflected the importance of radio. With heavy-handed propaganda the British film *Freedom Radio* tells the somewhat implausible story of a heroic attempt to set up a resistance radio transmitter within Nazi Germany. One scene in the movie has a ring of truth and foreshadows an incident in Hans Fallada's novel *Alone in Berlin,* showing an old woman arrested by the Gestapo after having been denounced by a neighbour for listening to a foreign radio station.

Despite the fact that there is a portrait of Adolf Hitler hanging in almost every interior shot, the German film *Wunschkonzert* wears its propaganda more lightly, following Goebbels's dictum that propaganda is more effective when it is not too obvious. The film presents radio as a unifying factor between military and civilian and all levels in German society.

Television had been developed in the 1930s in several countries, including Britain, France, Germany and the United States, but only began to play a significant role in moulding public opinion after the war.

Recording the popular British radio show ITMA. (Parade, *May 20 1940*)

German soldiers watching television in France. (Der Adler, *1942*)

Public television had been launched in Britain in 1936, but reached no more than a tiny elite and was closed down altogether at the outbreak of war. In line with the high hopes that the Nazi regime invested in superior German technology, the Germans continued to experiment with the medium. Theatre, opera and other musical entertainments were televised by the Germans in France for the benefit of the Wehrmacht and a very limited French public. Up to twelve hours of programmes a day were broadcast between 7 May 1943 and 16 August 1944.[5] On 30 June 1942 the magazine *Der Adler* ran an article on the new medium with illustrations of television studios and German soldiers watching a televised film.

1939, the year that war broke out in Europe, is often deemed to be the peak year in the history of Hollywood. It was the year of such hugely successful movies as *Gone with the Wind*, *The Wizard of Oz*, *Destry Rides Again*, *Stagecoach* and *Ninotchka*. On both sides of the Atlantic, tens of millions went to the movies every week, and only radio reached a wider audience. As usual, Goebbels was ahead of the game in perceiving the propaganda potential of the medium. Though the Hollywood 'moguls' were mostly of Russian or Hungarian Jewish origin, with the exception of the Warner brothers, they hesitated to take a stand against Fascist regimes for fear of endangering lucrative foreign markets.

Music was an integral part of nearly every sound movie, whether fictional, documentary or newsreels, the latter accompanied by a constant stream of music to heighten the impact of the images. The up-beat music used with images of warfare often strikes us now as highly incongruous.

The Hollywood studios employed their own house composers. During the 1930s émigré composers such as Max Steiner, Franz Waxman and Erich Korngold created the lush orchestral sound that we associate with the 'Golden Age' of Hollywood. Musically speaking, Hollywood was a world in itself and quite separate from the musical life of the East Coast of America. The East Coast musical establishment led by Aaron Copland disdained the Hollywood composers—even Korngold, who had had an important career as a 'serious' composer before arriving in Hollywood. Korngold's magnificently lush violin concerto, premiered in 1947, using music recycled from his movie scores, was notoriously and unfairly dismissed by a New York critic as 'more corn than gold'.[6] In turn, the moguls showed little interest in employing composers from outside the studio system.

Among the 'serious' composers who found very occasional employment were Alexandre Tansman, Ernst Toch, Darius Milhaud and Mario Castelnuovo-Tedesco, but none of them produced a significant body of work for the Hollywood film industry. Columbia's disastrous experience with Igor Stravinsky must have confirmed studio suspicions of composers with European reputations. Perhaps on the grounds that Norway is not far from Russia and presumably without being very familiar with Stravinsky's music, Columbia commissioned the great modernist to write the score for a film about the Nazi invasion of Norway. Stravinsky went ahead and wrote his score before the film itself was completed, expecting the filmmakers to fit in with his music. The score was rejected as unsuitable and later transformed by Stravinsky into his orchestral piece 'Four Norwegian Moods'.

In European countries the division between the classical music establishment and the film industry was not always so great. In Britain, Vaughan Williams, Lennox Berkeley and William Walton contributed to the war effort through their film scores. In Russia, Shostakovich and Prokofiev both wrote for films during the war. Prokofiev's scores for Eisenstein's movies, the pre-war anti-German *Alexander Nevsky* and the wartime *Ivan the Terrible*, are arguably the greatest film scores ever written.

In France most of the leading composers kept the pot boiling during the war by writing music for films. For composers as for directors and actors, working for the German-controlled studio Continental was regarded as a black mark at the end of the war. Among those who tarnished their reputations in this way were Georges Van Parys, perhaps the most prolific film composer of the war years, the songwriter Vincent Scotto, and the more serious composers Tony Aubin and Henri Sauguet. Otherwise, composing for the movies did not damage the professional standing of Claude Delvincourt, Georges Auric, Arthur Honegger, Francis Poulenc, Germaine Tailleferre, Maurice Thiriet, Jacques Ibert, Jean Francais, Marcel Delannoy and Henri Tomasi.[7]

The French film industry—which thrived under the German Occupation—also offered opportunities to Jewish composers who could not work under their own names. Under the pseudonym 'Georges Mouqué' Joseph Kosma provided music for the Charles Trenet vehicle *Adieu Léonard*, and for two masterpieces of Marcel Carné, *Les Visiteurs du Soir* in 1942 and *Les Enfants du Paradis* in 1944.[8] Roger Désormière bravely lent his name to Jean Wiener for work on the movie *Le voyageur de La Toussaint*.

With the coming of sound, the movie industry had done much to familiarize mass audiences with the sound of the symphony orchestra. The Hollywood sound of Steiner, Waxman and Korngold itself owed a huge debt to nineteenth- and early twentieth-century classical tradition and in particular to the music of Wagner, Tchaikovsky, Richard Strauss, Rachmaninov and Debussy. Real as well as pastiche classical music was used in a great many films.

In his book *Film and the Second World War* Roger Manvell notes that Western classical music was routinely used by Japanese filmmakers during the war. 'Haydn was used in support of scenes of the camouflage of planes in *Occupation of Sumatra*, Wagner's *Die Walküre* for scenes of parachuting arms and troops, Tchaikovsky to give emotional force to the wrecking of an airfield, and *Meistersinger* for the finale of destruction.'[9]

One of the most successful German movies of the Second World War, *Wunschkonzert*, makes extensive use of classical music, which is also integral to the plot. *Wunschkonzert* was seen by more people in Europe than any other film, after *Die grosse Liebe*. It shares several themes and situations with that film, making one aware of how formulaic and carefully calculated these films were. There is the same conflict between love and patriotic duty and a mildly homo-erotic subplot in the sentimental friendship between an officer and his junior side-kick. Despite the Nazi disapproval of homosexuality, male bonding was encouraged by the Nazis, just as it had been in ancient Greece, to aid the war effort.

The opening titles are accompanied by the fanfares from Liszt's 'Les préludes', familiar to German radio audiences from news bulletins of Nazi victories and also used to begin the regular Sunday afternoon broadcasts of the radio programme 'Wunschkonzert für die Wehrmacht'. The opening scenes, which take place during the 1936 Berlin Olympics, make use of footage from Leni Riefenstahl's film documentary of that event (as does the British film *Freedom Radio*). We see the famous moment of the blond athlete carrying the Olympic flame that so impressed the BBC commentator in 1936,

but with the soundtrack of Strauss's Olympic Hymn replaced by a new purpose-written hymn by the film composer Werner Bochmann.

The heroine Inge Wagner, played by the archetypal German girl-next-door Ilse Werner, and the hero, Flight Lieutenant Herbert Koch, played by Carl Raddatz, are brought together by chance and fall in love. They are separated when he is sent on a secret mission with the Condor Legion in the Spanish Civil War. They make contact again when Lieutenant Koch requests the Olympic Hymn to be played in a broadcast of 'Wunschkonzert'. After further mishaps and misunderstandings

The Nazis were happy to promote male bonding if not homosexuality.

the lovers are re-united at the end of the film but the concluding song, 'Denn wir fahren gegen Engelland' ('Now we go against England'), is a reminder that duty still takes precedence and that there will be further separations.

The film sets out to demonstrate the importance of music for all levels of German society both military and civilian. We see German soldiers at the front eagerly listening to concerts over the radio and sailors making their own music in a submarine. A young conscript in uniform plays Beethoven on an upright piano surmounted by a bust of the composer, and surrounded by members of his family who listen reverently before he goes to war. Later he dies a hero's death while playing the organ in a church in the midst of a battle, in order to guide his comrades and divert the enemy fire. The film ends with a potted version of a 'Wunschkonzert', demonstrating the range of music offered to the Wehrmacht in these concerts. Eugen Jochum conducts the Berlin Philharmonic in the Overture to Mozart's *Figaros Hochzeit*, Paul Hörbiger sings a song in Viennese dialect. The hyperactive Hungarian musical star Marika Rökk performs a number from one of her movies, and the operatic bass Wilhelm Strienz sings the sentimental 'Gute Nacht Mutter' at the request of a grieving mother whose son has been killed at the front.

The on-going discussion on both sides of the war about the relative merits of classical and popular music found its way into morale-boosting musical movies in Britain and Germany. In Vera Lynn's first movie, the 1943 *We'll Meet Again,* her diffident love interest is an aspiring composer of classical music. After a few pep talks about the value of popular music, he eventually finds success as a composer of popular songs for Vera Lynn. This plot line echoes that of a movie made the previous year in Germany called *Wir machen Musik,* in which the classical composer Karl Zimmermann (played by Viktor de Kowa) falls in love with the whistling songstress Anni Pichler (Ilse Werner) who performs with a female jazz band. While giving Anni a lesson on harmony, Karl angrily rejects *Gebrauchsmusik* (mu-

Ilse Werner as she appeared in the first scene of the film Wunschkonzert.

sic for use), jazz and popular songs as beneath him. She retorts that even Bach was prepared to write *Gebrauchsmusik* and expresses a pragmatic attitude to the use of music that would have been endorsed by Goebbels and indeed by certain left-wing American composers of the period. The issue of *Gebrauchsmusik* had been hotly debated by musical ideologues of differing political persuasions throughout the inter-war period, but it is surprising to find it cropping up in the middle of the war in an entertainment movie of singular silliness.

Karl's pretentious opera *Lucretia* is booed (or rather whistled) off the stage in a scene strangely reminiscent of the scene in *Citizen Kane* for which Bernard Hermann provided an aria from a mock opera entitled *Salammbo* in 1941. One wonders whether some covert borrowing went on between enemy composers or whether they were just thinking along parallel lines.

Wir machen Musik ends with a triumphant musical within a musical for which Karl has provided the music to display the singing and whistling talents of Anni, in an all-singing, big-band extravaganza that could have come straight from the studios of MGM.

A German film that makes conspicuous use of a pre-existing classical score is Leni Riefenstahl's *Tiefland*. The film is loosely based on Eugen D'Albert's opera, and music from the opera is heard in the background throughout. The controversy concerning this film centres on Riefenstahl's use of gypsy extras as stand-ins for Spanish peasants in scenes supposedly shot in the Pyrenees but actually shot in the Alps; many of them were later murdered at Auschwitz. Filming took place between 1942 and 1944, though after many setbacks the film was only released ten years later. The combination of D'Albert's haunting music and Riefenstahl's painterly photography creates some moments of extraordinary beauty, but the film is far from the masterpiece that it was claimed to be by admirers such as Jean Cocteau. Riefenstahl's clumsy handling of dialogue and character do not confirm her reputation as a great director and her own performance as the heroine Marta is embarrassingly bad.[10]

Tiefland compares interestingly with a near contemporary film by another legendary actor-director: Charlie Chaplin's *The Great Dictator* makes highly original use of classical music. Filming started in the first month of the European war, September 1939, when America was still officially neutral. Chaplin's outspoken attack on Fascism was brave and ahead of its time in a country in which 'premature' opposition to Fascism later came to be seen as 'Un-American'.

When Chaplin's Jewish barber (who shares a resemblance with the dictator Hynckel) shaves a customer in rhythm with Brahms's Hungarian Dance No 5, it is a comedic *tour-de-force*. The scene in which Hynckel (alias Hitler) dances with a balloon of the world to the strains of the Prelude to Act I of Wagner's *Lohengrin* is breathtaking as a performance (Chaplin is certainly a more graceful dancer than Riefenstahl) and is at the same time incomparably brilliant and effective as a piece of filmmaking.

Leni Riefenstahl, who directed and starred in the notorious movie version of Tiefland.

Chaplin shared with Hitler not only the month of his birth (April 1889—what does that say about star signs?) and a toothbrush moustache but also a passion for Wagner. Chaplin's use of the *Lohengrin* prelude, not only in the scene with the balloon but to accompany his final message of hope, shows that he used Wagner's music not because of its association with Hitler but for its ability to uplift.

Another American movie completed in 1940 that made highly original if controversial use of classical music was Walt Disney's full-length animated cartoon *Fantasia*, with the conductor Leopold Stokowski (once again replacing the projected Toscanini) and the Philadelphia Orchestra. *Fantasia* reflected a common desire of the period to bring classical music to a wider and more youthful and popular audience. It made use of advanced and experimental sound techniques, including a version of stereo called 'Fantasound' that limited the number of theatres in which it could be shown and consequently its profitability. It was re-released in a shortened mono version in 1942 but did not break into profit until long after the war. For most of the eight musical segments, Disney and Stokowski played safe with popular classics such as Tchaikovsky's 'Nutcracker Suite' and Beethoven's 'Pastoral' Symphony, but the use of abstraction to go with Bach's 'Toccata and Fugue in D minor' and the inclusion of the most iconic work of musical modernism, Stravinsky's *Rite of Spring* was undoubtedly bold for the time.

Two outstanding 'biopics' of great composers came out in 1942. The Austrian *Wen die Götter lieben* ('Those whom the Gods love'), which cashed in on the Mozart fever of the previous Mozart anniversary year, and the French *La symphonie fantastique* celebrated Hector Berlioz. Apart from a scene of heroic pathos in which the ailing Mozart passes on the torch of German music to the young Beethoven (played by René Deltgen, an actor with a permanent frown), *Wen die Götter lieben* wears its nationalist ideology lightly; it concentrates on Mozart's love life and in particular on his relationship with the sisters Aloysia and Constanze Weber. For the background music, the film composer Alois Melichar trawled through Mozart's oeuvre to find fragments and themes, which he blended into a musical soup that owes more to Wagnerian music drama than it does to any musical form that would have been recognised by Mozart. Along the way we are treated to more respectfully handled extracts of Mozart's works presented as performances within the movie, with the participation of the Vienna Philharmonic Orchestra and the singers Erna Berger (who provides the voice of Aloysia Weber) and Karl Schmidt-Walter. Visually the film is all silks and satins and shiny rococo as is the treatment of Mozart's character. Its hagiographic nature is emphasized by the way that the camera constantly hones in on Mozart's profile, recalling countless commemorative medallions and postage stamps.

Berlioz is presented more vividly by the actor Jean-Louis Barrault, who takes the composer through from callow youth to stoical old age. Fragments of the 'Symphonie fantastique' are used to accompany the action and amongst the musical treats offered are a lengthy extract from the monumental *Requiem*, performed—as the credits proudly boast—by 750 musicians, and two tantalisingly short excerpts from the lovely 'Absence' from the song cycle 'Nuits d'Eté' for which the voice of the actress Renée St Cyr is dubbed by a very fine but unacknowledged soprano. Goebbels found this movie sufficiently stirring to be alarmed by it. He wrote a stinging rebuke to the German official in charge of its production, Alfred Greven: 'I am very unhappy that our offices in Paris seem to be teaching the French how to represent nationalism in images.'[11] Other historic composers and musicians who were represented in wartime movies included Chopin, Liszt, Robert and Clara Schumann, Brahms, Bizet and the diva, Maria Malibran.

Not to be outdone by the Europeans, the Americans celebrated their own musical hero George Gershwin in *Rhapsody in Blue*, an exceptionally lavish 'biopic' made in 1944 by Warner Brothers. A degree of authenticity was ensured by the employment of Gershwin's close friend Oscar Levant to play himself and give advice on Gershwin's life and music. Other well-known personalities who made cameo appearances in the movie, playing themselves, included Paul Whiteman, Al Jolson and George White. In the words of Levant, 'It got very Pirandelloish'.[12]

One of the most successful pieces of 'classical' music used in a wartime movie was in fact a fake. This was the 'Warsaw Concerto' composed by the British composer Richard Addinsell for the 1941 film *Dangerous Moonlight*. Like *Die grosse Liebe* and *Wunschkonzert*, the story concerns a conflict between love and patriotic duty, only in this case it is a three-way conflict with the added ingredient of music, as the hero is a famous Polish pianist-composer Stefan Radetzky, played by Anton Walbrook. With considerable chutzpah the film studio RKO approached Rachmaninov with a request for a mini piano concerto for the movie. When the great Russian turned down their request and the rights to his existing concertos proved too expensive (though the makers of *Brief Encounter* were willing to pay for the use of his Second Piano Concerto in 1945), the studio had to make do with fake Rachmaninov by the British composer of light music Richard Addinsell.

In the late 1930s, Addinsell had already produced scores for several successful movies including *Fire over England*, *Goodbye Mr Chips* and *Gaslight*, and he was to make a modest contribution to the war effort with songs composed for Joyce Grenfell, but no one can have predicted just how successful Addinsell's concerto would turn out to be. Something of its extraordinary impact can be ascertained from the numerous references to it in Joyce Grenfell's diaries of her overseas tours, entertaining troops with the pianist Viola Tunnard. In Kirkuk, 'Viola did Albeniz, Chopin, Rachmaninoff, Moeran, Bach and Warsaw.' In Haifa, 'Viola played Warsaw in response to the usual requests and we ended on "Nellie Dean" with all the pub effects.' In Beirut, 'Viola gave 'em Chopin and Liszt and Moeran and finally, when asked for, Warsaw.' At a small military camp in Persia 'Viola played Warsaw afterward; and I had to do "Yours", both requests.' At the same camp Grenfell met a young airman who told her he was planning to have the Warsaw Concerto played at his wedding. 'He was, he said, crackers about it. Seen the picture four times just for the tune. That's just one of a dozen incidents, all relating to the magic the piece has over the boys.'

Thanks to its universal popularity the Warsaw Concerto rubbed shoulders with some unusual forms of entertainment. Grenfell described an amateur show put on by the navy in Bombay with the title 'Men only'. 'There were chorus girls—male ratings with knobbly knees or, once or twice, rather alarmingly feminine graces. There was a robust baritone who sang from one side of his face and made very nice noises indeed. There was a fakir who threw himself about on broken glass and ate a razor blade and an electric light bulb *and* fire. That was impressive but revolting and gave me hiccups ... And the peak of horror from my point of view was a performance of Warsaw in total darkness with the exception of a back set representing the bombed capital with flashes of fire and gun effects to drown the piano at stated intervals. The pianist was glib at runs and he had the music there with him in the inky blackness but he played a version entirely his own and did things to the rhythm and the note values and like everything else it went on far, far, far too long. Needless to say it was a big success.'[13]

Noel Coward's *Middle East Diary* confirms the Warsaw Concerto's universal popularity with overseas troops. Coward heard it at a concert given in Tripoli by the Royal Artillery Band on 27 September 1943, and remarked: 'The Royal Artillery Band was certainly catholic in its choice of music. It left no stone unturned from Brahms and Debussy to Sousa. The best item was really Dick's Warsaw Concerto. This fairly tore the place up.'[14]

In January 1945, when Warsaw was liberated by the Russians, the conductor André Kostelanetz and his soprano wife Lily Pons were in the foothills of the Himalayas entertaining Allied troops. On 19 January Kostelanetz noted in his diary: 'Joint US-British audiences that night. The British applauded "Stars and Stripes Forever" vociferously. That day there was a news flash of the capture of Warsaw and I made an appropriate announcement before we played the Warsaw Concerto, which was greeted very warmly.'[15]

The playing of a piece of film music written by a British composer in imitation of an American-naturalized Russian to celebrate the 'liberation' of Warsaw after the Russians had deliberately held back to allow its final and almost total destruction by the Germans, was one of the odder pieces of musical symbolism to come out of the war. The runaway success of the Warsaw Concerto spawned a plethora of cinematic piano concertos including Hubert Bath's 'Cornish Rhapsody' composed for the 1944 movie *Love Story* and 'The Dream of Olwen' composed by Charles Williams (Isaac Cozerbreit) for *While I Live*.

On all sides in the Second World War musical films were valued and encouraged as morale-boosters. The need for such movies was all the greater within the Reich after the war turned against Germany in the winter of 1942-43. *The Adventures of Baron Munchhausen*, filmed in colour with special effects that were spectacular even by Hollywood standards, was premiered on 3 March 1943 and must have helped to distract minds from the implications of the surrender of the 6th Army at Stalingrad exactly one month earlier. Film stars with musical talents such as Marika Rökk, Lizzi Waldmüller, Willy Fritsch and Johannes Heesters were kept busy before the cameras until the very end of the war. The sumptuous colour film of *Die Fledermaus* with the Dutch tenor Johannes Heesters, one of the most expensive films made in Germany up to that point, was still in production as the war ended and only released afterwards.

It is striking how many of the most popular stars of German musicals were not actually German. There was the Viennese contingent of stars like Lizzi Waldmüller, Paul Hörbiger and Hans Moser, but most came from outside the Reich. Until 1943 the number one musical film star was the Swede Zarah Leander. Her films were melodramatic rather than light-hearted, but usually contained at least one cheerful song that could be used as a morale-booster outside the context of the film. Other popular musical stars included the energetic Hungarian singer and dancer Marika Rökk who made eleven German movies between 1939 and 1944, and the 'Chilean Nightingale' Rosita Serrano who, like Leander, left Germany and fell out of favour with the regime in 1943. (While on tour in Sweden, Serrano performed in aid of a charity for Jewish refugees. The Nazi authorities responded by accusing her of spying and threatening her with arrest. Serrano wisely decided not to return to Germany.) The Dutch tenor Johannes Heesters remained to the bitter end, making a total of fourteen films between 1939 and 1944. (In 2008, aged 105, he caused widespread outrage with his unrepentant remarks about the Nazi era on Dutch TV.) Even Ilse Werner, famous for her whistling skills and regarded by Goebbels as the epitome of young German womanhood, was half Dutch and held a Dutch passport.

In France, the three most popular musical film stars of the war years were the Corsican heartthrob Tino Rossi who appeared in *Mon amour est près de toi* in 1943 and *L'île d'amour* in 1944, the quirky and brilliant Charles Trenet who appeared in *Romance de Paris* in 1941, *Frederica* in 1942 and *Adieu Léonard* in 1943, and the queen of French swing Irène de Trébert, whose most popular film was the 1942 *Mademoiselle Swing*.

By 1942 Germany and by proxy Vichy France were already at war with the United States, but Hollywood still held sway even if American films were no longer to be seen in the cinemas. French

Ebullient Hungarian musical star Marika Rökk.

Until 1943 the Swedish star Zarah Leander was the number one box office draw in Nazi-occupied Europe.

The 'Chilean nightingale' Rosita Serrano.

Charles Trenet reached the height of his popularity during the war.

illustrated magazines continued to feed a voracious public appetite for gossip about Hollywood celebrities such as Shirley Temple and Marlene Dietrich. What is most striking about *Mademoiselle Swing* is that it seems to have been virtually cloned from American models. Not only does the swing of Irène de Trébert and her bandleader husband Raymond Legrand sound thoroughly American, but the plot and the tone of the movie show its makers' familiarity with the films of Judy Garland and Deanna Durbin. *Mademoiselle Swing* offers harmless escapist entertainment. There is no mention of the war and only the eagle-eyed would spot the references to the Occupation through the fleeting appearances of the collaborationist newspaper *Les Nouveaux Temps* and of the premises of Radio Paris.

In Britain the three most popular musical film stars were George Formby, Gracie Fields and Vera Lynn. The humble working-class origin and eccentric teeth of all three were an integral part of their appeal to British audiences, but limited their attraction for Americans who required more glamour from their stars.

As far as musical movies were concerned it was Hollywood that led the way with bigger budgets and far slicker production values than anything that could be produced in Europe, even in the Neu Babelsberg studios of Berlin.

Dutch operetta star Johannes Heesters made 14 German movies between 1939 and 1944.

The French movie Mademoiselle Swing *closely followed Hollywood models.*

From the end of 1941, after America had entered the war, Hollywood musicals tended to take on a more patriotic tone and to end with big flag-waving finales. Hollywood turned its attention to the entertainment of troops and this in itself became the subject of a series of all-singing, all-dancing portmanteau movies that included *Thank Your Lucky Stars*, *This Is the Army*, *Thousands Cheer*, *Follow the Boys*, *Stage Door Canteen* and *Hollywood Canteen*.

Top American musical stars of the war years included Betty Grable, more famous for her 'million dollar' legs and for a pin-up photo distributed to five million GIs than for her singing and dancing skills; the 'Brazilian Bombshell' Carmen Miranda who acted as a colourful ambassadress in the American wartime charm offensive towards its southern neighbours; Bing Crosby who not only sang the best-selling song 'White Christmas' in the 1943 film *Holiday Inn*, but mined a rich vein of religious sentimentality in *Going My Way* and *The Bells of St Mary's*; and Judy Garland. In 1944 she appeared in *Meet Me in St Louis*—a film with no obvious connection to the war but that was, in the words of John Kobal, designed to 'quicken the heart of the man in the trenches' with its idealized picture of American values and family life.[16]

It took a little ingenuity to construct appropriate wartime roles for some bankable musical stars such as Fred Astaire, who was well past military age, or the sweet and youthful Deanna Durbin. The 1943 movie *The Sky's the Limit* cast Astaire as a rather elderly fighter pilot who sings 'My Shining Hour' as he sets out for the war. Durbin matured rapidly to take on a dramatic role in *The Amazing Mrs Holiday*, rescuing children caught up in the Pacific War while socking it to her audiences with 'Mighty lak' a rose' and Tosca's 'Vissi d'arte' in her gorgeous soprano voice. Durbin probably served the war effort more effectively by continuing to play lovable all-American small town girls in a series of movies in which she presented pot-pourris of popular, classical and patriotic songs as well as the odd tribute to America's allies. In *His Butler's Sister* in 1943 she sang a medley of Russian songs in what sounds like plausible Russian, accompanied by balalaikas. For *Nice Girl?* she shot alternative endings for American and British audiences, singing 'I give my thanks to America' or 'There'll always be an England'.

The need to engage America's significant black audience, now expected to play its part in the war, resulted in 1943 in two all-black musicals, *Cabin in the Sky* and *Stormy Weather*. Between them they presented a spectacular array of Afro-American musical talent including Ethel Waters, Lena Horne, Louis Armstrong, Bill Robinson, Cab Calloway and Fats Waller.

Despite fears at the start of the war that the big Hollywood studios would suffer financially, the wartime craving for entertaining and uplifting movies brought high attendance figures and record profits.

In addition to radio and film, the humble gramophone record played an important role in the musical life of the Second World War. The introduction of the electrical recording process in the 1920s had greatly enhanced the frequency range and quality of sound but in terms of format and convenience there had been little progress since the First World War. 78 rpm records on shellac were heavy and fragile. They rarely carried much more than four minutes of music per side and with the use of steel or brass needles they wore out rapidly. Nevertheless, they were regarded as a valuable commodity to be used at the front to entertain troops and on the radio to fill gaps between programmes and news bulletins. The Germans organized the theft of gramophone

Betty Grable was more famous for her legs than for her vocal or acting talents.

Hollywood Canteen *was one of a number of movies in which Hollywood stars were lined up to entertain the armed forces.*

Down Argentina Way. *With the help of the Brazilian star Carmen Miranda, Hollywood launched a charm offensive towards the United States's southern neighbours.*

Judy Garland in Meet Me in St Louis *and Deanna Durbin in a number of movies as a small town girl embodied everything that Americans believed they were fighting for.*

records along with musical instruments on a vast scale in the occupied territories. An article in *Der Adler* of 9 September 1941 illustrates German soldiers on the Russian front listening to gramophone records. We are told that the gramophone was 'discovered' in the ruins of a Russian aircraft hangar but assured that the records they are listening to are German.

Radio Paris boasted a collection of around 30,000 discs, amounting to something like 4,000 hours of music. This might not be much more than could be accommodated on a modern laptop or iPod, but in the words of Georges Preuilly in an article in *Les Ondes* in August 1943 it constituted 'a museum of voices and sound! A conservatoire of all who sing and act! A magic box for the radio!' Although Radio Paris could draw upon an exceptionally rich pool of musical talent for live broadcast, Preuilly estimated that 50 percent of broadcast time was taken up by the playing of records. 'Everyone knows that the record is one of the most important elements in broadcasting. Sometimes the star, sometimes merely useful, it triumphs one day and is the understudy the next. It fills the silences. It creates atmosphere. It is

The record library at Radio Paris.

German soldiers listen to records at the front on a looted gramophone.

universal. You can say what you like about recorded music. The air-waves would not be the same without it ...'

In Britain the lending of gramophone records was organized by ENSA as described by its director Basil Dean.

One of [Walter] Legge's schemes had been the formation of record libraries in each region, boxed into programmes of various types, such as symphony concerts, chamber music, piano recitals and so forth. There were also libraries of individual composers' works, catalogued under their names, for use at lecture-recitals, also scores for the use of those who wished to follow the music while the records were being played. Each box was provided with programme notes specially written by Edward Evans, the distinguished music critic (and brother of Dame Edith Evans). In these an effort was made to interest the prospective audiences in the lives of the composers and the meaning of their work. They were admirably done, quite simple and completely free from music jargon.

Distribution was controlled by the music advisers—usually their assistants acted as librarians—and more than once did I encounter a music adviser on the road with boxes of records stacked in the back of his car, like some itinerant village salesman. In due course distribution became so extensive that we had to institute a system of self-help, the various military units and factories exchanging the programmes among themselves by motor-cycle, or other means, and a time-limit had to be placed on the retention of each set—just like a lending-library. When the scheme was in full operation each regional library contained many thousands of records, and was continually being extended. In the London District alone the number exceeded ten thousand, because it was from this pool that the regional libraries were kept supplied. Recitals for civilians were often given under unusual conditions: during the London Blitz *The Magic Flute* (in German), with

310

Beecham conducting, was played in an air-raid shelter from the recordings made by Walter Legge in Berlin in 1938— so successfully that it was repeated the following night.[17]

Walter Legge later devised special vans in order to take concerts of gramophone records to soldiers at the front. According to Basil Dean:

> ... he began to pester our broadcasting engineers with his dream of taking music to men in the fox-holes. Giving way to his persuasion, the engineers eventually worked out designs for a rediffusion van, and the first prototype was built. This was a heavy-duty vehicle, equipped with its own power supply, a double turn-table for gramophone records, a microphone for the operator's announcements and two loudspeakers fitted to the roof of the truck, together with additional speakers on long leads, so they could be hung on the walls of buildings or in the trees when large audiences were assembled. Specially designed racks provided space for a library of 500 records. The amplifiers were designed to withstand rough usage and tropical conditions.
>
> The prototype was given exhaustive trials. Its success aroused great enthusiasm among our people. Soon there was a positive clamour from overseas for these rediffusion vans, which after the gremlins had been chased out of the first set of equipment, were supplied in considerable numbers not only to the Second Front but to Italy, the Middle East, Burma and Singapore. The record libraries which each truck carried included classical music and light music and variety programmes ...[18]

Now that music has become so easily and casually accessible, it is touching to read in letters and diaries of the war years how people sat down solemnly together to listen to gramophone records.

Shortages of shellac led several countries to institute schemes for the exchange of old records for new ones. Early in 1942 the War Production Board in America stopped the production of radio receivers and gramophones for personal use. Nevertheless, despite the exigencies of war an extraordinary quantity of new recordings was made during those years in Germany, France, Italy and Britain. Vera Lynn's autobiography describes the kind of difficulties encountered by recording artists in wartime conditions:

Even though shellac was in short supply there were still records to be made. Except that the faces of the orchestra kept changing, the routine for recording was much the same as it had always been; the difficulty lay in getting to the studios. One session for Decca at their West Hampstead studio had been booked for a nine o'clock start on a morning which just happened to follow a particularly heavy air raid.

After a nightmare journey through bomb-wrecked and burning streets, Vera Lynn arrived at the studio with just ten minutes of the recording session to go:

> My eyes were red and my voice was thick from the smoke and I was a bundle of nerves. But the orchestra had rehearsed the two numbers we were to do right down to the last dotted crochet, and the engineer had got the balance all sorted out, so Harry Sarton, who was taking the session, suggested that I went in anyway and did a couple of takes. I sang through both songs once, and that was it. Both sides were released, but the biggest irony is that I don't remember which ones they were.[19]

Most combatant countries were prepared to divert the necessary resources when it came to prestigious recording projects. In Italy, the fiftieth anniversary of the first performances of Mascagni's two most successful operas, *Cavalleria Rusticana* and *L'Amico Fritz*, were celebrated with complete recordings in 1940 and 1941, both conducted by the composer. (By 1941 it was no longer possible to present a sympathetic Jewish character in an Italian opera. The jolly marriage-broker Rabbi David in *L'Amico Fritz* is Aryanised and lauded with cries of 'Bravo Dottore' rather than of 'Bravo Rabbino'. It is sad to think of the great composer—who had used his last personal audience with Mussolini in 1939 to plead the cause of the Jewish composer Alberto Franchetti—lending his authority to this pusillanimity in the face of official anti-Semitism.) Verdi's lengthy *La Forza del Destino* was recorded near complete on 35 sides in 1942. Giordano's *Andrea Chenier* was recorded complete in 1942 and Verdi's *Un Ballo in Maschera* in 1943, both with Beniamino Gigli still close to the peak of his powers. In France there were the recordings of *Pelléas et Mélisande* and major works of Berlioz. In occupied Bohemia there were two complete recordings of Smetana's epic patriotic tone poem

'Ma Vlast'. In Britain William Walton's 'Belshazzar's Feast', modest in length but vast in resources needed, was recorded and in Germany Beethoven's Ninth Symphony, Mozart's *Requiem* and two recordings of Bach's *St Matthew Passion*.

Wartime conditions in the recording industry presented an unexpected bonus to several minor British composers. A number of works were recorded that would rapidly disappear from the repertoire after the end of the war, such as E J Moeran's Symphony in G Minor (recorded in 1942), Hamilton Harty's 'A John Field Suite' (recorded in 1943), John Ireland's Piano Concerto (recorded in 1942), and Holst's 'The Hymn of Jesus' (recorded in 1944).

America was the great exception, with a ban on new recordings from August 1942. This had nothing to do with the war, but was caused by a strike of musicians organised by the union leader James Petrillo. The strike lasted until 1944 and robbed jazz lovers of records of the early development of bebop, and classical music lovers of recordings of Lotte Lehmann and Lauritz Melchior in their final good years. Popular singers like Bing Crosby and Frank Sinatra got round the ban by using vocal instead of instrumental backing.

The ban occasionally caused a great deal of hardship to many musicians but could occasionally work quite spectacularly in their favour. In 1943 Duke Ellington went to the offices of his agent William Morris hoping to negotiate a loan of $2,500 to tide him over a lean period. To his surprise he found an envelope waiting for him with a cheque in it:

> And I looked at it because the cheque was supposed to go to William Morris, and I slipped it back in and said, Damn. 'That's $2,500! That's what I need.' I said I'd better check again, it's liable to be $22.50. It was $22,500. And I put that thing back in the envelope and ran out there [sic] like a stick-up man! What had happened, this was after the recording strike, after the recording strike we hadn't recorded anything, so we had no records, but a record we had recorded instrumentally in 1939, 'Never No Lament,' Bob Russell had now put a lyric to it and it was now doing very well by the Ink Spots and also another band. And this was what the cheque was for, the accumulated royalties, their release of our instrumental under a new title. [20]

It might seem extraordinary that such a ban with its potential impact on wartime morale was allowed to drag on for so long. However, Petrillo did allow musicians to go ahead with the recording of 'V-Discs', which were specially produced for United States military personnel overseas. These were 78 rpm discs made from the lighter and less fragile material of vinyl. A vast range of musical material was recorded with musicians from Frank Sinatra to Toscanini. The agreement was that the masters should be destroyed and the records never sold commercially. Happily, a great many V-discs survive and have become available on CD.

1   Joseph Goebbels, *Tagebücher*, Band 3: 1935-1939, p. 1302.
2   Giorgio Gualerzi and Carlo Marinelli Roscioni, *50 Anni di opera lirica alla RAI. 1931-80*, 1981.
3   P J Kavanagh, *The ITMA Years*, 1974.
4   Roy Plomley, *Desert Island Discs*, 1984.
5   Thierry Kubler, Emmanuel Lemieux, Cognac Jay, *La télévision française sous l'occupation*, 1990.
6   Irving Kolodin, *New York Sun*, March 1947.
7   Jacques Siclier, *La France de Pétain et son cinema*, 1981.
8   Maurice Fleuret, *Joseph Kosma*, 1988.
9   Roger Manvell, *Film and the Second World War*, 1974, p. 135.
10 Steven Bach. *Leni*, 2007, pp. 236-44, 291-4.
11 Pierre Armon, *Le monde du cinema sous l'occupation*, 1997, p. 97.
12 Sam Kashner and Nancy Schoenberger, *A talent for genius. The life and times of Oscar Levant*, p. 272.
13 Joyce Grenfell, *The Time of my Life*, p. 196.
14 Noel Coward, *Middle East Diary*, p.110.
15 James S Drake and Kristin Beall Ludecke, *Lily Pons: A centennial portrait*, 1999, p. 146.
16 John Kobal, *Gotta Sing Gotta Dance*, 1970, p. 221.
17 Basil Dean, *The Theatre at War*, 1956, p. 222.
18 Ibid., p. 291
19 Vera Lynn, *Vocal refrain*, p. 86.
20 Stuart Nicholson, *A portrait of Duke Ellington*, 1999, p. 253.

Chapter 12
WAR SONGS

During the Second World War, popular songs were potent ammunition in the war of words carried on over the airwaves. They were needed to pad out the news bulletins and the propaganda broadcasts, to attract listeners, and themselves often became part of the war of words.

These songs cover the gamut of human experience, but the songs that evoke the war most vividly are sentimental rather than patriotic or warlike. The most important single theme was the separation of loved ones. No war had ever displaced so many people. The resolutely cheerful 'Wish me luck as you wave me goodbye', sung by Gracie Fields in the film *Shipyard Sally*, appeared with perfect timing in 1939 just before the outbreak of war and the first departures of British troops to France. Soon after that, in the last months of 1939, 'Somewhere in France with you' was written by Michael Carr with the British Expeditionary Force specifically in mind. Despite its initial popularity it was obviously a song that was not sung very often between Dunkirk and D-Day.

Wartime songs of separation can be written from the viewpoint of either servicemen and women thinking about loved ones left behind, or else from that of those left behind. Many songs take the form of letters sent home—albeit heavily censored—that played such an important role in maintaining wartime morale. 'Don't Sit Under the Apple Tree (with anyone else but me)' expresses a common fear of infidelity that was often exploited negatively in demoralising propaganda broadcasts.

> Don't sit under the apple tree
> With anyone else but me

315

With anyone else but me,
Till I come marching home.

The charming lullaby 'Ninna nanna (Papa Sta in Guerra)' ['Daddy has gone to War'], recorded by Margherita Carosio in 1942, is sung from the point of view of a young mother left behind, assuring her baby that papa will be victorious and will come home soon.

The first great separation of the war was of urban children from their families, with the mass evacuation from the city centres that began even before the official declaration of war, and in Britain alone involved the movement of over three and a half million people in the first few months. This event, traumatic and heart-breaking for so many, is commemorated in the song 'Goodnight, children everywhere' by Gabriel Roger and Harry Philips. If the words seem mawkish today, they are sung with touching simplicity and sincerity by Vera Lynn, accompanied by a Wurlitzer organ in tremolo mode, on a record made in 1940.

Goodnight children everywhere,
Your mummy thinks of you tonight.
Lay your head upon your pillow.
Don't be a kid or a weeping willow.
Close your eyes and say a prayer.

Many of the most successful World War II songs concern the separation of lovers and families and their longing to be re-united. The bottomless appetite for such songs worried those elements in authority on the Allied side that feared an excess of sentimentality would undermine the morale of the troops. The BBC went so far as to set up an 'anti-slush' committee to counter the influence of Vera Lynn and her like. The efforts of the committee were in vain. Not for the first or last time the power of music proved stronger than the dictates of authority and the demand of the troops for Vera Lynn's sentimental songs proved impossible to repress.[1]

The war not only separated lovers but brought them together as well. It provided unprecedented opportunities for romantic and sexual adventures of all kinds—brief encounters, fumbled contact with strangers in the blackout, whirlwind romances and over-hasty marriages. Hurried courtship was the order of the day, as we hear in the lyrics of the Mills Brothers record 'I met her on Monday':

O I met her on Monday
The meeting was grand
The next day was Tuesday and I held.
Wednesday night I met her dad and mother
And gave a nickel to her freckle-faced brother.
I kissed her on Thursday at quarter to ten
Met her on Friday and kissed her again
What'ya think happened on Saturday night?
Mm, mm, that's right! We met the preacher
Mm, mm, that's right!

The promiscuity engendered by the war led to epidemics of venereal diseases that seriously threatened the war effort, necessitating campaigns of educational pamphlets and posters with slogans such as 'Fool the Axis—use prophylaxis'. The comedienne Bea Lillie describes performing some of her trademark suggestive songs at a military hospital: 'I'd spent a hour or so in one ward, wondering to myself why every patient had an odd look in his eyes and why he laughed so hard at the "suppose I move in" line. As I left, I said to the medical office at the door, "They're all so wonderful, these poor men. They've sacrificed so much for us. What ward is this?" "Venereal diseases," he said coolly.—Blackout!'[2]

Anglo-Saxon attitudes to sex meant that wartime sexual encounters could only be treated as a smutty joke or else veiled in the sanitized romance of a song like 'A Nightingale Sang in Berkeley Square', launched in the 1940 revue *New Faces*. A splendid example of the former, dating from the same year, is Florence Desmond's 'The deepest shelter in town'. As though accosting a passer-by in a bombing raid she sings:

I've got a cosy flat
There's a place for your hat
I'll wear a pink chiffon gown
And do I know my stuff
But if that's not enough
I've got the deepest shelter in town.

The Second World War brought together many couples, including the author's parents.

Even smuttier is the text of 'Blackout Bella' by the popular female impersonator

Lady with curls and Becky Sharp bonnet is Douglas Byng as he appears in "Revivals." He has half a-dozen quick changes in this sketch. Binnie Hale helps him struggle into his tight-fitting Empire gown.

Douglas Byng gets into drag.
(Parade, *19 February 1944*)

Douglas Byng. The British had a traditional liking for cross-dressing music hall artists and gave them a licence in sexual matters that would not have been accorded to straight performers. In fact, Byng's 'cross-dressing' was more often metaphorical than literal as he usually performed in a smart dinner suit. Byng was particularly proud of 'Blackout Bella' and included the full text in his autobiography.

I wrote my war song 'Blackout Bella' with an old-fashioned music hall flavour ... The song ended with me walking all round the Café [Café de Paris] floor in a blackout, with 'Come up and see me sometime', Mae West's famous motto, in luminous paint on my small white cape. I sang it at every troop concert all through the war and in India and Burma, also in cabaret and variety; so I think the old girl should be included here after missing all those bombs:

Blackout Bella

Of all the lovelies in the town, there's none as smart as Bella
I've almost won as much renown as Mr C's umbrella.
I'm a girl who serves her country and can raise the nation's hopes,
Like Prunella Stack, the Union Jack and Dr Marie Stopes.
In pre-war days with light ablaze they thought me rather shady,
But now that there's a blackout I am treated like a lady.
With sandbags on my chest, I have bumped into the best,
I'm blackout Bella
The whitest girl in town, the whitest girl in town.

A girl who knows the game,
Who's groped her way to fame.
Every fella salutes me on the beat
A'doin a bomps-a-daisy all down Regent Street.
I've popped in here, but not to profiteer,
My cover charge is less than half a crown.
I'm the only bag of lard that doesn't need a ration card
I'm blackout Bella, the whitest girl in town.

There was an objection to Byng's smutty double entendre, which happened while he was touring the Far East. 'One helper in the YMCA objected to my songs; but was told by the army authorities that if he complained again he would immediately be sent back to England and silence was golden.'[3]

It was surprisingly different in continental Europe and particularly in Germany. The texts written by the gay poet Bruno Balz for Germany's most popular musical star, Zarah Leander, frequently celebrate casual sexual encounters in a frank and straightforward way that would have been unthinkable in any mainstream English language song of the period. Zarah Leander always insisted that Bruno Balz understood how to write for her better than anyone else. With hindsight, the gay subtext of the songs is obvious. It would be interesting to know how much Leander and everyone else involved in her films understood of this at the time. The text of the song 'Kann die Liebe Sünde sein?' (Can love be a sin?), written by Balz in collaboration with the composer Lothar Brühne for the 1938 movie *Der Blaufuchs*, reads like a plea for tolerance from Balz, who was twice imprisoned by the Nazis for his homosexuality.

A year later, shortly after the outbreak of war, Leander sang 'Heut' Abend lad' ich mir die Liebe ein' with a text by Balz and music by Nico Dostal in the film *Lied der Wüste*. The song could equally well express the feelings of a persecuted homosexual or a lonely woman in wartime Berlin:

> Heut' Abend lade ich mir die Liebe ein.
> Heut' will ich glücklich sein die ganze Nacht.
> Es gibt doch nichts was ich heut; wissen will
> Weil ich nur küssen will die ganze Nacht.
> … und darum lade ich nun die Liebe ein
> Darum will ich glücklich sein die ganze Nacht.
> Oft hat mir ein Mund
> Seeligkeit un Vergessenheit gebracht
> Und weil es soviel soviel Freude macht
> Deshalb habe ich niemals 'no' gesagt.
> Jetzt mein typ ist sehr gefragt bei vielen Herren.
>
> (Tonight I shall invite love in.
> Tonight I want to be happy all the night.
> I don't want to know anything tonight

Because I want to kiss the whole night long
And this is why I want to be happy all the night
How often a mouth has brought me happiness and
  forgetfulness
And because it gives pleasure to so many I have never said
  'no'
My type is much in demand with the men.)

In the same movie the lovely 'Ein Paar Tränen werd' ich weinen um dich' (I'll shed a few tears over you), also by Balz and Dostal, is a gentler celebration of the joys and sorrows of a fleeting relationship.

Ein Paar Tränen werd' ich weinen um dich
Aber du wirst es nicht seh'n
Denn beim Abschied will ich lächeln
Als wär weiter nichts geschehen.

(I shall shed a few tears over you.
But you won't see it
Because when it comes to goodbye
I shall smile as though nothing had happened.)

At the beginning of Leander's most successful wartime movie *Die grosse Liebe*, released in 1942, she attracts the interest of the young hero played by Viktor Staal, by singing 'Mein Leben für die Liebe—jawohl!' (music Michael Jary, text Bruno Balz).

Mein ganzes Glück ist Liebe—jawohl!
Ich kann nun mal nicht anders
Ich muss nun mal so sein.
Ein Herz wie mein Herz ist nich gern allein.
Und Nächte ohne Liebe, O nein!
Sie sollt'es gar nicht geben. O nein!

(My whole happiness is love—O yes!
I can't help it, it has to be.
A heart like my heart doesn't want to be alone.
And nights without love
—O no! they shouldn't happen—O no!)

The hero hangs around the stage door after her performance and picks her up in the U-Bahn. After some token resistance, she invites him into her flat during an air raid and they spend a night of love together—an experience that must have been shared by countless couples in Berlin and London during the war.

Balz's most frenetic and explicit expression of wartime promiscuity is in the text for the song 'Jede Nacht ein neues Glück' (music by Lothar Brühne) written for Leander's final wartime film, *Damals*:

Jede Nacht ein neues Glück
Und neue Liebeleien
Jede Nacht ein andre Mund
So sol es bei mir seien.

(Every night a new pleasure
And new love affairs.
Every night another mouth.
That's how it has to be with me.)

The scene in which Leander sings this song in the movie is a masterpiece of Freudian high camp. It is set in a sleazy nightclub, in which for complicated reasons Leander's character, a brilliant and dedicated doctor, has been reduced to appearing in a cabaret act. Wearing a black dress that is all frills and bare flesh she staggers drunkenly on stage clutching a champagne glass, and sings the song leaning on a vast ship's figurehead in the form of a muscular nude merman with bifurcated tails wide open and crotch-covered by a conch shell—thrust suggestively forward. Her heartbroken admirer, played by the 23-year-old Rossano Brazzi, made up as a tragic clown, watches her tearfully from the wings. It is always interesting to observe how songs change their meaning in translation. The French version of 'Jede Nacht ein neues Glück' recorded by Rose Avril as 'Chaque soir j'attends l'amour' has less brutal connotations.

The title of this song, 'Every night a new pleasure', took on an ironic meaning for Leander when she made the studio recording of it in April 1943 after a night spent in an air-raid shelter during a particularly destructive bombing raid on Berlin.

War Songs: Vera and Zarah

The most widely loved songs of the Second World War in Britain and Germany were respectively 'We'll Meet Again' sung by Vera Lynn, and 'Ich weiss es wird einmal ein Wunder geschehen' sung by Zarah Leander. The two songs offer an interesting mirror image of one another. Both concern the separation of loved ones and their hopes of being re-united. An element of ambiguity, resulting from the contradiction between the message of hope and an underlying sense of tragedy, is essential to the appeal of both songs. The 'don't know where, don't know when' in Vera Lynn's song hints that it might be in the next world rather than this that the lovers will meet again.

There is a splendid irony in the fact that the music of 'Ich weiss es wird einmal ein Wunder geschehen' was composed by Michael Jary, a Pole masquerading as German, with the text by the gay poet Bruno Balz. Balz conceived the text while in the custody of the Gestapo because of his homosexuality and it clearly had a very specific personal meaning for him. In a TV interview given towards the end of her life, the splendidly raddled and chain-smoking Leander talked about the different interpretations that people gave to 'Ich weiss es wird einmal ein Wunder geschehen' during the war:

> I know that a miracle will happen—in the middle of the war. We meant that peace would come again, that calm would return, that there would be something to eat. Human beings would be able to lead a normal life again. That was something those men up there didn't understand. Instead they interpreted it as 'I know that one day a miracle will happen—we are going to rule the world.' That was not at all what we meant.[4]

No doubt the song took on both these meanings as the war situation deteriorated for the Germans, but Leander seems to be speaking with hindsight here. In late 1941 when *Die grosse Liebe* was being filmed, few would have believed that it needed a miracle for Germany to win the war. Though much is made in the movie of the scarcity of 'Bohnenkaffe' (real coffee) the privations of war had hardly begun to bite in Germany at this date.

Scenes from the most successful German movie of the war Die grosse Liebe.

The beauty of 'Ich weiss es wird einmal ein Wunder geschehen' is that the text allowed each listener to read his or her personal meaning into it. For the actress Grethe Weiser, for example, who plays Leander's maid in the movie and who is shown in the climactic scene listening, deeply moved, to the song, it can hardly have failed to evoke thoughts of her half-Jewish son from whom she was separated for the duration of the war and the longing which she later confided to Lale Andersen to be re-united with him.[5]

'We'll Meet Again' was recorded for the first time by Vera Lynn in 1939. Though she is associated with many of the best and most memorable British songs of the Second World War, such as 'The White Cliffs of Dover', 'Yours' and 'It's a lovely day tomorrow', it was above all 'We'll Meet Again' that caught the mood of the moment and established Vera Lynn as the 'Forces' Sweetheart'. Born in the east of London, the daughter of a plumber, Lynn never tried to hide her humble origins, unlike slightly older stars such as Jessie Matthews and Gertrude Lawrence, who affected cut-glass accents and upper-class mannerisms. Her very ordinariness was always an essential part of her appeal. In the late 1930s, Lynn began to make a name for herself as a vocalist with various popular dance bands. It was the war that gave her the opportunity of a lifetime. In her autobiography, Lynn quoted a comedian who quipped: 'The Second World War was started by Vera Lynn's agent', and also an anonymous writer who said 'During the war years, Vera Lynn had History working for her as an agent.' She comments: 'They were two ways of expressing the same thing; what I was doing, and the way I was doing it, just happened to be right at the time.'[6]

Vera Lynn, the 'Forces' Sweetheart'.

Vera Lynn's records still give pleasure. She had a pleasing and instantly recognisable timbre with a very distinctive catch in the voice. She also had sound musicality, an infallible sense of pitch and, most importantly, a rare quality of naturalness and sincerity that triumphed over the most banal and sentimental material. All of these qualities, however attractive, would not have been enough to set her apart from many other talented vocalists of the time, were it not for the significance of the moment that enabled her to achieve a very special kind of greatness. Vera Lynn was a simple and unpretentious girl who rose splendidly to the challenge of history. As is clear from her engaging and down-to-earth autobiographies she did not allow her sudden importance to turn her head. She retained her courage and moral integrity into old age, suing the extreme right-wing British National Party in 2009, when she was 91, for misuse of her image. Lynn has long since attained the status of 'national treasure'.

Amongst her wartime achievements were the highly successful radio request programme 'Sincerely Yours', extensive tours of the Middle and Far East under the aegis of ENSA, and four movies. The first and best of these, *We'll Meet Again*, released in 1943, took its title from Lynn's most famous record.

Zarah Leander possessed a face of luminous beauty made for close-ups on the big screen.

Zarah Leander was ten years older than Vera Lynn and was fully established as a major star well before the outbreak of war. Her initial breakthrough came in 1931 in an updated Stockholm production of *The Merry Widow*, for which permission was required from the astonished composer Franz Lehar for some radical downward transpositions for Leander's low-lying 'whisky baritone' voice.

In the mid-thirties Leander was being hailed as the 'new Garbo' but wisely turned down invitations to go to Hollywood. Even with the kind of makeover imposed on Garbo and Dietrich it is doubtful whether she could have been fitted into the Hollywood mould either physically or as a screen personality. She may have been discouraged by the fate of Lillian Harvey, her predecessor as Europe's number one musical film star, whose Hollywood venture ruined her career. In any case, as Leander later admitted in an interview, she preferred to be a big fish in a small pond and did not want to be 'number ten' in Hollywood.

Between 1937 and 1943 Leander made ten highly successful films for the principal German film studio of UFA. All of these films—with the exception of *Die grosse Liebe*—were set in exotic places or in historical periods. Leander's film persona could hardly have been more different from that of Vera Lynn. Leander was the 'femme fatale' and Lynn the girl next door--or as she is rather crushingly called by her love interest in *We'll Meet Again*, 'the pal'. With her lanky figure and toothy smile, Lynn was pleasingly attractive but never aspired to be glamorous.

Apart from the bronze splendour of her voice, Leander's chief asset on film was a face of luminous beauty made for close-ups on a giant screen. Like Garbo or Dietrich, she did not need to express anything. It was enough for a glycerine tear to slide down her perfect cheek and the public could project their own emotions onto the mask of her face. The famous 'veiled' look that gave an air of mystery to her performances was largely the result of the extreme short-sightedness that necessitated the wearing of dark glasses for interviews and public appearances. No one would have imagined for a minute that Vera Lynn could have been a spy or double agent, but many such rumours about Leander have persisted until now, based on little more than confusion between her screen and her real life personae.

All of Leander's roles had a tragic dimension. When asked about this she said that she could do tragedy and 'hysterical' gaiety but not much in between. Her records show clearly why the studio executives chose the former. Her post-war rendition of Cole Porter's song 'Wunderbar' was voted the second worst record of all time in a competition sponsored by Capital Radio in the 1970s.

Both Lynn and Leander were primarily singers who could act a little. (Leander always maintained that her wealth was not based on her movies but on the sales of the recordings of the songs she sang in them.) Their screen roles were carefully tailored to what they could and couldn't do. The exceptional success of both in *Die grosse Liebe* and *We'll Meet Again* lay partly in the fact that neither had to act at all, just to play a version of themselves.

326

Leander never achieved the status of 'national treasure', if only for the obvious reason that Germany lost the war. After her return to Sweden in 1943 she was shunned by her fellow countrymen. If Lynn came to signify the pride of the British in their 'finest hour', Leander was far too visible a symbol of the shame of a nation that had collaborated too willingly with Nazi Germany in the early years of the war, by supplying cheap iron ore and vitally-needed ball bearings for the Nazi war effort and by allowing German troops to cross Swedish territory into occupied Norway. A contemporary joke ran that Denmark was conquered in a night, Norway in a month and Sweden by telephone.

Leander claimed to be a political idiot. By and large she seems to have been clever enough to avoid excessively compromising situations. At the end of the war her critics had little that was specific to accuse her of other than that she had lent her talents to the Nazi entertainment industry. An accusation that she had sung for German troops in occupied France seems to have been based on a still from a scene in *Die grosse Liebe*. There was one widely publicised appearance in a 'Wunschkonzert für die Wehrmacht' ('Request concert for the army') on 1 December 1940. The significance of her sombre black costume and prominently displayed white handkerchief has been debated, but there probably was none.

Leander's German public proved a great deal more forgiving. After the war there were a handful of moderately successful German movies in which she played mature women with a shady past, and later on there were popular television appearances. From the 1970s she was riding high on the so-called *Nostalgie-Welle* and widely regarded by the German public with indulgent affection. It was an affection that was reciprocated. Leander continued to declare her devotion to the nation that had adopted her, and if she never became a national treasure at least she became the number one icon for German-speaking gays and lesbians.

The films *Die grosse Liebe* and *We'll Meet Again* were premiered a year apart, in 1942 and 1943 respectively, and make a fascinating comparison. There are many parallels as

Michel Jary, composer of Germany's most popular wartime song 'Ich weiss es wird ein Wunder geschehen'.

well as differences that highlight different attitudes in the respective countries. In her autobiography Vera Lynn comments ruefully that the British were not good at making musicals. No doubt she was thinking of the much slicker production values of the Hollywood musicals of the period. The technical excellence of the Hollywood movies of the 1940s owed a great deal to the numerous technicians imported from Germany between the wars or who had fled from Nazi persecution. But there was enough expertise left behind to ensure the high technical quality of wartime German movies. *Die grosse Liebe* has a visual sumptuousness and fluidity that makes *We'll Meet Again* look provincial by comparison. Though modern audiences may have moments of queasiness or *fou rire*, *Die grosse Liebe* still looks good. It is easy to see why it was the most successful European-made movie of the war, seen by 27.8 million people in the Reich and in occupied and neutral countries.

Both films contain documentary or quasi-documentary footage of bombing raids on London and Berlin, of wartime public entertainment, air-raid shelters and many fascinating glimpses of daily life. It is interesting to see the interior of Berlin's famous Scala musical theatre before its destruction, and Vera Lynn in full evening dress singing to an unseen audience via a microphone in a BBC sound studio furnished with Bauhaus tubular metal furniture.

In *We'll Meet Again* Vera Lynn's character Peggy Brown has her first success as a singer entertaining an audience, trapped in a theatre during a German bombing raid, with the cheerful 'Be like the kettle and sing' accompanied by Geraldo and his orchestra. In a plot twist that echoes the story of 'Lili Marleen' she achieves sudden fame through the accidental playing of a record on the radio. Later we see her creating a radio request programme for the troops, much like her own real life 'Sincerely Yours'.

Both movies show civilian populations struggling through under difficult conditions. Both movies have a strong propaganda and morale-boosting content. This is more obvious in *We'll Meet Again* where the propaganda element is less well integrated and characters tend to make speeches. The key speech in *We'll Meet Again* is made by Peggy to her friend Ruth urging her to be more supportive of her fiancé.

> Can't you see, Ruth, he's in the forces. His life is not his own any more. You can't change that no matter what you do. It's up to us now more ever to stand by those men of ours—

letting them know they can depend on us whatever happens
so we must make our loyalty—our sacrifice—equal to theirs.

The essential message of *Die grosse Liebe* is exactly the same. The
Danish singer Hanna Holberg, played by Zarah Leander, falls in love
with a young pilot Paul Westlandt, played by Viktor Staal. She is hurt
when he disappears without warning but mollified when she discovers
that he has not been with another woman but merely bombing England.
She breaks off their relationship when he postpones their wedding for
the second time and is mortified when she discovers that he has the *bona
fide* excuse that he has been invading Russia. Hanna sings the hit song
'Ich weiss es wird einmal ein Wunder geschehen' in a stage musical at a
point when she believes she may have lost Paul forever.

The lovers are temporarily reunited in the final scene of the movie.
Paul has been wounded and asks Hanna to visit him in hospital.
Looking handsome in full Nazi uniform and with his arm in a sling,
Paul reclines on a deck chair on a balcony overlooking a spectacular
view of the Alps. When Hanna arrives in a gorgeous fur coat Paul asks
if she still wants to marry him. In contrast with *We'll Meet Again,* the
moral that women must be willing to sacrifice personal feeling to the
war effort is made in gestures and looks and not in speeches. As he
asks her if she still wants to marry him Paul raises his eyes to a stream
of German bombers flying overhead through the Alpine skies towards
Russia and then transfers his gaze questioningly to Hanna. Her gaze
follows his upwards before she drops her head in a submissive nod
and the two look off into the distance to a reprise of the melody of the
'Ich weiss es wird einmal ein Wunder geschehen' sung by wordless
angelic choirs.

In view of the gay subtext of so many of Bruno Balz's songs for
Leander it is interesting to note the discretely closeted homo-erotic
sub-plot of Paul's relationship with his best friend Oberleutnant
v. Etzdorf, the first movie role for the actor Wolfgang Preiss and a
strangely prophetic one. After the war he would make a substantial
international career playing German army officers in films as varied
as *The Longest Day, Is Paris burning?, The Train, Von Ryan's Express, The
Boys from Brazil* and *A Bridge Too Far,* as well as providing the voice for
the Nazi Major Strasser in a dubbed version of *Casablanca.*

In the scene in which the two friends watch Hanna's act at the Scala,
they lean affectionately against one another like a pair of lovers. They
banter together in a beach scene clearly designed to show off Viktor

Staal's magnificent physique, and in a final scene when they prepare to set off on a mission during which Etzdorf will be killed, they delicately and with slight embarrassment probe each other's feelings. Etzdorf admits that he has always had problems with women and says that the only woman who has ever really loved him is his mother. If this homo-erotic sub-text of male bonding was indeed as deliberate as it now seems, it is highly unlikely that the Nazi censors would have been aware of it any more than the enforcers of the Hays Code would have understood the highly charged lesbian undercurrents in the scenes between Bette Davis and Mary Astor in the exactly contemporary Hollywood movie *The Great Lie*.

Finally, the songs are the thing in both *We'll Meet Again* and *Die grosse Liebe*.

Vera Lynn sings a selection of her hits both cheerful and sentimental, and briefly strays into what feels more like Leander's territory when she sings Schubert's 'Ave Maria' from the organ loft of a country church. Lyrics such as 'When you're up to your neck in hot water, be like the kettle and sing' or 'Sunshine again will greet the world with a smile. Life seems worthwhile after the rain' are clearly meant to lift the morale of audiences. The song 'We'll Meet Again' is the final number of the movie. Vera Lynn sings it in what looks like documentary footage of an actual concert, given out of doors with an audience of troops, who sway rhythmically and sing along.

Leander's morale boosting number, the text of which must have taken on increased urgency as the war situation deteriorated, was 'Davon geht die Welt nicht unter.'

> Davon geht die Welt nicht unter
> Sieht man sie manchmal auch grau
> Einmal wird sie wieder bunter
> Einmal wird sie wieder himmelblau.
>
> (It won't be the end of the world
> Even if the world sometimes seems grey.
> One day it will be brighter
> One day blue skies will return.)

Leander sings this song to an audience of German soldiers in occupied France. This scene is clearly staged, and the rococo Festsaal in which it takes place looks decidedly German rather than French, but the audience of soldiers sways and sings along exactly as it does in *We'll Meet Again*.

The climactic scene in which Leander sings 'Ich weiss es wird einmal ein Wunder geschehen' can only be described as a monument of *Edelkitsch*. The song itself, with its lurches into purple chromatic harmony and its quasi-operatic climaxes and heavenly chorus, is far removed from the unpretentious sentimentality of 'We'll Meet Again'. Leander sings on stage (apparently once again inside Berlin's Scala theatre though the scene is supposed to take place in Rome). She stands on an elaborate platform of Baroque curlicues in front of a grandstand of tiered angels. The filming of this scene involved an episode worthy of a Mel Brooks movie. It proved impossible to find sufficient female 'angels' of a size and height not to be dwarfed by the statuesque Leander. A highly practical and economical solution was found in the use of members of Hitler's personal SS guard or *Leibstandarte*, who had the great advantage of being of uniform height, and who were kitted out in wigs, wings and sparkling nightgowns. Inspection of the long shots with the aid of a computer to bring them into closer focus, reveals some very strange looking 'angels'.

War Songs: Lili Marlene

If 'We'll Meet Again' was *the* song of the war for the British and 'Ich weiss es wird einmal ein Wunder geschehen' for the Germans, the only song to appeal equally to Germans and British, and indeed to most of the combatants in the war, was Norbert Schultze's 'Lili Marleen'. The story of how this song crossed front lines and conquered the world is one of the strangest and most convoluted of the war. It is a prime example of something seen many times over during the war: of how a song could become freighted with new and contradictory meanings in turbulent times.

The text was written during the First World War by a young conscript in the German army called Hans Leip, who was involved with two young women: their names were fused to create Lili Marleen. The poem was published in a 1937 collection titled *Die kleine Hafenorgel*. Hans Leip composed his own melody to the text, which he can be heard singing in a fragment of an interview in the superb and comprehensively documented publication on 'Lili

Lale Andersen

Marleen' by the German company 'Bear Family Records'.[7]

Next in line was a Hindemith pupil called Rudolf Zink (1910-1983). Zink's version of the song was taken up by a little-known singer called Lale Andersen, who was appearing in the Munich cabaret 'Simplicissimus'. This is an attractive and appealingly melodic song, but failed to take off. In her autobiography Andersen recounts how she invited a young sentry from a local barracks to come and hear her perform the song. His verdict, which seems to have been shared by most of those who heard this version of the song, was that the text was good but the music too arty and complicated.[8]

The celebrated and final setting by Norbert Schultze was the result of a commission from the bass Jan Behrens. Though still in his twenties Schultze was a well-established composer. His charming children's opera *Schwarzer Peter*, in the popular and folksy style favoured by the Nazis, had been a great success at its premiere in 1936 and was well on its way to becoming a repertory piece. Behrens, who sang a small role in the 1938 Berlin premiere of *Schwarzer Peter*, was currently also appearing in a monthly radio programme of sea songs. Behrens needed new material for the programme and Schultze was happy to oblige by setting ten of the poems from *Die kleine Hafenorgel*.

Schultze claims in his autobiography that the melody came to him spontaneously when first shown the poem by Behrens in a noisy Berlin drinking place, his compositional musings being interrupted by the sounds of the anti-Semitic riots of *Kristallnacht*. This would date the birth of the famous melody quite precisely to the evening of 9 November 1938.[9] (This version of the story has been disputed by a former colleague who claimed that Schultze had used the melody previously for a jingle for a toothpaste advertisement.)

Everyone involved in the remarkable story of 'Lili Marleen' has remembered the sequence of events differently. Even the detailed accounts of Schultze in his autobiography *Mit dir, Lili Marleen* and of Lale Andersen in her autobiography *Leben mit einem Lied* differ significantly. But even if the idea of Lili Marleen being born in the midst of the *Kristallnacht* riots seems far-fetched, such is the ring of truth of much of Schultze's book that the reader is inclined to follow him.

Schultze's book should be essential reading for anyone seeking to get to grips with how millions of people in Europe's most 'civilized' country could have been swept into involvement in history's most monstrous crimes. Schultze was evidently a charmer and it would take a very stern reader to dislike him, however much they might disapprove of his actions. Inevitably, though, one asks how was it possible for an essentially decent, easy-going, pleasure loving and tolerant man to become the most pliable and prolific musical servant of the Nazi regime? How could he bring himself to write music for a string of propaganda movies and to compose celebratory marches for the latest Nazi aggression at the drop of a helmet? How could he unthinkingly provide a refined piano trio for the movie *Ich klage an*, that he only later realised was a blatant attempt to prepare German public opinion for a planned programme of euthanasia? In his book Schultze does not provide the answers to these questions, but neither does he dodge them. It is clear that he spent the last fifty years of his life ceaselessly putting them to himself. In the end it probably came down to the simple fact that he was prepared to do anything to avoid serving on the Eastern Front and that, as he comments at one point, once caught up in the web of Nazi evil, there was no escape.

Schultze's Leip songs were rejected by Jan Behrens as unsuitable for his purpose, and despite his burgeoning reputation as a composer Schultze met with little interest in his new songs. Schultze claims that as the texts were written from a man's point of view it did not occur to him to offer them to a female singer. Though many male singers did eventually record the song, it works better with a female singer who seems to embody the girl being addressed.

According to Lale Andersen, Schultze admitted when he tried to persuade her to take on the songs that he had already offered them to Germany's three most popular female vocalists: the Swedish Zarah Leander, the Hungarian Marika Rökk and the Chilean Rosita Serrano. Schultze and Andersen differ on how and where she was approached about the songs. He had known her since her Munich days, and by 1939 they were both based in Berlin where Andersen was appearing at the Kabarett der Komiker. Initially reluctant to take on songs that were already in her repertoire in the Zink versions, Andersen soon discovered that the public responded more warmly to Schultze than to Zink.

Around this time, with her popularity beginning to grow, Andersen was in negotiations for a recording contract with two different companies, Telefunken and Elektrola. She chose Elektrola because Telefunken already had the glamorous Rosita Serrano under contract and she felt she would be likely to come a poor second in the company's priorities.[10]

Andersen's first recording of 'Lili Marleen' was made on 2 August 1939, exactly one month before the outbreak of war. She was accompanied by a small orchestra and male chorus. The conductor was Bruno Seidler-Winkler, a prolific house conductor for various pre-war German record companies, whose name is familiar to all collectors of vocal 78s. The versatile Seidler-Winkler, who was more usually associated with classical music, introduced a number of changes to the song that were to play a significant role in its subsequent success. Firstly, the song acquired a new title. With 'Lili Marleen' as a subtitle, it became 'Lied eines jungen Wachtpostens' ('Song of a young sentry'). Seidler-Winkler also introduced the song with a bugle call based on the Prussian Last Post and added march rhythms. Neither feature was particularly original. Bugle calls had featured in two of the greatest international hits of the inter-war period: Marguerite Monnot's 'Mon Légionnaire' of 1936 which tells the story of liaison between a soldier and a prostitute from the woman's point of view, and Robert Stolz's cheerful 'Adieu, mein kleiner Gardeoffizier' which also had march rhythms.

The record initially had virtually no impact and sold a mere 700 copies. Were it not for historical events and a series of coincidences the recording would have passed into oblivion and probably Norbert Schultze and Lale Andersen as well.

On 19 April 1941 during their triumphant Balkans campaign, the Germans seized the radio station in Belgrade with the intention of using it to broadcast to the entire Mediterranean theatre of war. Musical entertainment was needed to sweeten the diet of propaganda and news bulletins, but once all the records with undesirable Jewish or Serbian associations were removed there were only 54 records left in the archive of the radio station. A certain Richard Kistenmacher was sent on an urgent mission to the nearest Nazi-controlled radio station in Vienna to bring back more records of entertainment music. In a case

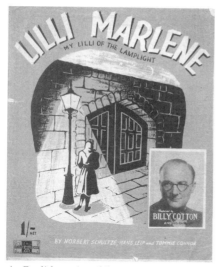

An English version of the song.

The most popular French recording of the
song was by the deep-voiced Suzy Solidor.

Suzy Solidor sings the song in a
television broadcast.

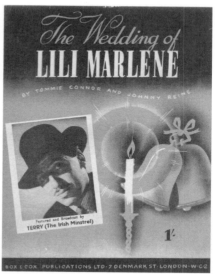

A post war follow-up.

2. The car stops outside *Radio Belgrade. From it spring armed guards, men carrying cases. Nazi propagandists have arrived to take over the Jugoslav radio. The year is 1941—for Germany, a year of gloating triumph, frenzied exhilaration. Her armies have swept all before them, Belgrade is latest city to be martyred by their bombs and bayonets.*

3. *From Belgrade the Nazis broadcast 'Deutschalandsender', a German Forces Programme, aimed to cheer the Afrika Korps fighting on the other side of the Mediterranean. They bring records with them; all but one is broken on the way. The announcer plays the surviving disc. It is "Lili Marlene" sung by Swedish cabaret crooner, Lala Andersen.*

LILI MARLENE
The Song Eighth Army Captured

4. *So successful is "Lili Marlene" that it becomes the regular "goodnight" record of Radio Belgrade. "Front and Homeland now say farewell to each other. The sentinel closes his logbook. And once more the strains of 'Lili Marlene' float through the night." Men of the Afrika Korps in the desert listen to their radio station's closing announcement.*

5. *The girl who sings "Lili Marlene" becomes a star. The Army keep the news of Lala Andersen until Russian one, and German soul. But how it is broadcast and the sound of German troops no longer playing.*

6. *Georg Bonnerman, actress wife of Herman Goering, sings for a gathering of high Nazis at Berlin's Kroll Opera House during her reign in "Lili Marlene". Although closely nearth to the song by a man—she weeks restores the feelings of a young sentry standing aloof. No, got back home—the song has always been associated with women singers.*

7. *To a Berlin nightclub has come a fashionable throng to hear "Lili Marlene" sung by the girl who made it famous. The lamp, the sentry, the barrack gate—all are represented in the stage set while a pointed name winks down approvingly from the backcloth sky. Pat Hughes (who plays Lala Andersen in the film is a London cabaret artiste.*

8. *The German officers and civilians laugh and clap as Lala finishes her act, but soon there will be little gaiety in Berlin. It is now 1943—for Germany, a year of disaster. When Von Paulus capitulates before Stalingrad on February 2, Goebbels bans all entertainment for three days. For the first time in five hundred nights "Lili Marlene" is off the air.*

The German 'Lili'
THE MUSIC FOR "LILI MARLENE" WAS WRITTEN BY NORBERT SCHULTZE, A HACK SONGWRITER. TUNE IS SOMEWHAT SIMILAR TO GERMAN LAST POST.

In the dark of evening
Where you stand and wait
Hangs a lantern gleaming
By the barracks gate.
We'll meet again by lantern shine
As we did once upon a time.
We two, Lili Marlene.
We two, Lili Marlene.

Our shadows once stood facing,
A tall one and a small.
They mingled in embracing
Upon the lighted wall
And passers-by could see well tell
Who kissed my shadow there so well,
My girl, Lili Marlene.
My girl, Lili Marlene.

Then came the trumpets blowing
Retreat to you and me
"My love I must be going,
Or else three days C.B."
And so I whispered "Cheerio !
Oh darling how I hate to go—
My sweet, Lili Marlene.
My sweet, Lili Marlene."

The B.B.C. 'Lili'
THE B.B.C. USED A SPECIAL VERSION OF THE SONG FOR PROPAGANDA BROADCASTS TO GERMANY. WORDS WERE VERY DIFFERENT FROM THE ORIGINAL.

My heart is full and weary
As I write this today
For life is grey and dreary
Since drums marched you away.
You say "war's duty !"—that's no rhyme
For true love, once upon a time.
Still waiting by the lantern
Is your Lili Marlene.

Your man is dead—I hear it
"His grave the Russian snow"
You die you must, I fear it
For Hitler wills it so.
Oh that we two might meet once more
In a new Germany purged of war
You and your Lili Marlene.
You and your Lili Marlene.

Führer, I thank you and greet you
For you are good and wise,
Widows and orphans meet you
With hollow silent eyes.
Hitler the man of blood and fear
Hang him on the lantern here
Oh may he swing from the lantern
Of your Lili Marlene.

Scenes from the British propaganda movie The True Story of Lili Marlene.

of unwanted records, Kistenmacher came across Lale Andersen's 'Lili Marleen'. Schultze surmises that it had been rejected in Vienna for reasons of local patriotism because of the Prussian bugle call.

Initially, through a continuing shortage of material, the record was broadcast twice or more an hour. After a short time the staff at Radio Belgrade were sick of the song and it was dropped. To their surprise Radio Belgrade received a deluge of protest from listeners. Schultze's insinuating melody had caught the fancy of Rommel's Afrika Korps in North Africa and of other listeners all over Europe. Later attempts for various reasons to drop Andersen's record or to replace it with other versions always met with the same irresistible wave of protest. Eventually the record was used every night to sign off Radio Belgrade programmes before the 10 pm news bulletin. By this time the melody had jumped across enemy lines and gained the affection of the troops of the British 8th Army as well. Every evening at 9.55 brought a brief truce between the opposing German and British armies encamped within hearing distance of one another. Lale Andersen claimed that her song saved hundreds of lives in this way.

Werner Hoffmeister, a former member of the Afrika Korps, remembered: 'And when we sat in a circle in the evenings, silently listening, suddenly from the other side about 80 meters away there was a murmur and a voice called out "comrades, louder please!" It was the English and this song had long since won them over. In this way, night after night we had a real fire truce, and in this time no shots rang out and it remained quiet for a while after.'[11]

By the time Noel Coward reached Tripoli in September 1943 while entertaining troops in North Africa, 'Lili Marlene' had become ubiquitous as a kind of victory song. At the Del Mahari hotel where he was staying, Coward wrote, 'A 3-piece orchestra was squealing away at the end of the courtyard. At a given moment the band played "Lily Marlene". This was received with tremendous applause and had to be repeated over and over again. Everyone joined in and sang it loudly with nightmarish effect in that mysterious, echoing place.'[12]

On both sides there were concerns about the impact the song might have on the war effort. Like the bigwigs at the BBC in the early days of Vera Lynn's success, Goebbels worried that sentimental songs would undermine the army's fighting spirit. Goebbels loathed 'Lili Marleen' in particular and dismissed it as 'defeatist' and as 'smelling of the corpse'. But just as he was forced to accept the popular appetite for swing, he grudgingly came to accept the need for sentimental songs such as 'Lili Marleen'. In his diary, on 4 October 1941, he concluded that these songs fulfilled a need, writing: 'Troops at the front want—and this is in some way somewhat odd and in other ways understandable—above all somewhat sentimental songs that give expression to the longings for home ... One can understand that a German soldier in the endless landscape of the Steppes in the East feels this longing for home all the more.'

Amongst the 197 versions of 'Lili Marleen' issued in the Bear Family CD set there are seventy-five recorded during the war years, in languages as diverse as English, Dutch, Bulgarian, Czech, Slovak, Hungarian, Portuguese, Spanish, French, Italian, Danish, Swedish and Finnish, which demonstrates the song's universal appeal.

As Lale Andersen's long forgotten record began its conquest of the world from Radio Belgrade, she herself was entertaining military personnel on a lengthy tour of German-controlled ports from Oslo to Bordeaux. Her first intimation that something extraordinary was happening was when she sat in a café on her return to Berlin and was accosted by a group of nurses who wanted her autograph, not as Lale Andersen but as 'Lili Marleen'. When she attempted to open the front door of her apartment, she found it was jammed by the sheer volume of fan mail that had arrived in her absence.[13]

Norbert Schultze's explanation for this phenomenal success was pragmatic. 'It was quite simply the time. It was war and ever more soldiers were suddenly overcome with home-sickness.' Lale Andersen's answer was more poetic: 'Can the wind explain why it becomes a storm?' Taken separately, neither the text nor the music of the song are particularly distinguished. But they are a perfect match for one another. Schultze crafted his song immaculately. The slightest deviation from his melodic line changes the emotional impact of the song, as we hear in the versions by low-voiced singers such as Anne Shelton and Suzy Solidor who cannot manage the awkward upward leap in the refrain on the words 'mit dir, Lili Marleen'. Without that interval the song loses something of its freshness and innocence.

Much of the initial success of 'Lili Marleen' was down to Lale Andersen's performance. Once again there is a perfect match between singer and material. If Schultze really approached Zarah Leander, Marikka Rökk and Rosita Serrano, he was lucky they all turned him down. Leander would have been too matronly, Rökk too skittish and Serrano far too genteel.

The Scottish soldier-adventurer Fitzroy Maclean heard Lale Andersen's record over the radio countless times both in North Africa and later fighting with Tito's partisans in Yugoslavia. In his memoirs *Eastern Approaches* his description captures the effect of her rendition very precisely. 'Husky, sensuous, nostalgic, sugar-sweet, her voice seemed to reach out to you, as she lingered over the catchy tune, the sickly sentimental words.'[14] The sugary sweet sensuality is in the timbre of the voice but also in her phrasing. The repeated use of gently downward portamenti creates the lingering quality remarked on by Fitzroy Maclean.

Other singers would later appropriate the song. Most successful of all was Marlene Dietrich, to the point that many people are surprised to discover it was not written for her. In fact, Dietrich turns the song into something quite different. Her Lili Marleen is older, tougher, more world weary and less feminine than Lale Andersen's.

Lale Andersen's world success was a thorn in the flesh for the Nazi hierarchy. The Nazis were fully aware that her loyalty could not be relied upon and that she maintained contact with her Jewish lover Rolf Liebermann (years later the distinguished Intendant of the Hamburg and Paris opera houses) in Switzerland. In the summer of 1942 while Andersen was on tour in Italy, she wrote a letter to Kurt Hirschfeld, the director of the Zurich Schauspielhaus in which she indicated she wanted to move to Switzerland. When the letter was intercepted it caused considerable alarm. The defection of Lili Marleen to a neutral country was a potential propaganda disaster to be avoided at all costs. Andersen was arrested at the Brenner Pass and taken into the custody of the Gestapo and 'Lili Marleen' removed from the German airwaves.

While under house arrest in Berlin, Andersen made a suicide attempt. Shortly afterwards she was imprisoned. It says much for the effectiveness of British intelligence as well as for the importance with which Lale Andersen was regarded that both events were rapidly announced over the BBC. On 3 April 1943 the BBC German Section played the famous record and asked listeners: 'Has it occurred to you that you have not heard this record recently? Why not? Perhaps because Lale Andersen is in a concentration camp.' Goebbels was forced into a public denial that possibly saved Andersen's life. She was released from prison and under strict constraints (including not singing THAT song) was able to resume her career.

Both before and after her arrest Andersen was a reluctant cog in the German propaganda machine, making English language versions of 'Lili Marleen' to attract Allied troops to German radio stations. Her autobiography contains a very graphic account of a nightmarish tour of Poland for one of Goebbels's 'Wunschkonzerte' alongside such famous artists as Grethe Weiser, Marika Rökk and the great Wagnerian contralto Emmy Leisner, all of whom were forced by Goebbels's henchman Hans Hinckel to go on a macabre sight-seeing tour of the Warsaw Ghetto. Andersen describes how she tried to calm Leisner who was reduced to a state of hysterical grief and guilt at the (rather unlikely) prospect of running into one of her pre-war Jewish friends or patrons.[15]

Throughout the war popular songs were given new texts. These were either more or less faithful translations of the original text into languages of other combatants or else satirical propaganda versions. Probably no song in history has been given quite so many variant texts as 'Lili Marleen' (or 'Lili Marlene', as it became).

As it was via the British 8th Army in North Africa that 'Lili Marleen' jumped the front line and reached out into the world, it is not surprising that the earliest foreign language versions and the largest number were in English. First in the field was the translation by the British collaborator Norman Baillie-Stewart, recorded by Charlie Schwedler on 12 January 1942 and later in the year by Lale Andersen.

> Listen to the bugle
> Hear its silv'ry call
> Carried by the night air
> And telling one and all
> Now is the time to meet your pal
> To meet your girl.

Marlene Dietrich came up with her own version, which is less coy and clichéd than the official American and British versions:

> Outside the barracks
> By the corner light
> I'll always stand
> And wait for you at night.
> We will create a world for two
> I'll wait for you
> The whole night through
> For you, Lili Marlene
> For you, Lili Marlene.

Bugler, tonight don't play the army call
I want another evening with her charms
Then we say goodbye and part
I'll always keep you in my heart
With me, Lili Marlene,
With me, Lili Marlene.

The standard American version recorded by Bing Crosby, Perry Como, Hildegarde and others, runs:

Underneath the lamp post
By the barrack gate
Standing all alone
Every night you'll see her wait
She waits for a boy
Who marched away
And though he's gone
She hears him say
Promise you'll be true
Fare thee well, Lilly Marlene
Till I return to you
Fare thee well, Lily Marlene.

The British version sung by Anne Shelton is equally bland:

Underneath the lantern
By the barrack gate
Darling, I remember
The way you used to wait.
It was there that you whispered
Tenderly
That you love me
And you'd always be
My Lily of the lamplight
My own, Lily Marlene.

Wisely, it was decided not to record the song with Britain's most popular vocalist Vera Lynn, who would never have been believable as the kind of girl who would hang around barracks at night. The best-selling British version by Anne Shelton made in 1944 was scarcely more believable. The march rhythms and with them the grittiness of the first version were jettisoned in favour of smooth sophistication.

Shelton sings gorgeously but sounds as if she were standing under the lamppost in an elegant evening gown.

Of the several French recorded versions with a text by Henri Lemarchand, the most successful was by Suzy Solidor, one of the few singers apart from Marlene Dietrich with a personality strong enough to impose itself on the song. Her dusky, vibrant voice and her overt lesbianism gave an entirely new dimension to this song about longing for a young woman. Leaning on a black piano and surrounded by a selection from her famous collection of over 200 portraits, the statuesque Solidor gave the first ever televised performance of the song for the somewhat limited audience of the Nazi-controlled Paris-Télévision in the summer of 1944.[16] Unlike the British and the Americans who adopted 'Lili Marleen' joyfully as their own, the French continued to associate the song with the German Occupation. Solidor's close identification with 'Lili Marleen' caused her problems at the end of the war.[17]

As Andersen herself discovered during her 1942 Italian tournée, the Italians were amongst the most enthusiastic fans of the song. A version recorded by the great operatic mezzo Gianna Pederzini, who had sung in the 1937 production of Cilea's *L'Arlesiana*, is sadly not included in the near comprehensive Bear Family compilation. Particularly attractive recordings were made by the elegant 'tenor of charm' Carlo Buti, and by the unjustly forgotten Meme Bianchi, who made a great many delightful Italian language versions of popular American songs at about this time.

Satirical and propaganda versions of 'Lili Marleen' appeared early on and were used by both sides. At the beginning of 1942 there was a Dutch radio broadcast of 'Lili Marleen' with a Nazi propaganda text attributed to Jacques van Tol. Ironically, van Tol's chief claim to fame was the text of the pre-war hit 'De kleine man', written for the Jewish cabaret star Louis Davids—a song that van Tol himself parodied in an anti-Semitic version entitled 'De jodenman'.[18]

The Dutch 'Lili Marleen' was preceded by a spoken introduction:

> I am now going to play a song from my own repertoire to you. The motif has been sent in by one of the hundred thousand listeners and it is called 'You'll see. Lili Marlene'. Occasionally I will drink a glass of beer in 'De Vergulde Roemer', a small pub somewhere in Amsterdam. Behind the bar works a lovely young lady called Lili Marlene, a name

you no doubt will have heard more often lately. She is a very tactful girl who never gets into arguments with her clients. Until recently she had to listen to a lot of that OZO chat [OZO was short for Oranje Zal Overwinnen—Orange will be victorious] but they have become quieter recently. A sign of these new times is that you will hear different sounds from now on as well. This song is a conversation between a punter and Lili Marlene. The punter talks and Lili Marlene nods and listens.

These are unstable times mankind is experiencing now,
Continents are battling each other and the whole
world trembles,
But before the hour of peace will chime,
England will have lost the battle
You'll see, Lili Marlene, you'll see, Lili Marlene.

England's blockade tortures the civilians,
No pork chops are to be had, but we are still eating
But before the hour of peace will chime
All of Europe shall be eating Russian wheat
You'll see, Lili Marlene, you'll see, Lili Marlene.

British plutocrats, who, with Yankee money,
Let others do their fighting are almost out of breath
Because, before the hour of peace will chime
The British pound will be worth six cents
You'll see, Lili Marlene, you'll see, Lili Marlene.

In front of the BBC building a big fat Jew stands eating
parasite bread in this misery
But when the hour of peace will chime
The Jew will go to the ghetto
You'll see, Lili Marlene,
You'll see, Lili Marlene.
                    (Translation: Eva Broer)

When 'Lili Marleen' was appropriated by the British 8th Army in North Africa and became 'Lili Marlene', triumphant English texts were devised to go with the melody.

There was a song that the Eighth Army used to hear,
In the lonely desert, lovely, sweet and clear
Over the ether came the strain,
The soft refrain each night again
With you—Lili Marlene.

Africa Corps has vanished from the earth
Smashed soon the swine that gave it birth
No more we'll hear that lilting strain
That soft refrain, each night again
With you, Lili Marlene.

As the war situation deteriorated in Germany and resentments grew against Nazi authority, bitter and sarcastic 'Lili Marleen' parodies proliferated in Germany itself. The Bear Family publication presents three of them, including:

Unter der laterne, vor der Reichskanzlei
Da hängt unser Führer und auch der Robert Ley.
Und alle die vorüber gehen
Wollen auch die andern hängen sehen
Die andern der Partei.[19]

(Under the lantern, in front of the Reichs Chancellery
Hangs our Führer and also Robert Ley.[20]
Everyone who passes wants to see
The others hanging there
The others from the Party.)

A similarly subversive parody circulated in occupied France.

Près d'une caserne, un soldat allemande
Qui montait la garde
Comme un grand faignant.
Je lui disais pourquoi pleures tu?
Il m' répondit: 'Nous sommes foutus.'
Hitler sera pendu.[21]

The theme of Hitler being hanged from the lamppost was taken up in a German language version, recorded by the émigré actress Lucie Mannheim and broadcast by the BBC in April 1943, in the wake of Germany's defeats in North Africa and at Stalingrad.

We see and hear her singing an English translation of this text in a remarkable propaganda documentary directed by Humphrey Jennings in 1944 for the British Ministry of Information, called *The True Story of Lili Marlene*. In its way, this short film is a minor masterpiece. The narrator was the British actor Marius Goring (then married to Lucie Mannheim), who after the war would play almost as many Nazis in movies as Wolfgang Preiss.

Marius Goring begins: 'Lili Marlene is the name of a song. The story of Lili Marlene—well, it's a sort of modern fairy story really—only it's a true story as well.' The film purports to tell that story, which it does with some degree of accuracy apart from the pardonable liberty of describing Lale Andersen as 'a little Swedish girl'.

There is a hilarious vignette of Goering's wife Emmy dressed as a Wagnerian heroine singing 'Lili Marleen' in over-blown operatic style with coloratura flourishes, on stage at the Berlin State Opera: that was probably inspired by the similar scene in Orson Welles' *Citizen Kane*. (In contrast to his arch rival Goebbels, Goering apparently loved 'Lili Marleen'. We can hear Emmy Goering prompting their three-year-old daughter Edda in the song on the soundtrack of a 1942 newsreel.)

The highlight of *The True Story of Lili Marlene* is a reconstruction of Lucie Mannheim's propaganda broadcast over the BBC the year before. This time we hear the words in English

> Führer, I thank and greet you
> For you are good and wise.
> Widows and orphans
> Meet with hollow silent eyes.
> Hitler, the man of blood and fear
> Hang him up on the lantern here
> Hang him up from the lantern
> Of your Lili Marlene.

In the closing scene of the film, Marius Goring again addresses the audience:

> Lili Marlene was born in the docks in Hamburg and then she went to Berlin and then flew to Belgrade. She was sent to the desert and was captured and she was transformed and marched with the armies of liberation into the heart of Europe.

After a lengthy virtuoso tracking shot through the street markets of London's docklands, Goring concludes: 'When the blackout is lifted and the lights are re-lit and the shining domes of Stalingrad are being rebuilt, then the true people and the real joys of life will come into their own again. And the famous tune of "Lili Marlene" will linger in the heads of the Eighth Army as a trophy of victory and as a memory of the last war, to remind us all to sweep Fascism off the face of the earth and to make it really the last war.'

A curious little postlude to the story of 'Lili Marlene' is offered by the 1949 song 'The Wedding of Lili Marlene'. The text evokes Lili Marlene as though she were a real person getting married after the war.

> There were tears in the crowded congregation
> There were hearts that had love but all in vain
> 'Twas good-bye to the sweetheart of the nation
> At the Wedding of Lili Marlene.
> Men who'd marched where the desert sands are burning
> From Tobruk down the road to Alamein,
> In their hearts tender mem'ries were returning,
> At the Wedding of Lili Marlene.

Another bizarre attempt to flesh out the character of Lili Marlene was made in 1950 with the truly terrible British film, *Lilli Marlene*, which purports to tell the story of a patriotic French girl (played by the British actress Lisa Daniely) who inspires the song. The film offers enough fake accents and ludicrous clichés to fill an episode of the TV parody *'Allo 'Allo*. The heroine gets to sing 'Lili Marleen' in German, French and English as well as a sentimental version of 'We'll Meet Again', and reprises 'Lili Marleen' at the end in the Albert Hall accompanied by 8,000 veterans of the North African campaign. Norbert Schultze's authorship of the song is nowhere acknowledged and the film's score is attributed to Stanley Black [Solomon Schwartz]. Never was the opening disclaimer of resemblance to real persons living or dead more truthful.

War Songs: Humorous, Patriotic and Military

Unlike 'Lili Marlene', humour signally failed to cross national and political lines during the Second World War. All sides used humour to bolster morale and to diminish the enemy but its use was only effective for home consumption.

Since the outbreak of the war, generations of British schoolboys have continued to sing a scurrilous text about the Nazis to the tune of the Colonel Bogey March. In one of its many variants it runs:

> Hitler has only got one ball
> Goering has two, but his are small
> Himmler's are very sim'ler
> And Goebbels's got no balls at all.

The *Ur*-version of the song, which began 'Goering has only got one ball', has been attributed to Toby O'Brien, an employee of the British Council in 1939. (Did employees of the British Council really have nothing better to do with their time at the outbreak of war?) Lyrics of such earthy vulgarity could never have been broadcast by the high-minded BBC or recorded commercially at this date, but no doubt the song did a great deal to sustain British spirits through the darkest hours of the Blitz. An article in *Time Magazine* on 10 April 1939 commented on British squeamishness after the Lord Chancellor of the day, Lord Clarendon, had banned a song entitled 'Even Hitler had a mother', which ran:

> Though we may get furious with Hitler
>   if we're not of Aryan race
> Let's remember that when he was littler
>   someone called him Angel Face.
> Though we may not idolize the Duce when
>   the news gets rather grim,
> Someone called hoochy-koochy-koochy,
>   that was how she humoured him.
> Even Hitler had a mother,
> Even Mussolini had a ma;
> When they were babies they were cross,
>   perhaps,
> But all they needed was a change of
>   naps—maps—

Don't be hard upon the Black Shirts, they
  may be rather Swastika,
But even Hitler had a mother and even
  Mussolini had a ma.

About the time that this song was banned, the periodical *Truth*, which supported the policy of appeasement, ran an article entitled 'Hitler the artist' which asked rhetorically but without a hint of irony if it could be 'possible that the real Hitler, the genuine little Adolf, is a sensitive child, intensely occupied with his own shy moods?' The continuing nervousness of the British authorities about making fun of the Nazis in song was demonstrated when Arthur Askey was banned from recording a song entitled 'It's really nice to see you, Mr Hess' after the flight of the Nazi deputy leader to Britain in 1940.

A humorous song of engaging daftness that achieved great success on both sides of the Atlantic was Oliver Wallace's 'Der Fuehrer's Face' written for a Walt Disney cartoon in which Donald Duck was mobilized in the propaganda war against Hitler. Though not as obscene as 'Hitler has only got one ball' it was given an earthy vulgarity in the extremely popular studio recording made by Spike Jones and his City Slickers by the use of an instrument described as a 'birdaphone', which simulated the sound of a 'raspberry' being blown every time the word 'Heil!' is called out.

Used against the enemy in World War II, musical humour tended to be a blunt weapon. Bumptious songs like 'We're gonna hang out the washing on the Siegfried Line' or 'It's just too bad for nasty Uncle Adolf', recorded in the first months of the war, backfired when the war went badly for the Allies in 1940.

Perhaps no song expresses more ironically the false optimism of the Phoney War than 'We're gonna hang out the washing on the Siegfried Line':

We're gonna hang out the washing on the Siegfried Line
Have you any dirty washing, mother dear?
We're gonna hang out the washing on the Siegfried Line
'Cause the washing day is here.
Whether the weather may be wet or fine
We'll just rub along without a care.
We're gonna hang out the washing on the Siegfried Line
If the Siegfried Line's still there.

The Germans' humorous reply to 'We're gonna hang out the washing on the Siegfried Line' was unlikely to raise many laughs either:

> Yeah my boy, you thought it would be too easy
> Having a great washing day at the German Rhine!
> Well, have you peed in your pants already?
> No need for you to be so sad!
> Don't worry, we're coming to face-wash you all over!
> And once the German washing day is going to be over
> You won't need any laundry anymore!

The song spawned a further gloatingly contemptuous response to a different tune from Charlie Schwedler.

> Dear Ma, I'm feeling rather done.
> My washing on the Siegfried Line has done a bunk
> and gone ...
> I couldn't bring a souvenir for Mary,
> 'Cos I met a German soldier who sent me back to Tipperary.

There were three further German parodies, including one with a grossly anti-Semitic text.

> It's alright, hanging washing on the Siegfried Line,
> If you've got a change of clothing you can spare.
> It's alright, hanging washing on the Siegfried Line
> If the Yiddish clothes would wear.[22]

The German and British senses of humour tended to be like ships passing in the night. The dry humour of Sir Thomas Beecham was regarded as so brilliant by the British that a book has been published of his collected witticisms. But when questioned by the author about what it was like working with Beecham at Covent Garden in the pre-war seasons, the German soprano Erna Berger replied that she admired him musically but could detect no sense of humour. The lumpish sallies of Charlie Schwedler's English lyrics raise an entirely unintended kind of laughter from English-speaking audiences and the wartime broadcasts of Charlie and his Band to Britain must have contributed to the myth—widely believed in that country—that Germans have a defective sense of humour.

Goebbels was decidedly unamused when he saw the propaganda short that still tickles the humour of British people: the clever doctoring of excerpts from Leni Riefenstahl's *Triumph of the Will*, so that the Nazi hierarchy are made to dance the Lambeth Walk.

Probably the most effective example of musical humour being used as an attack weapon was between French speakers in the war of words and music waged between the French Section of the BBC and the German-controlled Radio Paris. The usual pattern on both sides was to add satirical words to a popular song. In 1942 Maurice Van Moppès in London transformed Charles Trenet's pre-war hit 'Boum' into a jaunty celebration of the mounting intensity of Allied bombing raids on Germany.

> Tout' l'Angleterr' dit Boum!
> Lorsque les bomb's font Boum, Boum!
> Mais Boum!
> C'est en Allemagn' que, Boum!
> Hambourg, Berlin font Boum!
> C'est la RAF qui passe!
> Boum! Jour et nuit, badaboum![23]

In February 1943 following the German capitulation at Stalingrad, Van Moppès turned in a witty parody of 'Tout va très bien, Madame la Marquise' with Hitler cast in the role of the disaster-prone Marquise and Goebbels as the unctuous servant.

In 1943 the French team at the BBC was joined by Pierre Dac. Dubbed 'Le Roi des Loufoques' ('the king of the crazies') Dac was considered to be one of the most original French humorists of the twentieth century. Among the songs he parodied for propaganda purposes were 'Ça fait d'excellents français', sung earlier by Maurice Chevalier to boost French morale during the *drôle de guerre*, and Werner Richard Heymann's 'Les gars de la marine':

The brilliant French humorist Pierre Dac was an asset to the Free French in radio broadcasts from London.

Voilà les gars de la vermine
Chevalier de la bassess'
Voilà les Waffen SS

350

Voyez comme le genr'
Crapuleux
Ce qui s'fuit d'mieux
Avant qu'on ne les extremine
Regardez les consciencieus'ment
Voilà les gars de la vermine
Du plus p'tit jusqu'au plus grand
Du simple voyou á Darnand
ILS SONT ALLEMANDS.[24]

Wartime musical humour was most effective when confined to the role of cheering people up. No one did more to cheer up the British during the war than cheeky Lancashire comedian George Formby with his little ukulele and his rude songs. The indefatigable Formby was more often than not the first star to enter a war zone and it is estimated that he performed for around three million serving men and women. A single eight-week tour in 1943 took in thirteen countries, 24,000 miles, and 225,000 troops.[25]

Formby was the number one cinema box office attraction in Britain through most of the war, though his brand of humour failed to cross the Atlantic. The appeal of the dentally-challenged Formby was probably as incomprehensible to the Americans as it would have been to the Germans. The mixture of the coy and the smutty was peculiarly British and also very much of its time. After the sexual revolution of the 1960s, the *double entendre* of songs like 'When I'm cleaning windows' and 'With my little stick of Blackpool rock' came to seem as quaintly dated as the naughty seaside postcards of Donald McGill.

The ubiquitous gas mask that happily never fulfilled its intended purpose provided Formby with the theme of a wartime hit in which he comes up with a variety of suggestive alternative uses for it.

Now I'm getting very fond of my gas mask I declare.
It hardly ever leaves my sight.
I sling it on my back and I take it everywhere.
It even comes to bed at night.
It's been a real good pal to me I must confess.
And helped me out of many a mess.

My sister had a lot of socks to mend
So she gave me a fat bouncing baby to tend.
And when I felt it leaking at one end
Well I did what I could with my gas mask.

I bought a farm because I like fresh air.
At milking time I tried to do my share
And when I found the bucket wasn't there
Well I did what I could with my gas mask.

The lady living next door, Mrs 'Icks
She heard the sirens blow one morn at ten to six
She dashed outside in nothing but her nicks.
But she knew what to do with her gas mask.

In 1943, many British people suffered a sense of humour failure when Noel Coward launched his song 'Don't let's be beastly to the Germans'. Winston Churchill saw the joke but many others didn't:

Don't let's be beastly to the Germans
When our victory is ultimately won.
It was just those nasty Nazis
Who persuaded them to fight.
And their Beethoven and Bach
Are really far worse than their bite!

Let's be meek to them
And turn the other cheek to them,
And try to bring out their
latent sense of fun.

Some of the song's lines have dated and would need to be explained to anyone under a certain age. Others still retain something of their original outrageousness:

Let's be sweet to them
And day by day repeat to them
That sterilisation simply isn't done.

By the summer of 1943 when Coward wrote this song, it was clear that Germany was heading for ultimate defeat and that it was merely a matter of time. Coward was evidently picking up on the current widespread debate about how the Germans should be treated at the end of the war.

Exactly such a discussion had taken place as early as 8 March 1941, at the Prime Minister's country house of Chequers, when it took considerably more optimism to envisage German defeat. Churchill's private secretary John Colville reported in his diary: 'Duncan Sandys [Churchill's son-in-law and a Conservative member of parliament who had previously been a leading proponent of appeasement] was bloodthirsty. He wanted to destroy Germany by laying the country to waste and burning towns and factories, so that for years the German people might be occupied in

I'VE JUST COME OUT FROM ENGLAND
By NOEL COWARD

The humour of Noel Coward's song 'Don't let's be beastly to the Germans' misfired as did the superior tone of his Middle East Diary.

reconstruction. He wanted to destroy their books and libraries so that an illiterate generation might grow up. The PM said he was in no way moved by Duncan's words. He did not believe in pariah nations, and he saw no alternative to the acceptance of Germany as a part of the family of Europe.'[26]

'Don't let's be beastly to the Germans' was probably written in immediate response to the publication of an official report on what to do with Germany at the end of the war. *The Daily Herald* reported on 2 July 1943 on the 'Latest contribution to the controversy about what shall be done with Germany after the war' and quotes from the report produced by the Royal Institute of International Affairs at Chatham House.

> *Are the Germans to be permanently kept down by force and deprived of economic resources?*
> *Are they to be befriended and helped back as soon as possible to equality with other nations and full share of world prosperity?*
> The Chatham House group report says no to both these questions. And then sets out to find a middle way.

In the same month it was announced that the issue would be debated at the forthcoming Trades Union Conference with British workers expected to take a more benign attitude to their German fellow workers, though it was hardly likely that Coward would pay attention to anything as vulgar as a Trades Union Conference.

When 'Don't let's be beastly to the Germans' was broadcast shortly before Coward set off on a tour of North Africa and the Middle East, the BBC received sacks full of protest mail from listeners who had entirely missed the irony of Coward's words and thought he was actually advocating a conciliatory approach to the Germans at the end of the war. The BBC and the record company HMV panicked and banned the broadcast or sale of Coward's record.[27] Worse was to come. On 30 July 1943, in his weekly column entitled 'Listening Post' in the popular newspaper *The Daily Herald*, the musician and critic Spike Hughes excoriated Coward and his song. Spike Hughes's articles were frequently acerbic, especially towards the BBC, but the vitriolic tone of his article about Coward suggests personal animosity. Coward's reaction in his diary was: 'His attack was over-personal and far, far too long. Vituperation is an ineffective lesson unless it is handled with consummate skill.'

Hughes did not fall into the trap of imagining that Coward meant what he said about being kind to the Germans. Instead he accuses Coward of poor taste and taking an irredeemably trivial approach to a problem of vital importance.

> … I am not worried about Mr Coward's flimsy little cocktail-party song about the German people. He has never struck me as being a particularly clever satirist; an author in his position should have been savage about the Nazis ten years ago, and could perhaps have influenced his large public to adopt a more realistic view of things. But in those days Mr Coward's talent was more preoccupied with debutantes than Dachau, with 'Design for Living' than Hitler's designs for living room. Though it was all undoubtedly very witty and all that, the broadcasting of this song showed a mischievous disregard of public feeling at a time when most of us are trying to look ahead to see if we can't bequeath a little sanity to the world our children will have to live in. (*Daily Herald*, 30 July 1943, p. 2)

Hughes was expecting too much from a clever but superficial entertainer, but he was essentially right about the dangerous irresponsibility of Coward's views on the subject. These were revealed in all their unpleasantness in the diary that Coward wrote while on his Middle Eastern tour.

'Personally I have little respect or admiration for a race, however cultured, sensitive and civilised, that willingly allows itself time and time again to be stampeded into the same state of neurotic bestiality and arrogance, apparently—if we are to believe the Germanophiles—against its will. If its will is so weak and malleable I can't feel that, as a race it is much good anyway. I suppose it is hopeless to expect our amiable sentimentalists sodden with nostalgia for those dear dead summers in Bavaria and the beer gardens of Heidelberg, to face the unpalatable fact that sadistic tendencies and an unregenerate passion for world dominance have been inherent in the German people from the beginning.'[28]

So extreme was Coward's Germanophobia that he would not even allow himself his usual harmless pleasure of lusting after young servicemen if they happened to be German. When taken to inspect German prisoners of war he wrote: 'I scrutinized their faces carefully as we walked up and down the lines and was fully prepared to find that a large percentage of them were at least fine physical specimens. In this I was wrong. There were few healthy-looking bodies among the lot of them and their eyes were uniformly repellent.'[29]

Happily, at the end of the war, the imperatives of the Cold War took precedence. The vengeful ideas of Noel Coward and Duncan Sandys were consigned to the dustbin and the Allies were not condemned to repeat the mistakes they had made at the end of the previous war.

By the time that Coward returned to Britain after his North African and Middle Eastern tour, the fuss stirred up by 'Don't let's be beastly to the Germans' had begun to die down. Coward concluded ruefully: 'I am willing to admit that, as a nation, we have never been especially good at recognising satire, but the satire of "Don't let's be beastly to the Germans" was surely not all that subtle. I must be more careful in the future and double dot my Is and treble cross my Ts.'[30]

Coward exercised his wit less controversially in a song entitled 'Could you please oblige us with a bren gun?' that affectionately mocks the Home Guard.

> Could you please oblige us with a bren gun?
> Or failing that a hand grenade will do.
> We've got some ammunition
> In a rather damp condition
> And Major Huss has an arquebus
> That was used at Waterloo.

Coward's best and most enduring Second World War song was 'London Pride'—a tribute to the fighting spirit of London and its citizens during the Blitz, in which for once he drops the mask of humour. To a simple tune reminiscent of a children's nursery rhyme Coward evokes the spirit of the city poetically, though his clipped and artificial diction brings a whiff of condescension to lines such as 'Every Blitz your resistance toughening from the Ritz to the Rose and Crown' that may be grating to some. Joyce Grenfell had an unexpected success with the song on her Middle Eastern tour in October 1944 when she scheduled it amongst her more light-hearted items. 'Noel's "London Pride" goes over well. It has even more meaning out here and we've worked it up into quite a spectacular with me speaking the middle part against the piano! There was a lot of nose-blowing at the end which amazed me.'[31]

Hitler can at least be credited with causing a war that did more to undermine the rigidities of the British class system than any other event in history. The classes were thrown together in ways that were not always comfortable. The well-born Joyce Grenfell smirked privately in her diary at the very thought of the ersatz upper-class Noel Coward being taken for truly posh.

A call for social cohesion was made with the song 'We must all stick together':

> We march along together
> And sing with all our might.
> We must all stick together, all stick together
> And the clouds will soon roll by.
> We must all stick together, all stick together
> Never mind the old school tie.
> United we shall stand
> Whatever may befall
> The richest in the land
> The poorest of us all.

In Britain far more than in Germany, there were a great many popular songs that made more or less humorous reference to the everyday realities of the war—evacuation, rationing, official warnings about 'careless talk', gasmasks and the blackout. The blackout in particular inspired a great many songs. 'Goodnight (got your torchlight)' puts the blackout into its everyday context:

'Good night, *goodnight (spoken), Got your torchlight? *Yes*. Got your gas mask? *Yes,* Alright, alright, Good night, *goodnight,* Goodnight, *goodnight,* Got your tin hat? *Yes,* Got your food card? *Yes.'*

Songs about the blackout could be comic like 'Where does poor Pa go in the blackout', or romantic like 'They can't blackout the moon', or Evelyn Künnecke's 1940 hit 'Haben Sie schon mal im Dunkeln geküsst?' ('Have you ever kissed in the dark?'), but whereas the former refers to air-raids and falling over things in the dark, the latter makes no specific reference to the war.

Songs about the blackout could also be wistful or optimistic. An example of the former is 'When the lights go on again':

When the lights go on again all over the world
And the boys are home again all over the world
And rain or snow is all that may fall from the skies above
A kiss won't mean Good-bye but Hello to love.

The vicissitudes of civilian conscripts in the armed forces also provided a rich vein of humour for songwriters to mine in songs such as 'Kiss me good-night, Sergeant-Major.'

Don't forget to wake me in the morning
And bring me round a nice hot cup of tea.
Kiss me good-night, Sergeant-Major
Sergeant-Major, be a mother to me.

One song defies categorisation and that is Gracie Fields's special wartime version of her masterpiece of comic quirkiness 'The biggest aspidistra in the world'. The original version, first recorded in 1928, caught the imagination of the British public with its whimsical and slightly Freudian imagery.

For years we 'ad an Aspidistra in a flower pot
On the whatnot, near the 'at stand in the 'all.
It didn't seem to grow, till one day our brother Joe,
Had a notion that he'd make it strong and tall.
So 'e crossed with an acorn from an oak tree
And 'e planted it against the garden wall.
It shot like a rocket till it nearly touched the sky.
It's the biggest Aspidistra in the world.

Restored to public favour after a vicious newspaper campaign against her when she married an Italian national and moved to America in 1940, 'Our Gracie' re-recorded her most popular song in 1941, giving it a new final verse with a topical, humorous, propaganda slant.

> Me brother's in the army
> He's in the home defence.
> With the biggest aspidistra in the world.
> The Colonel says that's topping
> Now we'll start the big advance.
> With the biggest aspidistra in the world.
> When Goering sees it from afar
> He'll say to his old frau
> Young Joe has got his blood up.
> War will soon be over now.
> But they're going to string old Hitler
> From the very highest bough
> Of the biggest aspidistra in the world.

When in 1942 the British set up a highly successful secret radio station to disseminate disinformation and propaganda in Germany, its gargantuan triple antenna, 110 meters high, was almost inevitably named 'Aspidistra' after Gracie's beloved song.

'Biggest aspidistra in the world' is typical of the Second World War in that its jingoism is firmly tongue in cheek. There were a great many martial songs written during the war, but apart from the humorous ones very few have survived in the collective memory of the conflict. One of the most notorious German songs was Norbert Schultze's 'Bomben auf Engelland'—a song that even he was anxious to forget after the war.

> Hört ihr die Motoren singen:
> Ran an den Feind!
> Hört ihr's in den Ohren klingen:
> Ran an den Feind!
> Bomben! Bomben!
> Bomben auf Engelland!
>
> (Can you hear the engines singing;
> Attack the enemy!
> Do you hear it in your ears ringing:
> Attack the enemy!
> Bombs! Bombs!
> Bombs on England!)

358

'When I hear this song again today, it cuts me to the heart. What? Did you compose that? It pains me often the whole day long and keeps me awake at night with horror and shame—even today.' So wrote Norbert Schultze, 55 years later in his autobiography, about 'Bomben auf Engelland'.[32] The song was written for a propaganda documentary called *Feuertaufe* ('Baptism of Fire') filmed during the German invasion of Poland in September 1939.

Schultze had every reason to be ashamed of his association with this sickening film that celebrates the sheer brutality and destructiveness of Nazi war tactics and was a blatant attempt to terrorize anyone else who might have the temerity to stand up to Germany. Schultze should perhaps have been rather more ashamed of the ecstatic Wagnerian score he devised to accompany images of gleaming bombs raining down on the hapless Poles than of his trite little ditty. Strangely, the Polish pianist Wladyslaw Szpilman, who was on the ground at the receiving end of these German bombs, described the sight in similarly aesthetic and even sensuous terms. 'Rarely an hour passed without seeing the silvered silhouettes of the bombers surging up into the incredible blue skies of that autumn, followed by the rings of white smoke produced by our anti-aircraft fire.'[33]

Schultze's song occurs twice in the movie, firstly as 'Bombs on Poland' as German bombers fly into action against Poland, and then in the closing scene as 'Bombs on England' as the bombers prepare to do to London what they have just done to Warsaw. 'Bomben auf Engelland' was much the most successful and frequently performed of Schultze's many wartime marches. The song delighted Goering, the commander-in chief of the Luftwaffe, but Goebbels remarked caustically that it reminded him of the song 'Schenkt man sich Rosen' from Zeller's operetta *Der Vogelhändler*. There is indeed an operetta-like jollity about it, and it would not be hard to imagine General Boum singing such a tune in Offenbach's 1867 satire on German militarism, *La Grande Duchesse de Gérolstein*.

Schultze gives a hair-raising account of writing a march under extreme pressure of time and with constant supervision and interference from Goebbels, to go with Operation Barbarossa, the Nazi invasion of the Soviet Union. As Schultze remarks, it was extraordinary that Goebbels should involve himself in the minutiae of a march at such a time.[34]

Schultze's march 'Panzer rollen in Afrika', written for the Afrika Korps, is drearily conventional and certainly did less for Rommel's troops than 'Lili Marleen'. A song entitled 'Vorwärts mit General Rommel' ('Forward with General Rommel') commissioned as a gift for Rommel's birthday on 15 November 1942, had to be abandoned. Schultze was so delayed by changes to the text that, as he dryly put it, Rommel was going backwards rather than forwards by the time it was completed.[35]

A hard core within the Nazi party wanted to impose a strict diet of patriotic and marching songs for the armed forces and the German public. Vast quantities of this kind of music were indeed recorded and broadcast but the appetite of the German people for it was limited. It produced an effect of numbing monotony on all but the most hardened Nazis. Eventually, the Nazi hierarchy was forced to accept that, just like young people everywhere else, young Germans thirsted for sentimental songs and swing.

The scenes of jubilation that marked the outbreak of the First World War were not repeated at the beginning of the Second. Memories of the killing fields of Flanders were too fresh in people's minds. Though some of the patriotic marching songs from the First World War were revived during the Phoney War, the most successful songs of the Second World War were rarely jingoistic or martial in character.

On 11 December 1939, France's most admired operatic tenor Georges Thill recorded four patriotic marching songs. Three of these, Louis Ganne's 'Marche lorraine', Frédéric Bentayoux's 'Alsace-Lorraine' and Camille Robert's 'Quand Madelon' date from the First World War or earlier. It must be said that French composers showed a particular flair for this kind of music and these marches are far more attractive musically than anything produced by their German equivalents, including Schultze. The 'Marche lorraine', with its trumpet flourishes, flow of graceful melody and its cooing female chorus that sounds as though drafted in from the Folies-Bergère, is especially delightful.

The fourth march recorded by Thill in the same session 'Ils ne la gagneront pas!' (roughly translatable as 'They will not win'), by Lucien Carol and Georges Krier, was brand new and an official commission. One would never guess that it was written in 1939. It sounds as though it was left over from the previous war. It also has a jaunty tuneful charm with Thill sounding like a boisterous teenager on a picnic. Unfortunately the Germans did win, and marched into France before Thill's record had time to sell many copies, and it has remained one of his rarest. In 1944 a new edition of the song was published with the references to Pétain deleted and a new verse celebrating the tenacity, courage and temerity of De Gaulle.[36]

A great many songs were written to celebrate the British and American armed forces or particular sections of them. 'Sons of the Old Contemptibles' refers to young fighting soldiers whose fathers had been part of the British Expeditionary Force in the First World War, notoriously dismissed by Kaiser Wilhelm II as 'contemptible'.

'Lords of the air' published in 1939 anticipated the key role that the Royal Air Force was shortly to play the Battle of Britain.

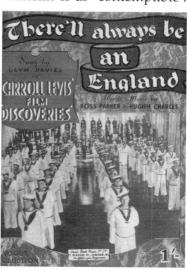

> The British Empire proudly
>   stands
> As in the days of old,
> Our fathers fought o'er land
>   and sea,
> Their history is told
> In our new battle-field the
>   sky,
> Prepare to do or dare
> Let this be our new battle-cry,
> 'Britannia rules the air.'

'There'll always be an England' became an unofficial anthem to at least one part of the United Kingdom.

By and large though, the most successful and widely remembered British patriotic songs of the Second World War, such as '(There'll be bluebirds over the) White Cliffs of Dover' and 'There'll always be an England', tended to be nostalgic and sentimental rather than militaristic, evoking history and the beauty of the British countryside and coasts.

'There'll always be an England' by Ross Parker and Hugh Charles, who later wrote 'We'll Meet Again', was written for a movie in the summer of 1939 and took off after the outbreak of war, with sheet music sales of 200,000 in the first few months and a best-selling record by Vera Lynn. Despite its

'This is worth fighting' for expressed the restrained patriotism of Britain's 'finest hour'.

overt patriotism, the tone of the song is nostalgic and defensive rather than aggressive.

> There'll always be an England
> While there's a country lane,
> Wherever there's a cottage small
> Beside a field of grain.

The final verse is a direct quotation of Shakespeare's most famous patriotic speech from the play *Richard II*, written when England had recently survived an invasion threat from the Spanish Armada.[37]

The Scots were understandably irritated at being subsumed with the English or excluded altogether, and sang their own versions of this song. 'There'll always be an England, while there's a country lane' became 'There'll always be an England as long as Scotland's there.' It is ironic that this famous patriotic song fits in with the German notion of the British being *Engländer*.

War Songs: The Chanson

The rich tradition of the popular *chanson* dating back to the nineteenth century enabled French songwriters to embrace a far greater range of emotional, sexual, social and political subject matter than their American and British counterparts, and to deal with it in a far more adult and sophisticated way. From the *drôle de guerre* through the Occupation and on to the Liberation, French songs continued to provide a (sometimes) oblique commentary on events and developments in France. Nazi oppression and censorship failed to stifle the creativity of the French songwriters, and some of the greatest of all *chansons*, such as Piaf's 'Le vagabond' and Trenet's 'La mer', were written under the Occupation.

During the *drôle de guerre* the renewed Anglo-French alliance was celebrated in cheerful morale-boosting songs such as 'Bonjour Tommy!'

> Bonjour, bonjour Tommy!
> Tu reviens donc en France.
> Nous voici réunis,
> Après vingt ans d'absence.
> Tu vas revoir ici

De vieilles connaissances
Toute la France
Crie: Bonjour, Tommy!
Et bonne chance![38]

Bonjour, bonjour Tommy!
So you've come back to France.
Here we are re-united
After twenty years of absence.
You will meet old acquaintances
The whole of France
Shouts: Bonjour, Tommy!
And good luck!

*Reda Caire's version of
'Bonjour Tommy' must have
raised a few eyebrows.*

The best-known version of this song was recorded by Léo Marjane in November 1939. A second version recorded a month later by the male 'chanteur de charme' Reda Caire has outrageously camp connotations to modern ears. As a former member of Mistinguett's notoriously louche entourage, Reda Caire can hardly have been unaware of the homosexual implications.

*The irresistibly funny
Fernandel.*

A number of French language versions of British hits of the period appeared, including 'We're gonna hang out the washing on the Siegfried Line' ('On ira pendre notre linge sur la ligne Siegfried'). Gracie Fields's song, 'Wish me luck as you wave me goodbye', was recorded by the sweet-voiced Eliane Célis as 'Souris-moi et dis-moi bonne chance!'

Hitler's humble origins as a housepainter were mocked by Georgius in the song 'Il travaille du pinceau' ('He works with a brush'); the horse-faced comedian Fernandel warned humorously against false rumours in the song 'Francine' which he performed for French troops at the Maginot Line.[39]

Whether written with impending war in mind or not, certain songs such as Damia's 'Un avion tout blanc' ('Mon amour est parti dans un avion tout blanc') ['My love has left in a white plane'] recorded in May 1939, and Lucienne Boyer's plaintive 'Partir sans laisser d'adresse'

('Gone without leaving an address') would have taken on new significance with the outbreak of war and the call-up of troops.

The fears and anxieties of the *drôle de guerre* are touchingly expressed in 'Mon p'tit Kaki'—subtitled 'Lettre de femme'—with words by Roger Bernstein and music by Georges Van Parys, sung by Lucienne Boyer in the cabaret Chez Elle in November 1939. Like so many wartime songs it takes the form of a letter to a conscripted soldier from his wife.

> Mon p'tit Kaki
> Mon grand chéri!
> Ta p'tit femme sera bien sage
> Ell' pense á toi
> Et c'est pourquoi
> Ell' t'en aime encor' davantage
> Ell' tiendra l'coup
> Et jusqu'au bout
> Car pour avoir du courage
> Elle a ta photo sur son coeur jour et nuit
> Mon chéri!
> Mon p'tit Kaki![40]

> (My little Kaki
> My great love!
> Your little woman will be good
> She thinks of you
> And that's why she still loves you
> She holds out to the end
> To give her courage
> She has your photo on her heart night and day.)

The following year after the fall of France, Georges Van Parys wrote a new version of the song to words by Jean Boyer, with the wife writing to her soldier husband who is now, with more than a million others, a prisoner of the Germans.

Georges Van Parys also wrote the music for 'Ça fait d'excellents français' sung at the Casino de Paris by Maurice Chevalier in the morale-boosting revue *Paris-London*—intended to celebrate the renewal of the Anglo-French alliance, which presents an altogether more up-beat picture of conscription.

Le Colonel était dans la Finance
Le Commandant était dans L'Industrie
Le Capitaine était dans lAssurance
Et le Lieut'nant était dans l'Epicerie...

Et tout ca, ça fait
D'excellents Français
D'excellents soldats
Qui marchent au pas ... [41]

(The Colonel was in finance
The Commander was in industry
The Captain was in insurance and the Lieutenant was
    a grocer ...

And all this makes
Excellent French men
Excellent soldiers
Who march in step.)

The subsequent verses describe their differing political convictions and even the medical conditions that are typical of their class and rank. (At this date, the French were evidently as class-conscious as the British.)

When Georges Van Parys wrote this song, he was himself a conscripted soldier. While entertaining troops at the front with a varied and distinguished group of performers, he was half amused and half horrified how accurate his song had been in listing the social divisions and hierarchical attitudes within the French army. Only members of the Comédie Française were deemed worthy of dining with the generals. Though world famous because of her pre-war international hit 'Parler-moi d'amour', the singer Lucienne Boyer as a singer of 'Variétés' was considered of lower rank and dined instead with the colonels, one of whom made knee-trembling advances to her all through the meal. George Van Parys and the comedian Pierre Dac were consigned to the captains but were relieved not to have to fight off sexual advances. [42]

After the French defeat Van Parys wrote bitterly in his diary on 23 August 1940: 'This war couldn't have ended in any other way. This is precisely what I thought when I heard Chevalier sing; "Et tout ça, ça fait d'excellents Français". How do you expect matters to end with soldiers like that?' [43]

The most enduring and widely loved chanson to come out of the *drôle de guerre*, Michel Emer's 'L'accordéoniste', was launched by Edith Piaf at the Bobino music hall in Paris in February 1940. With a gritty and tragic narrative, punctuated with refrains of frenetic gaiety, it belongs in the tradition of the *chanson réaliste* but was out of step with both the forced optimism of the *drôle de guerre* and the pious family values of Vichy. A young prostitute falls in love with an accordion player at a dance hall she frequents between clients. When he goes off to war she dreams of his return and of setting up a *maison* (brothel) where she will work as a cashier and he will be the boss. Even this modest dream is shattered when he fails to come back. It has to be said that such a song with English lyrics would have been unthinkable either on Broadway or in the West End of London. Sung with a complete absence of false pathos by Piaf, it is a small masterpiece.[44]

With the defeat of France and the great exodus from Paris in June 1940, the theatres and cabarets closed and the singers were dispersed—several not to return until after the war. Jean Sablon, the first singer to introduce the American style of crooning with a microphone, spent the war years in the Americas. Josephine Baker, who had worked hard to entertain French troops during the *drôle de guerre*, like many others moved south to Marseilles, and then on to North Africa. Several pre-war stars, such as Mireille, Marie Dubas, and Renée Lebas, were forced to avoid Paris and the occupied zone because of their Jewish ancestry.

Mireille, the composer and performer of such naughty and witty songs as 'Couché dans le foin' ('Sleeping in the hay'), eventually found refuge in a convent, where she involved the nuns in her schemes to recycle British parachutes as underwear and brassieres, and put on theatrical performances to raise money for the Resistance. She was mildly embarrassed to be asked to perform some of her songs for the nuns, accompanying herself on a harmonium. 'I was not admired, or appreciated. No, I was contemplated. The gaze, the blossoming, the expression of these figurines, the silence that followed, moved me, touched me and meant more to me than any applause. And then I was proud. Through me, my sisters had discovered the CHANSON.'[45]

Marie Dubas and Renée Lebas sought refuge in Switzerland and continued their careers there for the rest of the war. But plenty of talent remained. One by one the big stars—Chevalier, Mistinguett, Trenet, Tino Rossi, Suzy Solidor and Léo Marjane—returned to the stage as the theatres and cabarets reopened from the autumn of 1940.

New talent emerged, too, under the Occupation, including André Claveau, Géorges Guétary, Roland Gerbeau, Georges Ulmer and Yves Montand.

Cabaret and concerts of popular songs continued to play an important role in Parisian cultural life throughout the Occupation. The weekly cultural magazine *Comoedia* carried a regular section entitled 'Variétés et Chanson' alongside its reportage of high culture. Though French lovers of classical music welcomed visiting German musicians and continued to listen to masterpieces of the Austro-German tradition, German popular music had little impact, apart from a handful of songs popularised by the German musicals that replaced American movies in French cinemas. One of the greatest hits of the first year of Occupation was a bilingual Franco-German version of the jaunty song 'Bel Ami' by Theo Mackeben from the movie of the same name, sung by Eva Busch. Busch had arrived in Paris before the war as a refugee. For a while it seemed she would be able to continue her Parisian career unaffected by the defeat of France and even to profit by her ability to slip effortlessly from French into German, but she soon fell foul of the German occupiers and landed in Ravensbruck concentration camp. The great exception to the generally lukewarm French response to German popular songs was of course 'Lili Marleen', which was a special case in France as elsewhere.

The ubiquitous theme of separation was perhaps more keenly felt in France than in most other countries. From June 1940 there were 1.8 million French soldiers in German captivity who were only gradually returned in exchange for French workers who went to Germany to replace conscripted German men. Between 1940 and November 1942 France itself was divided between the occupied zone

The Franco-German hit 'Bel Ami' was popular throughout Europe.

The popular French crooner Jean Sablon.

'J'attendrai' song sheet.

The French caption asks whether the girl is listening to Tino Rossi or Lili Marlene. Pin-ups of Hitler and Maurice Chevalier inside her cupboard make odd companions.

and the Vichy zone, and the border between the two was not always easy to cross.

'J'attendrai', the most evocative of all French wartime songs of separation and longing, was strictly speaking neither a French nor a wartime song. It originated in Italy in 1937 as 'Tornerai' before being introduced into France by the Italian singer Rina Ketty and taken up by Tino Rossi and Jean Sablon. The French pianist and singer Fania Fénelon arranged the song for the women's orchestra in Auschwitz and wrote in her memoirs of how much it meant to the musicians of the orchestra. 'Written for those absent in 1939-40 [*sic*], it symbolised all returns for us, theirs and ours. Every time we played the arrangement we were secretly jubilant. It was amusing to be able to sing a song of hope under their [the Nazi guards'] noses.'[46]

A great many songs written under the Occupation deal with the theme of waiting and longing for loved ones. These include 'J'écoute la pluie', sung by Lys Gauty at the ABC music hall.

> Et pour toi, mon amour
> Jusqu'au jour de ton retour
> J'écoute la pluie
> J'écoute le vent qui fuit.[47]

> (And for you, my love
> Until the day you come back
> I'm listening to the rain
> I'm listening to the rushing wind.)

In March 1941 Léo Marjane sang 'Attends-moi mon amour':

> Attends-moi, mon amour
> Avec un peu de chance
> Je serai bientôt de retour
> Prenons patience … [48]

> (Wait for my, my love
> With a bit of luck
> I'll be home soon
> Be patient.)

Similarly, in 1943 the handsome young star Georges Guétary recorded 'Mon coeur est toujours près de toi' ('My heart is always near to you').

> Malgré que tu sois, mon amour loin de moi
> Mon coeur est toujours près de toi.[49]

> (Although my love, you are far away
> My heart is always close to you.)

The absence of French husbands and lovers and the presence of German soldiers over such a lengthy period led inevitably to what has been dubbed 'collaboration horizontale'. For a regime whose motto was *Travail, Famille, Patrie* ('Work, Family, Fatherland'), infidelity and the disruption of family life was of the gravest concern. The Vichy authorities even passed a law in December 1942 to criminalize those who committed adultery with the wives of prisoners of war, designed 'to protect the dignity of the household from which the husband is absent due to circumstances of war.' As this law was completely unenforceable against the German military, it was counterproductive. The official estimate of the number of children born to French women by German soldiers up until October 1943 was a staggering 85,000.

In song at least, the High Priestess of collaboration *horizontale* was Léo Marjane, who sang a number of songs expressing the 'état d'âme' that led so many French women to seek consolation in the arms of German soldiers. The most notorious of these was 'Seule ce soir' ('Alone tonight').

> Je suis seule ce soir
> Avec mes rêves
> Je suis seule ce soir
> Sans ton amour
> Le jour tombe, ma joie s'achève
> Tout se brise dans mon coeur lourd.[50]
> (I'm alone tonight
> With my dreams
> I'm alone tonight
> Without your love
> The day ends, my joy is over
> Everything is shattered in my heavy heart.)

Leo Marjane's song titles and her facial expressions reflect the changing situation of French women under the Occupation.

Léo Marjane was at the height of her popularity during the late 1930s and the war years. With a mellow voice and relaxed American style of crooning, she succeeded all too well in accommodating the rapidly changing political situation in France.

Before the war she had recorded a string of American hits, including the Yiddish titles 'Bei mir bist du schön' and 'Mazeltov': this cannot have stood her in good stead under the Occupation. During the Phoney War she welcomed the British troops with 'Bonjour Tommy' and a bilingual version of 'It's a long way to Tipperary'. In February 1940, with French husbands and lovers already conscripted but not yet long-term prisoners, she prays to her guardian angel to help her resist temptation in the song 'Mon ange'. After defeat and German Occupation she continues to catch the changing moods and attitudes of the time with her songs. 'Attends moi, mon amour' ('Wait for me, my love') gives way to 'Seule ce soir' in which the guardian angel seems to have been dismissed, and she moves on to the all too aptly titled 'J'ai vendu mon âme au diable' ('I've sold my soul to the devil').

She adapted her facial expression to these changing moods on the covers for the sheet music of the three songs.

The very title of one of Marjane's last hit records, the 1944 'Rose, noir ou gris' ('Pink, black or grey') evoked, for some, associations with the black market, the grey uniforms of the Germans and with a period that people soon wanted to forget. It was these associations as much as changing post-war musical tastes that prevented Léo Marjane from regaining her former level of success after the war. Once malicious and lurid accusations against her from a disgruntled former employee were dismissed, judges during the *Épuration* had little to reproach her with other than the usual charges of having

The First World War hit 'It's a long, long way to Tipperary' was revived to celebrate the renewal of the Anglo-French alliance.

'Pour fêter ton retour'.
To celebrate your return.

Entre sa femme et son frère.

A returning French prisoner of war is re-united with his family.

sung to French prisoners and factory workers in Germany, broadcasting on Radio Paris and performing in clubs frequented by the German military. When asked by a judge how she could sing in front of so many grey uniforms, Marjane replied simply that she suffered from myopia—a reply that could have been used by a great many artists who continued to earn a living in wartime Germany and the occupied countries.

There were, of course, also plenty of songs that stressed the faithfulness of the women left behind, such as 'Pour fêter ton retour' recorded by Annette Lajon in 1943.

Pour fêter ton retour
Je me ferai trés belle!
Pour fêter ton retour
Je t'offrirai mon coeur fidèle![51]

(To celebrate your return
I'll make myself beautiful
To celebrate your return
I'll offer you my faithful heart.)

Reactions to defeat and Occupation, as reflected in French songs, veered between nostalgic regret and forced optimism. Songs such as 'Ça sent si bon la France' sung by Maurice Chevalier to French prisoners in a German camp in November 1941, 'Ah! Que la France est belle' ('How beautiful France is') from the 1942 operetta *Valses de Paris*, and Trenet's 'Douce France', celebrate France as a kind of lost paradise.

Other songs such as 'Ça revient', sung by Johnny Hess at the ABC in November 1940, encouraged the French people to make the best of the situation and to get on with their lives.

Ça revient
La vie recommence
Ça revient
Comme une romance.[52]

(It comes back
Life starts again
It comes back
Like a romance.)

Mistinguett put across the same message when she appeared in the revue *Toujours Paris* at the Casino de Paris in November 1941, with the song 'La Tour Eiffel est toujours là' ('The Eiffel tower is still there').

The 1941 revue Toujours Paris *brought the indestructible Mistinguett back to the Paris stage.*

Mistinguett assures her Parisian audience that the Eiffel Tower is still there.

Paris, mon Paris t'as change de physionomi'
Tes ru's sont calm's et tes taxis
Sont à la retraite.
Dans l'Av'nu' du Bois les femm's avec leur souliers d'bois
Quand ell's march'nt sur les pave d'bois
Font des claquettes
Mais ton ciel est toujours aussi leger
Oui, pour moi ton Coeur n'a pas change
Pour le voir il suffit je crois
De regarder au tour de soi.[53]

(Paris has changed its face
Your streets are quiet and your taxis
Have retired
On the Avenue du Bois the women
With wooden shoes go click clack
But the sky is as light as ever
Yes, for me your heart has not changed
You only have to look around to see that.)

The authorities in Vichy wanted the French people to embrace the 'New Order' in Europe as a positive development rather than to view it as a defeat for France. In the first year or so of the Occupation at least, a number of popular French songs advocated precisely that. Soon after the debacle, Raymond Asso and Marguerite Monnot, who had created the great pre-war hit 'Mon légionnaire' for Marie Dubas and many songs for Piaf, produced 'Vive demain' which comes close to being a Vichy manifesto.

> Debout la France, pour la moisson
> Qu'on apercoit á l'horizon,
> Dans le ciel monte radieux
> Un avenir plus merveilleux
> Belle jeunesse, que ton drapeau
> Flotte sur le monde nouveau
> Hier est mort. Vive demain
> Une autre France est en chemin.[54]

> (Arise France, for the harvest
> That we can see on the horizon,
> In the sky a more marvellous future
> Rises radiantly
> Beautiful youth,
> Let your flag float over a new world
> Yesterday is dead. Long live tomorrow.
> Another France is on the way.)

At this stage of the war France had effectively changed sides with the passive support of the bulk of the population. Resistance was negligible during the first year after defeat. There were those who congratulated themselves on now being on the winning side and who looked forward to France playing a leading role in the new order.

'What does Hitler want from us?' asked the distinguished French writer Jean de la Hire.

In a pamphlet entitled 'Hitler, que nous veut-il donc', the well-known author Jean de la Hire argued that France needed to be on the winning side and that was clearly Germany. He assured his readers that Hitler desired that France would 'take her great natural place in a pacified, reconciled and united Europe, for the march forward into the new era.'

With superb irony De la Hire dated his text 15 November-8 December 1941. If he had finished two days earlier he would have been correct. There was little prospect for anything other than a German victory. But after Pearl Harbor on 7 December, far-sighted observers—such as Mussolini's

374

son-in-law and foreign minister Count Ciano, realized that with Russia undefeated and America in the war, ultimate victory for Hitler was impossible. This was not to be generally understood in France for another year and in the meantime French songs continued to reflect the ethos of the Vichy regime.

Maurice Chevalier clearly lent his charisma and influence to the new order when he sang 'La chanson du maçon' ('Song of the mason'), a transparent call for unity behind the national rebirth envisaged by Vichy.

> Si tout l'mond' chantait comm' les macons
> Si chacun apportait son moellon
> Nous rebâtirions notre maison
> Qui deviendrait;
> Bon Dieu!
> La maison de Bon Dieu![55]

> (If the whole world could sing like the masons
> If everyone carried his building block
> We would rebuild our house
> Which would become
> God willing
> The house of the Good Lord.)

Chevalier's version was the most popular but the archives of Radio Paris contained no less than ten different versions with which to ram home the message.

'La France de demain' ('The France of tomorrow') recorded by the tenor André Dassary in June 1941 includes in its final verse the rallying cry of Vichy: *Travail, Famille, Patrie*. It was Dassary too (presumably to his later embarrassment) who recorded in the same month the best-known version of the song that became an unofficial anthem of the Vichy regime: 'Maréchal,

'The Song of the Mason' exhorted the French to pull together behind the policies of Vichy.

André Dassary recorded the best-selling version of the Petainist hymn 'Maréchal, nous voilà'.

nous voilà!' acclaiming Maréchal Petain as the saviour of France.

Tu as lutté sans cesse
Pour le salut commun,
On parle avec tendresse
Du héros de Verdun.
En nous donnant ta vie
Ton genie et ta foi,
Tu sauves la patrie
Une seconde fois.[56]

(You have struggled ceaselessly
For the common good,
We speak tenderly
Of the hero of Verdun
In giving us your life,
Your genius and your faith
You save the fatherland for a second time.)

As Vichy lost popularity and authority, parody and Gaullist versions of the song proliferated. The refrain of 'Maréchal nous voilà!':

Devant toi, le sauveur de la France,
Nous jurons, nous tes gars,
De servir et de suivre des pas.
Maréchal, nous voilà!

(Before you, the saviour of France
We swear, us, your lads
To serve and follow in your footsteps
Maréchal, here we are!)

became:

Général, nous voilà!
Résolus à lutter pour la France
Car tous les braves gens
Marcheront sous de Gaulle au combat!
Général, nous voilà!

(General, here we are!
Determined to fight for France
Because all the good people
Will march under de Gaulle to the fight!
General, here we are!)

Mounting dissatisfaction with Vichy and resentment of the increasing rapaciousness of the German Occupation could only be expressed through songs in oblique ways. Charles Trenet's 'Si tu vas à Paris' was conceived and first presented in Marseilles in 1942 when France was still divided into zones and Marseilles was full of former Parisians seeking the relative safety of the unoccupied zone. The song was taken up rapidly by French refugees elsewhere, by Irène Hilda in New York in 1942 and by Marie Dubas the following year in Switzerland.

Si tu vas à Paris
Dis bonjour aux amis
Et dis-leur que mon coeur
Et toujours fidèle.[57]

(If you go to Paris
Say hello to our friends
And tell them that my heart
Remains faithful.)

'Si tu vas à Paris' was immediately banned after the Germans moved into the southern zone in November 1942.

The shortages and privations that helped to turn French opinion against the German Occupation also inspired many songs. Initially the shortages were taken in good humour. By the end of 1940 leather ceased to be available for shoes. Like the hat makers whose inventiveness helped to compensate for restrictions on fabrics for dresses, shoemakers showed great inventiveness and style in exploiting unorthodox materials. An article in *L'Illustration* in July 1941 celebrated 'The great changeover from leather to wood':

It's a big and a good surprise. At the beginning of spring Parisians were astonished by the strange shoes in unexpected forms and styles that began to appear in the shop windows on the Boulevards. Then, alerted by the joyous sound of clacking, they turned round to follow the

Fashions of 1941. Elegant shoes made without leather.

sometimes awkward steps of the elegant ladies, with a slightly mocking eye.

'La symphonie des semelles' evokes the sound of wooden shoes.

In 1942 Vincent Scotto wrote two light-hearted songs about the sound of wooden shoes worn by women who were no longer able to obtain leather. 'La symphonie des semelles en bois' ('Symphony of the wooden shoes') was written for Maurice Chevalier and 'Un bruit de sabots' for André Claveau. Later in the war there were harsher songs about food shortages and the black market, such as 'Dans son sac à main' and 'Marché rose'.

Songs expressing more overt criticism and resistance to Vichy and the Germans could only be heard via foreign radio stations. The BBC in London did its best to promote 'Le chant des partisans' by the Russian-born Anna Marly as a song of French national resistance, from 1943 onwards. The original Russian text was freely translated into French by the writer Joseph Kessel and his nephew Maurice Druon for the popular singer Germaine Sablon, sister of the suave crooner Jean Sablon. Involved in the Resistance in the early stages of the war, all three had made an adventurous escape across the Pyrenees and had presented their services to the Free French in London. The song was whistled twice daily in the broadcast 'Honneur et Patrie'. There is an element of artifice about the commercial recording made by Germaine Sablon in 1944. As she sings the repeated short phrases with increasing fervour, there is an elaborate orchestral accompaniment somewhat reminiscent of Ravel's 'Bolero', and sounds of marching feet and whistling partisans create a cinematic effect. The song was in fact filmed with Germaine Sablon in a propaganda short made by Alberto Cavalcanti in 1943 called *Three Songs about the Resistance*.

As the war turned against Germany, neutral Switzerland was emboldened to allow the broadcast of critical songs on Swiss radio stations. The provocative song '14 Juillet' (Bastille Day celebrations having been suppressed by the Germans) was broadcast from Radio Lausanne by Marie Dubas in 1943 and recorded by Renée Lebas in Switzerland in the same year.

The great Marie Dubas, France's most popular female performer before the war, irresistibly funny and with a brassy soprano voice not dissimilar to that of Gracie Fields, sang the moving 'Ce soir je pense à mon pays' ('Tonight I am thinking of my country') on Radio Lausanne in the spring of 1944 in a frail voice that was a shadow of its former self.

Ce soir je pense à mon pays
A tous mes amis, là-bas.
Ce soir, je rêve à toi cheri
Et murmure ton nom tour bas
C'est que je n'ai qu'un seul espoir
L'espoir si doux de te revoir
Ce soir, je pense à mon pays
A tous mes amis, là-bas.[58]

Though a fervent Catholic, the much loved Marie Dubas was forced to take refuge in Switzerland because of her Jewish ancestry.

(Tonight I'm thinking of my country
Of all my friends, over there
Tonight, I'm dreaming of you my love
And murmuring your name quietly
The sweet hope of seeing you again
Tonight, I am thinking of my country
Of all my friends, over there.)

The most gifted French composer of popular songs of the war years was undoubtedly Charles Trenet. Greatly influenced by his friendship

Trenet's youthful energy was always part of his charm.

Trenet's 'Douce France' stirred the hearts of the French under German occupation.

with the Surrealist poet Max Jacob, who would later die in Nazi custody, Trenet wrote songs that have a poetic and whimsical quality that earned him the nickname 'Le fou chantant' ('The singing madman'). The years of his greatest popularity, 1938-1944, coincided exactly with those of Léo Marjane, but despite being on the receiving end of some harsh criticisms after the Liberation he went on to enjoy another half century of a successful career.

Like so many others, Trenet walked a moral and political tightrope under the Occupation. Rumours of his Jewish ancestry based on an apparent resemblance to Harpo Marx and a suggestion that Trenet was an anagram of the Jewish name Netter forced him to produce documentation of Aryan ancestry, something for which he was later reproached. Trenet was probably as apolitical as it was possible to be in these years. It would seem that he had neither political insight nor strong convictions but merely wanted to carry on with his career as an entertainer. Nevertheless, he repeatedly showed an uncanny ability to divine the mood of the moment and whether he intended it or not his songs became invested with political meaning. His song 'Si tu vas à Paris' became the song that expressed the aspirations of French exiles whereas songs like 'La marche aux jeunes' and the lovely 'Douce France' could be interpreted as expressing the political aspirations of Vichy.

One did not, of course, have to be a Petainist to appreciate the tender and nostalgic evocation of traditional France in 'Douce France'. Frenzied applause that greeted the public performance of the song during the Occupation could have been understood as anti-German demonstrations. Roland Gerbeau, who gave the song its first public performance, at the Bobino in October 1943, said: 'To sing "Douce France" in that year, at the height of the Occupation, was to be assured of an attentive and delighted public!'[59] The French politician Valéry Giscard d'Estaing, then fighting with the Maquis, recalled that he used to hum this song to give himself courage.

At the end of the war Trenet was reproached with having written a Petainist hymn, the 1942 song 'La marche aux jeunes'. The rather bland text celebrates youth, health and optimism.

> Ah! Qu'il fait bon d'avoir vingt ans
> Et de marcher le coeur content,
> Vers le clocher de son village!
>
> (Oh, but it's good to be 20 years old
> And to march with a happy heart
> Towards the village clock tower.)

As Trenet's biographer Richard Cannavo quite reasonably points out, youth, health and optimism had always been essential elements in Trenet's personal appeal. That said, it is easy to see why the song was chosen for the B side of a 1941 recording of the anthem 'Maréchal, nous voilà!'.

Perhaps the greatest accolade of Trenet's career was the use of his song 'Verlaine', a bluesy setting of Verlaine's poem 'Chanson d'automne' that had outraged conservative critics in 1941, as a signal to the French underground that the 1944 Allied landings in Normandy were imminent.

Twice more Trenet scored bull's-eyes with songs that seemed to anticipate events by a couple of years. The first of these, 'Quand tu reverras ton village' ('When you see your village again'), was probably intended to refer to returning French prisoners exchanged for factory workers, when it was first performed at the ABC in 1942 by Tino Rossi.

Quand tu reverras ton village
Quand tu reverras ton clocher
Ta maison, tes parents, les amis de ton áge
Tu diras; 'Rien chez moi n'a change.[60]

(When you see your village again
When you see your church tower
Your house, your parents, your friends
You will say 'Nothing has changed.')

The words gained greatly in poignancy when people returned to their homes at the end of the war.

According to Roland Gerbeau (who was the first to record Trenet's 'La mer' in December 1944), Trenet's most popular song was composed without the aid of pen, paper or piano, in a railway carriage on a journey between Montpellier and Perpignon in 1943, though it was not till the end of the war that it took off and became a world success. Gerbeau described how Trenet himself had his first success with 'La Mer' at a concert given for members of the Resistance of the 12th Arrondissement in Paris just after the Liberation: 'He sang about twenty of his songs, with his usual triumphant success of course, and at the end he said "Well, let's try 'La mer'!" And there for the first time, and in a very mysterious way, this song that he had performed without success so many times under the Occupation was a triumph with the public.'[61] It had become, as Richard Cannavo puts it, 'the hymn of regained happiness'.[62]

Naturally, the euphoria following the Liberation of Paris in August 1944 also found expression in song though none of these celebratory songs could be recorded in Paris itself until the end of the year when, after a gap of several months, recording was resumed.

Maurice Chevalier, anxious to counter the accusations of collaboration—that he had only survived through the protection of Louis Aragon and the Communist Party—got in on the act early by singing 'Fleur de Paris':

C'est une fleur de Paris
Du vieux Paris qui sourit
Car c'est la fleur du retour,
Du retour des beaux jours
Pendant quatre ans dans nos coeurs

'When you see your village again' —
a song that anticipated the end of hostilities.

With 'Fleur de Paris' Maurice Chevalier hoped
to re-establish his credibility as a Frenchman.

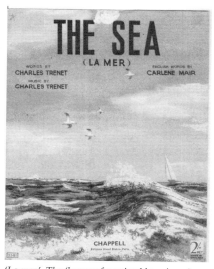

'La mer'. The 'hymn of regained happiness'.

Elle a gardé ses couleurs
Bleu, blanc, rouge
Avec l'espoir elle a fleuri
Fleur de Paris.[63]

(It is the flower of Paris
Of the old Paris that smiled
Because it's the flower of return
The return of the good days
During four years our hearts
Had kept its colours
Blue, white and red
With hope, it bloomed
The flower of Paris.)

'Oh! La! La!' Communications between the French and their 'Anglo-Saxon' liberators were not always straightforward.

In August 1944 within days of the Liberation of Paris, Jean Nohain wrote a new, politicised text to his 1942 song 'Et ouf, on respire!'

Depuis quatre ans sans rien dire
Notre pauvre vieux Paris
Avait perdu son sourire
Sans un flot de vert de gris
Et puis soudain tout explose
C'est un bonheur sans pareil
On revoit la vie en rose
On chante sous le soleil.[64]

(Over four years without saying a word
Our poor old Paris
Had lost her smile
Under a flood of grey-green
And suddenly everything exploded
You see life 'en rose' again
You sing under the sun.)

General Leclerc's 2nd Free French Armoured Division, the first Allied troops to penetrate the city on 25 August 1944, were celebrated in their own song, the 'Marche de la 2e D.B.', recorded by two leading opera singers, the baritone Pierre Nougaro and the tenor José Luccioni.[65] For a short time at least the Anglo-Saxon liberators also basked in the Parisian mood of good will as we hear from the 'Franglais' of 'Oh! La! La!'

Oh! La! La!
Good morning Mademoiselle,
Oh! La! La!
I go à l'Opéra
Oh! La! La!
Je speak pas very well.

Oh! La! La!
C'est-y là ou pa là
En souriant la petit' Parisienne
Dit gentiment
Justement j'vais par là.[66]

Gratitude towards the Anglo-Saxon liberators had not figured in the triumphal speech given by General de Gaulle on 28 August 1944 at the Paris Hôtel de Ville. De Gaulle's greatness lay in the power of his rhetoric. On a practical level he had done little but hamper the war effort with his tantrums. Even in the headiness of the moment there must have been those who realised that his claim that the

'Lily bye bye'. A French song that salutes American sacrifice.

GENERAL DE GAULLE'S TRIUMPHANT ENTRY INTO PARIS AFTER ITS LIBERATION.

GENERAL DE GAULLE INSPECTING THE FRENCH ARMOURED DIVISION AFTER THE LIBERATION OF PARIS : ON HIS RIGHT IS GEN. LECLERC, AND BEYOND, GEN. KOENIG.

In his triumphant speech from the Paris Town Hall De Gaulle failed to acknowledge any debt to the Americans and the British.

French had liberated themselves through their own efforts was absurd and that France owed a debt to her Anglo-Saxon allies. This was indeed acknowledged in a number of songs such as 'Lily bye bye!' This tells the tale of the handsome Texan Jimmy, 'King of the lasso', who says goodbye to his lady love in order to fight in France :

> Tout un mois en Normandie sur le front
> Le Jimmy se battit comme un vieux Lion
> Fou de joie il ecrivait tous les jours
> Ma Lily, ma Lily, à bientôt mon cher amour.
> Mais un soir, emporté par son élan
> Il tomba au milieu d'un guet-apens.[67]

> (For a whole month in Normandy on the front
> Jimmy fought like an old lion
> Mad with joy, he wrote every day
> My Lily, my Lily, see you soon, my love
> But one evening carried away by his courage
> He fell into an ambush.)

When the Americans arrived they brought their own songs with

The triumph of American popular music.

them, as seen from the sudden proliferation of music of American origin sold as sheet music at the end of the war. The *chanson* continued to thrive for another generation in the hands of Piaf, Trenet, Georges Brassens, Jacques Brel, etc., but its golden age was over and the death knell had sounded. The new American hegemony was celebrated in songs such as 'Le rythme americain', 'La danse atomique' and French versions of American hits such as 'In the Mood' ('Dans l'ambiance').

War Songs: America

On the popular music front, America had won the war before it had begun. The conquest of the rest of the world by the American entertainment industry was well under way in the decades between the wars, aided by the creation of the great Hollywood movie factories in the 1920s and by the proliferation of radio in the 1930s. American dance crazes swept the world and however much the Nazi hierarchy might rail against 'Jewish-Negro' culture there was simply nothing they could do to stem the tide of popular American music. Michael Jary and Bruno Balz were no match for Irving Berlin, George and Ira Gershwin, Jerome Kern, Rodgers and Hart, and the seduction of swing. For millions of people, not only in America, the sound of the Andrews Sisters in 'Boogie Woogie Bugle Boy' or Glenn Miller's 'In the Mood' became the sound of the Second World War.

American dance bands reached their zenith at this time, but they also suffered from wartime restrictions. Military conscription brought constant changes of personnel, the Petrillo recording ban diminished incomes, and travel became harder for peripatetic musicians. Rex Stewart, a member of the Duke Ellington Band recalled: "Things got really tough; the phonograph ban started and there was no recording … this cut down our income. Then the record companies weren't even pressing the hits because shellac was hard to come by. Food rationing meant the fare was even worse in the greasy spoons that catered for us. Going on the road was tough. Trains were commandeered; the armed forces, of course, took precedence, while we scrambled to our gigs however possible."[68]

Irving Berlin, a musically illiterate émigré from Siberia who began

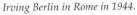

Irving Berlin in Rome in 1944.   *Irving Berlin's show* This Is the Army.

his career as a singing waiter in New York's Chinatown, became probably the most successful and prolific songwriter of the twentieth century. He had the rare distinction (shared to some extent with the Welsh composer Ivor Novello) of serving his country musically in both world wars. The famous newspaper headline 'Army takes Berlin!' of 1917 was a pun too good to miss, and was used again in the Second World War with headlines of 'Berlin goes to Rome' when Irving Berlin entertained troops in Italy towards the end of the war.

While serving in the army during the First World War, Berlin was commissioned to create a patriotic musical show entitled *Yip, Yip, Yaphank* for which he originally conceived the song 'God Bless America'. It was unaccountably dropped from the show and it had to wait for another world war to become something like a second national anthem, performed and recorded by numerous American singers including Kate Smith and Deanna Durbin.

During the Second World War, as the grand old man of popular American music, Irving Berlin became something of a musical ambassador for his country. It was while he was on a morale-boosting visit to Britain in 1944 that the former singing waiter found himself engaged in a testing lunch party conversation with Winston Churchill who was under the impression that he was talking to the philosopher Isaiah Berlin.[69]

Irving Berlin's most important musical contribution to the Second World War, apart from countless performances of his earlier evergreen songs, was the 1942 musical *This Is the Army*. This show (also turned into a movie), included songs such as 'This is the Army, Mr Jones', 'I Left My Heart at the Stage Door Canteen' and 'With My Head in the Clouds'. Opening in New York on 4 July 1942 with a cast comprised entirely of enlisted men, *This Is the Army* proved a smash success. It toured the major American cities, before being transformed into a movie in 1943 with added plot and female characters. It then travelled the world in the wake of the triumphant American army, from London to North Africa, Naples, Rome, and on to Australia and the Pacific. At each stop, Berlin added a song calculated to play to the sentiments of local audiences. In London, 'My British Buddy' brought tears to the eyes of Queen Elizabeth. For the Australians, Berlin composed 'I Get Along with the Aussies'.

But even more widely loved than all these crowd-pleasers was the song 'White Christmas' from the 1942 movie *Holiday Inn*. Neither the film nor the song had anything directly to do with the war, but Christmas had taken on a special significance for both sides. The sentiment engendered by separated families in wartime must have contributed to the phenomenal sales of Bing Crosby's bland recording of one of Berlin's less distinguished inspirations.

Berlin's slightly older contemporary Jerome Kern, who had pioneered the Broadway musical in the 1920s, was largely engaged with writing songs for movies during the war years. The songs he wrote for Rita Hayworth in *You Were Never Lovelier* and *Cover Girl*, and for Deanna Durbin in *Can't Help Singing*, helped to lift the spirits of the war-weary. The sentimental 'Smoke Gets In Your Eyes' written for the 1933 musical *Roberta* fitted the mood of the time and continued to be a big wartime hit. But apart from the forgotten 'And Russia Is Her Name' commissioned for the propaganda movie *Song of Russia*, Kern wrote only one song directly inspired by the war, the very lovely and poignant 'The Last Time I Saw Paris'. Though America was not yet in the war, Oscar Hammerstein II wrote the text spontaneously in response to the news of the fall of Paris and presented it to Kern, who promptly set it to music. The song was interpolated into the 1941 movie *Lady Be Good* and won the Academy Award for best song that year even though it was not strictly eligible as it had not been written expressly for the movie. Kern wrote a note on the manuscript that the song should be sung 'not sadly', a wish observed in the nicely judged recording by Hildegarde but not by the tearful sounding Tony Martin. Kern also wrote a message on the score for Hammerstein, asking him to contact Ira Gershwin to see if they could borrow the taxi horns used by George Gershwin in *An American in Paris*.[70]

Another great American songwriter at the height of his powers in the war years, and certainly one who would have identified with the sentiments of 'The Last Time I Saw Paris', was Cole Porter. Despite being severely disabled and in constant pain after a riding accident in 1937, Porter completed scores for five Broadway musicals and five Hollywood movies between 1939 and 1944. The war years culminated in the apotheosis of the composer in a much sanitized 1945 film version of his life, entitled *Night and Day*, intended to provide inspiration to injured and disabled war veterans. After reading the script Porter commented that it was 'as if I was reading about someone I know slightly.'[71]

The war gave Porter the opportunity to combine patriotism with his taste for handsome young servicemen in songs such as 'I'm in Love with a Soldier Boy' from the 1942 show *Something for the Boys*. He was also capable of writing crassly jingoistic lyrics such as those for the 1943 *Sailors of the Sky*:

> So beware you Huns,
> Whether Japanese or German
> 'Cause we've got guns
> For exterminatin' vermin.'[72]

Such songs may have raised a quick laugh but probably did a great deal less for the war effort than his more durable pre-war hits such as 'Night and Day' and 'Begin the Beguine'. Porter's biggest wartime hit was 'Don't Fence Me In', sung by Roy Rogers in the 1944 movie *Hollywood Canteen*. A version recorded by Bing Crosby and the Andrews Sisters made in late 1944 headed the 'hit parade' for eight weeks and sold over a million copies. The song had been written some years before and may well have had a personal meaning for the married but homosexual Porter. One contemporary critic read a more political meaning into the song, believing that it advocated a rejection of a 'coalition of Evil … trying to fence in the whole world and enslave its people' showing that virtually any song could be given a political meaning in war circumstances.[73]

During the war Porter wrote two particularly fine songs that seem to reflect his own history of fleeting relationships and unsatisfied longings. 'You'd Be So Nice To Come Home To' from the 1943 film *Something to Shout About* was inspired by his on/off affair with a young dancer called Nelson Barclift who had been conscripted into the army. The lovely 'Ev'ry Time We Say Goodbye' from the 1944 *Seven Lively Arts* was a song that every service man and woman separated from their partner would have been able to identify with.[74]

> Ev'ry time I say goodbye I die a little
> Ev'ry time I say good bye I wonder why a little
> Why the Gods above me who must be in the know
> Think so little of me,
> They allow you to go.

The youngest of the great American songwriters of this generation, Richard Rodgers, did not deal directly with the Second World War until much later with his ground-breaking musical *South Pacific*. But the song 'You'll Never Walk Alone' from the 1945 show *Carousel* must have provided comfort to many war widows in a best-selling version recorded that year by Frank Sinatra.

The American songs of the Second World War with the greatest popular currency were probably not those by any of these great masters of song-writing, but by composers closer in age to the combatants. These younger and less established writers had been given an unexpected leg-up due to a long-running dispute between ASCAP and the broadcasting industry, which had resulted in Irving Berlin, Cole Porter, Richard Rodgers and Jerome Kern disappearing from the airwaves in 1941.

Among the most popular songs were those dealing with the theme of separation and longing, such as 'I'll Be Seeing You', 'Every Night About This Time', 'Counting the Days', 'Sentimental Journey', 'I'll Walk Alone', 'I'm Stepping Out with a Memory Tonight' and 'You Are My Sunshine'.

The bizarre Lester Young record 'Bitzkrieg Baby' expresses the truculent isolationism of many Americans prior to Pearl Harbor.

Blitzkrieg Baby
You can't bomb me
'Cos I'm pleadin' neutrality.
Got my gun out
Can you see.
Blitzkrieg Baby you can't bomb me.
Blitzkrieg Baby you look so cute
All that stuff in your parachute.
Let that propaganda be
Blitzkrieg baby you can't bomb me.
I'll give you warning
'Cos I'm afraid I'll have to.
So take my warning or else
You'll get the hand grenade.

The privations of daily wartime life were hardly the kind of pressing issue that it was for Europeans, but the vicissitudes of military life being experienced by millions of Americans for the first time inspired a great many songs, such as 'Ma, I Miss Your Apple Pie', 'Boogie Woogie Bugle Boy' and 'The GI Jive':

This the GI jive, Man alive!
It starts with the bugler blowing reveille over your bed
When you arrive, Jack, that's the GI drive
Pootily toot, jump into your suit
Make a salute!

The titles of 'Coming in on a Wing and a Prayer' and 'Praise the Lord and Pass the Ammunition' became popular catch-phrases of the war.

Once America was in the war, there was plenty of jingoism but usually with a light-hearted and humorous touch. Bing Crosby and the Andrews Sisters sang:

There'll be a hot time in the town of Berlin
When the Yanks go marching in.
I want to be there, boy
And spread some joy
When they take old Berlin

When the Brooklyn boys begin
To take the joint apart
And tear it down.

They're gonna take a hike
Through Hitler's Reich
And change that 'Heil!'
To 'What'cha know, Jo!'

Ethel Merman's record of 'We'll Be Singing Hallelujah Marching Through Berlin' begins in comic fashion. She dismisses a spoof Hitler radio rant with 'Get back in your trunk, skunk!' and then delivers an idealistic message in gospel style.

We'll be singing Hallelujah
Marching through Berlin.
When we drive those sons of Satan
From their place of sin
When we get there we're gonna see
The world has peace and liberty
That's the way it's gotta be
'Cos a man's no good unless he's free!

The war on the other side of the Atlantic, carried on in the name of freedom, justice and human dignity, encouraged many African-Americans in their struggle at home for the same things. 'In 1943, the title of Duke Ellington's extended jazz composition *New World A-Comin'* expressed the hopes of many. Ellington's involvement with various anti-fascist organisations such as the Joint Anti-Fascist Refugee Committee and the Artists' Front to Win the War earned him the suspicion of the FBI which tended to regard all such organisations as "Communist fronts".'[75]

The anti-Fascist songs of Leadbelly, Woody Guthrie and Josh White carry a universal meaning that goes beyond the defeat of Hitler. To the tune of 'When the saints go marchin' in' Woody Guthrie sings 'When we set this whole world free. I want to be in that number, when we set this whole world free.' With pardonable historical inaccuracy, since 1933 would not have rhymed with 'Jew', Leadbelly intones mournfully:

The great African-American bass and civil rights activist Paul Robeson.

'As Time Goes By', a pre-war song that became inextricably associated with the war thanks to the movie Casablanca.

Hitler started in 1932
When he started out he took
the home from the Jew
We're gonna tear Hitler down
We're gonna tear Hitler
down some day.

In January 1942, less than two months after America's entry into the war, Paul Robeson recorded a set of seven songs published as *Songs of Free Men* in Columbia's Masterworks series. In order to emphasize the universality of the struggle against Fascism he chose two American songs—Marc Blitzstein's 'The Purest Kind of a Guy' and Earl Robinson's 'Joe Hull', 'Moorsoldaten', a song from a German concentration camp by the German Jewish refugee Hanns Eisler, a Spanish Civil War song, and two Russian songs. The velvet magnificence of his bass voice, and the granite nobility and integrity of his interpretations make these records an intensely moving experience, but it seems they received more exposure on Russian radio than they did in his own country.

Of course many of the most popular American songs of the period had nothing at all to do with the war and owed their popularity to that very fact. The most idolized singer of the time was Frank Sinatra and one would never know that there was a war on from most of his records.

One much loved American

394

song that conjures up vivid associations with the war is a special case and that is 'As Time Goes By'. Written by Herman Hupfeld in 1931 at the height of the Depression for a play entitled *Everybody's Welcome*, it became a hit in the recorded version by Rudy Vallee. It was later incorporated into a play called *Everybody Comes to Rick's* by Murray Burnett and Joan Alison, which in turn became the basis for the most iconic of all Second World War movies, *Casablanca*. During the war, perhaps even more than during the Depression, audiences wanted to be reminded that

> The fundamental things apply
> As time goes by.[76]

1   Vera Lynn, *Vocal refrain*, 1975, p. 99.
2   Beatrice Lillie, *Every Other Inch a Lady*, 1972, p. 252.
3   Douglas Byng, *As You Were*, 1970, pp 149-151.
4   *Ich bin der Leander—Das muss reichen*, TV documentary: Dokumentation Deutschland, 1974
5   Lale Andersen, *Leben mit einem Lied*, 1974, p. 159.
6   Lynn, p. 96.
7   Horst Bergmeier, Rainer Lotz and Volker Kühn, *Lili Marleen. An allen Fronten. Das Lied. Seine Zeit, seine Interpretationen und seine Botschaften*, 2005.
8   Andersen, p. 119.
9   Norbert Schultze, *Mit dir, Lili Marleen*, 1995, pp. 58-9.
10 Andersen, p. 120.
11 Bergmeier et al., p. 48.
12 Noel Coward, *Middle East Diary*, 1944, p. 103.
13 Andersen, p. 143.
14 Fitzroy Maclean, *Eastern Approaches*, p. 208.
15 Andersen, p. 162.
16 Marie-Hélène Carbonel, *Suzy Solidor. Une vie d'amour*, 2007.
17 Thierry Kubler and Emmanuel Lemieux, *Cognaq Jay, 1940, La télévision française sous l'occupation*, 1990, p. 181.
18 Bergmeier et al., p. 68.
19 Ibid., p. 88.
20 Robert Ley was head of the Deutsche Arbeitsfront and instigator of the 'Kraft durch Freude' schemes.
21 This text was given to me by Christine Petit.
22 Horst Bergmeier, Rainer Lotz, *Hitler's Airwaves*, 1997.
23 Martin Pénet, *Mémoire de la chanson*, Volume II, 2004, p. 1283.
24 Jacques Pessis, *Pierre Dac*, 1992, p. 263.
25 Alan Randall and Ray Seaton, *George Formby*, 1974, p. 160.
26 John Colville, *The Fringes of Power*, Volume I, 1985, p. 432.
27 Sheridan Morley, *A Talent to Amuse*, 1974, p. 289.
28 Coward, *Middle East Diary*, p.118.
29 Ibid., p. 85.
30 Ibid., p.118.
31 Joyce Grenfell, *The Time of My Life*, 1989, p. 127.
32 Schultze, p. 70.
33 Wladyslaw Szpilman, *Le Pianiste*, 1998, p. 24.
34 Schultze, pp. 84-5.
35 Ibid., p. 90.
36 Pénet, p. 1147.
37 William Shakespeare, *The Tragedy of Richard II*, Act II, scene i.
38 Pénet, p. 1141.
39 Ibid., p. 1145.
40 Ibid., p. 1152.
41 Ibid., p. 1142.
42 Georges Van Parys, *Les jours comme ils viennent*, 1969. p. 256.
43 Ibid., p. 273.

44 Pénet, p. 1170.

45 Mireille, *Avec le soleil pour témoin*, 1981, p. 145.

46 Fania Fenelon, p. 129

47 Pénet, p. 1199.

48 Ibid., p. 1209.

49 Ibid., p. 1368.

50 Ibid., p. 1251.

51 Ibid., p. 1372.

52 Ibid., p. 1188.

53 Ibid., p. 1257.

54 Ibid., p. 1205.

55 Ibid., p. 1216.

56 Ibid., p. 1236.

57 Ibid., p. 1316.

58 Robert de Laroche and Francois Bellair, *Marie Dubas,* 1980, p. 234.

59 Richard Cannavo, *Monsieur Trenet,* p. 341.

60 Pénet, p. 1307.

61 Cannavo, p. 341.

62 Ibid., p. 339.

63 Pénet, p. 1408.

64 Ibid., p. 1407.

65 Ibid., p. 1445.

66 Ibid., p. 1449.

67 Ibid., p. 1444.

68 Stuart Nicholson, *Reminiscing in Tempo: A Portrait of Duke Ellington,* p. 239.

69 Colville, Volume II, p. 91.

70 Gerald Bordman, *Jerome Kern*, 1980, p. 385.

71 William McBrien, *Cole Porter*, 1998, p. 290.

72 Ibid., p. 259.

73 Ibid., p. 273.

74 Ibid., p. 287.

75 Nicholson, p. 242.

76 Richard E Osborne, *The Casablanca Companion*, 1997, p. 76.

Chapter 13
RETRIBUTION AND AFTERMATH

The crimes of the Second World War were so enormous and so complex—largely, but by no means exclusively, on the Axis side—that we are even now only beginning to understand them. In the immediate aftermath of the war, blame and retribution were often as arbitrary and unjust as anything that had taken place during the war itself.

The Italian baritone Tito Gobbi wrote: 'In no country did the cessation of hostilities bring anything like a happy ending. But in the musical worlds of Germany and Italy the confusion that succeeded the end of the war produced one particularly unpleasant feature. Artists who felt they had been unjustly neglected during the previous years now moved into the operatic scene with the determination to oust, if possible, those who had been more successful. It was easy to say, or hint strongly, that success in their rivals had been due to political rather than artistic reasons. Tempers understandably ran high and in the general atmosphere of bitterness and recrimination some artists of mediocre attainment took a flying leap up the ladder of success by employing some very questionable means.'[1]

Though he was discrete about what happened to him, Gobbi was clearly speaking from personal experience. Between November 1943 and June 1944 Gobbi, together with Beniamino Gigli and Maria Caniglia, took part in an extended operatic season in Rome: it concluded with a performance of Verdi's *Un Ballo in Maschera* that ended at one o'clock in the morning on 3 June. By 8 am the same morning, the Germans had evacuated the city and twenty-four hours later the American Fifth Army arrived. Ten days later Gigli and Verdi had been replaced at the Rome Opera by Irving Berlin's *This Is the Army* just as Wagner would

Beniamino Gigli. "Having 'sung for the Germans' I now discovered, to my astonishment, that I was a traitor."

Tito Gobbi. Self portrait in the role of Scarpia.

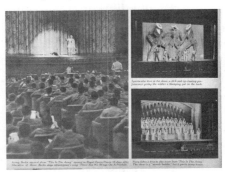

Irving Berlin's This Is the Army *replaced Verdi at the Rome Opera House.*

be replaced by Cole Porter at the Festspielhaus in Bayreuth shortly after.

With his customary naivety Gigli wrote: 'Having "sung for the Germans", I now discovered, to my astonishment, that I was a traitor. The accusation did not come from the Allies, but from my own countrymen. Threatening crowds besieged my house in Rome; for months I did not dare leave it.' Gigli's honeyed voice, however, brought him rapid forgiveness. 'By the spring of 1945, things were calmer. I began to appear in public again. On March 12th I sang at a concert in the Teatro Adriano, in aid of refugees. Many people asked me afterwards, "When are you coming back to the Opera?" To myself I thought "I'll wait till I'm asked." I did not have to wait long.'[2]

Not every artist was so favoured. The conductor Gino Marinuzzi, who had been closely associated with the Fascist regime, died in August 1945 and was widely believed to have been assassinated by partisans, although that was denied.

The twin Paris opera houses, the Opéra and the Opéra Comique, were notorious at the best of times for an atmosphere of petty jealousy and vicious intrigue. When the much-respected veteran director Jacques Rouché was dismissed from his post on suspicion of collaboration, it was an opportunity for feuds to be pursued and scores to be settled, and once again for the talented to be supplanted by the less talented. By coincidence the first two post-war productions at the Opéra were Gounod's *Roméo et Juliette* and a ballet on the same subject danced to Tchaikovsky's tone poem. The chronicler of the Paris Opéra Charles Dupêchez commented: 'The partisan battles within the Paris Opéra have never so much resembled the fratricidal duels of Verona.'[3]

An entry in Noel Coward's diary for 14 November 1944 gives some sense of the snap judgements that were being made. 'Pierre Fresnay is out of prison as he did not denounce anyone, and he now admits miserably that he was wrong. Yvonne Printemps apparently behaved well and will be allowed to play again. Sacha Guitry has been very bad; Gaby Morlay idiotic; and Marcel Achard allowed himself to be flattered by the Germans. Chevalier has been very questionable.' When Chevalier pleaded his case personally with Coward a couple of weeks later Coward wrote in his diary: 'I believe him and at all events it is not for me to judge.'[4]

In Germany and Austria the process of *épuration* or 'de-nazification' was carried out by the occupying Allied forces. The soprano Elisabeth Schwarzkopf complained bitterly of the 'brutality' of the interrogations. In her case this was probably due to her repeated attempts to lie herself out of trouble.[5] On the whole, the process, while far from perfect, was carried out with greater lenience and fairness by the Allies than it was in the newly-liberated countries by their own people.

Once the hasty and somewhat half-hearted process of de-nazification was over, West Germany, dead-set on economic recovery and encouraged by the United States anxious to use Germany as a bastion against communism, plunged into a period of denial and something like a conspiracy of silence for the best part of a generation. The Communist East had its own agendas and narratives that involved a different kind of deception. Just how difficult it was to talk about the immediate past is illustrated by a radio interview given in Cologne on 13 February 1951 by the conductor Fritz Busch after an absence of nearly eighteen years from his native country. Both the interviewer and the conductor tie themselves up in painful circumlocutions. After paying Busch extravagant compliments the interviewer asks for his impressions on returning to his native land, adding, '… as you are, I would like to say, only a guest in Germany, unfortunately.' Stumbling over his words Busch answers: 'First of all I would like to say how happy I am to be back in my old homeland of Germany. I am of course, depressed when I see … ah … um … the destructions that have appeared …'[6] as if the destruction of the German cities was the result of a natural disaster for which no one was to blame.

The conspiracy of silence is even more apparent in a collection of radio talks published as a book in 1963 entitled *Das musikalische Selbst-Portrait* in which 50 prominent German musicians discuss their careers. Those who stayed and those who left both show an equal reluctance to refer to the Nazi period in anything other than the most oblique terms. Bruno Walter states baldly: 'When Hitler came, the French offered me citizenship,' without explaining the dramatic circumstances of his departure from Berlin in 1933 and from Vienna in 1938.[7] Others such as Michael Raucheisen and Max Lorenz manage to narrate their careers with no mention whatsoever of the Nazi period and the war.

Nowhere is the post-war state of denial more blatant than in the titles of the autobiographies of musicians and stars who were at their zenith under the Nazis: Peter Kreuder, *Schön war die Zeiten* ('Beautiful were the times'), Gustav Frölich, *Waren das Zeiten* ('Those were the times'), Zarah Leander, *Es war so wunderbar* ('It was so wonderful') and Ilse Werner, *So wird's nie wieder* ('It will never be like that again').

In more recent years, German scholars have taken up the process of investigating the past with admirable honesty and rigour. Ernst Klee's *Kulturlexikon zum Dritten Reich* presents the evidence of the collaboration of German artists with the Nazi regime with a meticulous and chilling thoroughness. The book makes it clear that it was almost impossible for any artist to survive under such a comprehensively evil regime without being in some way morally contaminated.

Invaluable though the *Kulturlexikon* is as a research tool (not least for this book) it is important to remember that it only presents the case for the prosecution. There are no shades of grey. All is black and white, or perhaps one should say that it is all black. There are no mitigating circumstances and there is no counter-evidence. It may take another generation for a more nuanced picture of the accountability of German artists to be possible. Klee's *Kulturlexikon* is an important and absolutely necessary work but not the last word on the subject.

In trying to defend the reputation of the conductor Clemens Krauss, Ida Cook highlighted the difficulties of making judgements in the post-war period. Cook and her sister Louise had rescued 29 German Jews with the help of Krauss and his wife, the soprano Viorica Ursuleac. Krauss's stance throughout the Nazi regime had been one of abject opportunism but clearly the Cook sisters saw another side to his behaviour. Of course, one could also argue that the very fact that Krauss evidently knew that Nazi racial policies were wrong and understood what the consequences would be for the victims made his opportunism even more distasteful. Ida Cook concluded: 'Almost the only way to do strict justice in an "inquest" of this kind is to reject all spiteful generalisations and accept only well authenticated particulars and to add to those, one's personal experience. In the case of Krauss and Ursuleac, we had personal and extensive experience, and I cannot say less than they behaved well and actively helped us and several of our friends.'[8]

The Dutch conductor Mengelberg was never able to perform in public again after the war.

The thoroughly arbitrary nature of the justice meted out at the end of the Second World War is illustrated by the fate of four famous conductors: Wilhelm Furtwängler, Willem Mengelberg, Herbert von Karajan and Karl Böhm. That Furtwängler and Mengelberg were judged so much more harshly is largely down to their greater pre-war prominence. It could be argued that their greater fame and authority required a higher level of moral responsibility. Furtwängler, though flawed and compromised, exhibited a degree of conscience and attempted, however ineffectively, to mitigate Nazi criminality, which is more than can be said of Karajan and Böhm—or even Sir Thomas Beecham.

For Furtwängler the process of de-nazification was long drawn out and painful. His defence of his behaviour during the Third Reich was self-serving and not very convincing. 'I knew Germany was in a terrible crisis: I felt responsible for German music, and it was my task to survive this crisis, as much as I could.'[9] In the spring of 1947 Furtwängler was allowed to resume his career but his reputation was irreparably damaged. He encountered protest and hostility in Switzerland where he had taken refuge at the end of the war. In America the protests of many Jewish artists, including Arthur Rubinstein, Vladimir Horowitz and Isaac Stern, led to the withdrawal of an invitation to conduct the Chicago Symphony Orchestra. The director of the Metropolitan Opera in New York, Rudolph Bing, wished to invite him to conduct there, but this was flatly rejected by the Metropolitan board. Bing commented that it was the 'only time in twenty-two years that I was told whom I could or could not hire.' He added: 'What is so odd about this incident in recollection is that I was personally extremely sensitive to the question of whether or not an artist had collaborated with the Nazis, and there were many I flatly refused to hire because of my feeling that they had taken sides against the decent people of the world.'[10]

Two Jewish musicians who had supported the struggle against Hitler in every way they could, the violinist Yehudi Menuhin and the pianist Myra Hess, went out of their way to welcome the conductor back into the fold of respectable musicians and attracted a great deal of criticism themselves in doing so. Myra Hess's argument in favour of performing with Furtwängler and the Berlin Philharmonic was: 'Either we close off Germany and exterminate the Germans or we find our common ground again through the arts.'[11]

As a life-long advocate of Mahler's music and someone who had forged warm and lasting working relations with Jewish artists such as Myra Hess and the Dutch baritone Willem Ravelli—who sang the part of Jesus in his famous Easter performances of the *St Matthew Passion*, Mengelberg cannot be accused of supporting Nazi racial ideology. It is claimed that, like Furtwängler, he used his influence to help and protect Jewish musicians. However, Mengelberg's case differs from that of Furtwängler in two key respects. Firstly, though half German, he held Dutch nationality and secondly, he was more than willing and even eager to perform in occupied territories during the war. Nevertheless, his post-war punishment seems excessively harsh. He was banned from performing in his native Holland for life. Though this ban was later reduced to six years it made no difference as Mengelberg died two months before the ban was up.

Two singers attracted special opprobrium at the end of the war— Germaine Lubin and Kirsten Flagstad. In each case it is hard to avoid the conclusion that they were singled out more because of their repertoire than because of anything they did. Both were outstanding interpreters of Wagner's more heroic roles and it was too easy to identify these statuesque blonde women with Nazi ideology. Both had been accorded the status of goddesses—Lubin in France and Flagstad in America—and there was also perhaps an element of iconoclasm in the viciousness of the attacks to which they were subjected after the war.

Parallels could be drawn with the particularly savage treatment of two French film stars, Mireille Balin, reputedly the most beautiful actress in 1930s France, and Corinne Luchaire. Their collaboration was no more significant than that of many others who eventually resumed their careers. Both Balin and Luchaire socialized prominently in collaborationist circles. Balin's chief error was to take an Austrian lover and Luchaire's to be the daughter of the notorious journalist Jean Luchaire. It would seem that the extreme hostility to these women had more to do with the screen images they projected—Balin as the bejewelled temptress who lures Jean Gabin to his doom in *Pépé le Moko* and Luchaire as a delinquent teenager in *Prison without Bars*.

By all accounts Germaine Lubin was a jealous and ungenerous colleague, deeply disliked by many of her soprano rivals. The Australian soprano Marjorie Lawrence, who sang at the Paris Opéra in the interwar years, offers an amusing account of Lubin's bad behaviour on stage when they sang in *Lohengrin* together. 'War between me and Lubin was on. At the end of the act when we took our bows together she refused to shake my hand when I extended it to her and being more practised than I in the tricks of the opera trade, she was able to edge herself in front of me and behaved as though all the cheering was for her.'[12] Such antics won Lubin no friends and cost her dear in her hour of trial, with colleagues queuing up to repeat spiteful and preposterous rumours. 'Except for having eaten the flesh of children, there was nothing I was not accused of,' she later claimed. 'I was aware that two prima donnas—everyone knows their names, but I will not stoop so low as to mention them—had always loathed me for being the reigning diva and getting all the plum parts. They saw the opportunity to destroy me, and they succeeded.'[13]

There is in fact no reason to believe that Lubin's behaviour *vis-à-vis* the Germans was any worse than that of most of her colleagues. Unlike Piaf and Chevalier she resolutely refused all invitations to sing in Germany during the war. The left-wing and passionately anti-Nazi soprano Irène Joachim did not hesitate to socialize with Lubin during the Occupation (they had no roles in common) and credited Lubin with using her influence to save the life of Jewish singer Marya Freund.[14] Indeed, this was part of the problem. Through her friendship with Winifred Wagner and her amicable relations with the German authorities, Lubin was able to pull strings on behalf of others, and like the film star Arletty and the great actor-playwright Sacha Guitry, every time she did so she compromised herself more. She sang in a concert to mark the opening of Arno Breker's exhibition at the Orangerie in 1942, but this was in order to secure the release of Maurice Franck,

The consequences of film star Mireille Balin's 'collaboration horizontale' were terrible.

Corinne Luchaire was tainted by association with her journalist father who was executed for collaboration.

Arletty

the Jewish 'Chef de Chant' at the Opéra.

At her trial in 1946 it could not be proved that she had committed any more serious misdemeanours than singing Isolde with the visiting Berlin Staatsoper in 1941 and being on friendly terms with the occupiers—and possibly more than that with one German officer although she claimed never to have been interested in sex. For this the punishment was draconian. She was sentenced to *dégradation nationale* ('loss of civil rights') for life, confiscation of property, and was banned from performing. Once the initial fury of the *épuration* had passed, the performance ban and the *degradation nationale* were reduced to six years, but Lubin had been robbed of the last good years of her career. A recording made during a concert in Italy in 1954 shows the voice of the 64-year-old singer in splendid form—huge, voluptuous in quality and steady as a rock. But the suicide of her son the year before had undermined her will to continue. Lubin lived on into an embittered old age and an interview given to Lanfranco Rasponi in 1978 shortly before her death reads like a long howl of anguish.

Kirsten Flagstad faced her accusers with quiet dignity and 'Norwegian stubbornness'.

Between 1935 and 1941 Kirsten Flagstad had conquered America with her incomparable interpretation of the heavy Wagner roles. Hers was probably the most magnificent voice that had ever been heard in these roles. Flagstad became the most admired and highest paid soprano in America. She even took on the mantle of Ernestine Schumann-Heink as 'mother of the nation' when she sang 'Silent Night' over the radio at Christmas after the latter had died in 1936.

Her determined decision to return to occupied Norway to be with her husband in April 1941 was at first admired, but after America entered the war it was perceived as some kind of betrayal. Despite the fact that Flagstad's husband was later accused of collaboration with the Quisling government, Flagstad's own behaviour during the war was irreproachable as was eventually acknowledged by her countrymen after the first bitter post-war recriminations. She had refused all invitations to sing in her occupied native land or in the German Reich. Illogically, three Swedish tenors who had all stooped to singing in Germany during the war, Jussi Björling, Torsten Ralf and Set Svanholm, were welcomed to the Met immediately after the war with no hint of protest. Though America had suffered less than any other major protagonist in the war, it was the Americans who were most unforgiving towards Flagstad. When she returned to the United States in 1947 Flagstad encountered a campaign of protest and vilification that amounted to a witch-hunt. Over several seasons she faced down her accusers with courage and dignity. After being heckled and booed throughout a concert in Philadelphia she commented: 'Of course the more they booed between numbers, the more stubborn I got, and you know how stubborn a Norwegian can get.'[15]

One American who took a more sanguine view of the Flagstad affair was the journalist Vincent Sheean, author of the political memoir *Personal History* that inspired the Alfred Hitchcock movie *Foreign Correspondent*. Sheean wrote: 'I never did see any reason why a lady should not go home to her husband in troubled times and stay with him at home, even if he were a Nazi sympathiser or collaborator. It would seem to me a somewhat private matter ... by what reason it came to be supposed that Mme. Flagstad had "betrayed" us I never really began to guess; she was a perfectly free adult woman, not in peonage to the Metropolitan, and as long as she did not help the Nazis in their monstrous schemes (as I believe she did not) it was her own business what she did.'[16]

In London, Flagstad was approached by the United Jewish Relief Appeal and asked to sing at a charity concert in aid of Jewish orphans. She hesitated for fear of being accused of buying her way back into public favour through charity, but eventually built a warm relationship with London's Jewish community.

In fact Flagstad had no need to curry favour with the British public. In contrast to America, Britain welcomed her back with open arms, both in her old Wagnerian repertoire and as Purcell's Dido. Flagstad agreed to sing the role for a token fee of a pint of stout per performance, out of friendship for the actor Bernard Miles who staged the performance of *Dido and Aeneas* at his Mermaid Theatre, but also perhaps in gratitude for the respect shown her by the British public.

In 1951 Flagstad was eventually invited back to the scene of her greatest triumphs, the Metropolitan Opera in New York. She reported in her memoirs that these late Met performances gave her little pleasure other than the satisfaction of being there despite her enemies. Rudolf Bing, who extended the invitation in the face of fierce opposition, justified Flagstad's return with the caustic comment: 'It seemed to me peculiar that an artist like Erna Berger—who had sung all through the war for the pleasure of the Nazi big-wigs in Berlin—could be acceptable at the Metropolitan, while Miss Flagstad had to be banished.'[17]

The coloratura soprano Erna Berger was the first major German singer to be welcomed to the Met after the war, in 1949, just as she had been at Covent Garden in 1947. Berger was apparently one of Hitler's favourite singers (for which she can hardly be blamed) and had indeed sung on many official Nazi occasions during the war. She can be glimpsed in newsreel film of Hitler's birthday concert in 1942, smiling as she takes a bow after the Ninth Symphony of Beethoven. She seems to have occasioned no protest in America. The difference between Flagstad and Berger was that the former represented Brunnhilde and the latter Verdi's Gilda. It was impossible to identify Berger's diminutive and charming figure and her girlish voice with Nazi aggression.

In old age soprano Erna Berger asked herself how much she knew about Nazi crimes.

When I spent the best part of two days in the summer of 1988 discussing Berger's career with her, I was utterly disarmed by her gentle and ingenuous manner. It was as if Gilda had survived the last act of *Rigoletto* and lived into a mellow and contented old age. I was dimly aware that she had been close to great evil but lacked the courage or the initiative to ask her about it. She might possibly have given me some truthful answers. Few singers of her generation were able to face up to the reality of what they had lived through and the regime that they had served. In her autobiography, Berger certainly makes many of the usual excuses—of being apolitical and only living for her art, etc. She also exhibited a touch of the solipsism so characteristic of artists. She begins her chapter on the Second World War with the sentence 'When Hitler marched into Poland, it temporarily ended my international career.' However, she had already gone a lot further than most of her colleagues when she questioned herself about Nazi atrocities: 'Did we not want to know? Should I not have guessed?' To these rhetorical questions she offered neither answers nor excuses.[18]

Elisabeth Schwarzkopf successfully put her past behind her and established herself as Germany's most admired post-war soprano.

Such an admission of self-doubt would have been unthinkable from Berger's younger contemporary Elisabeth Schwarzkopf. There are many remaining mysteries about Elisabeth Schwarzkopf's wartime career, but even given the most favourable interpretation, it is clear that her complicity with the Nazi regime was incomparably greater than that of Lubin or Flagstad. Like Karajan and Böhm, she was able to brush aside her post-war difficulties with remarkable speed and go on to a brilliant international career. Rudolf Bing's refusal to cast her in Stravinsky's *Rake's Progress* 'for reasons I would rather not discuss in writing'[19] was one of the rare occasions that she encountered any impediment to that career. It was only late in her life after a probing and meticulously researched biography was published by Alan Jefferson that her past came back to haunt her. After trawling through a mass of bureaucratic correspondence, Jefferson concluded that Schwarzkopf's career at the Deutscher Oper was fast-tracked with the help of a 'high-ranking' Nazi official. Schwarzkopf's 'protector' is not named in the book but the clear implication is that it was Goebbels.[20] Threatened litigation never materialized. Madame Schwarzkopf may well have feared what a court case would have brought to light.

Schwarzkopf did not help herself with an autobiography which appeared in French ghosted by the distinguished French opera critic André Tubeuf, in which she comes across as even more arrogant and disagreeable than in Jefferson's critical but admiring portrait. Without a hint of contrition, Schwarzkopf dismisses her membership of the Nazi Party as necessary for her career. Even if one accepts this argument (and there were plenty of singers and musicians of her generation who made careers in Nazi Germany without party membership) it would surely have behoved her to acknowledge that membership of the Nazi

410

Party was something to be ashamed of and that it was an organisation that caused untold harm to millions. It was a wise decision not to publish the book in German or English translations.

By dint of hard work and ruthless ambition Schwarzkopf transformed ('brick by brick' as she put it)[21] an essentially second rate and uninteresting voice into a highly individual if somewhat artificial instrument that enabled her to establish herself as the most important and influential German soprano of the post-war period. The competition in the field was fierce. Amongst the many sopranos with better voices, more natural techniques and little or no Nazi baggage, were Elisabeth Grümmer, Irmgard Seefried, Sena Jurinac, Lisa Della Casa, Hilde Gueden and Hilde Zadek. Schwarzkopf was able to leapfrog all of them through her alliance and marriage with the equally ruthless recording impresario Walter Legge. Using a powerful man to further her career was a clever trick to pull off twice. It is not a story of virtue rewarded and there was to be no happy ending.

There is a bizarre coda in the form of a booklet entitled *The Schwarzkopf tapes: an artist replies to a hostile biography*, published in 2010, four years after Schwarzkopf's death and a few months after that of her unwelcome biographer. The transcriptions of her conversations about Jefferson's book present a sad picture of an angry and irascible old woman. Schwarzkopf's desperate attempts to fault Jefferson on trivial detail, her near pathological aversion to others 'peering' into her life and her insistence that, as she puts it 'it is the result that matters. Not the way up there', do little to allay the suspicions about her early career that he raised.[22]

Whether we like it or not, we live in the shadow of Hitler. From the Middle East to the Far East, history is still driven by memories of the Second World War. Over the past 65 years many composers have attempted to deal with the events of that war and few have succeeded. We are still perhaps too close and the scale of the tragedies too momentous. In trying to deal through art with events that involved tens of millions of deaths, there is an abiding danger of bathos.

The most powerful musical expression of loss and grief to have come out of the war was Richard Strauss's 'Metamorphosen', a 'Study for 23 solo strings', based on a musical quotation from the slow movement of the Eroica Symphony of Beethoven. It was composed in the final weeks of the war and premiered in Zurich on 26 January 1946 by Paul Sacher. The work is deeply tragic in mood, but what exactly is being mourned? The trigger for its composition seems to have been the destruction of the German cities and in particular their opera houses. Strauss wrote to his some-time librettist Joseph Gregor in March 1945: 'I am inconsolable. The Goethe House, the most sacred place on earth, destroyed! My lovely Dresden—Weimar—Munich, all gone!'[23] The destruction of the German cities was undoubtedly a tragedy and a loss to humanity but one would like to believe that the overwhelming sorrow of 'Metamorphosen', possibly the greatest music to be inspired by the Second World War, is about more than the destruction of buildings, and that whether Strauss consciously intended it to be so or not, it is about the greater destruction of German culture through Nazi barbarism as well as by Allied bombs, and about the sorrow and loss of war in general. It is perhaps part of the power of this music that its meaning is general and not specific.

One of the first major composers to attempt to deal more specifically with the Holocaust was Arnold Schoenberg with his six minute monodrama 'A Survivor from Warsaw', written in 1947. It is an impressive work but too terse and rarefied in its musical language for widespread impact.

Franz Waxman, who had experienced Nazi brutality at first hand and who showed such a remarkable ability to express menace and horror in his film scores, should have been the man for the job. Sadly, Waxman's setting of poems of child victims in Terezín, 'The Song of Terezín', fails to live up to the expectations one might have had of this gifted composer.

As late as 2002, when Nicholas Maw's ambitious opera *Sophie's Choice*, dealing with the experiences of a concentration camp survivor, was premiered in London, the critic of *The Guardian* complained of the 'gaps between subject, score and staging'.

Perhaps the most successful musical memorials to the Second World War have been the ones in which the composer has taken a step backwards and dealt with the tragedies from a certain emotional distance and in a universal rather than a specific way. Benjamin Britten's pacifist *War Requiem* was premiered in the newly dedicated and rebuilt Coventry Cathedral in 1962; it was intended to be performed with Russian, German and British soloists so as to rise above patriotism and specific politics. It is significant too that the English texts that intersperse the Latin of the Requiem Mass derive not from the Second World War but come from the First World War poet Wilfred Owen.

Messiaen's awesome 'Et expect resurrectionem mortuorum', with its great craggy outcrops of brass, woodwind and percussion, premiered in 1965 in the sublime and mysterious space of the Sainte Chapelle in Paris; it similarly attempts to commemorate the dead of both world wars in a monumental religious context. Each of the five movements is prefaced by a quotation from the Old or the New Testament.

Another composer who sought to universalise his musical commemorations of the Second World War and to remove them from close association with actual events was Krzysztof Penderecki. The work that made his international reputation, 'Threnody for the victims of Hiroshima', was originally given the purely abstract title of *8'37"*. Penderecki claimed that it was only after it was performed and recorded that he was 'struck with the emotional charge of the work'. He explained: 'I thought it would be a waste to condemn it to such anonymity, to those "digits". I decided to dedicate it to the Hiroshima victims.'[24]

One of the most joyous musical legacies of the Second World War is the record 'Echoes of France', made on 21 January 1946 in EMI's Abbey Road studios in London by the great jazz musicians Django Reinhardt and Stéphane Grappelli with a re-constituted 'Hot Club of France'. Reinhardt and Grappelli had been separated by the war for almost six years. According to one witness, when they re-met in the august premises of the Atheneum Club the first thing they did was to improvise an ecstatic jazz version of the French national anthem.[25] A few days later this became 'Echoes of France' in their first recording session together since the fall of France in 1940. What better way could there have been of celebrating the joy of liberation and the end of six long years of war?

1   Tito Gobbi, *My Life*, 1979, p. 79.

2   Beniamino Gigli, *The Memoirs of Beniamino Gigli*, 1957, p. 213.

3   Charles Dupêchez, *Histoire de l'Opéra de Paris*, 1984, p. 248.

4   Noel Coward, *The Noel Coward Diaries*, 1982, p. 82.

5   Alan Jefferson, *Elisabeth Schwarzkopf*, pp. 63-72.

6   Busch, CD.

7   Joseph Müller-Marein and Hannes Reinhardt, *Das musikalische Selbstportrait*, 1963, p. 18.

8   Ida Cook, *We Followed our Stars*, 1950.

9   John Ardoin, *The Furtwängler Record*, 1994, p. 59.

10 Sir Rudolf Bing, *5000 Nights at the Opera*, 1972.

11 Marion McKenna, *Myra Hess*, 1976, p. 225.

12 Marjorie Lawrence, *Interrupted Melody*, 1952, p. 123.

13 Lanfranco Rasponi, *The Last Prima Donnas*, 1994, p. 92.

14 Brigitte Massin, *Les Joachim*, p. 286.

15 Louis Biancolli, *The Flagstad Manuscript*, 1952, p. 180.

16 Vincent Sheean, *First and Last Love*, 1957, p. 244.

17 Bing, p. 204.

18 Erna Berger, *Auf Flügeln des Gesanges*, p.59.

19 Elisabeth Schwarzkopf, *Les autres soirs*, 2004, p. 47.

20 Jefferson, pp, 45-53.

21 Schwarzkopf, p. 47.

22 Alan Saunders (ed.), *The Schwarzkopf tapes*, p. 16.

23 Matthew Boyden, *Richard Strauss*, p. 352.

24 Quoted in the notes for the Naxos CD *Penderecki; Orchestral Works*, Vol. 1.

25 Paul Balmer, *Stéphane Grappelli: with and without Django*, 2003, p. 137.

BIBLIOGRAPHY

Almeida, Fabrice, d', *La vie mondaine sous le nazisme*, Paris: Perrin, 2006.

Andersen, Lale, *Leben mit einem Lied*, Munich: Deutsche Taschenbuch Verlag, 1981.

Ancelin, Pierre, *Henri Sauguet, l'homme et l'oeuvre*, Paris: La Revue musicale, 1983.

Antheil, George, *Bad Boy of Music*, Garden City, N.Y.: Doubleday, Doran & Co Inc., 1945.

Antonietto, Alain and François Billard, *Django Reinhardt, Rythmes futures*, Paris: Fayard, 2004.

Ardoin, John, *The Furtwängler record*, Portland, Or.: Amadeus Press, 1994.

Arsand, Daniel, *Mireille Balin, ou La Beauté foudroyée*, Lyon: La Manufacture, 1989.

Aster, Misha, *The Reich's orchestra, the Berlin Philharmonic 1933-1945*, London: Souvenir, 2011.

Bach, Steven, *Leni: the life and work of Leni Riefenstahl*, London: Little Brown, 2007.

Bach, Steven, *Marlene Dietrich: life and legend*, London: HarperCollins, 1993.

Bacharach, A L,.(ed), *British music of our time*, Penguin, 1946.

Bachmann, Robert C, *Karajan: notes on a career*, trans. Shaun Whiteside. London: Quartet, 1990.

Baker, Josephine and Bouillon, Jo, *Josephine*, trans. Mariana Fitzpatrick. New York: Harper & Row, 1977.

Baillie, Isobel, *Never sing louder than lovely*, London: Hutchinson, 1982.

Balmer, Paul, *Stéphane Grappelli: with and without Django*, London: Sanctuary, 2003.

Barnett, Andrew, *Sibelius*, New Haven, Conn., London: Yale University Press, 2007.

Barron, Stéphanie, with Sabine Eckmann, *Exiles + emigrés, the flight of European artists from Hitler*, exh. cat., Los Angeles County Museum of Art, 1997.

Barrot, Olivier and Raymond Chirat, *La vie culturelle dans la France occupée*, Paris; Gallimard, 2009.

Bauman, Janina, *Winter in the morning: a young girl's life in the Warsaw Ghetto and beyond, 1939-1945*, London: Virago, 1986.

Beckmans, José, *Prisonnier de son art: mémoires*, Paris: Librarie Séguier, 1989.

Beevor, Antony, *Stalingrad*, London: Viking, 1988.

Benatzky, Ralph, *Triumph und Tristesse: aus den Tagebüchern von 1919 bis 1946*, Berlin: Parthas, 2002.

Berger, Erna, *Auf Flügeln des Gesanges: Erinnerungen einer Sängerin*, Zurich: Atlantis Musik-buch-Verlag, 1988.

Bergmeier, Horst, Lotz, Rainer E, Kühn, Volker, *Lili Marleen, An allen Fronten, Das Lied, seine Zeit, seine Interpretatione, seine Botschaften*, Hambergen, Bear Family Records, 2005.

Bergmeier, Horst, and Lotz Rainer E, *Hitler's Airwaves*, New Haven, Conn., London: Yale University Press, 1997.

Berr, Hélène, *Journal*, trans. David Bellos, London: MacLehose, 2008.

Bie, Oscar, *Wir von der Oper*, Munich: Verlag F. Bruckmann, 1932.

Bing, [Sir] Rudolf, *5000 Nights at the Opera*, London: Hamilton, 1972.

Blackwood, Alan, *Sir Thomas Beecham: the man and the music*, London: Ebury, 1994.

Block, Geoffrey, *Richard Rodgers*, New Haven, Conn., London: Yale University Press, 2003.

Böhm, Karl, *Ma vie*, (Translation from German, Elisabeth Bouillon),
    Paris: Jean-Claude Lattès, 1980.

Bordman, Gerald, *Jerome Kern: his life and his music*, New York,
    Oxford: Oxford University Press, 1980.

Boyden, Matthew, *Richard Strauss*, London: Weidenfeld and Nicolson, 1999.

Braithwaite, Rodric, *Moscow 1941, a city and its people at war*, London: Profile, 2006.

Briggs, Susan, *Those Radio Times*, London: Weidenfeld and Nicolson, 1981.

Bruyas, Florian, *Histoire de l'opérette en France, 1855-1965*, Lyon: Emmanuel Vitte, 1974.

Burbank, Richard, *Twentieth Century Music, A Chronology*,
    London: Thames and Hudson, 1984.

Burgess, Muriel, with Tommy Keen, *Gracie Fields*, London: W.H. Allen, 1981.

Burton, Humphrey, *Leonard Bernstein*, London: Faber & Faber, 1994.

Burton, Richard D E, *Francis Poulenc*, Bath: Absolute, 2002.

Busch, Eva, *Und trotzdem: Eine Autobiographie*, Munich: Albrecht Knaus Verlag, 1991.

Byng, Douglas, *As you were: reminiscences*, London: Duckworth, 1970.

Cadars, Pierre and Francis Courtale, *Le cinéma nazi*, Paris: E. Losfeld, 1972.

Cain, John, *The BBC: 70 years of broadcasting*, BBC, 1992.

Calvet, Louis-Jean, *Cent ans de chanson française, 1907-2007*, Paris: Archipel, 2007.

Cannavo, Richard, *Monsieur Trenet*, Paris: Lieu Commun, 1993.

Carbonel, Marie-Hélène, *Suzy Solidor: une vie d'amours*, Marseille: Autres temps, 2007.

Carpenter, Humphrey, *Benjamin Britten: a biography*,
    New York: Charles Scribner's Sons, 1992.

Carroll, Brendan G, *The Last Prodigy, a biography of Erich Wolfgang Korngold*,
    Portland, Ore.: Amadeus Press, 1997.

Casanova, Nicole, *Isolde 39: Germaine Lubin*, Paris: Flammarion, 1974.

Castle, Charles, *Noel*, London: Abacus, 1974.

Chappell, Connery, *Island of barbed wire: internment on the Isle of Man in World War Two*,
    London: Robert Hale, 1984.

Chevalier, Maurice, *With Love: the autobiography as told to Eileen and Robert Mason Pollock*,
    London: Cassell, 1960.

Chimènes, Myriam, *La vie musicale sous Vichy*, Brussels: Complexe, 2001.

Cité de la Musique, *Le 3e Reich et la Musique*, exh. cat., Paris: Fayard, 2004.

Closel, Amaury du and Philippe Olivier, *Déracinements, exil et deportations des musiciens sous
    le Troisième Reich*, Paris: Éditions Hermann, 2009.

Closel, Amaury du, *Les voix étouffés du 3e reich*, Paris: Éditions Actes Sud, 2005.

Coeuroy, André, *Histoire générale du jazz*, Paris: Denoël, 1942.

Cointet, Michèle, *Vichy Capitale, 1940-1944*, Paris: Perrin, 1993.

Cointet, Michèle et Jean-Paul, *Dictionnaire historique de la France sous l'occupation*,
    Paris: Tallandier, 2000.

Colville, John, *The fringes of power: Downing Street diaries 1939-1955*,
    London: Hodder and Stoughton, 1985.

Cook, Ida, *We followed our Stars*, London: Hamish Hamilton, 1950.

Coward, Noel, *Middle East Diary*, London: Heinemann, 1944.

Coward, Noel, Graham Payne and Sheridan Morley eds., *The Noel Coward Diaries*,
    London: Weidenfeld and Nicolson, 1982.

Council for the Encouragement of Music and the Arts, *The Arts in Wartime*,
    London: CEMA, 1943.

Crist, Elizabeth, *Music for the common man: Aaron Copland during the Depression and war*, Oxford: Oxford University Press, 2005.

Dachs, Robert, *Sag beim Abschied*, Vienna: Verlag der Apfel, 1994.

Danielson, Virginia, *The voice of Egypt: Umm Kulthum, Arabic song, and Egyptian society in the twentieth century*, Chicago, London: University of Chicago Press, 1997.

Darmon, Pierre, *Le monde du cinema sous l'Occupation*, Paris: Stock, 1997.

Dean, Basil, *The Theatre at War*, London: George G. Harrap & Co., 1956.

Dean, Basil, *Mind's eye: an autobiography*, London: Hutchinson, 1973.

Delannoy, Marcel, *Honegger*, Paris: P Horay, 1953.

Laroche, Robert de, *Marie Dubas: comédienne de la chanson*, Saint-Cyr-sur-Loire: C. Pirot, 1980.

Del Mar, Norman, *Richard Strauss*, London: Barrier & Rockliff, 1962.

Depaulis, Jacques, *Reynaldo Hahn*, Biarritz: Atlantica, 2007.

Dickinson, Peter (ed.), *Samuel Barber remembered: a centenary tribute*, Rochester, N.Y.: University of Rochester Press, 2010.

Doctor, Jenny and David Wright, (eds), *The Proms: a new history*, London: Thames and Hudson, 2006.

Drake, James A and Kristin Beall Ludecke, *Lily Pons: a Centennial Portrait*, Portland, Ore.: Amadeus, 1999.

Dupêchez, Charles, *Histoire de l'Opéra de Paris: un siècle au palais Garnier 1875-1980*, Paris: Librairie académique Perin, 1984.

Dutilleux, Henri, *Mystère et mémoire des sons*, Paris: Belfond, 1993.

Eck, Hélène, (ed.), *La guerre des ondes: histoire des radios de langue française pendant la Deuxième Guerre mondiale*, Paris: Armand Colin, 1985.

Egk, Werner, *Die Zeit wartet nicht*, Munich: Wilhelm Goldmann Verlag, 1981.

Ellis, Mary, *Those dancing years: an autobiography*, London: Murray, 1982.

Fallada, Hans, *Alone in Berlin*, trans. Michael Hofmann, London: Penguin Books, 2009. [Original title *Jeder stirbt für sich allein*, 1947.]

Farneth, David, with Elmar Juchem and Dave Stein, *Kurt Weill: a life in pictures and documents*, London: Thames and Hudson, 2000.

Fawkes, Richard, *Fighting for a laugh: entertaining the British and American Armed Forces 1939-1946*, London: Macdonald and Jane's, 1978.

Fay, Laurel E, *Shostakovich: A Life*, Oxford: Oxford University Press, 2000.

Fechner, Eberhard, *Die Comedian Harmonists*, Weinheim: Quadriga, 1988.

Fénelon, Fania, trans. Judith Landry, *The musicians of Auschwitz*, London: Joseph, 1977.

Fifield, Christopher (ed.), *Letters and diaries of Kathleen Ferrier*, Woodbridge: Boydell Press, 2011.

Fisher, John, *George Formby*, London: Woburn Press, 1977.

Flagstad, Kirsten, as told to Biancoli, Louis, *The Flagstad manuscript*, New York: Putnam, 1952.

Fleuret, Maurice, *Joseph Kosma 1905-1969: un homme, un musicien*, Paris: Revue musicale, 1988.

Foreman, Lewis, *From Parry to Britten, British Music in Letters, 1900-1945*, London: B T Batsford Ltd, 1987.

Fragny, Robert, *Ninon Vallin*, Lyon: Éditions et Imprimeries du Sud-Est, 1963.

Fransman, John, *A Jewish child survivor's recollection of the Holocaust. From Zachor*. Published by the Child Survivor's Association of Great Britain, 2011.

Fry, Helen P, *Music and men: the life and loves of Harriet Cohen*, Stroud: History Press, 2008.

Garban, Dominique, *Jacques Rouché: l'homme qui sauva l'Opéra de Paris*, Paris: Somogy, 2007.

Geissmar, Bertha, *The baton and the jackboot: recollections of musical life*, London: Columbus, 1988.

417

Gigli, Rina, *Beniamino Gigli, mio padre*, Parma: Azzali, 1986.

Gilbert, Susie, *Opera for everybody: the story of English National Opera*, London: Faber, 2009.

Gobbi, Tito, with Ida Cook, *My life*, London: Macdonald and Jane's, 1979.

Gold, Trude (ed.), *The Diary of Dr Johannes Paul Kemer*, The Holocaust Education Trust and the London Jewish Cultural Centre (incorporating the Spiro Institute). Lesson Resources, 2011.

Greenberg, Rodney, *George Gershwin*, London: Phaidon, 1998.

Grenfell, Joyce, *The time of my life: entertaining the troops: her wartime journals*, London: Hodder and Stoughton, 1989.

Grenfell, Joyce, *Joyce Grenfell requests the pleasure*, London: Macmillian, 1976.

Grun, Bernard, *Prince of Vienna: the life, the times and the melodies of Oscar Straus*, London: WH Allen, 1955.

Gualerzi, Giorgio and Carlo Marinelli Roscioni, *50 anni di opera lirica alla RAI,1931-1980*, Turin: ERI, 1981.

Halbreich, Harry, *Arthur Honegger*, trans. Roger Nichols, Portland, OR: Amadeus Press, 1999.

Hamann, Brigitte, *Winifred Wagner: a life at the heart of Hitler's Bayreuth*, trans. Alan Bunce, London: Granta, 2005.

Haney, Lynn, *Naked at the feast: a biography of Josephine Baker*, London: Robson 1986.

Hardy, Phil and Dave Laing, *The Faber companion to 20th-century popular music*, London: Faber, 1990.

Herf, Jeffrey, *Nazi propaganda for the Arab world*, New Haven, Conn.: Yale University Press, 2009.

Horowitz, Joseph, *Understanding Toscanini*, London: Faber, 1987.

Hillesum, Etty, *Une vie bouleversée*, (trans. Philippe Noble, from the Dutch *Het Denkende hart van de barak*), Editions du Seuil, 1995.

Huggett, Frank E, *Goodnight sweetheart: songs and memories of the Second World War*, London: WH Allen, 1979.

Iskin, René, *Dans un camp, Basdorf 1943*, Paris: Didier Carpentier, 2005.

Jackson, Julian, *France: the dark years 1940-1944*, Oxford: Oxford University Press, 2001.

Jacobi, Jutta, *Zarah Leander: das Leben einer Diva*, Hamburg: Hoffmann und Campe, 2006.

Jadin, Philippe, *Jean Sablon: le gentleman de la chanson*, Saint-Cyr-sur-Loire, C. Pirot, 2002.

Jefferson, Alan, *Elisabeth Schwarzkopf*, London: Gollancz, 1996.

Joliffe, John, *Glyndebourne; an Operatic Miracle*, London: John Murray, 1999.

Jolivet, Hilda, *Avec ... André Jolivet*, Paris: Flammarion, 1978.

Jones, Michael, *Leningrad: state of siege*, London: John Murray, 2008.

Kashner, Sam, and Nancy Schoenberger, *A talent for genius. The life and times of Oscar Levant*, Los Angeles: Silman-James Press, 1994.

Kavanagh, Ted, Introduction by P J Kavanagh, *The Itma Years*, London: Futura, 1974.

Kennedy, Michael, *Barbirolli: conductor laureate: the authorised biography*, London: Hart-Davis, 1971.

Kennedy, Michael, *Richard Strauss: man, musician, enigma*, Cambridge: Cambridge University Press, 1999.

Klabunde, Anja, *Magda Goebbels*, trans. Shaun Whiteside, London: Time Warner, 2001.

Klee, Ernst, *Kulturleben zum Dritten Reich*, Frankfurt/M, Fischer Taschenbuch Verlag, 2009.

Kobal, John, *Gotta sing, gotta dance: a pictorial history of film musicals*, Feltham: Hamlyn, 1970.

Knopp, Guido, *Hitler's women—and Marlene*, trans. Angus McGeoch, Stroud: Sutton, 2003.

Koppes, Clayton R and Gregory D Black, *Hollywood goes to war: how politics, profits and propaganda shaped World War II movies*, London: Tauris, 1988.

Krauser, Ernst, *Werner Egk*, Wilhelmshaven: Heinrichshofen's Verlag, 1971.

Kreimer, Klaus, *Une histoire du cinema allemande, La UFA*, France: Flammarion, 1992.

Kreuder, Peter, *Schön war die Zeit*, Bertelsheim Lessering, 1961.

Kubler, Thierry and Emmanuel Lemieux, *Cognacq Jay, 1940, la télévision française sous l'Occupation*, Paris: Editions Plume, 1990.

Künnecke, Evelyn, *Sing Evelyn sing: Revue eines Lebens*, Hamburg: Hoffmann und Campe, 1982.

Kutsch K J and Leo Riemens, *Grosses Sängerlexikon*, Berne: Franke Verlag, 1987.

La Hire, Jean de, *Hitler, que nous veut-il donc?*, Paris: Éditions du livre moderne, 1941.

Lacombe, Nicole and Alain, *Frehel*, Paris: Pierre Belfond, 1990.

Lambert, Constant, *Music Ho!, a study of music in decline*, with new introduction by Angus Morrison, London: Hogarth, 1985.

Lasker-Wallfisch, Anita, *Inherit the truth 1939-1945, the documented experiences of a survivor of Auschwitz and Belsen*, New York: St Martin's Press, 2000.

Lassimonne, Denise and Howard Ferguson (eds), *Myra Hess by her friends*, London: Hamish Hamilton, 1966.

Lawrence, Marjorie, *Interrupted Melody*, London: Falcon Press, 1952.

Leander, Zarah, *Es war so wunderbar! Mein Leben*, Hamburg: Hoffmann und Campe, 1975.

Legrand, Raphaelle and Nicole Wild, *Regards sur l'opéra-comique: trois siècles de vie theâtrale*, Paris: CNRS, 2002.

Leider, Frida, *Playing my part*, trans. Charles Osborne, London: Calder and Boyars, 1966.

Leonard, Maurice, *Slobodskaya: a biography of Oda Slobodskaya*, London: Gollancz, 1979.

Larry Lesueur, *12 Months that Changed the World*, New York: Alfred A Knopf, 1943.

Levi, Erik, *Music in the Third Reich*, Basingstoke: Macmillan, 1994.

Levi, Erik, *Mozart and the Nazis: how the Third Reich abused a cultural icon*, New Haven, London: Yale University Press, 2010.

Levi, Trude, *A cat called Adolf*, London: Valentine Mitchell, 1995.

Lifar, Serge, *Ma vie*, Paris: R. Julliard, 1965.

Lillie, Beatrice, *Every other inch a lady*, Garden City, NY: Doubleday, 1972.

Lucas, John, *Thomas Beecham: an obsession with music*, Woodbridge: Boydell, 2008.

Luchaire, Corinne, *Ma drôle de vie*, Paris: Daulpha Éditions, 1949.

Lumeau, Aurélie, *Radio Londres 1940-1944: les voix de la liberté*, Paris: Perrin, 2005.

Lynn, Vera, *Vocal refrain: an autobiography*, London: WH Allen, 1975.

Lynn, Vera, *Some sunny day: my autobiography*, London: HarperCollins, 2009.

MacDonald, Malcolm, *Schoenberg*, Oxford: Oxford University Press, 2008.

Maclean, Fitzroy, *Eastern Approaches*, London: Jonathan Cape, 1949.

Manvell, Roger, *Films and the Second World War*, London: Dent, 1974.

Marcus, Kenneth H, *Musical metropolis, Los Angeles and the creation of a music culture*, New York: Palgrave Macmillan, 2004.

Massin, Brigitte, *Les Joachim: une famile de musiciens*, Paris: Fayard, 1999.

Matzner, Joachim, *Furtwängler: Analyse, Dokument, Protokoll*, Zurich: Atlantis Musikbuch Verlag, 1986.

McBrien, William, *Cole Porter: the definitive biography*, London: HarperCollins, 1998.

McClung, Bruce D, *Lady in the Dark, biography of a musical*, New York, Oxford: Oxford University Press, 2007.

McKenna, Marian C, *Myra Hess: a portrait*, London: Hamilton, 1976.

Milhaud, Darius, *Ma vie heureuse*, Paris: Éditions Belfond, 1973.

Mirambeau, Christophe, *Albert Willemetz: un regard dans le siècle*, Paris: Rampe, 2004.

Mireille, *Avec le soleil pour témoin*, Paris: R. Laffont, 1981.

Moore, Gerald, *Am I too loud?: Memoirs of an accompanist*, London: Hamish Hamilton, 1962.

Mooser, R-Aloys, *Regards sur la musique contemporaine, 1921-1946*, Lausanne: Librarie F Rouge, 1946.

Morrison, Richard, *Orchestra: the LSO: a century of triumph and turbulence*, London: Faber and Faber, 2004.

419

Morrison, Simon, *The people's artist: Prokofiev's Soviet years*,
    Oxford: Oxford University Press, 2009.
Müller, Melissa and Reinhard Piechocky, *A Garden of Eden in Hell: the life of Alice Herz-Sommer*, trans. Giles McDonogh, London: Macmillan, 2007.
Müller-Marein, Josef and Hannes Reinhardt, *Das musikalische Selbstportrait von Komponisten, Dirigenten, Instrumentalisten, Sängerinnen und Sängern unserer Zeit*,
    Hamburg: Nannen Verlag, 1963.
Naegele, Verena, *Viktor Ullmann: Komponieren in verlorener Zeit*, Cologne: Dittrich, 2002.
Napier-Tauber, Diana, *Richard Tauber*, London: Art and Educational Publishers, Ltd, 1949.
Naso, Eckart von, *Schlusnus, Mensch und Sänger*, Hamburg: W Krüger, 1957.
Newman, Richard, with Karen Kirtley, *Alma Rosé: Vienna to Auschwitz*,
    Portland, OR: Amadeus Press, 2000.
Newton, Ivor, *At the piano—Ivor Newton: the world of an accompanist*,
    London: Hamish Hamilton, 1966.
Nicholson, Stuart (compiled by), *Reminiscing in tempo, A portrait of Duke Ellington*,
    London: Sidgwick & Jackson, 1999.
Novick, Peter, *L'Epuration française, 1944-49*, Paris: Ballard, 1985. (translated from the English by Hélène Ternois.)
O'Connor, Garry, *The pursuit of perfection: a life of Maggie Teyte*, London: Gollancz, 1979.
Olivier, Philippe, *Charles Munch: une biographie par le disque*, Paris: Belfond, 1987.
Opperby, Preben, *Leopold Stokowski*, Tunbridge Wells: Midas, 1982.
Orff, Godela, *Mein Vater und ich: Erinnerungen an Carl Orff*, Munich: Henschel Verlag, 2008.
Osborne, Richard E, *The Casablanca Companion: the movie classic and its place in history*,
    Indianapolis, Ind: Riebel-Roque Publishing, 1997.
Pander, Oscar von, *Clemens Krauss in München*, Munich: Verlag C.H. Beck, 1955.
Partner, Peter, *Arab voices: the BBC Arabic Service 1938-1988*, London: BBC, 1988.
Parys, Georges van, *Les jours comme ils viennent*, Paris: Plon, 1969.
Pénet, Martin (ed.), *Mémoire de la chanson: 1200 chansons du moyen-âge à 1919*,
    Paris: Omnibus, 2004.
Pessis, Jacques (ed), *Pierre Dac*, Paris: Éditions François Bourin, 1992.
Pinza, Ezio, with Robert Magidoff, *Ezio Pinza: an autobiography*,
    New York, Toronto: Rinehart & Co., 1958.
Plomley, Roy, *Desert Island Discs*, London: Hutchinson, 1984.
Pople, Anthony, *Messiaen, Quatuor pour la fin du temps*,
    Cambridge: Cambridge University Press, 1998.
Potter, Tully, *Adolf Busch: the life of an honest musician*, London: Toccata, 2010.
Previn, André, *No minor chords: my days in Hollywood*, New York, London: Doubleday, 1991.
Prieberg, Fred K, *Musik im NS-Staat*, Frankfurt/M: Fischer Taschenbuch Verlag, 1982.
Prieberg, Fred K, *Trial of strength: Wilhelm Furtwängler and the Third Reich*,
    London: Quartet, 1991.
Puritz, Gerd, *Elisabeth Schumann*, edited and translated by Joy Puritz,
    London: Deutsch, 1993.
Randall, Alan and Ray Seaton, *George Formby: a biography*, London: WH Allen, 1974.
Rasponi, Lanfranco, *The Last Prima Donnas*, London: Gollancz, 1994.
Reid, Charles, *John Barbirolli: a biography*, London: Hamilton, 1971.
Reid, Charles, *Malcolm Sargent: a biography*, London: Hamish Hamilton, 1968.
Reinhardt, Gottfried, *The Genius, A Memoir of Max Reinhardt*,
    New York: Alfred A Knopf, 1979.
Riefenstahl, Leni, *A Memoir*, New York: Picador, 1995.
Ringold, Daniel, *Maurice Chevalier, le sourire de Paris*, Paris: TFI Éditions, 1995.
Roncigli, Audrey, *Le cas Furtwängle: un chef d'orchestra sous le IIIe Reich*, Paris: Imago, 2009.

Rosenthal, Harold, *Two Centuries of Opera at Covent Garden*, London: Putnam, 1958.

Rosvaenge, Helge, *Mach es besser, mein Sohn: ein Tenor erzählt aus seinem Leben*, Leipzig, 1963.

Ryding, Erik and Rebecca Pechefsky, *Bruno Walter: a world elsewhere*, New Haven, Conn., London: Yale University Press, 2001.

Sachs, Harvey, *Toscanini*, London: Weidenfeld and Nicolson, 1978.

Sachs, Harvey (compiled, edited, and translated by), *The Letters of Toscanini*, London: Faber and Faber, 1989.

Sachs, Harvey, *Reflections on Toscanini*, London: Robson, 1992.

Sackett, Susan, *Hollywood sings*, New York: Billboard Books, 1995.

Šafránek, Miloš, *Bohuslav Martinů: His Life and Works*, trans. Roberta Finlayson-Samsourová, London: Allan Wingate, 1962.

Sanders, Alan, *The Schwarzkopf Tapes: an artist replies to a hostile biography*, Richmond: Classical Recordings Quarterly & the Elisabeth Schwarzkopf/ Walter Legge Society, 2010.

Sanjek, Russell, *Pennies from Heaven: the American popular music business in the twentieth century*, New York: Da Capo Press, 1996.

Schwarzkopf, Elisabeth, *Les autres soirs*, Paris: Tallandier, 2004.

Scotland, Tony, *Lennox & Freda*, Norwich: Michael Russell, 2010.

Secrest, Meryle, *Somewhere for me: a biography of Richard Rodgers*, New York: Alfred A. Knopf, 2001.

Segond, André, *Georges Thill, ou, l'âge d'or de l'Opéra*, Lyon: Jacques-Marie Laffont et Associés, 1980.

Seib, Philip, *Broadcasts from the Blitz: how Edward R Murrow helped lead America into war*, Washington, DC: Potomac, 2007.

Seiler, Paul, *Zarah Diva, Das Portrait eines Stars*, Berlin: Albino Verlag, 1985.

Seiler, Paul, *Ein Mythos lebt, Zarah Leander*, Berlin: Graphische Werkstätten, 1991.

Seltsam, William (compiled by), *Metropolitan Opera Annals: A chronicle of artists and performances*, New York: H W Wilson Co, Metropolitan Opera Guild, 1942.

Shaw, Arnold, *Sinatra*, London: Allen, 1968.

Sheean, (James) Vincent, *First and Last Love*, London: Gollancz, 1957.

Sherman, A J, *Mandate days: British lives in Palestine, 1918-1948*, London: Thames and Hudson, 1997.

Shostakovich, Dmitri, *Testimony: the memoirs of Dmitri Shostakovich as told to and edited by Solomon Volkov*, trans. Antonina W Bouis, London: Hamish Hamilton, 1979.

Siclier, Jacques, *La France de Pétain et son cinéma*, Paris: Henri Veyrier, 1981.

Slonimsky, Nicolas, *Music since 1900*, London: Cassell, 1972.

Smith, Cyril, as told to Joyce Eglinton, *Duet for Three Hands*, London: Angus & Robertson, 1958.

Spotts, Frederic, *Bayreuth: a history of the Wagner festival*, New Haven, London: Yale University Press, 1996.

Spotts, Frederic, *The shameful peace: how French artists and intellectuals survived the Nazi occupation*, New Haven, London: Yale University Press, 2008.

Spycket, Jérôme, *Nadia Boulanger*, Paris, Lausanne: Lattès, Payot, 1987.

Stapleton, Michael, *The Sadler's Wells Opera*, London: Adam & Charles Black, 1954.

Stolz, Robert and Einzi, *Servus Du: Robert Stolz und sein Jahrhundert*, Munich: Blanvalet, 1980.

Strachan, Alan, *Secret Dreams: the biography of Michael Redgrave*, London: Weidenfeld and Nicolson, 2004.

Strauss, Richard, *The Correspondence between Richard Strauss and Hugo von Hofmannsthal*, trans. Hanns Hammelmann and Ewald Osers, London: Collins, 1952.

Stuckenschmidt, H H, *Zum Hören geboren: ein Leben mit der Musik unserer Zeit*, Munich: Piper, 1979.

Sullivan, Rosemary, *Villa Air-Bel:, the Second World War, escape and a house in France*,
    London: John Murray, 2006.
Szpilman, Wladyslaw, *Le pianiste*, (translated from English by Bernard Cohen),
    Paris: Éditions Robert Laffont, 1998.
Tegel, Susan, *Nazis and the cinema*, London: Hambledon Continuum, 2007.
Ténot, Frank, *Celui qui aimait le jazz*, Paris: Foundation Frank Ténot/
    Éditions du Layeur, 2009.
Térrier, Agnes, *L'orchestre de l'Opéra de Paris*, Paris: Martinière,
    Opéra national de Paris, 2003.
Teyte, Maggie, *Star on the Door*, London: Putnam, 1958.
Thomas, Tony, *Music for the movies*, London: Tantivy Press, 1973.
Tierney, Neil, *The unknown country: a life of Igor Stravinsky*, London: Hale, 1977.
Tierney, Neil, *William Walton: his life and music*, London: Hale, 1984.
Tillion, Germaine, *Le Verfügbar aux enfers: une opérette à Ravensbrück*,
    Paris: Editions de la Martinière, 2005.
Tippett, Michael, *Those twentieth century blues: an autobiography*, London: Hutchinson, 1991.
Trapp, Agathe von, *Memories before and after the Sound of Music*,
    London: HarperCollins, 2010
Traubner, Richard, *Operetta: a theatrical history*, Oxford: Oxford University Press, 1989.
Vries, Willem de, *Sonderstab Musik: music confiscations by the Einsatzstab Reichsleiter
    Rosenberg under the Nazi occupation of Western Europe*,
    Amsterdam: Amsterdam University Press, 1996.
Vayne, Kyra, with Andrew Palmer, *A voice reborn*, London: Arcadia, 1999.
Vaughan Williams, Ursula, *R V W: a biography of Ralph Vaughan Williams*,
    London: Oxford University Press, 1964.
Varnay, Astrid, with Donald Arthur, *55 years in Five Acts: My Life in Opera*, Boston:
    Northeastern Universty Press, 2000.
Walton, Chris, *Othmar Schoeck: eine Biographie*, German trans. by Ken W Bartlett,
    Zurich: Atlantis Musikbuch-Verlag, 1994.
Webb, Paul, *Ivor Novello: a portrait of a star*, London: Stage Directions, 1999.
Weinschenk H E, *Künstler plaudern*, Berlin: W. Limpert, 1938.
Wilson, Sandy, *Ivor*, London: Joseph, 1975.
Wolff, Stéphane, *Un demi-siècle de l'Opéra-comique, 1900-1950*, Paris: André Bonne, 1953.
Zuckmayer, Carl, *Geheimreport*, Munich: Deutsche Taschenbuch Verlag, 2004.
Zuhur, Sherifa, *Asmahan's secrets: woman, war and song*, London: Saqi, 2000.

Journals

Der Adler
Ciné Mondial
Comoedia
Illustrated London News
L'Illustration
Match
Les Ondes
Parade
Sept Jours
Signal
Vedette

INDEX

Index

Griller Quartet 211
Grümmer, Elisabeth 411
Grynszpan, Herschel 219
Gueden, Hilde 411
Guitry, Sacha 401, 405
Gulenkampf, Georg 134
Guller, Youra 103
Gurlitt, Manfred 141
Guthrie, Tyrone 192, 193
Guthrie, Woody 393

Haas, Michael 248, 259
Haas, Pavel 28, 248, 259
Haba, Alois 239
Haendel, Ida 209
Hahn, Reynaldo 60, 79, 102, 103, 104, 202
Haitink, Bernard 28
Halbreich, Harry 91, 93, 94
Hallé Orchestra 198, 203, 204
Hall, Henry 7, 272
Hambourg, Mark 197, 209
Hammerstein, Oscar 160, 168, 169, 389
Hammes, Karl 30
Hammond, Joan 176, 194, 195, 199, 202, 210, 215
Handel, George Frideric 15, 17, 18, 42, 59, 63, 203
Hani, Pierre 276, 277
Hanke, Karl 57
Hanson, Howard 165
Harris, Roy 153, 155, 156, 165 et seq.
Harrison, Julius 216
Hart, Lorenz 142, 146, 168, 281, 387
Hart, Moss 168
Hartmann, Karl Amadeus 118
Harty, Hamilton 203, 208
Harvey, Lillian 254, 326
Haskil, Clara 103
Hatikvah 226
Hayworth, Rita 389
Hecht, Ben 151
Heesters, Johannes 303
Heger, Robert 26, 124
Heifetz, Jascha 160, 170, 242, 244
Heine, Heinrich 21, 126, 256
Helian, Jacques 61
Henderson, Roy 210
Hermann, Bernard 165, 298
Herz-Sommer, Alice 29, 258
Hess, Johnny 277, 278, 279, 372
Hess, Myra 4, 197, 198, 201, 203, 207, 209, 211, 213 et seq., 404
Hess, Rudolf 214, 348
Hewitt, Maurice 68, 99, 291
Heydrich, Reinhard Tristan 11, 150
Heydrich, Richard Bruno 11

Heymann, Werner Richard 135, 142, 169, 350
Hildegarde 341, 390
Hillemacher Brothers 86
Hillesum, Etty 257
Himmler, Heinrich 255, 347
Hinckel, Hans 340
Hindemith, Paul 114, 118, 184, 208, 239, 332
Hitler, Adolf 17, 22, 24, 26, 31, 35, 36, 37, 38, 39, 40, 41, 44, 46, 47, 49, 52, 55, 57, 67, 72, 105, 106, 112, 115, 116, 118, 119, 120, 121, 122, 127, 128, 131, 134, 135, 195, 198, 207, 208, 218, 231, 239, 240, 243, 249, 258, 261, 266, 277, 283, 292, 293, 299, 331, 344, 345, 347, 348, 350, 354, 356, 358, 363, 374, 393, 402, 409, 411
Hoerée, Arthur 83, 92
Hoffmeister, Werner 337
Hofmann, Joseph 211
Hofmannsthal, Hugo von 123, 130
Holbrooke, Joseph 209
Hollaender, Friedrich 142, 169
Honegger, Arthur 16, 17, 68, 70, 73, 74, 75, 76, 84, 85, 87, 91, 92, 93, 94, 95, 98, 105, 106, 208, 295
Hope, Bob 242
Hörbiger, Paul 297, 303
Horenstein, Jascha 111
Horne, Lena 307
Hornstein, Eva 32
Horowitz, Vladimir 160, 170, 211, 403
Hotter, Hans 126
Houseman, A E 216
Huber, Kurt 28, 117
Hughes, Spike 354
Hülphers, Arne 272, 273
Humby, Betty 159
Hupfeld, Herman 395
Hüsch, Gerhard 54

Ibert, Jacques 103, 105, 220, 295
Inghelbrecht, Désiré-Emile 60, 100, 101
Iskin, René 253
Iskoldoff, Eugene 195
ITMA 292

Jacob, Max 380
Jadlowker, Hermann 229
Jana, La 30
Jansen, Jacques 81, 82
Janssen, Herbert 44, 56, 157
Jarred, Mary 210
Jarry, Michael 273
Jaubert, Maurice 30, 88

427

1

Index